1939

Also by Frederick Taylor

Dresden: Tuesday, 13 February 1945

The Berlin Wall: 13 August 1961 – 9 November 1989

Exorcising Hitler: The Occupation and Denazification of Germany

*The Downfall of Money: Germany's Hyperinflation and
the Destruction of the Middle Class*

Coventry: Thursday, 14 November 1940

1939

A PEOPLE'S HISTORY
of the
COMING OF WORLD WAR II

FREDERICK TAYLOR

W. W. NORTON & COMPANY
Independent Publishers Since 1923

First published in the UK by Macmillan Publishers International Limited under the title
1939: A People's History

For information about permission to reproduce selections from this book, write to
Permissions, W. W. Norton & Company, Inc., 500 Fifth Avenue, New York, NY 10110

For information about special discounts for bulk purchases, please contact
W. W. Norton Special Sales at specialsales@wwnorton.com or 800-233-4830

Manufacturing by Lake Book Manufacturing

Library of Congress Cataloging-in-Publication Data

Names: Taylor, Fred, 1947– author.
Title: 1939 : a people's history of the coming of the Second World War / Frederick Taylor.
Other titles: 1939 | People's history of the coming of the Second World War
Description: First American edition. | New York : W. W. Norton & Company, 2020. |
Published in England as: 1939: a people's history : 'the war nobody wanted.' |
Includes bibliographical references and index.
Identifiers: LCCN 2020000207 | ISBN 9781324006794 (hardcover) |
ISBN 9781324006800 (epub)
Subjects: LCSH: World War, 1939-1945—Public opinion. | World War, 1939-1945—
Causes. | Europe—Politics and government—1918-1945. | Europe—History—1918-1945.
Classification: LCC D810.P8 T39 2020 | DDC 940.53/1—dc23
LC record available at https://lccn.loc.gov/2020000207

W. W. Norton & Company, Inc., 500 Fifth Avenue, New York, N.Y. 10110
www.wwnorton.com

W. W. Norton & Company Ltd., 15 Carlisle Street, London W1D 3BS

1 2 3 4 5 6 7 8 9 0

For Alice, always.

CONTENTS

LIST OF ILLUSTRATIONS

German Territorial acquisitions under Hitler, before the Second World War

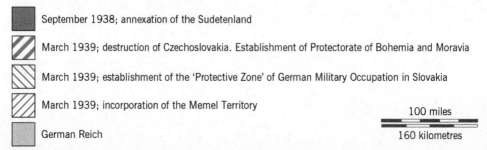

September 1938; annexation of the Sudetenland

March 1939; destruction of Czechoslovakia. Establishment of Protectorate of Bohemia and Moravia

March 1939; establishment of the 'Protective Zone' of German Military Occupation in Slovakia

March 1939; incorporation of the Memel Territory

German Reich

100 miles

160 kilometres

Europe on the eve of the Munich Conference, September 1938

IRELAND

Dublin•

UNITED
KINGDOM

London•

North
Sea

Amsterdam•

NETHERLANDS

BELGIUM

Brussels•

Frankfurt•

Atlantic Ocean

Paris•

Freiburg•

200 miles

320 kilometres

Bay of
Biscay

F R A N C E

SWITZERLAND

Guernica•

FRANCOISTS

Ligurian Sea

•Madrid

REPUBLICANS

Barcelona•

Corsica

SPAIN

REPUBLICANS

Valencia•

Balearic Islands

Sardinia

M e d i t e r r a n e a n   S e a

INTRODUCTION

'All the systems evolved by human beings for living
on this earth were now shown to be either delusory,
destructive, sadly outdated or at risk.'

*— Booker Prize-winning British author Penelope Fitzgerald
recalls her thoughts as a 22-year-old at Christmas time 1938.*

'I tremble for my happiness, the future of my fatherland,
for life, freedom, health and work — I am fearful of
all those things in these minutes.'

*— Erich Ebermayer, successful Nazi-era scriptwriter and
playwright, confesses his true thoughts to his diary
during the final moments of 1938.*

In the crucial year between the autumn of 1938 and the autumn
of 1939, the nations of Europe slid from the promise of peace
into the horror of total war. This book's title, *The War Nobody
Wanted*, reflects the fact that, when this happened, there was no
mass outbreak of enthusiasm for war as there had been a quarter
of a century earlier, in 1914. Moreover, Hitler had hoped initially
to limit the conflict. So perhaps even he did not want the war
that he got.

There is, of course, another issue here. While few in Britain
or Germany wanted a war, it is a historical fact that the mass
of the people in both countries eventually tolerated one, and

participated, if not with enthusiasm, then with a grim determination. This is especially true of the journey undertaken by
the mass of the public in Germany, which had been deeply
reluctant go to war in September 1938 over the Sudetenland,
but a little less than a year later allowed itself to be persuaded
that conflict with Poland was legitimate and necessary. The
propaganda campaign undertaken by the Nazi regime to this
end provides a near-perfect example of how, when a government
exercises total control of information, an entire nation can be
bent to its will.

*

How did all this happen? The broad diplomatic and political events
of 1938–9, and the roles of the elites involved, have been described
and analysed many times since. But what did it feel like, as an
'ordinary' person in Britain or Germany, to be living through
this time of tension, fear, uncertainty, and – ultimately –
catastrophe? What was occurring day by day far away from the
diplomatic drawing rooms and the conferences and the cabinet
meetings? To gain a deeper insight into this under-reported aspect
was my main motivation for researching and writing this book.

In my research on the bombing of Dresden, the building of
the Berlin Wall, the air raid on Coventry – books dealing with
crises in human affairs – I have tried to take a fresh, 'ground-up'
view of such great and terrible events. *The War Nobody Wanted* is
in that tradition. Yet in building up a vivid, humanly graspable
picture of lives that were lived over that fateful year, I have had
to hunt more avidly and more widely than ever for sources that
enable such an approach to the past.

Historians working now, eighty years after the events described,
are acting at the limit of human memory. When I first began to
write this kind of history, almost twenty years ago, people who
as adults had taken part in, or been eyewitnesses to, the Second
World War were relatively plentiful; now, most surviving eyewitnesses were children at the time I am writing about. This fact
affects the lens through which their memories are viewed. I did
indeed interview a substantial number of people in their nineties

in Britain and in Germany, the oldest of whom was ninety-six. There was nothing wrong with their ability to remember, or to describe what they recalled, but the memories were those of children, unaware of or protected from the greater, more frightening events occurring outside the home. All were fascinating and often delightful partners for conversation, but in most cases their views were limited. In particular, one of the things that I instinctively suspected but found clearly confirmed by these encounters was that peace, however desirable, is altogether less memorable than war; it is monaural rather than stereo, black and white rather than colour, at least as far as ease of recollection is concerned. A child does not remember the news of the Munich conference, but children recall the experience of a bombing raid. There are, of course, dramatic exceptions to this rule, as readers will see from this book, and those exceptions justify all the extra effort.

Fortunately, there turned out be no shortage of other sources that bear witness to the everyday experiences of life just before the Second World War. In Britain, there is the Mass Observation Archive, with its precious diary material supplied by hundreds of 'ordinary' civilians of differing ages and classes, some of it directly related to the great crises of the day, much of it not, but yet equally valuable and informative for this book's purposes. There is a host of diaries, memoirs and newspapers (particularly popular newspapers such as the *Daily Mirror* and the *Daily Express*) that all provide lively and often surprisingly unmediated insights into the everyday lives, fears, hopes and prejudices of the British population during the year covered by this book. The press also contains fascinating and quirky, sometimes unsettling, detail that has been lost in the great sweep of historical narrative but proves, if one is prepared to put in the necessary hours of searching newspapers' inside pages, recoverable. There is also the astonishing trove of audio interview recordings available at the Imperial War Museum, London, and online, much of it taped twenty or thirty or more years ago. And there is a mass of published diaries and memoirs.

In Germany, there was no equivalent of Mass Observation – unless one is allowed to count the apparatus of the Nazi police state, which reported on citizens' opinions, complaints and fears, as well as goings-on in the Reich's small towns and great cities alike, and was often surprisingly willing to admit the uncomfortable aspects of those goings-on. The SS Security Service, the Gestapo and the local Party organizations all collected reports on public opinion; I have dipped into some direct archive material and also drawn on published collections of such documents. The German press of the time, although of course thoroughly controlled by the regime, also reveals a surprising amount – sometimes inadvertently – about the anxieties that preoccupied both the average citizen of the Third Reich and the men (I can safely say that, because Nazi rule was exclusively male) who dictated what their fellow Germans heard and read and were expected to think. A month's issues of a German newspaper from the Baltic coast city of Stettin, for instance, centring on the horrors of the November 1938 anti-Jewish pogrom that is familiar even to English-speaking readers by its German name, *Kristallnacht* – 'the night of broken glass' – shows more intensely and terrifyingly, because it is so localized and specific, how such events affect a seemingly average, workaday place; one, moreover, that is scarcely mentioned in most history books of the time. It is all too clear that the destruction of Stettin's synagogue, first by fire and then by dynamite, occurred while the city's life went on around it, with its bustling restaurants, shops, bars and nightclubs, its theatres and newly built cinema complexes, chillingly similar to their twenty-first-century equivalents. I also gained access to diaries and memoirs from the period, which are held by the remarkable Deutsches Tagebucharchiv (German Diary Archive) in Emmendingen, near Freiburg in south-west Germany. Most of these are evidence of the extent to which, no matter how much they desired peace, 'ordinary' people accepted and lived with – in some cases passionately embraced – the Nazi regime and its everyday demands. Other published diaries and memoirs, especially those of Ruth Andreas-Friedrich and Erich Ebermayer, also provide precious insights into the private worlds that somehow survived within a monolithic totalitarian structure.

*

I have, I think, ended up writing a different book from the one I would have conceived even just a few years ago. Before the disastrous economic and political events of 2008–9, it was possible to blithely assume that we had left the brutal and unpredictable world of the 1930s behind us. However, just as the economic crisis of 1929–31 summoned up the demons described in this book, so our own time's economic and social problems – excessive national and private debt, globalization leading to unemployment and low wages for the majority but high profits for the few, and uncontrolled mass movements of populations – have led to similarly destabilizing and demoralizing developments in Europe, America, and parts of Asia. At the same time, large-scale abuse of data, accompanied by manipulation of online information and social media, has placed persuasive power into the hands of twenty-first-century authoritarian disrupters to an extent that their predecessors in the 1930s could only have dreamt of.

The rebellion against membership of the European Union, culminating in the British 'Brexit' referendum on 23 June 2016, represents a new high-water mark for anxious and distrustful popular sentiment. A little more than seventy years after the war against extreme nationalism appeared won, a small but clear majority of those who chose to vote essentially reaffirmed the near-absolute primacy of nationalism over internationalism, reversing the political direction in which the United Kingdom and the rest of Europe had appeared to be travelling since 1945. In the United States, a phrase with dubious historical pedigree, 'America First', has become current once more.

What we are living through is not, of course, precisely a repeat of the 1930s. However, the study of the 1930s reminds us of the dangers of crass inequality, of international 'beggar-my-neighbour' competition, of the capacity of marginalized social groups for extreme violence based on the scapegoating of minorities, and of the many other consequences that flow from irresponsible and often sadly misjudged notions of national self-interest.

As for us, the 'ordinary people' of today, like our grandparents and great-grandparents in the late 1930s, we are sure that we

want all the advantages of prosperity, safety, a roof over our heads
and the conveniences of fast travel and communication. And, like
them, we want the gift of international peace, which guarantees
all these good things. However, many of us also seem to think
we can combine these benefits with crude national self-
aggrandizement while remaining immune to the consequences.

No one really expects another war in Europe. However, it is
also true that for the first time in almost three-quarters of a
century, no one really rules it out.

In this trend lies the chilling similarity between our world and
the experience of the people living day by day, week by week,
through the chaotic and unpredictable time immediately preceding
the outbreak of the Second World War. This is how it felt to be
human beings existing in the thick of a fateful and ultimately
catastrophic phase in European history, their experience unmediated by hindsight. Like most of us today, our grandparents and
great-grandparents were largely preoccupied with private daily
duties and routines, preoccupations and gratifications. They could
not, of course, foresee the future. Wider dangers remained unseen
or half-seen, individual and communal hopes for peace and continuing prosperity had not yet been dashed.

Britain was quite 'modern' (if the term makes sense) by the
end of the 1930s. Germany, it should be said, was also a typical
Western consumer society in many, often quite disarming, ways.
However, with the active encouragement of the Nazi governing
apparatus, the country was also a pressure cooker of passions.

A regime such as Hitler's, which follows a major peaceful
diplomatic victory (the Munich Agreement) in short order with
a state-sponsored savage and murderous attack on a law-abiding
section of its own population (the *Kristallnacht* outrages against
Germany's Jews), is not one whose leader's actions on the international stage can be viewed in a value-free way as 'pragmatic'.

There is, it seems to me, something much more powerful and
compulsive at work here in the German national psyche at that
time – turmoil within, that eventually became reflected in turmoil
without. Piecing together a mosaic of public and private feeling,
and judging its often hidden power, seems to me a way of

redressing the imbalances of a 'top-down' view that can end up looking at major political actors' machinations in a kind of arid, almost laboratory isolation. Perhaps some similar history will be written years from now about present-day Britain and America – especially the latter – in this fascinating and unnerving context.

Most books about the pre-war era that try to balance a 'top-down' narrative with a 'bottom-up' element tend to confine themselves to sketching what ordinary people are doing when they are fearing the imminence of a war that, with hindsight, we know lies just over the horizon. *The War Nobody Wanted* will establish what they were doing when the threat of war was *not* presently on their minds – working, spending time with family, worrying about money or their personal appearance, eating and going dancing or to the cinema – so allowing us to enter fully their world of eight decades ago.

*

The closing weeks of 1938 appeared to draw a line under the post-war era, satisfying most of Germany's grievances about the injustices of the Treaty of Versailles, securing more just and potentially more stable borders for the states of Central Europe. There were high hopes of permanent peace. The problem and ultimate tragic causality lay – as we know now but millions alive at the time did not – in the sinister nature of Hitler's true ambition.

Austria, having lost its centuries-old empire, had tried to join with newly democratic Germany in 1918 but been prevented by the victors from doing so. In 1931 the small and impoverished republic tried again, this time in the form of a customs union with its 'big brother' to the north. Again, the great powers blocked this in many ways sensible move, for political reasons. Even in the case of the Sudetenland, the German-speaking districts of Bohemia and Moravia (which had also tried to join Germany in 1918), there was a cultural logic to their incorporation into a single German-speaking state in October 1938.

The German public, even those portions of it still unsympathetic to Nazism, approved. So, more unexpectedly, did the populace in Britain, France and other democratic countries.

Opinions had changed since 1918. Their governments had denied these concessions to the mostly benign democratic politicians of Weimar Germany right through the 1920s, but now, belatedly, had come to view the post-war settlement as unjust and unsustainable. The recipient of their resulting largesse was not, however, a rational statesman – it was too late for that – but an insatiable dictator.

The ruling elites in Britain and France failed to realize in time that they were not dealing with a slightly more excitable version of Weimar's Gustav Stresemann or Heinrich Brüning. Hitler was a new phenomenon: an ideologically driven leader who sought not reasonable national satisfaction but absolute power. How did so many people miss seeing this catastrophe in the making until it was (almost) too late?

Professional property and industrial developers use (when they can get away with it) a clever but none-too-moral method of gaining permission from the planning authorities for dubious projects. This entails applying for – and being granted – a succession of minor, apparently reasonable, and not necessarily dangerous-looking permissions until, in effect, these accumulate into a permitted project that would not have been allowed had the authorities been presented with the overall plan from the start. This is known in the business as 'salami slicing'. With hindsight, we can see that Hitler was adept at the 'salami-slicing' technique in his relations with the British, French, Czechoslovaks, Poles and other interested parties during the later 1930s.

By 1939, showing his characteristic mixture of boldness and guile, the Führer had accumulated what he needed, in territory, diplomatic clout and military strength, in order to dominate Europe – not to mention, potentially, the Eurasian lands to the east. During this same year, the democratic powers began to realize the true extent of his aims. Of course, by then it was far too late to thwart him without resorting to massive force.

Following on from this, the populations of the European nations (soon to be joined by the Americans and Russians) were drawn into a vast and bloody worldwide war of extermination that just three or four years earlier no one had imagined could ever happen.

The price ultimately paid on both sides was a terrible one: in blood, in senseless destruction, and in the nightmare that was the Holocaust. On a material, perhaps less essential level, it also delayed what might be called the modern project. Had war not intervened, shattering so much peaceful promise, Europe might not only have been spared immeasurable horror, but would also have been able to enjoy the harmless pleasures and securities of prosperous consumerism in the 1940s, rather than having to wait until the 1950s and 1960s. That thwarted promise of a better material life also forms part of this book's theme.

*

During the fateful first days of September 1939, most adult Europeans were, of course, aware of the appalling cost of the previous war. Many millions dead. The collapse of historic nations. Destruction. Hunger. Revolution. Few, apart from a minority of fanatics, wanted another conflict of that type.

The two decades that had elapsed since the Great War ended had seen hyperinflation, disorder and economic depression – a roller-coaster ride of social and political instability. As the world approached the mid-1930s, however, the international economic climate had improved. Despite continuing poverty and unemployment in some parts of Europe, a phenomenon that we would see as recognizably modern had begun to emerge: a mass consumer society. Before 1914, just about all of what could be called luxury had been confined to the topmost segment of society; in 1939, the spread, while still relatively limited, was far greater. More people shared in the comfort and convenience of material things than ever before, in a way that caused changes in how society functioned and in its members' expectations.

By 1938, the level of consumption had risen in all the advanced countries of Europe. There was radio in millions of households, there were telephones, there were fairly sophisticated electrical appliances for the home, there was commercial air travel as well as the established rail network. Private car ownership, though still much rarer than in America, was no longer the preserve of the rich and privileged. There was even television, which came first to Germany in 1935, in good part for the very modern reason that the Olympic Games were due to take place the next year in Berlin. Britain followed in 1936 (with better-quality pictures).

*

In peacetime, Nazi Germany, for all its cruelties and intolerance, was not Soviet Russia. American and other foreign films were shown throughout Germany (unless the directors or stars were well known to be Jewish). Foreign newspapers were on sale in German cities (so long as they were not clearly socialist or communist). Newspapers carried the schedules of foreign radio stations as well as German ones (a situation that would change radically once war was declared, after which listening to non-German transmissions became a serious, potentially capital, offence).

The facade of relative normality and prosperity that the country presented to the casual view was, of course, deceptive. The mass of the German public might have continued to hope for peace. It had, however, voted for Adolf Hitler, a naked militarist and racist, in sufficient numbers to make the Nazi Party the largest in the country and its leader, on 30 January 1933, Chancellor. Once in power, while throwing hundreds of thousands of dissidents and political opponents into concentration camps and beginning a consistent policy of pogroms and discrimination against German Jews, the obnoxious but to many of his people spellbinding Austrian-born adventurer had appeared to miraculously solve the problem of high unemployment.

Hitler's programme of rearmament and national self-assertion (while still proclaiming peaceful intent, a trick perhaps learned from Soviet propaganda) gained him further popularity and served to mask the regime's contradictions. True, German industrial workers were distinctly less well off than their equivalents in Britain, France, and certainly the USA, and were forced to work even harder (a compulsory sixty-hour week was introduced in early 1939). However, at least they had jobs, as their government constantly reminded them. There were compensations for loyalty in the form of the Party's 'Strength Through Joy' pleasure and leisure organization, and a wide range of government-supported training and further education courses for the ambitious worker. Of course, for those bold enough to suggest that all this was still not quite enough, there was always the threat of the Gestapo, the Geheime Staatspolizei, to enforce acquiescence.

Almost six years after Hitler had seized power, he seemed more popular than ever. The fact nonetheless remained that Germany, though outwardly strong and prosperous, was storing up problems. Falls in foreign currency reserves and raw materials shortages threatened to bankrupt the country. So long as the economy remained Nazified and therefore in normal economic terms unsustainable, these problems could only be 'solved' by acquiring new territory and resources – with or without war.

*

By contrast, Britain in the late 1930s, although gradually losing its grip on Empire and suffering from setbacks to its traditional mining and heavy industrial sectors, was on the whole in good shape economically. The decision to abandon the gold standard in 1931 had permitted a more flexible economy than in other advanced countries, and thus a speedier recovery.

High unemployment in the still depressed north of the country – leading to desperate popular protests such as the Jarrow March – contrasted with rising living standards in the English south and Midlands, where modern consumer-directed manufacturing (including motor-vehicle production, electrical equipment, radio communications and latterly aircraft production) and new service industries brought unheard-of prosperity. Owing to cheap credit, the 1930s was also an era of enormous expansion in house building, leading to a booming construction sector.

From 1936, and with reluctance, after it grew clear that Germany was rearming, the British government paid reluctant heed to expanding its armed forces. Local city and town officials were primed with providing a basic civil defence infrastructure, for it was clear that a new war would involve devastating aerial bombardment. However, many, especially those controlled by the broadly anti-war Labour Party, dragged their feet in imposing what was decried as a 'militarization of everyday life'.

The great majority of the British population did not favour war. Britain was no longer the almost limitlessly wealthy super-power it had been before 1914. The country's continuing world-power status now relied on the maintenance of a rules-based international order, with its guarantees of the global status quo (and especially of Britain's precious Empire). A world war would make British power vulnerable to Germany, and to Germany's allies, Italy – in the Mediterranean and the Middle East – and Japan (in the Far East). This prompted much of the reasoning behind Neville Chamberlain's so-called 'policy of appeasement'.

In Germany, whatever the private feelings of some citizens (which they were usually wise enough to keep to themselves), there was not much obvious opposition to rapid remilitarization, or the building of air-raid shelters and imposition of rigorous air-raid drills. All these began to be implemented almost imme-diately after the Nazi seizure of power. There was little active desire for war, but unlike the case in Britain, little or no oppo-sition to restoring the ability to wage it – especially as rearmament created much-needed jobs. In short, what many Germans wanted was the fruits of war without the need for actual conflict, which does not quite equate to wanting peace. The contradiction between these twin desires – for peace on the one side yet aggressive expansionism on the other – obvious as it might seem to many observers outside Germany, did not seem so to many of the Führer's subjects, even during the final months before war broke out. The regime deceived, with its message of Hitler as a 'man of peace', and found millions of Germans all too ready to be accept the lie.

Moreover, the suspicion that the Western powers were 'encir-cling' Germany as they had supposedly done before 1914 also fed a powerful popular undertow even among Germans who did not actively support the Nazi regime. Anything that smacked of defiance of the hated Versailles Treaty was broadly favoured by most Germans.

So, the Nazis' exit from the League of Nations, followed by such coups as Hitler's remilitarization of the Rhineland in 1936 (which, as a breach of the Treaty of Versailles, could have provoked a legitimate Anglo-French armed response), increased the Führer's popularity, providing the twin satisfactions of defying the Allies and at the same time increasing Germany's defensive capability. And these 'wins' were achieved without war. The same proved true of the forced annexation of Austria in March 1938 and of Hitler's management of the crisis that preceded the Reich's acquisition of the Sudetenland in October of the same year, at which point our narrative proper begins.

The War Nobody Wanted describes a breakdown of hope, accompanying a collapse in what remained of the European political order. In its conclusion, with the German invasion of Poland, it also marks the beginning of a terrible transformation in the attitude of a large section of the German people, from passive, even sullen, accepters of the Führer's will to accomplices in genocidal horror. The means by which this change of heart was effected – a continual, ruthless and mendacious campaign of vilification in the captive German press and other media against all the ethnic groups and countries, large or small, that stood in the way of Nazi ambitions – forms a key theme of this book.

Frederick Taylor
St Keverne, Cornwall
October 2018

ONE

September 1938
'So, No War!'

On Tuesday 27 September 1938, Europe held its breath. Just under twenty years since the end of the 'Great War' – supposedly the conflict to end all conflicts – matters in the troubled centre of the Continent had come to a head. After weeks of disturbances, leading to wild accusations of violence and maltreatment of German-speakers in the western provinces of Czechoslovakia – a few of them justified, most not – the German dictator, Adolf Hitler, had made a dark promise: unless his demands were met, he would send his Wehrmacht into Bohemia and Moravia to 'rescue' the country's German-speaking minority from supposed state-sponsored violence and to punish the Czech government and people for their real and imagined crimes. Britain and France had publicly sworn to go to war if he did so.

Among the anxious millions was Ann Magnus, a twelve-year-old English schoolgirl living in tranquil rural Essex, experiencing a first serious intimation of how dangerous her world had become. Her father, a City stockbroker, had moved out of London in response to the German bombing raids on the capital in the final years of the First World War. By now, after years of commuting, he had retired. He led her outside after dark to view a novel spectacle. 'We saw searchlights over London,' she recalled. Together, they watched from their farmhouse garden as the beams played eerily over the distant British capital for the first time since 1918. Her mother had refused to leave the house, finding the idea of another war and more bombing too distressing.[1]

On 26 September 1938, in a speech at the Berlin Sportpalast, Hitler had told a huge audience of Nazi believers that the die was cast. Unless Czechoslovakia gave in to all his demands before 1 October, he would take the country by force. To show he meant business, a demonstration of Germany's military power was planned for the next day in the heart of the Reich capital.

In Berlin, as the afternoon of 27 September wore on, trucks filled with troops, tanks and artillery pieces rumbled along the wide thoroughfare of the Wilhelmstrasse and through the Wilhelmplatz. Here they passed the grandiose facade of Hitler's recently completed New Reich Chancellery. From its purpose-built second-floor balcony the Führer was expected imminently to view this impressive array of forces that he had publicly vowed to send against Czechoslovakia.

Dusk began to fall. There was always a bit of a crowd in front of the Chancellery – mostly provincial tourists, hoping for a sight of the Führer. Today's gathering was larger than usual, reflecting the dramatic international atmosphere and the attraction of a major parade.

Directly across the street stood Berlin's oldest, grandest, hotel, the Kaiserhof, where Hitler had lived and established his headquarters in the weeks before he seized power almost six years earlier. In its elegant bar sat two equally elegant women in their thirties, celebrating the end of their working day with one, two, and then three Martinis. One of these women, Ruth Andreas-Friedrich, would record her experiences of that day – as she did for all the terrible days and years that followed. Just turned thirty-seven years old, she married young and divorced before thirty. She had a teenage daughter, a career as a magazine journalist and reviewer, and a partner, 'Andrik' (real name Leo Borchard),* who

---

* Leo Borchard (1899–1945) was born in Moscow of German-Russian heritage. In the mid-1930s he was still allowed to make recordings, but not to appear in public

was a well-known orchestral conductor (currently touring Scandinavia). Her wide circle of artistically inclined Gentile and Jewish friends had at least one thing in common: they shared a loathing of the Nazi regime.

Andreas-Friedrich's companion in the bar of the Kaiserhof, named in her account as 'Karla Simson' (real name, Susanne 'Susy' Simonis), was three years younger, also a journalist and an active anti-Nazi. Both women were fully aware of the dangers the world faced that autumn day. Simonis, in particular, was well connected inside the German Foreign Office, through her cousin, Erich Kordt (his name changed to 'Erich Tuch' for Andreas-Friedrich's account), a senior aide to Hitler's Foreign Minister, Joachim von Ribbentrop. Kordt was actually inside the room at the Chancellery that very evening.

Simonis drained her third Martini, then fished the olive out of her cocktail, popped it in her mouth, and said thoughtfully: 'I think we're in the wrong place. World history is being made outside.' Andreas-Friedrich nodded. 'Okay, let's mingle with the people.'[2]

Outside on the Wilhelmplatz, the two friends found the crowd surprisingly subdued. There was a certain febrile anxiety abroad in the early evening air. They did not have long to wait for the great moment. The curtains on the second floor parted, the high windows opened, and out onto the balcony stepped Adolf Hitler. He advanced towards the balustrade, followed at a respectful distance by a gaggle of senior officers, and surveyed the crowd below. Andreas-Friedrich glanced at the faces of the people surrounding her in the crowd. They looked, she wrote later: 'like whipped dogs'. No one was shouting support for the Führer, as was otherwise usual when he presented himself to the people.

---

in Germany. Andrik Krassnow was a cover name he used for his Resistance activities. He survived the war and was appointed Director of the Berlin Philharmonic, only to be shot and killed by an American sentry while returning from a performance when his car (driven by a British officer) failed to stop at a sector border post in occupied Berlin.

Her friend plucked at Andreas-Friedrich's coat and whispered in her ear: 'All dressed up and nowhere to go.'

The tanks went on rumbling past while the crowd remained near-silent. After a few more moments, Hitler turned on his heel and disappeared back into the building. White-gloved SS-men shut the door behind him and closed the curtains. A young worker in the crowd muttered: 'If this doesn't mean war, I'll eat a broom-stick.' 'And more fools us,' said a middle-aged postman, still in uniform. He glanced around nervously, astounded at his own temerity.

After they parted, a depressed Andreas-Friedrich was unwilling to go back to her little apartment in suburban Steglitz. She walked around for some time in central Berlin before ending up, after midnight, 'looking by' Hiller's restaurant in Unter den Linden. There she met a habitué of the place, the Jewish journalist Heinrich Mühsam, an old friend and former colleague at the magazine where she worked. Mühsam was not a conventionally attractive man, with his lank hair, crumpled suit and bulbous, shiny nose, but he was wise and charming and a fine writer. Andreas-Friedrich sometimes wished her affection for him could find physical expression, but it could not. 'As we sit at the table together,' she wrote, 'we are almost in love. I just can't kiss him. But I don't dare tell him that. One cannot cause further hurt to people who already have things hard enough'. There they stayed until 3 a.m., when they shared a taxi to their respective homes.

*

In the meantime, unknown to the general public, the crisis over the Sudetenland had begun a further series of twists and turns that would change everything, at least for the immediate future. Hours earlier, the crowd on the Wilhelmplatz, including Andreas-Friedrich and Susy Simonis, had seen the Führer disappear wordlessly back into his Chancellery. Almost everyone who witnessed this had echoed the man in the crowd – 'This means war.'

In fact, however, on his return to the room full of officials and high officers, Hitler had been filled with gloom at the evident lack of popular enthusiasm for the planned military action against

Czechoslovakia. 'With a people like this,' he confided to his intimates, casting a sour glare at the Propaganda Minister, Joseph
Goebbels, 'I cannot make a war yet.'

That morning, Hitler had spoken in the Chancellery with Sir
Horace Wilson, a senior British civil servant, foreign policy
adviser to and emissary of the British Prime Minister, Neville
Chamberlain. Wilson had told him that France would support
Czechoslovakia in case of a German invasion (indeed, was bound
by treaty do so). Should this mean war, Britain would be obliged
to fight too. Hitler had responded uncompromisingly, insisting
that he would 'smash Czechoslovakia' if his terms were not
accepted. He had prepared for all emergencies. And not for
nothing had he spent four and a half billion Reichsmarks forti-
fying Germany's western border.

Nevertheless, at 10.30 on the evening of that same day –
Tuesday 27 September – within a few hours of the Führer's
disappointing encounter with German public opinion, Chamberlain
received a letter from Hitler. In it, the Führer promised him that
German forces would not move beyond the territory that the
Czechs had already agreed to cede to the Reich, that a plebiscite
in the territories would be a free vote, and that Germany was
prepared to guarantee the integrity of what remained of the
Czechoslovak state.[3]

It was true that Chamberlain had also shown signs of not being
entirely behind the firm line that Wilson had conveyed to Hitler.
In a broadcast on BBC radio that evening, the Prime Minister
referred to the many desperate letters, pleading for peace, which
he had received from the general public. He continued in a vein
that would become notorious:

> If I felt my responsibility heavy before, to read such letters has
> made it seem almost overwhelming. How horrible, fantastic,
> incredible it is that we should be digging trenches and trying
> on gas-masks here because of a quarrel in a far-away country
> between people of whom we know nothing. It seems still more
> impossible that a quarrel which has already been settled in
> principle should be the subject of war . . .

. . . However much we may sympathise with a small nation
confronted by a big powerful neighbour, we cannot in all circumstances undertake to involve the whole British Empire in war
simply on her account. If we have to fight it must be on larger
issues than that.[4]

It did not quite amount to a volte-face – any more than did
Hitler's temporary change of tactic – but it came close. The
bizarre assertion that the crisis was taking place 'in a far-away
country between people of whom we know nothing' seemed
especially egregious. If such ignorance about Czechoslovakia – a
key country in the chain of Eastern European alliances set up to
help contain Germany after the First World War – was indeed a
fact, then the Prime Minister needed to sack his foreign policy
advisers – or possibly himself. The Czechoslovak crisis had dominated everyone's thoughts, not to mention the newspaper
headlines, in Europe and beyond since the early months of 1938.
Chamberlain had already flown to Germany twice with his French
counterpart, Édouard Daladier, to tackle the problem in direct
encounters with Hitler.

At the first set of crisis meetings, on 15 September, at the
Führer's mountaintop home, the Berghof, near Berchtesgaden,
they had discussed the Sudeten question in great detail.
Chamberlain had surprised his host by agreeing in principle to
an adjustment of the Czech borders so long as this was confined
to German-speaking-majority districts. He met the Führer again
a week later at Bad Godesberg, in the Rhineland. Here Hitler,
sensing his opponents' strategic indecisiveness and ever the
gambler, stepped up his demands. As a result, perhaps unexpectedly so far as the Führer was concerned, he encountered a strong
level of resistance from the French and the British. The Western
allies issued new guarantees of the Czech state's right to existence,
leading to a new European crisis and the most serious danger of
war so far.

The Czechs mobilized their considerable army. Over the
previous twenty years, the Czechoslovak state had constructed
an elaborate and sturdy defence system throughout the moun-

tainous Sudetenland – an area which in the previous century the great German chancellor Bismarck had described as 'a fortress built by God in the heart of Europe'. Hitler moved seven divisions of the Wehrmacht up to that same border, from Saxony in the north, Bavaria in the middle, and his recently acquired new province of Austria in the south.

In Britain, gas masks were distributed (gas, the great terror weapon of the First World War, seemed for many, including those in authority, a greater danger than bombs). Slit trenches were dug to provide rudimentary protection against bomb shrapnel, public buildings sandbagged, and many thousands of children were evacuated from the major cities. For almost a week, war seemed likely, if not inevitable.

*

The British Prime Minister, sixty-nine years old, had long been the 'strong man' of the Conservative-dominated so-called 'National Government', which had been formed in November 1931 in response to the Great Depression. As Chancellor of the Exchequer for five and a half years, Neville Chamberlain had engaged in ruthless cost cutting, engineering a budget surplus that most voters accepted put the country in a much better financial and economic situation than had seemed possible in the depths of the downturn. Chamberlain had been the natural successor to Stanley Baldwin. The veteran three-time Tory Prime Minister, aging and unwell, had resigned in May 1937, following his successful resolution of the crisis that led to the abdication of Edward VIII and the accession of his brother, George VI.

At the Treasury, Chamberlain had presided over brutal cuts to the military budget. However, from 1935 onwards he had supported a renewed expansion of the Royal Air Force and a general increase in armaments production to cope with the possible threat from Hitler's Germany. This decision had been opposed by the opposition leader, Clement Attlee, and his Labour colleagues, who at the time condemned it as 'warmongering'.

Chamberlain was, in fact, a surprisingly ruthless politician. With the aid of his harshly disciplinarian chief whip, David

Margesson, he kept the parliamentary Tory Party under strict control, showing 'an icy ruthlessness in bending Tory MPs to his and the government's will'.[5] Any rebels against the official line found themselves in serious political and sometimes personal trouble, not least because of the activities of the head of the Conservative Research Department, Sir Joseph Ball, a close friend of Chamberlain and frequent companion on the fly-fishing trips that took up a lot of the Prime Minister's spare time. A former senior official in charge of special investigations for MI5, Ball gathered information on the government's and Chamberlain's enemies, using methods that one historian has compared to those employed by President Nixon's 'dirty tricks department' thirty years later, including phone tapping.[6]

All this efficiency in power-wielding, and a powerful reputation for competence, belied Chamberlain's faintly comical air of wing-collared, umbrella-wielding Edwardian stuffiness. His professional toughness was further balanced out by eccentricities that imbued him with a certain human vulnerability. He was a skilled fly-fisherman and a fine shot, fairly conventional upper-class life skills, but also had a passionate love of trees, for example. His letters to his much-loved sister were full of mentions of whether they were in leaf and how much they flourished. In fact, according to his chauffeur, James Joseph Read, when staying at Chequers, his official country residence in Buckinghamshire, Chamberlain would often make energetic forays into the estate woods with a saw, for 'it worried him to see dead branches on a tree'. Although nearly seventy at the time, the Prime Minister would clamber into the upper reaches to do the necessary surgery.

One story told by Read had Chamberlain perched atop a tree just by the house when a terrified stag raced into view. Chamberlain called down to Read to open up the entrance to the estate's coal cellar, which lay across the yard. The animal duly dived into it and Read shut the door. Shortly after, the local stag hunt rode up. On Chamberlain's instructions, the chauffeur professed to have no idea of their quarry's whereabouts. The hunt galloped off, and the animal was saved. All this time, Chamberlain – the most powerful elected official in the British Empire – remained in the highest branches of the tree, saw in hand, silent and unobserved.[7]

Neville Chamberlain was also a martyr to gout, and Read became expert, he recalled, at easing the Prime Minister's swollen feet into his boots. The chauffeur even says that, when Chamberlain had occasion to fly to Germany for the first crisis meeting with Hitler, there were discussions as to whether he might be included in the party, in case a gout attack occurred during the crucial negotiations. In the end, it was decided that there was too little room for Read on the plane.

Before the end of 27 September, Chamberlain had already replied to Hitler's apparently emollient offer and agreed in principle to fly to Germany for a third time in a little more than two weeks, even going so far as to tell Hitler in advance: 'I feel certain that you can get all essentials without war and without delay.'[8] On the other hand, the British fleet was mobilized at just about the same time. The carrot-and-stick pressure for new talks mounted, and not just from the British side. During the small hours in London – still evening in America – President Roosevelt broadcast an appeal for a new conference on the Sudeten question.

By 11.30 next morning, 28 September, Chamberlain had contacted both Hitler and Mussolini and made a concrete proposal for a four-power meeting in Germany. Shortly afterwards, the German military mobilization, planned for 2 p.m., was postponed.

*

Understandably, after her late-night wandering and her even later tryst with Heinrich Mühsam, Ruth Andreas-Friedrich slept late the next day. It was almost 10 a.m. when, luxuriating in the shower, she heard the outside doorbell of the shared block ring four times, the signal that she had a visitor. She threw on a bathrobe and answered the door. It was her friend Susanne Simonis.

'Man alive – it's all off!' Simonis panted, having obviously run all the way there.

'What – where – who?'

'The war, of course!'

Andreas-Friedrich muttered something about needing to get

dressed and make herself a cup of tea before she could grasp anything at all. Simonis waited impatiently while her friend quickly dressed, brewed her tea, and fetched a slice of breakfast bread from the cupboard.

'So, no war!' Simonis explained then. 'Peace! Real, honest-to-God peace! They're going to negotiate a deal tomorrow. In Munich. Between Hitler, Mussolini, Daladier and Chamberlain. I got this from an authentic source!'

Among people like these, 'authentic' was a key word, meaning genuine information rather than rumour or propaganda. In this case, the source was Simonis's cousin on her mother's side, Erich Kordt, diplomat and right-hand man to Ribbentrop. Kordt was an insider, but as his friends knew, one with thoughts of his own that his boss and his comrades didn't know about and must never get to know. Although he had joined the Nazi Party the previous year, he was no supporter of the regime. Along with his older brother, Theo – currently chargé d'affaires at the German Embassy in London – he was plotting with senior Wehrmacht officers to get rid of Hitler if it came to war over Czechoslovakia.

Simonis told Andreas-Friedrich that her cousin had been inside the grand room at the Chancellery when Hitler had gone out onto the balcony the previous evening. He had seen everything from the window, even spotted the two familiar female faces in the crowd below. She repeated what Erich had told her in the interim:

So at that moment, the war was on a knife-edge. Hitler stepped out onto the balcony to salute his soldiers. Never before had he been so determined to take by force that which he had been refused in peace. We helped spoil that moment for him. With our glum faces and our unraised arms. For thirty minutes after stepping back into the room, he stood behind the curtain and took full account of our disfavour. Meanwhile, Goebbels, with his hat pulled down, cruised all over Berlin in a car with the blinds down and checked out the public mood. That put the lid on it. 'With the situation this way, we're going nowhere,' as the Berliners would say – especially when it came to running a war, and that was what the Nazis realised. So, they put their heads together again and postponed the thing. You just watch, from tomorrow those tormented Sudeten Germans will disappear from all the newspapers.[9]

Andreas-Friedrich felt little relief, only a flatness of mood, and it was clear to her that Simonis felt much the same. She went to the wireless and switched to Czech national radio. At first she got just the interval signal – a few bars of Smetana's patriotic symphonic poem *Vyšehrad* (The High Castle) – before Prague broadcast a funereal all-male choral piece.

For the rest of the day, as Andreas-Friedrich confessed to her diary, she wandered around in a daze. The high tension of the past weeks had somehow, it seemed, robbed her of the capacity for joy. 'War or peace?' she wrote. 'Both seem to me equally terrible and burdened with guilt.'

Seen from the point of view of oppositionists such as Andreas-Friedrich and her circle, this was true enough. As peace-loving human beings, they did not want war, but many were nonetheless beginning to suspect that only a war would rid the country of Hitler and his regime. The Kordt brothers – Erich, assistant to the Nazi Foreign Minister, Ribbentrop, and Theo, senior diplomat at the London Embassy – were part of a conspiracy involving leading military and political figures. Their aim was to stage a coup against Hitler in the case of war against Czechoslovakia, pleading overriding national necessity due to the Führer's insanity. Susy Simonis was also involved, as an occasional courier between her cousins, Erich in Berlin and Theo in London. She had been in London at the beginning of that same month, bearing a secret message that she had learned by heart to avoid any risk of interception.[10]

The originators of the plot were officers associated with the Abwehr, Germany's military intelligence, among them Lieutenant-Colonel Hans Oster and Major Helmuth Groscurth. Some of the Wehrmacht's most senior officers were loosely involved, including retired General von Witzleben, General Beck, until recently Chief of the General Staff, the army's Commander-in-Chief, von

Brauchitsch, and the Abwehr chief, Admiral Canaris. Leading civilian figures within the conspiracy's orbit included the Economics Minister, Hjalmar Schacht (the man who had defeated the hyperinflation of 1923), the conservative former Mayor of Leipzig and now head of overseas sales for the Bosch concern, Carl Goerdeler, and the State Secretary at the Foreign Office, Ernst von Weizsäcker (as such, the boss of the Kordt brothers). Most were old-style German conservatives, with a strong mix of monarchists, rather than democrats. Not all even wanted to overthrow or kill Hitler – more to 'bring him to his senses'[11] – but all believed that war at this time and for this cause would mean Germany's ruin. They were prepared to take drastic action to prevent it.

The British government was quite aware of this group's existence, and of its expressed aims. Theo Kordt appears on 6 September in the diaries of 53-year-old Sir Alexander Cadogan, permanent head of the British Foreign Office and the diplomatic service, as 'Herr X'.[12] On that day, Kordt had approached Sir Horace Wilson to inform him of Hitler's intention to move his forces against the Czechs on 19 or 20 September. This was a prediction that the German diplomat repeated the next evening in the presence of Cadogan and the Foreign Secretary, Lord Halifax – the Prime Minister was away fly-fishing in Scotland – after being secretly summoned to Downing Street ('through the garden entrance'). Kordt added a plea that the British publicly declare their intention to stand by the Czechs, come what may. He even suggested that London might make a specific warning radio broadcast to the German nation[13] – an idea that Cadogan thought potentially disastrous, adding that it 'almost makes me suspect', i.e. think that Kordt might in fact be some kind of agent provocateur.

Over the next days and weeks, Kordt and his friends would make desperate attempts to steel British resolve against Hitler's machinations. The opposition's plans depended on Franco-British firmness in the face of Nazi aggression, even – perhaps especially – if that firmness led to war in Central Europe. The problem was that, as Cadogan's reaction showed, the British could never quite work out whether this affair represented a genuine attempt at transnational cooperation against the Hitler peril or whether London was being, in the modern parlance, 'played' by some clever and devious Nazi diplomats.

In the final analysis, and perhaps sometimes with a certain regret, the British government chose to behave as if the opposition represented by Theo Kordt was not trustworthy. The British ruling class's distrust of its German equivalent had not, after all, suddenly sprung into being in 1933 when Hitler assumed power; it dated at the latest from these men's experiences of the First World War and the ever more bitter Anglo-German rivalries that had preceded it.

*

As for the British public, among most ordinary people, who knew only what they saw in the newspapers and heard on the radio, tensions still ran high. As the weekend approached, Leonard Grugeon, a 22-year-old bank clerk in Swindon and observer for Mass Observation, wrote of the atmosphere among colleagues at the bank where he worked: 'Meanwhile we wait anxiously while the statesmen confer . . . A great laziness affects the people. No work beyond that which is essential is undertaken. Letters remain unwritten, books unread, theatres unvisited, for none knows what tomorrow will bring – but everyone wonders.'[14]

Slightly earlier in the crisis, some had still tried to make light of it. Elizabeth Crowfoot, a young actress on tour with a repertory company, quoted her fellow company members discussing the latest news:

B.R. (actor, c. 30) came up and said, 'I shouldn't mind a war. Think of it – shan't have to bother about a job, no "keeping in touch", all costumes provided, no make-up, digs free –'
K.K. 'And [£]2/10 a day – it must be that because you get that on the dole.'
E.B., who was in the last war, just looked at them.

'K.K.' went on to say that he might apply to join the RAF, because there would be the delay of being trained – or the Navy, as that would be 'moderately clean'. He 'couldn't stand dirt or rats'.[15]

In Coventry, a centre for armaments manufacturing in the British Midlands and therefore a prime German bombing target, a reporter for Mass Observation mentioned hearing a sixteen-year-old youth telling a passer-by that if war broke out he would 'hare away home – wouldn't catch me staying in Coventry, I should put as much distance between me and Coventry as I could!' A friend of the reporter returning from Birmingham had told her that Barrow's, a large department store in the city's Bull Street, was 'coping with a rush of people only comparable to Christmas time'.[16]

The next day, after Chamberlain's trip to the Munich conference had been agreed, things relaxed perceptibly, though civilians encountered by the reporter spoke of digging trenches in case of air raids ('Bloody lot of good they'll be to us'). In Tunbridge Wells, 25 miles south of London, Miss Miller, a young schoolteacher and firm anti-Fascist, listened to the BBC six o'clock evening news after she got back from work. She wrote in her report:

> Chamberlain to go to Munich. Feeling of immense relief. Even catches excitement of parliament. At the same time suspense – Will England and France now make things impossible for Czechoslovakia? Will Mussolini demand our compliance re. Spain for his services? Still it is most hopeful news. After this, and lying on couch . . . to listen to news, I feel most refreshed and less tired.[17]

Miss Miller admitted that today she had also been intending to dig a trench in the garden and had purchased a pickaxe for the purpose. She had even decided at the weekend on a spot for the trench, 'but due to better news, lateness, etc., [I] postpone it'.

Back in Coventry, that evening there was a 'confused babble' of voices on the bus home, with a young shop worker in his early twenties declaring 'in a superior voice: "Well, what did I always say? I knew there'd never be a war. Come pretty close to it, but—"' and another young commuter was equally optimistic: 'Hitler may be a fool, but he's not as big a fool as to start a war – never thought it would come to war.'[18]

*

In Germany, it was also unclear to most of the population whether the new development meant certain peace or just a more complicated way to war. Wilm Hosenfeld, a 43-year-old First World War veteran, was a schoolteacher in the village of Thalau, in eastern Hessen. He combined being a faithful Catholic with enthusiastic membership of the National Socialist Party, and had attended the Nuremberg Rally two years earlier. Hosenfeld had nonetheless been disturbed by Hitler's aggressive speech on 26 September: 'He speaks without restraint, in a bullying way, you can say that his manner has little grace or superiority. Expressions such as "lying democratic toad" are unworthy of a great statesman who is representing a great people. He does not intend to compromise. We fear that there will be war.'[19] The next day there was even a hint of a political rethink. Perhaps dictatorships bring problems as well as advantages?

> Just now, despite everything, one is given cause to be aware that the political form of the pure dictatorship can also bring great danger. What is there to stop Hitler from remaining impervious and plunging the German people into war? A referendum? Big words, but in reality the people are not being consulted. Quite different to democracy, with a parliament.[20]

The next day, not being privy to the secret information that had cheered Ruth Andreas-Friedrich and her friends, the provincial schoolmaster was only marginally less gloomy. This was also a 'bad day' (*böser Tag*) in which the shadow of war seemed to darken further. 'This war,' Hosenfeld wrote in his diary, 'would be enormously bad in its consequences – every time there is news on the radio, we rush to the set to listen. A [Annemarie, his wife] is so downcast that the slightest emotional stress leads to tears.'[21]

In the south-west of the country, at Canstatt, just outside Stuttgart, a woman in her twenties, working as a gardener, was writing a diary entry for the day. As she went on, she switched from the subject of the exceptionally hot weather, now dominant for two weeks past, to the Sudeten Crisis and the meeting in Munich. Although clearly a keen supporter of Hitler, she wrote with evident concern about the situation and what it might mean for her father and brother:

> Certainly, if it must be, it will be each to his place, and trust in the Führer's lucky touch and in Italy's and Japan's readiness to help. Events are piling one on top of the other, today the Führer is meeting Chamberlain and Daladier in Munich for talks, and tension as to the result is getting higher all the time. Every few hours there is news on the radio and reports of the terror in Czechia, the tension is at bursting point.
>
> Will Papa have to go, and later Heinz? What will become of us if we all get dispersed? I am afraid for our future. The news from foreign radio stations, which we often listen to, only serves to confuse us the more, they are always different from ours, they are never pro-German. They are envious of our Germany's growing strength, that is all, and the Jews who have fled and now also are having to leave Italy will be doing their usual business.[22]

She then proceeded to describe going with a girlfriend to the Zarah Leander film that had reportedly won the Mussolini Trophy at Venice.*

In Berlin, meanwhile, 38-year-old Erich Ebermayer occupied

---

* *Zu neuen Ufern* (To New Shores), the Swedish-born actress's first film in Germany, was in fact only nominated for the prize, which was won by a French film starring Jean Gabin. Its director, Detlef Sierck, shortly afterwards fled Germany to join his Jewish wife in exile and eventually ended up in the USA, where he took a new name and transformed himself into the famous director of Hollywood melodramas, Douglas Sirk.

a curious position, close to the elite of the Third Reich and yet constantly on the edge of illegality. A successful novelist, playwright and screenwriter, he had been a prominent liberal voice in the Weimar era, and many of his works had been banned by the Nazis. However, he had contacts within Hitler's circle, including Reichsleiter Philipp Bouhler, one of Hitler's earliest supporters and from 1936 head of the Führer's political Chancellery, who was a cousin on Ebermayer's mother's side. Through another cousin, he was related by marriage to Dr Fritz Todt, Hitler's construction tsar and leader of the vast civil and military engineering behemoth named, after him, Organisation Todt. So Ebermayer would attend some glittering Nazi cultural festival one day, then be invited in for a tense 'chat' with the Gestapo on another – though it must be said that he never ended up in a concentration camp.

Fortunately for Ebermayer, his non-political plays were still performed, and he was permitted to write film scripts of a neutral, popular nature, to take on lucrative jobs as a (usually uncredited) 'script doctor', and to work as a theatre director. As a consequence, he still made a handsome living throughout the Nazi period. And he kept a diary. On 28 September, he wrote about Hitler's rabid, rabble-rousing speech of 26 September, of which he had just read a newspaper account ('I found it physically impossible to listen to it [on the radio]'):

> The mood of people in Berlin is interesting. If we disregard the fanatical masses who filled the Sportpalast . . . we see only miserable faces everywhere. No one wants war – but many would like the Sudetenland. All the same, things are going so well! We are getting paid so well! We have a car, a refrigerator, a radiogram – what do we want with a war? The 'Führer' has done the trick before without a war. He'll do it this time, too . . . [23]

As Ebermayer had observed, all depended, for most Germans, on the Führer's success in his latest, most crucial meetings with the Western powers. They had trusted him during these recent

years to gain all that Germany needed by peaceful means. He
had not, so far, let them down.

*

At 7.30 on the morning of Thursday 29 September, Sir Alexander
Cadogan and his daughter Gillian picked up Lord Halifax from
his London home, 86 Eaton Square, and drove him out to Heston
aerodrome, west of London. From here Neville Chamberlain was
preparing to board the American-built Lockheed 14 Super Electra
that would take him and his aides to Munich. It was the same
civilian-registered fourteen-seater aircraft, operated by British
Airways,* that had taken him to Bad Godesberg a week earlier.
In drizzly weather, they duly waved the PM off on his crucial
mission. It was, Cadogan judged, 'a good show'.[24]

For Cadogan, at least, the rest of the day was, as the overworked
civil servant recorded, 'easy' – 'the calm in the middle of the
typhoon!' It even included a cheering call from the American
Ambassador, Joseph Kennedy, who insisted he would 'tell the
P.M. that I'm the man for Washington!'† With Chamberlain away
in Germany, Cadogan even managed to enjoy dinner at home
with his family, 'the first in *days*'.

At 11.51, German time, Chamberlain and his negotiating team
landed at Oberwiesenfeld aerodrome, on the northern edge of
Munich, a place familiar to the Prime Minister from his trip
earlier in the month. He was met by Foreign Minister Ribbentrop
and a welcoming committee that included not just relatively
'respectable' Nazis such as General Ritter von Epp but also
SS-Brigadeführer Christian Weber, a burly former bar-room
bouncer. Weber was unofficial city boss of Munich, prominent
among the Nazi 'old fighters' (*alte Kämpfer*), the bruisers who had
guarded Hitler from his earliest days as a rabble-rousing small-
time politician in Bavaria. Also on the tarmac, by way of contrast,

---

* Not to be confused with the modern airline of the same name. It was absorbed
a year or so later into the larger state-supported conglomerate named BOAC.

† To be appointed as Ambassador to the USA was a long-held though never fulfilled
ambition of Cadogan.

was the Eton-educated British Ambassador to Germany, Sir Nevile Henderson.

Without delay, the British delegation was whisked to quarters at the Regina Hotel on the Maximiliansplatz. From there it was a distance of less than a kilometre to the so-called Führerbau, the recently completed administrative headquarters of the National Socialist Party and Hitler's political base when in Munich, where the crisis talks were scheduled to take place.

The discussions began at 12.30 p.m. in Hitler's study in the Führerbau. The event was carefully stage-managed, with Hitler deliberately seated with his back to the window, so that his face was in shadow. Chamberlain was on his left, while Daladier and Mussolini sat together on the sofa.[25] The document they were to agree upon had supposedly been originated by the Italians as 'honest brokers'. It had in fact been drafted by Göring and put into formal language by Foreign Office State Secretary and puta-tive Resistance leader Ernst von Weizsäcker, then sent off on a circuitous route via Rome before returning along with the Duce and his entourage to be placed before the negotiators in Munich as if it were their own work.[26]

The session went on into the afternoon, when there was a break. They reconvened at 10 p.m. to hammer out the final agreement. 'Poor P.M. must be half dead!' as Cadogan commented in his diary. When proceedings were complete, at 2.30 a.m., Hitler had got all that he had wanted (or rather, all that he had decided he wanted, for now, having been robbed of his excuse for invading Czechoslovakia). Only Daladier and his chief aide, Alexis Léger, raised fundamental anxieties about the future of Czechoslovakia, but this was little more than a rearguard action.[27]

Under the terms of the final agreement, German troops would be permitted to occupy the so-called 'Sudeten' territories on 1 October, a reversion to Hitler's original deadline. The borders were dictated by strategic rather than purely ethnic considerations – hundreds of thousands of Germans were left in the Czech rump state and almost a million Czechs absorbed into Germany. Anyone currently living in these areas, Czechs or German-speakers, who did not wish to become German, would have to leave by 10

October. They would be allowed to take nothing with them and receive no compensation. The impressive fortifications that the Czechs had built in the mountainous border areas facing Germany would pass to the Reich: the Czech lands beyond would, in effect, lie at the mercy of the Wehrmacht. The majority of the Czechoslovak republic's heavy and armaments industries would also be ceded to Germany.

*

On the afternoon of 29 September 1938, while the four-power discussions were grinding on at the Führerbau, Maria Jörg, a 23-year-old domestic servant, was cycling along a country road that cut through the Forstenrieder Park, an extensive forest reserve that had once been a royal hunting ground, 15 kilometres or so south-west of Munich's city centre. She had reached a gentle curve in the road close to where there stood a modest, hip-roofed nineteenth-century building – Forsthaus Oberdill – belonging to the forestry service. It was the only habitation in the immediate area.

At this moment a man in his early thirties, likewise on a bicycle, passed her, coming from the opposite direction. She pressed on, but almost at once strong arms grabbed her from behind and pulled her down from her seat. The oncoming cyclist had swerved around and attacked her. Within seconds, the man had successfully dragged her to the roadside. There he throttled her before shooting her in the back of the head with a small revolver. He then hauled her further into the woods and attempted to rape her, though later evidence would indicate that he ejaculated before he could manage penetration.

The attacker dismembered Maria Jörg's corpse with a knife and dug a hole in the soft forest floor. After depositing the body parts in the hole he covered it with a mixture of pine needles and soil. As for the young woman's bicycle, he hurriedly dismantled it and cast the bits into the undergrowth. He took with him a few of her possessions, including a purse, and was gone.

Fifteen kilometres and a world away in Munich the day's great events continued their course, and anxious humanity's gaze remained fixed upon the city. It would be some months, in

fact, before anything was found in the woods opposite Forsthaus
Oberdill. Maria Jörg had, it seemed, simply joined the ranks
of the disappeared. Only as the next year progressed would
the truth about her small but infinitely terrible fate begin to
come to light – as would be the case for much else of a fateful
nature, greater but just as terrible in its way, which took place
on 29 September 1938.

*

Vojtech Mastny, Prague's Minister to Berlin, and Hubert Masařik,
secretary to the Czechoslovak Foreign Minister, had been sent by
the Czechoslovak government to Munich as 'observers'. They too
had booked into the Regina Hotel, but on arrival in Munich were
intercepted by Gestapo officials, who effectively kept them pris-
oner at their hotel, thus preventing them from attending the
negotiations.[28]

Even before anything was agreed, the Czechoslovak state's
humiliation was complete, but that did not prevent further insults,
not just from acknowledged foes but also from supposed friends.
After Chamberlain returned to the Regina Hotel in the small
hours, with Daladier in tow, they invited the Czech representatives
to attend on them. It was now gone 2 a.m. and Chamberlain did
nothing to conceal his exhaustion, yawning openly as the
Agreement was briefly explained to the Czechoslovak representatives. It was made clear that their assent was not necessarily
required. If they did not agree to the terms, they would simply
be on their own. 'They were then finished with us,' Masařik said,
'and we were allowed to go.'[29]

For his part, Hitler appeared very pleased with the outcome,
even insisting that the visitors' book be brought over from his
old headquarters, the co-called 'Brown House', so that the leaders
could sign that too. However, in truth he cared little for the
Sudeten lands as such (although, as an Austrian, he probably cared
more than most Germans from the 'old Reich'). He actually
wanted Prague and all of Bohemia. So far as he was concerned,
he had been forced by the French and British to settle for less.
The Führer had been compelled, in other words, to stand by his

public claim (that his sole interest was the safety and right to self-determination of the Sudeten Germans) and abandon – or, as it turned out, postpone – his secret objective, which was the total destruction and occupation of Czechoslovakia by military means.[30]

On the morning after the signing of the agreement, Friday 30 September, Chamberlain left his hotel and drove in an open-topped car to Hitler's flat in an apartment block at 16 Prinzregentenplatz, just across the river Isar, where the dictator had kept his Munich residence since 1929. Chamberlain had requested an extra meeting, man-to-man and nation to nation, seeking a further bilateral assurance of peace. Britain's French allies had not been informed. The Prime Minister was loudly cheered by Munich locals during his short journey, a fact that thrilled Chamberlain but further angered his host. Nonetheless, for form's sake, Hitler humoured the 'man with the umbrella'.

The Führer engaged in an hour and a half of apparently friendly conversation before, along with Chamberlain, putting his name to a further document, the so-called 'Anglo-German Declaration'. This expressed the two countries' mutual desire 'never to go to war with one another again'. Significantly, so it seemed, the agreement promised formal machinery for assuring peaceful resolution of any problems occurring in future between Germany and Britain. However, according to Frank Ashton-Gwatkin, an Appeasement-supporting Foreign Office official, a German acquaintance claimed Hitler remarked afterwards that he had signed the second agreement because Chamberlain 'seemed like such a nice old gentleman, and I thought I'd give him my auto-graph as a souvenir!'[31]

In the afternoon, after a little more than twenty-four hours on German soil, Chamberlain climbed back into his Lockheed Electra and returned to London, landing once again at Heston aerodrome at about 5.30 p.m. Large crowds of well-wishers thronged the area around the runway. As Chamberlain faced the press after leaving his aircraft, he fished the Anglo-German Declaration from his pocket and read out a section to the assem-bled reporters and camera crews, who included, as a 'first', an outside broadcast team from the BBC's new television service. This was the famous – or, as it became, notorious – 'piece of paper'.

'My good friends,' the Prime Minister concluded, 'this is the second time that there has come back from Germany to Downing Street peace with honour. I believe it is peace for our time.'[32]

Sir Alexander Cadogan had commented in his diary for 30 September: '*Times* this morning publishes the Munich Agreement. Looks to me quite good.'[33] Held up by traffic on the Great West Road, he had raced to be present when Chamberlain landed. Cadogan failed at the time to see any particular significance in the Prime Minister's words. The F.O.'s mandarin of mandarins recorded the events matter-of-factly in his diary:

> Crashed through crowd at gates, brandishing the police pass, and constables opened up the crowd and let us right through on to the concrete where we arrived as the pilot switched off and P.M. stepped out. He shook hands first with Clarendon, who brought summons from the King, then with H. [Foreign Secretary Halifax] and me. He broadcast a speech and got away fairly quickly. Rain began again as he finished.

*

The separate so-called 'Anglo-German Agreement' that Chamberlain had brandished on his return to London may have impressed many back home in Britain, with its implication that Hitler genuinely desired peace between the two countries, but Joseph Goebbels, Hitler's Propaganda Minister, had an altogether more cynical explanation. He wrote in his diary on 2 October 1938, after discussing the matter with Hitler, that the Führer had signed the Anglo-German agreement mainly because 'at the time the agreement was being drawn up, we did not yet know if the Czechs would agree [to the terms of the broader Munich Treaty] and for that reason it was an excellent way of tying London's hands'.[34] He also wrote of the dramatic public events that followed the Munich Agreement:

The march of the German troops [into the Sudetenland] begins at 14.00 hours. What a happy day! You could hug yourself for joy. The Führer's reception by the city of Berlin is being given great attention and coverage in the entire world's press. The German press has been operating in exemplary fashion these past days.

A more jaundiced version of how the German media had actually functioned during the crisis was presented by Ruth Andreas-Friedrich, who described the mood at the press organization where she worked:

It is curious. Each day thousands of hundredweights of newsprint roll out of this building. Spewing a torrent of national socialist propaganda over humanity. And nonetheless there's scarcely anyone under this roof who actually concurs with what he writes, typesets, prints, edits, or as a messenger boy carries along the corridors. For as long as the walls still have no ears, people grumble in pairs or small groups behind every door. The few 'hundred-percenters' [convinced Nazis] are well-known, are sucked up to and – avoided. We warn of their approach, fall silent or change the subject as soon as they enter the room. No one, however, dares tell them to their face what he really thinks, what is really depressing him, what is making him anxious.[35]

It did not matter all that much to the almighty Goebbels, of course, so long as the impression given to the papers' readers and to any foreigners still influenced by what they saw in the German press was the one he favoured. Right up to the final hour in Munich, the German press – whatever journalists' personal feelings and including, as she herself admitted, Andreas-Friedrich and her colleagues – had maintained a universal, synchronized campaign of hysterical atrocity-mongering to keep up the pressure on the Czechs and their allies while the capitulation was being prepared. Reports of 'unimaginable terror' against innocent local Germans subsided, but now the emphasis switched to warnings about the treacherous Czechs and their alleged puppetmasters in Moscow.

On 29 September, the SS newspaper, *Das Schwarze Korps* (Black Corps), printed a grotesque cartoon of the Czechoslovak President, Edvard Beneš, as 'Stalin's ape', perched on the Russian dictator's shoulder while they were given instructions by an exaggeratedly Jewish caricature of the Soviet Foreign Minister, Litvinov.

On the same day, in the Rhenish shoe-manufacturing centre of Germany, Pirmasens, far from sophisticated Berlin, the headline in the local paper shrilled: 'Beneš Loots and Murders On'.

On 1 October, even as the news of the Munich Agreement was spreading through the world, there was no let-up. Goebbels's new line was that the Czechoslovaks might have swallowed the bitter pill of Munich, but they would now try to lay waste to the Sudeten territories before the Wehrmacht could take control. The *Bodensee-Rundschau*, down on Lake Constance, screamed: 'Prague Accepts and Begins Its General Work of Destruction'. The (mostly fictitious) claim that the Czechs were carrying out a scorched-earth policy was repeated in another report from Vienna, claiming: 'Huge Coal Depots Are Set Ablaze – Jews as String-Pullers behind the Czech Attacks'.[36]

All the same, once the Munich Agreement had been signed, the statesmen had gone home, and the Wehrmacht had moved over the border into the new territories, there was not merely a huge sigh of relief but a mass outburst of joy in Germany. The SS Security Service, the SD (Sicherheitsdienst), which along with the local Gestapo stations closely monitored the popular mood, was forced in its report on the year 1938 to admit the existence of widespread 'war psychosis' during this period, accompanied by a certain defeatism that had 'escalated into the strongest criticism of the "adventurous policy of the Reich"'.[37]

During the crisis, there were worries within the regime about panic, or a run on the savings banks, as had occurred in the summer of 1914. In one small Saxon town near Leipzig, a local agent of the SD was diverted from his usual reports on the political reliability or otherwise of local worthies to inquire of the local savings bank about this matter. He was able to conclude that money had continued to be paid into accounts in the usual amounts, and there had been no exceptional withdrawals because of the international political situation.[38] People, or at least the good folk of Naunhof, had trust in the Führer's judgement.

For the moment, the wave of anxiety receded. Hitler had triumphed again, and without a war. Or so it seemed.

TWO

October 1938
'More Popular than Hitler'

There was no question that in Britain, too, most of the general public found reason only for celebration in the Munich Agreement. The relief at the fact of 'no war' was enormous. Trenches had been dug, gas masks distributed, bomb shelters ordered, and family members evacuated away from the larger cities. Now all this could be put on hold – perhaps, if it was true that Hitler now had everything he wanted, eventually abandoned. One young woman whose father worked in Whitehall at the War Office reported: 'Apparently Wing-Commander Hodsoll, director-general of Air Raid Precautions . . . reported that there was quite a traffic in gas-masks to American tourists who wanted to take them home as "souvenirs" of the crisis!'[1]

As Cadogan had indicated, a messenger from the King greeted Chamberlain the moment he stepped from his plane at Heston. He bore an invitation for the PM to come directly to the Palace. For the first time since the armistice in 1918, so far as Cadogan recalled, a prime minister appeared on the balcony of Buckingham Palace, along with the King and Queen, to receive the plaudits of the public. 'The King Leads the Cheers', proclaimed the *Daily Mirror*, originally a paper aimed at the middle classes but now publishing in the new 'tabloid' format, copied from America, and on its way to becoming a highly illustrated, left-leaning paper for the workers. It carried a photograph of a beaming Mr and Mrs Chamberlain acknowledging the tumultuous applause, with King George and Queen Elizabeth standing, against protocol, off to one side as if to grant the triumphant Premier extra prominence. More photographs followed in the inside pages, of Mrs Chamberlain being mobbed by fans in St James's Park, and of her husband leaning out of a window at Downing Street to greet the crowds gathered there.

Dee Moss, a thirteen-year-old from Leyton, East London, was among the crowd outside Downing Street. She had been left with her father and uncle when her mother took her younger siblings off to the country at the beginning of the crisis. The family was very anxious about a new war, and with reason. Their house had been damaged by a bomb dropped from a Zeppelin airship in the first war – the blast had shattered the French windows, which had never been properly repaired. Dee was also confronted with the unfamiliar sight of searchlights probing the night over Bakers Arms, on the border between Leyton and Walthamstow. She could only ask nervously: 'What are they for? What are they doing?'

After the Munich Agreement was announced and the crisis seemed at an end, the Mosses went into central London to join the large, jubilant crowd outside the Prime Minister's residence. Dee saw Chamberlain entering Number 10 from a vantage point perched on her father's shoulders. This did not particularly interest her, as she found the Prime Minister old and boring-looking. However, she was very excited to see the dashing former Foreign Secretary, Sir Anthony Eden (a leader of fashion who even had a hat named after him, a type of black, silk-brimmed Homburg), who was then still very young for a senior politician at a mere forty-one. The impressionable young girl reported that she 'fell in love with him' on the spot. He was 'like a film star'.[2]

Not everyone in Britain was delighted by the Munich settlement. Vera Ines Elkan, a left-wing photographer who had made something of a reputation reporting from the Republican front line in the Spanish Civil War, was back in London at the time, working with Spanish refugees. She went with her fellow aid workers from the refugee centre on Tavistock Square to the Tavistock Hotel to hear Chamberlain speak on the radio. They were outraged at what he had to say.

> I felt so sick, and it was clear he was this fool of a man, didn't know what he was talking about even. So for the first and only time in my life — there was a demonstration soon afterwards — and I marched and I marched [sic] on this demonstration. It was three miles but seemed like three hundred. Beside me marched this enormous policeman on an enormous white horse and I thought, any minute he will step on me. I don't remember where we marched from but I remember we walked past Hyde Park and past Marble Arch and I think down Oxford Street and it was terrible, I hated it. We shouted all the time: Chamberlain-Must-Go! Chamberlain-Must-Go! And then he didn't go . . .[3]

While the anti-Fascists might have been expected to react in this way, deep cracks had also begun to develop within the fabric of government and the British establishment. George Patrick Jellicoe was the son and heir, born late in his father's life, of John, Admiral and First Earl Jellicoe. The Earl had commanded the British North Sea Fleet in the spectacular but inconclusive Battle of Jutland (known to Germans as the Skagerrak-Schlacht) in May 1916 and had later served as First Sea Lord and finally Governor General of New Zealand. He was fifty-eight when his son was born, and died in November 1935, which meant that George succeeded to the earldom at the age of seventeen, even before he went up to Cambridge University. George was, as he himself recalled, resolutely apolitical until Munich, which occurred just before he was due to begin his final year:

> I had been in Germany for a 'gap six months' and had some interest in what was going on and the rise of Hitler, but I was not greatly involved and I don't think most of my friends were. But the great exception was Munich. I think I became politically and internationally much more aware at that time. I felt very

strongly about it. I remember going to stay with a great friend
of mine, Archie John Wavell, son of the Field Marshal, General
Wavell as he then was. He was commander at Salisbury, and I
remember feeling strongly, right or wrong, about Munich,
deploring it, feeling very ashamed of it, and I think a lot of my
friends felt this . . . [4]

During the night of 29/30 September, in Munich Chamberlain
and Daladier struggled unsuccessfully to salvage something from
the (to them, at least) inevitable ruin of Czechoslovakia.
Meanwhile, the First Lord of the Admiralty in Chamberlain's
government, Duff Cooper, a well-known bon viveur, was attending
a dinner organized by The Other Club. This exclusive dining
circle, made up of politicians and other public figures of note,
met in the Pinafore Room at the Savoy Hotel. It had been founded
a quarter of a century earlier by Winston Churchill and the late
F.E. Smith, and unlike many such societies had a rule (which
Churchill claimed had been included at his insistence) that 'nothing
in the rules or intercourse of the club shall interfere with the
rancour or asperity of party politics'.

On this night, it lived up to that particular rule. Cooper
and the government's Minister of Health, Walter Elliot, found
themselves viciously attacked for their continuing support of
Chamberlain's 'Appeasement' policy. They came under with-
ering fire, first from Churchill and then, as the evening wore
on and yet more drink was taken, also by a group of Churchill's
political allies. Cooper himself actually represented a small
group within the government that was trying to steer a stronger
line against Hitler – Elliot, too, was a member of this group,
though less vociferous – but of course, although Cooper's fight
for increased naval spending in the face of the German threat
had become public knowledge, while he remained a minister
he was bound by 'cabinet responsibility' to defend its general
policies. Cooper was renowned for his fearsome temper, and
in the heat of the evening he gave as good as he got. As he
recalled in his memoirs: 'everyone insulted everyone else' in a
monumental battle of words that went on into the small hours.

Given the fact that they were beginning a new day, one of The Other Club's members reminded his fellow diners that the early editions of the newspapers would now be on the stands. Someone went out to get a paper. On his return, this was snatched from his hands by Duff Cooper, who read the headlines in silence and then the rest of the final report from Munich out loud, in a voice heavy with rage and disgust. The betrayal by Britain and France of the Czechs was complete and undeniable. He threw the newspaper on the table and stalked out of the room.[5] The next day, he resigned from the cabinet.[6]

*

The day after Chamberlain's return from Munich, 1 October, was a Saturday. It was the first weekend in months when it seemed that there would, could, be no war.

The theatres in the capital offered relieved Londoners the playwright and actor Ivor Novello in a glittering commercial production of Shakespeare's *Henry V* at Drury Lane, Sybil Thorndike and Emlyn Williams in Williams's own play, *The Corn is Green* at the Duchess, the stage version of *Goodbye, Mr Chips* at the Shaftesbury, and the long-running smash-hit musical *Me and My Girl* at the Victoria Palace, 'Home of "The Lambeth Walk"'. The novelty dance from the show had become internationally famous. A British journalist recalled people in Prague defiantly dancing the Lambeth Walk while they awaited their country's fate in that long, hot, late-summer crisis that ended, temporarily at least, with the Munich Agreement.[7]

Films on release in London included one of MGM's most successful of the year, Clark Gable, Myrna Loy and Spencer Tracy in the aeronautical thriller/romance *Test Pilot* (which had also premiered in Germany in mid-August 1938), *A Yank at Oxford* with Robert Taylor and Vivien Leigh, the Marx Brothers' comedy *A Day at the Races*, and the first feature-length Disney animation classic, *Snow White and the Seven Dwarfs* (which was banned from general release in Germany despite being a favourite of Hitler, who had his own copy).[8]

Saturday was, of course, the day when hundreds of thousands of British football fans – totalling around 22 million a year for

Football League matches alone, excluding cup ties and reserve matches – could see their teams play. This was a time when the maximum wage permitted for a professional footballer was £8 per week (£6 in the close season), but there seemed to be just as much excitement involved as today, and as much space devoted to the game in the paper's pages – though the articles were almost entirely about actual football rather than the players' lifestyle or private exploits. Given that they earned a mere three times the average industrial wage and were likely to arrive at the ground by bus along with the fans, and drink with them in the same pubs afterwards, this was hardly surprising. On BBC Radio there was motor racing, including coverage of the British Grand Prix at Donington. The twenty thousand or so owners of television sets close enough to London to receive broadcasts from the Alexandra Palace transmitter could enjoy *Look in and Laugh* with Queenie Leonard, followed by the Gaumont British News, and then by a serio-comic play about Saint Simeon Stylites, who in the fifth century AD spent thirty-seven years living on a platform atop a pillar in what is now Aleppo, Syria. The play had already been transmitted, live, on 23 September, and was now not just transmitted but also performed, again, since the first performance had not been recorded. After a four-and-a-half-hour break in transmission there was then a show called *Cabaret*.

The weekend's press, meanwhile, was almost unanimous in its praise for the Munich Agreement. The single-word headline 'PEACE!' was emblazoned across the front page of Lord Beaverbrook's pro-Appeasement *Daily Express* in two-inch type, along with the boast: 'The Daily Express declares that Great Britain will not be involved in a European War this year or next year either'.[9] The London *Times* waited until Saturday to deliver its full blessing in an editorial getting on for 1,500 words long. Under the headline 'A New Dawn', its leader-writer told his readers in gushing terms:

No conqueror returning from a victory on the battlefield has come home adorned with nobler laurels than Mr. Chamberlain from Munich yesterday; and King and people alike have shown by the manner of their reception their sense of his achievement. The terms of settlement in the Czech-German dispute, reached in the small hours of the morning and published in the later issues of The Times of yesterday, have been seen to deliver the world from menace of extreme horror while doing rough-and-ready justice between conflicting claims. Yet even this great service to humanity was already beginning to appear as the lesser half of the Prime Minister's work in Munich. He himself announced it as the prelude to a larger settlement. He had not only relegated an agonizing episode to the past; he had found for the nations a new hope for the future. The joint declaration made by Herr Hitler and Mr. Chamberlain proclaims that 'the desire of the two people never to go to war with one another again' shall henceforth govern the whole of their relationships.[10]

Apart from the communist *Daily Worker*, which declared that 'This Dishonour Will Not Bring Us Peace', the rest of the press gave Chamberlain more than the benefit of the doubt.

Like Hitler, the British Prime Minister had reached the pinnacle of his popularity. Toy shops sold Chamberlain dolls, booted up for fly-fishing and carrying a fishing rod and reel in one hand and a sign saying PEACEMAKER in the other. The Poet Laureate, John Masefield, had even written a mercifully short, not to to say arcane, poem in his honour, entitled 'Neville Chamberlain' and published in *The Times*:

> As Priam to Achilles for his Son,
> So you, into the night, divinely led,
> To ask that young men's bodies, not yet dead,
> Be given from the battle not begun.[11]

Two weeks after his return from Munich, Chamberlain wrote to his sister Hilda from the Scottish borders, where he was taking a ten-day fishing holiday at the invitation of the Earl of Home, that the 'very embarrassing' tide of public appreciation had shown no sign of flagging. In the past week, he said, he had been notified of the arrival of 'two cases (from different senders) of the finest German Rhine Wine, and flies and salmon rods, watches, lucky horseshoes, tweed for sporting suits and socks'. Moreover:

> The tide of letters, flowers, testimonials and gifts continues to flow in without much abatement. Annie [Mrs Chamberlain] is still getting some 70 letters a day and in the hope of coping with these and with arrears she has appealed, & with success, to Pearl and Hester to come & help her four paid secretaries. Not only have they come with enthusiasm but they have brought Mabel Catterson Smith as well, so I hope we shall now make some headway.[12]

In fact, so Chamberlain wrote, he had also received adulatory letters from Germany. 'I frequently hear', the Prime Minister continued gaily, revealing that the relatively harmless personal vanity of which he was often accused had begun to border on hubris, 'that I am more popular there than Hitler himself'.

*

There was indeed a notable, if brief, wave of affection for Mr Chamberlain, the 'old gentleman with the umbrella', among many Germans after the Munich Conference. Part of the reason was undoubtedly the fact that Chamberlain had taken the trouble to come to Germany to deal with the Sudeten Problem. This reflected well on the British leader, but, of course, also showed how important Hitler and, by implication, Germany, had now become.

Impressively, the Führer could apparently summon the world's statesmen into his presence at will. The hitherto doggedly monarchist, almost eighty-year-old grandmother of Irmgard Brester was overcome with a new pride: 'Right now the flags are flying and everyone has a happy face. My dear Immo, how fortunes turn – in the times of the last Kaiser there were no representatives of the world powers coming to us, instead we had to go to all the states begging. For this we have to thank our Führer . . .'[13]

According to her diary, the woman gardener in Canstatt was especially impressed that Chamberlain and Hitler had also reached a one-to-one agreement to solve problems between their countries peacefully, though she wondered: 'But Chamberlain is old. Do the other English think the same way?'[14]

What this diarist didn't know was that the whole agreement – Munich Treaty, Anglo-German pact, everything – was a ruse on the Führer's part. On the morning before the Munich conference, Hitler had met Mussolini's train at Kufstein, on the pre-Anschluss Austrian border with Germany, following which the Duce and his advisers joined Hitler in his private salon on the German dictator's specially adapted *Führerzug* to travel on to Munich.

During the 90-kilometre journey, according to the diaries of the Italian Foreign Minister, Count Galeazzo Ciano, Hitler and Mussolini pored over maps of the Czech borders and defences, and Hitler frankly admitted to the Duce that he wished to deal with the Czechs only so as to be able to turn his ever-strengthening forces against his enemies in the West. He viewed a European war as inevitable: 'A time will come,' he told Mussolini, 'when united we will have to fight against France and England; this might as well happen while at the head of our countries there is the Duce and I, still young and full of life.'[15]

Less than three days later, with the Munich Agreement now signed and sealed, the first Wehrmacht units duly crossed in strength from the south at various points on the former frontier with Czechoslovakia. It was 2 p.m. on 1 October 1938. This was the first step in an occupation planned to take place in five stages over the first ten days of the month. German soldiers found themselves greeted by huge crowds of enthusiastic, Hitler-saluting Sudeten Germans. Frontier posts were enthusiastically dismantled and barriers destroyed by members of the Sudeten German SDP (Sudetendeutsche Partei), which had begun its existence as a peaceful movement for German-speaking autonomy and ended as a paramilitary tool of the German government, its active members all but indistinguishable from Nazi Storm Troopers.

Meanwhile, many thousands of justifiably frightened Czechs and political opponents of the Nazis, who still included some among the German-speakers, had already begun a desperate withdrawal from the Sudetenland across the new border into the Czechoslovakian rump state. Large numbers of non-Germans living in these newly transferred districts would be expelled or even killed. Farms and holdings belonging to Czech and Jewish owners were confiscated and from 1940 onwards given to so-called Bessarabian and Dobruja Germans evacuated from Romania under the 'Home to the Reich' (*Heim ins Reich*) project.[16]

As State Secretary at the German Foreign Office, Ernst von Weizsäcker had been involved in planning an army coup against Hitler. At the same time, as the department's most senior career official, he had been largely responsible for the weasel wording of the Munich Treaty, whose acceptance by the Western powers had thwarted that very same coup. Equally paradoxically, Major Helmuth Groscurth, another plotter, had, as chief of the Abwehr's Department II, in charge of Sabotage and Subversion, been working hard through secret contacts inside the Sudetenland to create the chaos that Hitler used as his excuse for threatening Czechoslovakia.

As early as 27 August, Major von Groscurth wrote in his private diary, concerning a meeting with Karl Hermann Frank, Deputy Leader of the Sudeten German Party, who had just returned from a meeting with Hitler: 'Führer is set on war. Orders the bringing about of incidents in the CSR [Czechoslovakia].'[17] These incidents Groscurth and his Abwehr friends duly helped to arrange, along with massive financial help for the paramilitary so-called Sudetendeutsches Freikorps (Sudeten German Free Corps) that was mainly responsible for causing the trouble.[18] At least Groscurth had the basic honesty to admit – in the privacy of his diary – that 'the mendacity of the German propaganda is unbearable'.[19] After all, the deeply religious pastor's son belonged to the select few who were in a position to know. Like Canaris, Groscurth was not the first decent, honest man inveigled into working for a tyrannical liar, and neither would he be the last.

Of course, it was their positions of power and knowledge within the Hitler project that made Groscurth and his circle able and, because of their ultimate loathing of the regime's workings, willing to countenance the Führer's overthrow. All the same, it seems hard to deny that, had the already sceptical members of the British elite known precisely what their contacts within the German Resistance were up to in their official capacities, they would have been even more doubtful of their motives.

*

While cynical encouragement of unrest from across the border in Greater Germany played a key role in the weakening of the Czechoslovak state, the Sudeten Germans' discontent was also firmly rooted in the history of the region. As ancient constituents of the Austrian Empire, after its disintegration in 1918 these German-majority districts of Bohemia and Moravia had wanted to join the Austrian republic that was set up at the end of the war, but the victorious Allied powers forbade it.

Many of the German-speaking inhabitants of these districts had been accustomed, in the days of the Austrian Empire, to their language being the dominant one throughout Bohemia and Moravia. They now resented, sometimes bitterly so, being placed under the thumb of a nation (the Czechs) over which they had traditionally ruled.

True, the Germans in this new, democratic but overwhelmingly Slavic republic had the same basic civil rights as their Czech, Slovak, Polish, and Hungarian-speaking and Ukrainian compatriots. And though the Czechs made up roughly half of the CSR's population, the Germans were the second-largest national group (at 21 per cent of the total, more than the Slovaks, who made up only 15 per cent). For a while, things seemed to calm down. By the 1920s, extreme nationalist feelings had sufficiently subsided for moderate German groups, including the German Social Democratic Party, which had traditionally represented the workers in the Sudetenland's industrial towns, to participate in coalition governments in Prague.

Nonetheless, a degree of continuing Sudeten German resentment against the government was not without cause. Immediately after the foundation of the Republic in 1918, the Czech leader Edvard Beneš had purveyed the idea of a multicultural Czechoslovakia as a 'second Switzerland'. That was not quite how things turned out. From the outset of the new state's existence, in a backlash against centuries of German-speaking Austrian domination, there had been hostility to and discrimination against the Sudeten Germans on the part of the majority Czech population. The administration in the Sudetenland, including the education system, was being steadily 'Czechified'. Politicians in Prague openly preached an imposed (Czech) homogeneity as the answer to the problem of disunity, and in the twenty years between the end of the First World War and the Munich Agreement most formerly overwhelmingly German towns had acquired sizeable Czech minorities, including officials appointed by Prague and Czech military personnel. Both groups brought with them Czech-speaking dependants and stepped up the call for Czech-language schools and public facilities, increasing the German-speakers' sense of being beleaguered and under long-term cultural threat.

When the Depression hit in the early 1930s, the central government's tendency to discriminate in favour of Czechs increased. Moreover, since a great deal of the country's light-industrial capacity, reliant on exports and especially vulnerable to the slump in world trade, lay in the German-speaking areas, this caused an even more disproportionate rise in unemployment in the Sudetenland. In 1936, of the country's 846,000 unemployed 525,000 were German-speaking.[20] This brutal fact, and the lingering economic crisis, made Sudeten Germans, political and racial conflicts aside, look ever more enviously over the border into Nazi Germany, where by this time full employment was close to prevailing.

The dramatic deterioration of economic life in the German-speaking parts of the CSR was illustrated by the situation in Gablonz (Czech: Jablonec), a majority-German town in the mountains of northern Bohemia, close to the German border. Its hitherto prosperous industries, most importantly glass and artificial jewellery production, collapsed along with the stock market in 1929, and this led to great distress in the area.

Käthe Strenitz, who grew up in Gablonz as a member of a comfortably off, mainly German-speaking Jewish family, was in her early teens at the time. She recalled being only vaguely aware of political or social problems before then. She could speak Czech to a decent level, and even had a Czech piano teacher, though 'on the whole there wasn't much mixing' between the linguistic groups. After the economic crash 'there was nothing for people, they were starving, and it went on for quite a long time. So the ground was ripe for the Nazis to come in.' As for the darker aspects of this phenomenon, she did not remember any anti-Semitism at school or in the town, 'but my brother once came home with a swastika on his back. When he was very little.' Her mother was 'an old-fashioned liberal who believed everything was going to be all right and nothing bad would happen . . . it took me a long time to get over this idea'.[21]

By the mid-1930s the political landscape had changed drastically. The noisily nationalist SDP now dominated the German-speaking electorate. It had moved from being essentially a pressure group, making peaceful demands for more rights and autonomy for Germans, to a separatist movement with a more and more violent paramilitary wing. The separatists were urged on and heavily supported, financially and otherwise, by Hitler's government in Berlin, which had specifically instructed its protégés to provoke the Czechoslovak state at every opportunity, and to consistently demand more than that state could reasonably concede. This was the situation in the late spring and summer of 1938. Goebbels's propaganda machine slid into overdrive, filling the pages of the captive German press with lurid and shocking – and mostly fake – stories of atrocities against the Sudeten minority in Czechoslovakia.

The fastidious Major Groscurth was one German official who admitted privately that most of the dramatic stories of atrocities carried out against the Sudeten German population were wild exaggerations – in fact, the Czech authorities showed remarkable restraint in the face of systematic, often violent provocation by the SDP.[22] This campaign nonetheless culminated in the so-called 'Sudeten German revolt' of 12 September. In what appears to have been a spontaneous response to inflammatory remarks by Hitler at the Nuremberg Party Rally, armed nationalist extremists in the Sudetenland, abetted by SS and SA units from across the border in Germany, seized several German-majority towns. Czech and Jewish-owned homes and businesses were attacked and severely damaged, and Czech police units subjected to violent attack.

According to a report from the German Social Democratic Party in Exile (Sopade), which still had its headquarters in Prague and maintained an extensive network of informers in the Sudetenland, in the small town of Oberplan (Horní Planá) in a forested area close to the borders with both Germany and Austria, a reign of terror ensued:

> . . . the Henlein* people proceeded through the place as if they had already conquered it. They broke the window panes in the Czech school and the Residential Centre for Czech officials and daubed everything Czech, even the post boxes, with green paint. They smashed in all the windows of the businesses and homes belonging to the Jewish shopkeepers Kohn and Schwarz. Schwarz was in the process of taking his wife to the maternity hospital and had already got his car ready for the purpose. The Henlein people ripped to shreds the things in the car (feather mattresses, baby wear, and so on) and scattered everything all over the market square, slashed the tyres of the car and tipped the car over. The Czech police were present, but could do nothing about it.[23]

Franz Fühmann, then a student at the High School in Reichenberg in northern Bohemia and approaching his seventeenth birthday, was a keen admirer of Hitler. For some time he had been a member of the SDP's youth wing, which in the pre-annexation days was organized as a gymnastics club. He later became a writer and described the atmosphere among young German nationalists in those heady days of mid-September 1938 in a lightly fictionalized memoir:

---

* Leader of the SDP.

My friend Karli knocked on the window of my ground-floor student quarters at Frau Waclawek's on Gablonzer Strasse and yelled to me breathlessly that I had to come to the gymnasium quickly, it was an orange alert, today the Czechs would attack the gymnasium!

They all went to the gym and took up defensive posts, armed with dumb-bells. The Czech 'attack' turned out slightly differently from what they had imagined, however. It took the form of a wiry little police lieutenant and two constables, who on entering the building fixed the Germans with a firm but not necessarily hostile gaze and addressed the 'burly man' who led the youth group:

'And vat, pray tell, are you chentlemen doing?' asked the lieutenant. 'We're doing gymnastics,' the burly man said hoarsely. I felt the blood pounding in my temples; now the order would come to pounce upon the foe! 'Chymnastics, it is healthy,' said the lieutenant, raising his left hand and turning back his cuff with the right; 'it is very healthy,' he repeated and pushed back his cuff and said a third time, smiling, that gymnastics was very healthy, and added, looking at his watch, that he hadn't wanted to disturb us gentlemen and would be on his way again; he only wanted to point out, and he held up his watch to the burly man's eyes, that it was already a quarter after seven, and eight was curfew [. . .] and he pushed his cuff back over his watch, touched his hand to his kepi and turned round, saying as he turned: 'I vish the chentlemen an enchoyable efening' and strolled out the door, the two policemen following him at a leisurely pace.[24]

The next morning, the German radio station from across the border, to which they all listened assiduously, announced that a 'horde of brutish Czech police troops' had stormed the Reichenberg youth gym and carried out bloody assaults on the innocent schoolboys exercising there. Yet another example of why the Reich could not stand idly by while the 'Czech-Jewish-Marxist cut-throats' victimized the Sudeten Germans.

We listened to this report knowing every word for a lie and yet we listened with eyes aglow and it never crossed our mind that it was all just lies. 'Man, that little Goebbels sure knows his propaganda,' said Karli, head of my raiding party, and punched me in the ribs, 'no one's ever done propaganda like that before, that's just grand!' and Karli said that no other country but the Reich could pull off propaganda that grand, and I nodded. He was right.

Martial law was declared, following which the Czech authorities quite quickly managed to restore a semblance of order. The SDP leadership and many of their followers fled across the border into Germany. There had indeed been many injuries and dozens of fatalities on both sides, though nowhere near on the scale claimed by the Nazis – whose leaders and propaganda organs would routinely (and mendaciously) put German deaths in the hundreds.[25] All the same, on balance, Goebbels's propaganda won the day. Two weeks later, the Sudetenland lay at the Nazis' feet and what remained of Czechoslovakia was left all but defenceless.

*

Hitler made his triumphal entry into the Sudetenland before dawn on 3 October 1938. He had travelled by train overnight from Berlin to Hof, in the far north-eastern corner of Bavaria. From there it was less than 30 kilometres to the first Sudeten town, the border community of Asch (Aš). Here he was received at his makeshift headquarters by Lieutenant-General Heinz Guderian, whose tank units had moved into the area just hours previously.

Climbing into an open-topped Mercedes, Hitler then proceeded further into his new possession. He travelled along roads now lined with cheering Sudetenlanders, passing through villages and hamlets decked with swastika flags. As the Special Correspondent of the London *Times* reported, all morning 'hundreds of girls in gay local dress stood with bunches of flowers, which they threw at any motor-car coming from the direction of Germany'.[26]

In the nearby town of Eger (Cheb in Czech), which had been the scene of many disturbances over the previous weeks, Hitler met with his generals and with Konrad Henlein, the leader of the SDP, who had been appointed Reich Commissar for the Sudetenland. From a tribune in the sixteenth-century market square, Hitler then addressed a huge crowd, in a short speech punctuated by loud shouts of 'Heil!'

Ominously, in those same merry towns and villages through which the Führer and his troops passed that day, here and there houses could already be seen daubed in paint with the word *Jude*.

Many of the 50,000 or so Jews living in the Sudetenland had already anticipated what was coming. Some were refugees from Germany, while others had been resident there for generations. Those who had not already left did so almost at once – it was already clear that the Sudeten areas were going to break away from Czechoslovakia sooner rather than later. Käthe Strenitz's liberal Jewish family moved from Gablonz, where they had lived for generations, to Prague just before the Munich Agreement. Apart from their Jewishness, the fact that Käthe's 'old-fashioned liberal' mother had sheltered and entertained German political refugees during the previous few years must have played a part in the decision. On that account alone, they would have been marked out for retribution.[27]

Elsewhere in the German-speaking area, a young Jewish doctor, Anton Weliminsky, had been practising for just a year and a half. Weliminsky had qualified at the German University in Prague, where his father was an academic and researcher in bacteriology. Culturally wholly German in his upbringing, Weliminsky's command of Czech was extremely poor, so after finishing his post-university military service with the Czechoslovak army, he went into general practice in the German-speaking Sudeten ski resort of Gottesgab (Boži Dar in Czech). At an altitude of more than a thousand metres, and directly on the border with Saxony, it was the highest incorporated town in Central Europe.

Dr Weliminsky too left shortly before Munich. Reading the runes correctly, he resigned and returned to Prague, where his parents lived. When asked many years later if, despite Munich, he 'could have stayed' in Gottesgab – where, after all, he had a job – he paused for a long moment, then replied in a wry growl: 'Theoretically.'[28]

Reports to the headquarters of the exiled German Social Democratic Party in Prague during these days and weeks belie the impression that Goebbels's propaganda outlets, and even the British press, were attempting to convey an orderly handover from Czechoslovakia to Germany. Behind the celebrating civilians lining the streets, there had been wild scenes of panic and flight unfolding in the Sudeten territories and beyond. In the early weeks of the occupation, the Sudetenland was under military administration, which meant that the Wehrmacht held ultimate authority. According to the socialist exiles this put a stop to many unofficial acts of vengeance by SDP paramilitaries. However, in place of the Sudeten irregulars, large numbers of Gestapo officials soon appeared from across the border and, Wehrmacht or no, moved against perceived 'enemies of the *Volk*':

> All residences belonging to refugees have been sealed. They are opened up only if the refugee appears in person. The offices of the Social-Democratic Party have also been sealed, and in cases where they have been opened, the Gestapo is to be found, going through the documents. There are fresh arrests every day. There does not appear to be any particular system to this so far. RW-people [members of the German-speaking militia loyal to the Czech government], local government officials and figures of authority are almost without exception taken into custody. In Reichenberg, socialist comrades were driven through the streets with placards round their necks declaring 'I am a traitor to the *Volk*'. In Neuern [Nýsko], which has a socialist majority, 70 have fled and of those remaining 28 have been arrested. Unemployed men were herded together and forced into the Labour Service.[29]

Socialists, democrats and Jews were not the only political targets in the immediate post-Munich period, however. As Major Groscurth noted with distaste during his travels through the newly occupied areas during those days, some hundreds of SDP supporters, including leaders of the militias that had 'protected' German-speaking communities during the summer, had also been arrested by 'Gestapo hoodlums' (*Lausbuben der Gestapa*. The accused, some of whom had joined the SDP cause relatively recently, after years of supporting other, less extreme political groups, were suspected of being overly tied in to local loyalties.[30] A swift lesson on what it meant to invite invasion by a totalitarian state – not to mention the dubious benefits of 'answered prayers'.

*

On Saturday 1 October 1938, the day the Wehrmacht took possession of its first tranche of formerly Czech territory, the weekend edition of the *Daily Mirror* carried an article by a young female columnist named Eileen Ascroft. It was entitled 'To the Unhappy Brave Women of Prague' and began 'We, the women of England, send you our thanks to-day from the very bottom of our hearts for your heroic sacrifice in the cause of world peace'.[31]

Ascroft had recently taken over from star columnist Godfrey Winn, whose transfer to the rival *Daily Express* enabled him to claim the status of highest-paid journalist in Fleet Street. Her article was almost a pastiche of Winn's sentimental, whimsical style, a parade of saccharine condescension and faux sympathy that took several hundred words to explain to the unfortunate women of Czechoslovakia that the English felt very sorry for them in their 'many hardships and trials' – and please not to be bitter, for (capitals in the original final paragraph): 'WHATEVER HAPPENS IN THE FUTURE THERE WILL ALWAYS BE A VERY WARM AND GRATEFUL SPOT IN ALL OUR HEARTS FOR THE GALLANT LITTLE PEOPLE OF CZECHOSLOVAKIA'. The rest of the page was taken up by an advertisement for Black Magic chocolates.

Altogether grander spiritual guides were also active in the public sphere in the immediate aftermath of Munich. Cosmo Gordon Lang, the Archbishop of Canterbury, had resorted to BBC radio during the crisis, calling for the nation to pray that war might be averted. After the Prime Minister returned, the Primate of All England led the rejoicing. Taking to the airwaves

via the BBC once more on Sunday 2 October, Lang delivered a
long, almost ecstatic sermon on what he saw as the divine intervention that had secured peace for the world:

> I wonder whether ever in the history of our land there has
> arisen a greater tide of prayer. It has arisen from the hearts and
> homes of our people, and from our churches everywhere. We
> cannot doubt that God has answered. I have already said through
> the wireless that when the MPs came trooping out into the
> lobby, more than one said to me 'Here is the hand of God'. I
> read yesterday of an old farmer in my own Diocese who pointing
> upwards to the wide heavens above Romney Marsh said quietly
> 'There is a God up there'.[32]

Next day there was a debate in the House of Lords during
which the Archbishop allowed himself a rhetorical question that
mirrored Eileen Ascroft's fleeting expression of moral doubt,
albeit in a more sophisticated way: 'Is it right, can it ever be right,
to base any peace upon an act of injustice?' Lang's answer, for
the moment, was that, faced with the prospect of a war 'which
might destroy civilisation itself . . . almost any price was worth
paying to avoid that calamity'. In this response, but also in the
niggling doubt that preceded it, the Archbishop probably spoke
for most of his country's people.

By Tuesday 4 October, the Sudeten Crisis, and along with it
the danger of war, had started to recede from the news headlines.
The *Daily Mirror*'s main front-page headline reported ex-Foreign
Secretary Anthony Eden's warning about 'threats' from the dictatorships. In a box on the same page there was also a mildly
sarcastic comparison piece, headlined 'Three Days'. It contrasted
Chamberlain's near-euphoric pronouncements on his return from
Munich the previous Friday with his more cautious remarks to
the House of Commons on Monday. Almost certainly feeling
under pressure from his opponents within his own party, the
Prime Minister stressed that, although the new agreement with
Germany was a wholly positive thing, Britain would continue to
rearm:

No one must think that because of the agreement signed by
the Four Powers at Munich we can relax our re-armament
efforts . . . We must renew our determination to build up the
deficiencies in our armaments and defensive precautions so that
we may equip ourselves and make our diplomacy effective . . .

On page 4, meanwhile, the now ex-First Lord of the Admiralty,
Duff Cooper, explained his motives for resigning (with a picture
that included his glamorous and for many readers rather better-
known wife, the actress and socialite Lady Diana Cooper). Later
pages of the paper covered the usual sensationalist stories,
including that of a woman who 'DID THE LAMBETH WALK IN
HIGH-HEELED SHOES, THEN SLIPPED ON STAIRS, DIED',
as well as grave international crises that had been overshadowed
by Munich, such as the bloody, two-years-old Palestinian rebellion
in the Middle East.[33]

On Wednesday 5 October, in an attempt to conclude the House
of Commons debate on Munich, the Chancellor of the Exchequer,
Sir John Simon, moved 'That this House approves the policy of
His Majesty's Government by which war was averted in the recent
crisis and supports their efforts to secure a lasting peace'. Several
of the anti-Appeasement Tory rebels made speeches, but Winston
Churchill launched an especially fierce and telling attack on the
Munich settlement, calling it 'a total and unmitigated defeat' and
querying Chamberlain's supposed achievement:

> The utmost he has been able to gain for Czechoslovakia and in
> the matters which were in dispute has been that the German
> dictator, instead of snatching his victuals from the table, has
> been content to have them served to him course by course.[34]

Nevertheless, next day the motion was finally passed by 366
votes to 144, a government majority of 222, despite 30 absten-
tions by anti-Appeasement Tories. During the four days of debate,
Margesson, the Tory Chief Whip, and his acolytes had spread fear
among the rebels by threatening to withdraw the whip from them
(i.e. expel them from the parliamentary party) and possibly run

candidates against them in the next election.[35] As the firmly pro-Appeasement *Daily Express* had trumpeted the previous day, there were strong rumours that Chamberlain, banking on his popularity following the Munich Agreement, was considering calling a snap General Election.[36] Margesson's threat was therefore not merely theoretical, but potentially painfully immediate.

After the Commons vote, there were attempts to influence local Conservative Party organizations to 'deselect' leading rebels. These were unsuccessful, but the press, especially the *Mail* and the *Express*, launched unremitting attacks on the government's opponents, Tory and otherwise. So intolerant had the attitude of the pro-government press and the government's own enforcers become that Geoffrey Cox, who had just joined the *Express* as a foreign correspondent, recalled that in his newsroom the standard, angry answer to anyone expressing doubts about the Munich Agreement was that they must be a warmonger. Eventually, he said, the government's attitude towards its critics began to betray 'undertones of totalitarianism'.[37]

Despite the efforts of the government and the pro-Appeasement press, once the initial rejoicing at the avoidance of war had worn off there was a slow but steady growth of buyer's remorse among many members of a general public that had at first trusted Chamberlain's claim of 'peace for our time'.

Isabel Blackwell, who worked as a filing clerk in a trade union office, had been 'sick with worry' during the crisis. After the immediate danger passed, despite her relief, she had to admit that she 'did not trust Hitler' – another common feeling.

Similarly, a Mrs E. Dawson from Gateshead in north-east England, though 'relieved and glad for all the world' and thanking God for the Prime Minister's efforts, admitted that 'in my heart of hearts I wonder [underlining in the original]'.[38]

Cyril Dunn, a young journalist working for the provincial *Hull Daily Mail*, confided to his notebook: 'I'm dam' relieved war has at least been postponed . . . But I'm definitely unhappy about the Czechs and a bit uneasy about the loss of democratic prestige. I'm not alone in this.'[39]

Hardly anyone seemed to think that Hitler would, in the end, be satisfied with what he had gained. The only question was where he would go next; here the favourites were the rest of Czechoslovakia, Romania or Poland.

*

On Saturday 1 October 1938, the Aliens Police Regulation (*Ausländerpolizeiverordnung*) came into force throughout the German Reich. This stripped all foreign (or stateless) residents of Germany of any legal right to remain in the country, placing the onus on such residents to prove their suitability and thereby allowing the authorities to expel them without recourse. This new decree also applied to any resident who had previously been stripped of their status as a German citizen (which since 1933 had happened to many Jews and political opponents of the Nazis).

At 2 p.m. on Sunday 2 October, Poland's semi-dictatorial government sent troops to occupy the hitherto Czech-governed industrial district of the former duchy of Teschen (Těšín). The region, with a population of about 200,000, which had been in dispute between the two countries since 1919, was declared annexed to Poland. The country's nationalist press went wild. Showing rather more prescience, one of the Czech officers in charge of the surrender remarked bitterly to his Polish counterparts that they would be handing over the area to Germany before they knew it.[40] The international reaction was not positive. The occupation, exploiting a fellow Slavic people's moment of weakness, seemed to put Warsaw on the same low moral level as Berlin. Sir Alexander Cadogan of the British Foreign Office referred in his diary to the Polish Foreign Minister as 'that brute Beck'.[41]

On Wednesday 5 October 1938, while the British parliament continued to debate Chamberlain's foreign policy, a German government order was issued invalidating the passports of all Jewish citizens of the Reich. They were required to hand in their passports within fourteen days so that these could be modified to indicate their racial status by means of a letter 'J', after which they would be revalidated.

Also on 5 October, the Czechoslovak President, Edvard Beneš, announced his resignation. General Jan Syrový, a military hero and former commander of the Czech Legion in the First World War, had become Prime Minister of a national unity administration in late September. Syrový took over vital parts of the presidential role until the Catholic, conservative President of the Supreme Court, Emil Hácha, agreed to assume the post. It would soon become clear the Czech government was bowing to German pressure and taking a strong rightward turn. Before the month was out, Beneš would go into exile in London.

On Thursday 6 October, the Fascist Grand Council in Rome held discussions about the 'Jewish Question' and, among other things, officially forbade marriages between Italian Jews and non-Jews.

The same day, the Polish government, which had been pursuing anti-Semitic policies of its own since the death of the old, mostly tolerant strongman, Marshal Pilsudski, in 1935, stipulated that all Polish citizens who had lived abroad continuously for more than five years were deemed to have broken contact with their motherland. They would lose their citizenship unless they had a check mark put in their passports by the relevant consulates in their countries of residence. The deadline for this was 30 October.

The law enabling this sudden attack on the rights of Polish Jews living abroad had been passed at the end of March 1938 as a reaction to the German occupation of Austria. There were around 20,000 Jews living in the territory of the former Austrian Republic who were technically Polish citizens, and a further 30,000 in Germany. In some cases these individuals and families were second- or third-generation. They had been born, educated and now worked in Germany. They had certainly lived, in most instances, as if they were German. It was clear that the Polish law was aimed at rendering these expatriate Jews stateless and so preventing them from returning to Poland. Equally clear was that the Nazi state had no intention of being forced to harbour tens of thousands of foreign Jews who, within a matter of days, would be unable to return to their homeland, voluntarily or otherwise. A crisis began to brew, and its implications would be even more grave than most suspected.

On 9 October 1938, speaking in Saarbrücken, in the far
west of Germany, Hitler declared that the experiences of the
past eight months (since the Anschluss of Austria and the
Sudeten Crisis) had taught him that no effort should be spared
in order to protect the Reich. Therefore the fortifications on
the western borders (the so-called Westwall or 'Siegfried Line'
as it became known in England and America) would be further
extended.

Apart from making clear his continuing distrust of the West,
just days after a major international agreement in Munich that
had seemed to reduce international tension, Hitler's statement
signalled further major social and economic change in the border
areas facing France and the Low Countries. This already massive
engineering project would, as a side effect, bring a vast force of
workers (and military personnel) to the area, disturbing the peace
of a doggedly traditional rural society but also creating badly
needed jobs and economic stimulus. As one account of a struggling
grocery store in the village of Irrel, near Bitburg and close to the
border with Luxembourg, told it: 'Luckily for business owners,
the construction of the Westwall began in our area, and what
with the many workers that began to populate our district, an
economic upswing began.'[42]

On 10 October 1938, the so-called Sudeten German Free
Corps was officially dissolved and the next day the German
Reichsmark was declared a legal currency in the Sudetenland,
alongside – for the moment – the Czech Koruna or Crown.
Owing to the strict policies of the Czechoslovak Central Bank,
the Crown had been one of the hardest currencies in Europe.
Now the exchange rate was officially set at just over eight to the
Mark, which represented a real devaluation of at least a third.
Absolute prices for food and consumer goods in Czechoslovakia
were, in any case, lower than those in heavily taxed Germany.
The result was that, once word got around, the Sudetenland was
invaded once again, this time by hordes of tourists from other
parts of 'Greater Germany', even from as far away as the
Rhineland. They eagerly ate and drank and shopped while the
local Sudetenlanders looked on in irritated amazement:

And then they . . . went on eating and drinking, twenty pfennigs a portion, and when they couldn't choke down any more
to save their lives they got up and wobbled through the
streets . . . and clapped us on the shoulder and asked if we
were grateful they'd liberated us, and we said yes, and they
clapped us on the shoulder and said we should be very grateful
indeed, they'd spared no sacrifice to liberate us and it was only
right and proper for them to take a little breather here and
some coffee with cake and whipped cream, they hadn't had that
in the Reich in ages! Then they hit the shops again and their
bags filled with shoes and silk stockings and lingerie and soap
and cigarettes and cookies and sardines and sausage and Prague
ham and watches and jewellery, and then they hauled their bags
over the border that no longer was . . .[43]

Despite all these developments, to most Germans – even the
Sudeten Germans – and certainly to the outside world, after
Munich life appeared to be resuming a normal state. A new
normal, perhaps, but better than the catastrophic alternative.

*

'The most obvious reaction to the September Crisis on the part
of us keen enemies of the state,' noted Erich Ebermayer, typically
mingling mild self-mockery with mild self-aggrandizement, 'is a
generally discernible political disinterest. No one wants to be
bothered at all about politics. Any agitation about that side of
things just seems to one a waste of time. Long live private life!
That's now the motto of the moment. Everything else is futile.
We can change nothing. The triumphalist [Hitler] has succeeded
totally.'[44]

This truth applied even to the far from disinterested Ruth
Andreas-Friedrich, who ruefully remarked on the fact in her
diary, and scolded herself for it. Her old friend Heinrich Mühsam
jogged her out of her temporary dream of normality. She
described on 15 October 1938 an encounter with him at his usual
haunt, Hiller's restaurant on Unter den Linden. He had been far
from cheerful, gazing down at his notebook, which lay open

between his wine glass and uncleared dishes. 'I don't like this quiet,' Mühsam said. 'I like the quiet even less than the storm.' Andreas-Friedrich chided him gently: 'Just being grouchy all the time doesn't have any point either. What have you got to find fault with now?'

He shook his head. 'Absolutely nothing to find fault with! Just following logic. You see: What is a dictator without his successes? I mean, without visible successes he devalues his own currency. Only kings or liberal heads of state can afford to rest on their laurels. Tyrants, though, are driven beings. Restlessly wandering between being feted or crucified. If they are not to run out of breath themselves, they have to keep others breathless. The masses want circuses and bread. Once the big foreign policy number is over, out jumps the clown from his box. Do you know who the clown is? The German Jew!'[45]

THREE

November 1938
'We Are Being Hunted Like Hares'

At 9.45 on the grey, misty morning of 7 November 1938, a stateless seventeen-year-old by the name of Herschel Grynszpan entered the German Embassy in Paris. He demanded, so the story went, to speak to a senior official, preferably the Ambassador. He had important information to impart. The young Jew was in the end led into the office of a junior Embassy secretary, 29-year-old Ernst vom Rath, scion of an aristocratic family and a Nazi Party member. Grynszpan promptly pulled a gun out from under his raincoat and shot vom Rath five times in the stomach, shouting out, so the French police later claimed, that his victim was a 'filthy Boche'.*

For this desperate, angry young man, the shooting was an individual act of protest. He meant to draw attention to the plight of his family, and many thousands of others who were being treated as dispensable pawns in the era's escalating international power games. For the beleaguered Jews of Germany, however, already trapped in a country where their rights and basic safeties

---

* 'Boche' was First World War slang for a German, apparently originating in the northern French dialect word *caboche* (cabbage) or colloquially 'head' – an insulting term comparable with 'kraut' or 'square-head'.

were being systematically denied and eroded, what happened in
Ernst vom Rath's office that morning was the prelude to a racial
catastrophe unmatched in its vicious brutality since the Middle
Ages.

*

The first ten months of 1938 had been far from comfortable for
German Jews. Although Jews could still, officially, attend schools
and universities, socialize more or less normally and run businesses
in Germany, formal and informal restrictions were making life
harder all the time. One hundred and fifty thousand of them –
roughly a third of Germany's Jewish population in 1933 – had
now gone into exile – to other European countries, to America,
north and south, and in thousands of cases to Palestine. Now, as
the Third Reich turned the administrative screw ever tighter, the
problem was that potential places of refuge for the Jews who
decided – or needed – to emigrate were growing ever scarcer.

Appeals to the international community on behalf of Germany's
Jews had so far yielded meagre results. Between 6 and 15 July
1938, with the brutalities accompanying the Nazi Anschluss of
Austria still fresh in the world's memory and trouble already
brewing in the Sudetenland, representatives of thirty-two countries had met at the splendid Hotel Royale in the French spa town
of Évian-les-Bains, on the south shore of Lake Geneva. Their
purpose was to discuss the problem of Jews fleeing fascism, and
more precisely the increasing violence and intolerance of the
Hitler regime in Germany. The conference had been called chiefly
at the instigation of President Roosevelt – as many suspected,
because for domestic political reasons he needed some countries
other than the USA to take in desperate German Jews. He hoped
to persuade or shame them to do so by exposing the problem to
the world.

The imminent opening of the proceedings occasioned the
London *Daily Mirror*'s David Walker to invite readers' comments
on the Jewish refugee crisis that had led to the Évian Conference.
Having already expressed his sympathy for the plight of modern
Jews, Walker was clearly shocked by the vehemence of the letters

he received from members of the British public over the next couple of days. The majority, he was forced to admit, were decidedly, in many cases obscenely, anti-Semitic. Above all, they were passionately opposed to taking any refugees from Hitler into Britain: 'Instead of clearing these stinking people, we are taking Germany's scum', signed 'Jew baiter – and proud of it, E.15'.

'A lot of the letters were illogical and some of them indecent,' Walker wrote, 'but taken in the mass they prove a fact which MUST be made public.' He continued:

> If Évian is inconclusive, as it may well be, it will be up to us to decide for ourselves.
>
> I happen to think that all the accusations in these letters, put together, are still no excuse for a pogrom. But I am in the minority.
>
> The fact remains: if we don't start looking for a sane solution NOW, more blood will flow in the gutters, Christian as well as Jewish.[1]

The conference was indeed inconclusive. The delegates took pleasure cruises on the lake, gambled in the town's casino, enjoyed the spa facilities. Then, representative after representative stood up and expressed sympathy for the persecuted Jews before explaining why their particular country could not, sadly, take in any of these unfortunate people. Too full already, too poor, too little attuned to foreign immigration. The Australian delegate bluntly told the conference that 'as we have no real racial problem, we are not desirous of importing one'.[2] Others were less frank, but shared the universal reluctance. Golda Meyerson, who attended as an observer representing the Jewish Labour Movement in Palestine, wrote later:

> I don't think that anyone who didn't live through it can understand what I felt at Évian – a mixture of sorrow, rage, frustration, and horror. I wanted to get up and scream at them, 'Don't you know that these so-called numbers are human beings, people who may spend the rest of their lives in concentration camps,

or wandering around the world like lepers if you don't let them in?' Of course, I didn't know then that not concentration camps but death camps awaited the refugees whom no one wanted.[3]

Australia, in the end, did agree to take some 15,000 refugees over the next three years. Britain also promised to take a few, though not in the British Mandate of Palestine, on account of the low-level civil war going on there between Arabs and Jews. Lord Winterton, leader of the British delegation, made vague mention of allowing Jews to emigrate to Kenya, an idea that was never followed through. America also increased its immigration quota slightly, though by nothing like as much as the situation required. The democratic governments' reluctance was ignoble but understandable in view of public opinion. In a poll carried out by *Fortune* Magazine in the USA, over two-thirds of the respondents opposed allowing in any refugees 'with conditions as they are'.[4]

Jews were not popular, it was obvious. The only head of state to offer anything like a generous – wildly and, in fact, suspiciously generous – invitation to the Austrian and German Jews was General Trujillo, strongman ruler of the Dominican Republic. The Caribbean dictator said he would issue 100,000 visas. One of the stated reasons was that he wanted to increase the 'white' population of the country, most of whose people were mixed-race or black, with the latter group being rapidly augmented by a stream of immigrants from neighbouring Haiti. An unstated reason was that, as a ruler who during less than ten years in power had murdered thousands of unarmed civilians in cold blood, he was keen on some positive PR, especially in America. He even offered an entire village, with land attached, where the Jews could make a life through farming. Only a few hundred Jews accepted the invitation and the settlement, Sousa, was not an entirely happy creation.[5]

A Standing Committee was set up at the end of the conference, its remit widened, in view of the growth of anti-Semitic feeling in other European countries, to include a potential new Jewish exodus from Eastern Europe in general, including Poland. There was talk of raising money to this end, but little more.[6] This remained the situation until October, when a new crisis arose inside Germany.

On 27 October 1938, acting on orders of Gruppenführer Reinhard Heydrich, head of the Reich Security Police, Gestapo units began rounding up thousands of Polish Jews in Germany and transporting them to the Polish border. All Polish Jews – including Jews born in Germany who carried Polish passports – were to leave the country, or be deported, by 29 October. This was two days before the Warsaw government's own deadline, under which these same people would no longer be allowed to enter Poland on their Polish passports.

The ministerial order that had set the arrests and deportations in motion stated specifically that 'the greatest possible number of Polish Jews should be got across the border before the time stipulated'.[7] In the next two days, 18,000 Polish Jews were, in fact, rounded up – concentrating on adult males – throughout Germany and dumped on the Polish border at three different places – the lakeside town of Zbąszyń (German name Bentschen), west of Poznań, Chojnize (Konitz), up towards the Baltic in Polish Pomerania, and Beuthen (Polish name Bytom) in Upper Silesia.

The Polish authorities were, understandably, unable to cope. At first they were unwilling to let any deportees through, but over the next two days some 10,000 in possession of identity documents were allowed into the country, provided they had relatives willing to take responsibility for them. A thousand or so reached Warsaw within the next twenty-four hours or so, though many spoke only German and had difficulty finding their way. As for the rest, who either had no family to go to or who in the eyes of the Poles had no valid documentation, they were stuck.

The situation at Zbąszyń was the worst. Here the deportees were driven – according to press reports, in some cases by SS troops at bayonet-point[8] – along roads and across fields, and so ended up trapped in no-man's-land between the Polish town and the last railway station on the German side, at Neu Bentschen. Thousands were forced to camp out in conditions of great squalor, subject to the rapidly deteriorating late autumn weather. This would go on for weeks in one shape or form, in many cases for months.[9]

The overnight mass deportations, known as the *Polenaktion* (Polish Operation), exemplified in their scale, ruthless efficiency and utter disregard for human suffering a new phenomenon in modern European history – a dress rehearsal for even worse atrocities to come. They were also a first expression of the fact that the Nazi state would not be satisfied with anything as simple as success. In its radical brutality, it was taking a first step towards making an entire nation accomplice to criminality on a grand and breathtaking scale.

*

One curious fact is that there was no mention of the *Polenaktion* in the diaries of the most fanatically anti-Semitic of all the high-level Nazi leaders, Joseph Goebbels. His diary entries usually trumpeted such outrages – actions in which Goebbels was habitu-ally both co-originator and cheerleader – but there was an explanation for his silence. The ultra-loyal, workaholic Minister of Propaganda was at a crisis point in his private life and, during those fatal days, all but removed from the political equation in a way that had never occurred before and would not occur again. The cause was his unhappy marriage, and his lengthy affair with a beautiful Czech-born actress, Lida – 'Liduschka' as he called her – Baarová.

Twenty-four years old, and already a star of German cinema, Baarová was seventeen years younger than Goebbels. By the summer of 1938, the liaison between her and the propaganda minister, a notorious philanderer, had become widely known, especially in film circles. As the Sudeten Crisis peaked, Goebbels seemed ready to leave his wife, Magda, and their children for Baarová – in a point of fine irony, a lifelong citizen of the very nation that he and Hitler were eager to destroy.

In mid-August, Goebbels had confessed to his wife about his passion for the actress. Magda complained to Hitler, with whom she enjoyed a special, although almost certainly chaste, relation-ship of her own. Hitler told Goebbels to end the affair, and

Goebbels agreed, but actually found it impossible to give Baarová up.

By mid-October the minister had, he claimed, firmly decided to divorce Magda, even though she had just borne their fourth child. At a crisis visit by the Goebbels family to the Berghof, the Führer's Alpine eyrie, Hitler issued an ultimatum. If Goebbels left Magda for Baarová his political career was over.

Goebbels finally gave in and ended the relationship. He duly kept his job, though for weeks afterwards he suffered from terrible depression and psychosomatic symptoms. On a further order from Hitler, Goebbels, Magda and their children were subjected to a special photo session and the pictures released to the press with instructions to publish as widely as possible. The Führer was childless. The Goebbels clan, who had consequently been conscripted as the Third Reich's 'first family', were to be shown as solid, loving and forever united.

Goebbels had finally obeyed the Führer's command to stay with his wife, and thus salvaged his government position, but the tensions of the past weeks had damaged the relationship between the two men and potentially endangered Goebbels's standing in the Nazi hierarchy. He would have to prove himself all over again to the Führer to salvage the relationship of intimacy he craved. This meant he had to reinforce his indispensable role as the regime's radical engine, controller of public opinion, the driving force behind Germany's transformation into a totally united and – above all – 'Jew-free' nation. Goebbels's need for rehabilitation would have drastic effects far beyond the narrow, gossip-ridden social world of the Nazi elite.

*

The *Polenaktion* was a major international incident as well as an appalling spectacle of cruelty. Its origins lay as much in international rivalries and undercurrents of feeling as in German domestic pressures. At first sight, especially glimpsed from abroad, recent assaults on Germany's established, native Jewish population could, by comparison, seem mainly legal and administrative in nature – the pinprick measures against Jewish doctors and lawyers, the imposition of 'Jewish' passports, and so on – but in fact 1938 had witnessed a steady increase in acts of violence and destruction against Jewish individuals, properties and communities all over the Reich.

The Sudeten Crisis, seemingly directing all the population's thoughts to the sufferings of the German-speaking communities in Czechoslovakia, had also provoked, at least in committed Nazi circles, an increase in anti-Semitic outrages. From May 1938, the month in which the Hitler Regime, having ingested 6 million Austrians, launched a campaign of hate and blame against the Czechs, the frequency of racist incidents in the Reich increased noticeably. As ever 'the Jews' were blamed for causing the international tension, by allegedly whipping up foreign feeling against Germany. The SS Security Service's nationwide report for October 1938 observed with some satisfaction:

> The increasingly anti-Jewish attitude of the people, mostly caused by the provocative and insolent behaviour of individual Jews during the time of the international crisis, was most strongly expressed in actions against the Jewish population, which in the south and south-west of the Reich took on an almost pogrom-like character.[10]

The severest outrages did, in fact, occur in these regions, often in small towns and villages, and were often presented as part of the general campaign to rein in excessive Jewish economic influence. Individual Jews were roughed up. Jewish-owned shops attacked, windows broken in homes and businesses. Synagogues were set on fire.[11] As early as May 1938, in Hanau, east of Frankfurt-am-Main, the door of the synagogue had been bricked up overnight, on the eve of the Sabbath. When, some days later, at the request of the Jewish community, a local 'Aryan' building contractor unsealed the door and restored access, his firm was punished by having municipal contracts cancelled. 'Local glaziers have refused to refit window panes in the synagogue,' said a gleeful report by an SS Security Service official. 'After these events, it will scarcely be possible to find an artisan willing to take on work for the Jews.'[12]

On 21 June 1938, however, there was also a brief campaign of violence and repression in Berlin itself, largely at the behest of Goebbels in his capacity as Gauleiter* of the capital. Several hundred Jews were arrested, mostly rounded up in cafes around the Kurfürstendamm. The premises of Jewish lawyers and doctors were daubed with anti-Jewish insults in red paint, and there was plundering and wrecking of Jewish-owned shops. The next day, the operation was called off on Hitler's personal orders. With the Sudeten Crisis coming to a head, the Führer was anxious to avoid international public opinion being unfavourably influenced by such obviously regime-sponsored thuggery.[13]

Elsewhere, away from the spotlight, the inexorable tide of violence flowed on. A report by the office of the District Governor (*Regierungspräsident*) in Speyer, on the Rhine, listing anti-Semitic outrages during October 1938 summed up a strategy of cynical official disassociation from atrocities that were, in reality, covertly sponsored by the regime. It described how Jewish homes in Rülzheim, a small town nearby, were daubed with slogans in red paint such as 'Hang the Jewish Warmongers' and 'Jews Dead'. In another local town, the synagogue was broken into and sacred objects destroyed. Elsewhere homes were broken into and robbed of valuables. A Jewish cemetery was vandalized. The report noted that in no cases had the Jews affected brought charges, and concluded in a sneering tone:

> The perpetrators of all these incidents, which arose spontaneously out of the will of the general public, could not be identified. The people wish to have the Jews gone from the villages, and this is the way in which it avenges the insolent behaviour of the Jews during the time of tension in September.

This justification for the actions of the population resounds throughout the reports.

---

* Leader of a *Gau*, an administrative district instituted by the Nazi regime.

In the course of the deportation operation against Polish Jews on 27 and 28 October, 213 persons were transported from the area by means of a special train . . .[14]

On 1 November 1938, the headquarters of the SS Security Service in Berlin summed up the new measures by which the Nazis were contriving 'the solution to the Jewish problem on Reich territory'. 'Jews have been successfully excluded by law or ordinance from the following professions', the report concluded:

The auction trade
The security industry
Provision of professional information regarding property or
    personal matters
Dealing in property
Professional arrangement of property contracts and loans
Professional marriage bureaux and the tourist trade
Itinerant trade
The medical profession
Activity as lawyers[15]

Jews in Germany, often living in long-established communities, were being gradually but inexorably, through the ruthless operation of what now passed for law, robbed of any chance to earn a living or to function as normal citizens. It was also clear from the Security Service reports that government agencies were encouraging an undertow of violence, but in public washing their hands of responsibility and blaming the outrages on spontaneous popular anger. The appalling series of events that followed were thus not a surprise to the state authorities, but in fact represented a climactic paroxysm of violence that had long been planned by those same officials and their minions.

*

The most significant, and dangerous, consequence of the *Polenaktion* arose not on the eastern border, or even in Berlin, but hundreds of miles to the west, in Paris.

Herschel (also known as Hermann) Grynszpan was born in Hanover, Germany, in March 1921 to Yiddish-speaking Polish-Jewish parents, Sendel and Riva, who had emigrated from Poland, then part of the Russian Empire, in 1911. Herschel, an intelligent but solitary boy, prone to temperamental outbursts, left school in his home city at fourteen. Early on, he decided that he would like to emigrate to Palestine. Because of the racial clauses in the 1913 German nationality law, he could not apply for German citizenship, despite being born in the country. Markedly more religious than his parents, he attended yeshiva in Frankfurt-am-Main courtesy of a grant from Jewish community funds, then returned home and tried to apply for entry to Palestine through the local Jewish Emigration Office. He was told that at fifteen he was a year too young to travel alone. His parents, who lived off his father's modest tailoring business, were persuaded that in the interim, especially in light of increasing Nazi persecution in Germany, young Herschel should leave the country.

Equipped with a Polish passport and with a German re-entry permit, valid until April 1937, Herschel was able to enter Belgium, where residence rules were more lax. From there, however, the boy soon crossed into France and went on to Paris, where he initially stayed with an uncle and aunt. His situation in France was on the edge of illegality, since the law there demanded that he provide proof of being able to support himself, which he could not. Nonetheless, he stayed on in Paris.

After the spring of 1937, Herschel's re-entry visa became invalid, so he could no longer return to Germany. His Polish passport expired in January 1938. In July 1938 he was finally refused a residence visa in France and ordered to leave the country by the end of August. From then on, Herschel was essentially on the run.

Liable to deportation at any time, unable to work for fear of his illegal status being discovered, and with his impecunious relatives unable to offer financial support, Herschel, who had never learned much French, took refuge in an Orthodox-Jewish, Yiddish-speaking enclave in a depressed part of Paris. There he brooded on his situation. As October drew to a close, he heard even worse news from Germany. His parents and three surviving siblings had been deported along with other Polish Jews and dumped in no-man's-land at Zbąszyń. The press was full of the deportees' plight and the awful conditions in which they were being forced to live while held in limbo at the border.

And so it was that on the morning of 7 November 1938 Herschel Grynszpan walked into the German Embassy in Paris and shot down Ernst vom Rath. The young stateless Jew was quickly arrested by the French police and taken into custody. A photograph taken shortly afterwards shows a slightly pudgy but personable teenager wearing a suit and tie and a raincoat. 'I acted,' he told his interrogators at the police station, 'because of love for my parents and for my people who were subjected unjustly to outrageous treatment. It is not, after all, a crime to be Jewish. I am not a dog. I have a right to live. My people have a right to exist on this earth.'[16]

Vom Rath lingered for two days in hospital in Paris. Hitler's personal physician, Karl Brandt, was sent to join the French doctors at the diplomat's bedside.

Even as vom Rath's life hung in the balance, the Nazi regime's propaganda machine was running at full power, portraying the shooting not as the ill-thought-through act of a self-dramatizing seventeen-year-old victim of the times but as evidence of a world-wide Jewish conspiracy. 'Cowardly Murder Attempt of the Jew Grünspan [sic] against Embassy Counsellor Ernst vom Rath' and 'World Jewry Tears the Mask from its Face' were two headlines that Ruth Andreas-Friedrich noted on the morning of 9 November. Vom Rath's supposedly exemplary life story and his noble service to the German Volk were now highlighted in every newspaper. Medical bulletins were issued every hour.

In the meantime, as Andreas-Friedrich made her way into work, the atmosphere among Berliners on the bus was gloomily expectant rather than furious, but it was noticeable that along the fashionable shopping streets, the Kurfürstendamm and the Tauentzienstrasse, businesses marked out as Jewish-owned (which they now had to be by law) were even emptier than usual, increasing her foreboding. But at least she could still hope that the wounded diplomat might recover.[17]

The doctors failed, however. Ernst vom Rath died on 9 November 1938 at around 5.30 in the afternoon. Within a few short hours, as darkness fell in Berlin and at hundreds of locations across the territory of Greater Germany, something began to be heard that was already grimly familiar to many but would now become a signal of terror: the sound of breaking glass.

*

At seven o'clock on the morning of 10 November 1938, the downstairs doorbell rang at Ruth Andreas-Friedrich's apartment. Again and again . . . she counted nine or ten times . . . the rings came quickly and urgently. She went downstairs, opened the door, and there stood Dr Weissmann, a lawyer friend, and a Jew. 'Hide me, they're after me!' he panted. She stared at him. 'Who? What? I don't understand!'

Dr Weissmann rushed past her and up into her room. There he collapsed into a chair and put his head in his hands. Again, she asked in real bewilderment what had happened. His expression changed to one of bitter mockery.

Do you live on the moon? The devil is on the loose in Berlin! The synagogues are burning. Jewish blood is spurting from the knife. The SA* is on the march and smashing all the window panes. And you ask me what is happening?[18]

Understanding dawned. Out here, in this peaceful suburb, Andreas-Friedrich had seen and heard nothing of what was happening in the city. The day of reckoning they had all feared had arrived. Words tumbled over each other as Weissmann went on with his story:

We are being hunted like hares. They made me run the length of the Kurfürstendamm. Jewish swine! Mass murderer! Die, you asshole! they yelled at me. Pelted with stones and lumps of muck! Those louts, those hoodlums, those damned SA

* SA = Sturmabteilung, Storm Troopers or Brownshirts.

thugs . . . And the police just watched. Let what's burning, burn, and what should die, let it die!

Only now did Andreas-Friedrich realize that vom Rath must be dead, and her Jewish friend confirmed that this was so. 'And now they are celebrating his funeral mass – with burning torches and cans of petrol, sacrilege and mass murder. They nearly got me, but I slipped into a side street. So they got to beat up someone else, not me.'

Andreas-Friedrich told Weissmann to stay in the apartment while she went out and bought milk and bread. By nine, her friend had showered and breakfasted, kitted out in a pair of her partner Leo's pyjamas, and at nine-thirty she was on her way to work, leaving him there to rest in safety. On the bus, fellow commuters were silent and seemed to her quietly ashamed. As for the Kurfürstendamm, where she got off, it was a 'sea of glass fragments'. On the corner of the Ku'damm and Fasanenstrasse, near the entrance to her office, a crowd had come to a halt and was staring northwards along the street, unable to take its eyes from the burning ruins of the grand Fasanenstrasse Synagogue, the largest in Berlin, finished in 1912 and gifted with treasures by the then Kaiser himself.

'Damned scandal,' whispered a man standing near Andreas-Friedrich. She wanted to 'call him brother', but did not, for she had – to her shame – got used to keeping silent.

At the offices of the press group she worked for, all was chaos. Her boss sat distraught in his office. He had seen the Nazi thugs pouring petrol into the synagogue and noisily setting the building alight. He grimaced at the story the Nazis were now putting out, that the destruction was a result of 'popular anger', not state-sponsored. 'But . . . the facts?' Andreas-Friedrich asked. Wordlessly he showed her some typed sheets that carried the imprimatur of the government press agency, the 'German News Bureau' (Deutsches Nachrichtenbüro or DNB for short, controlled of course by Goebbels), and headlined 'Anti-Jewish Actions in Berlin and the Reich'. What was in these sheets was to be reproduced in the evening edition of all newspapers throughout Germany, with only a few cosmetic changes by editors on the margin so that not all papers' articles read exactly the same. He was duty-bound to sign it with his byline 'to make like I believe this pitiful rubbish'. The DNB's set screed began:

> After the announcement of the passing of Party Comrade vom Rath, the German diplomat struck down by the cowardly hand of a Jewish murderer, anti-Jewish demonstrations have developed spontaneously throughout the Reich. The profound anger of the German *Volk* also made itself apparent in strong anti-Jewish actions . . . In many places in Berlin the display windows of Jewish businesses were smashed and Jewish shop owners' display stands demolished. The Jewish business owners still possessed the insolence to make their Aryan employees remove the glass shards with their bare fingers, which provoked passionate protests from passers-by . . .

And so on for paragraph after paragraph.

'So now I know,' Andreas-Friedrich wrote. 'The Jewish War has begun.'

In fact, in other parts of Germany it had begun even before vom Rath's death. In the Hesse city of Kassel and in Dessau, in Thuringia, organized Nazi mobs had carried out attacks on Jewish homes, businesses and synagogues the previous day.[19] Goebbels had been informed of these disturbances. He was in Munich at the time, attending the Party event held annually to commemorate the failed coup of 9 November 1923 that had first put Hitler on the national stage. Late that afternoon, knowing that vom Rath had died, he met with Hitler at the Munich City Hall. Goebbels wrote afterwards in his diary:

> I tell the Führer about the business. He orders: Let demonstrations continue. Withdraw police. For once, the Jews should feel the anger of the people. That is right. I immediately instruct police and Party accordingly. Then I speak briefly in the same vein to the Party leadership. Wild applause. They all dash for the telephones immediately. Now the people will take action.[20]

It is evident from internal Nazi Party documents that Goebbels's furious appeal to the Party bosses assembled in Munich was, for all its malicious passion, carefully couched. Deniability was all. Nothing in writing. His aim was to enable the Party to orchestrate a pogrom while, to the outside world, maintaining the fiction that everything that happened on the night of 9/10 November 1938 arose out of spontaneous popular outrage.[21]

Most of the organizing and telephoning took place between 10 p.m. and midnight. Among the most important Nazi bosses to be prodded into action by Goebbels was Viktor Lutze, Chief of Staff of the SA, the Brownshirts who had terrorized the streets of German towns and cities before Hitler's rise to power.[22] Although reduced both in political importance and in numbers since 1933, shrinking from around 4 million to fewer than 2 million, the SA nonetheless still provided a huge reserve of trained bruisers willing and able to do the Party's bidding. Its members would play a major role in the horrors of the night to come.

A tide of destruction swept throughout the country in the few hours after midnight on 10 November. Businesses and homes were trashed, Jews beaten up and in some cases killed. Thousands of Jewish men were taken into so-called 'protective custody' (*Schutzhaft*). Synagogues were burned down by uniformed fire-setting squads plentifully equipped with petrol cans. Again and again in the newspapers, now all – down to the tiniest local news-sheet – subject to strict supervision by the Ministry of Propaganda, a similar line appeared when it came to describing the failure of the authorities to protect the synagogues.

The description in the *Pommersche Zeitung*, published in the major Baltic port of Stettin* at the mouth of the river Oder (population in 1939 around 270,000), was more or less typical in its cynical treatment of the city synagogue's wilful destruction – 'The fire brigade, which had arrived with numerous trucks and fire extinguishing equipment, had, in view of the rapid spread of the fire, to confine itself to the protection of neighbouring buildings.'[23]

---

* Now part of Poland and renamed Szczecin.

This echoed, deliberately or not, Goebbels's own comments in his diary about the destruction by fire of the Ohel Yaakov Synagogue on the Herzog-Rudolf-Strasse in the historic heart of Munich on that same night. Observing a 'blood-red sky' visible above the synagogue in the small hours of 10 November, he wrote: 'We only fire-fight as much as is necessary to protect nearby buildings. Otherwise let it burn down . . .'[24]

In the final paragraph of its report on *Kristallnacht* ('the night of broken glass'), the newspaper in Stettin listed almost casually the horrific damage done elsewhere in the region:

> In the provinces, in many places – among others, in Stralsund, Pasewalk, Swinemünde, Greifenhagen, Gollnow, Naugard, Pyritz, Köslin, Stolp, Neustetlin, Schneidemühl – the synagogues also went up flames. In various Jewish businesses the display windows were shattered. In Stralsund, the entire Jewish population was taken into protective custody. Mistreatment of Jews occurred nowhere, since the public, despite its understandable anger at the cowardly Jewish act of murder, in all cases remained level-headed throughout.

The official line on *Kristallnacht* insisted that the German public or 'racial comrades' (*Volksgenossen*) had risen up as one man in outrage at the murder of vom Rath. Damage had been done to Jewish-owned buildings and businesses, of course, and synagogues attacked, but with perfect Teutonic self-control the vengeance-seeking crowds had respected the stock in the shops, and, moreover, 'since the racial comrades exercised utmost discipline, they did not harm so much as a hair of a Jew's head'.[25]

The truth was quite different. Ninety-one Jews were officially estimated killed in the course of the *Kristallnacht* outrages – estimated, that is, in internal documents by the Nazi authorities themselves – though the true figure was probably much greater. Hundreds committed suicide. More deaths followed as many thousands were thrown into concentration camps, where they were systematically ill-treated, starved, brutalized and overworked. Over time, the total seems likely to have escalated well

into four figures.[26] The SA and its helpmeets may have been
licensed to commit violence, but in many places during the night
of 9/10 November the Brownshirts were out of control. Central
government itself may not have been aware of the full, shameful
extent of the massacre.

Ruth Andreas-Friedrich's lawyer friend, Dr Weissmann,
described to her how desperately he had fled to avoid physical
violence from the SA gangs scouring the Kurfürstendamm for
Jews to victimize. Erich Ebermayer, writer and man-about-Berlin,
was also out on the famous boulevard that same night. He
described how it felt to be in the middle of that hell on the late
evening of 9 November:

> We had dined in the city and afterwards were strolling along
> the Kurfürstendamm. Suddenly, trucks rolled up, packed full
> with SA-men. During the next few minutes, monstrous things
> happened in almost complete silence. One plate-glass display
> window after another on the Ku-Damm crunched and tinkled.
> Shards of glass tumbled out. We all stood stock-still. Responding
> to crisp, curt orders the SA squads proceeded from building
> to building. One of them carried a list and would call out the
> name of the next business due. Then more shattering glass. On
> the other side of the boulevard, another SA squad was 'at work',
> just as silently and precisely. A few people ran off and looked
> for policemen. But there were no policemen to be seen. The
> one at the Joachimsthaler Strasse junction, in charge of directing
> the traffic, did not seem to consider it his business. He just
> grinned.
>
> We finally continued on our way towards Halensee, walking
> over the fragments of glass that covered the wide pavement. Just
> as we had almost reached the Wilmersdorfer Strasse, where my
> car was parked, suddenly behind us and to our right a bright,
> shimmering glow appeared in the sky. We stared upwards. The
> flames themselves were not visible, but their reflection against
> the sky grew bigger and bigger with each minute. People were
> running towards us from the area where the great fire was raging:
> The synagogue is burning! SA-men have set fire to the synagogue![27]

Ebermayer's diary was just as clear when it came to the alleged probity of the 'racial comrades' regarding the contents of Jewish-owned shops and businesses. 'Since this morning [10 November] the plunder is in full swing. Everyone is taking from the demolished businesses whatever he needs. People are walking the streets shamelessly with coats, ladies dresses, dozens of neck-ties, draped over their arms.'[28]As for respecting the property and persons of private individuals, a story told by Ruth Adler stands for hundreds, perhaps more, of experiences that say otherwise. From an old Frankfurt Jewish family long prominent in the book-selling trade, Ruth Adler was then fifteen years old and living with her parents in Düsseldorf. On 9 November 1938 she had been separated from the adults, along with her younger brother. They were offered shelter by 'Aryan' acquaintances – an architect and his wife – to avoid the violence of *Kristallnacht*. However, forced to return home the next day (the concierge of the friends' building had informed the Gestapo of their presence), Ruth and her brother found a scene of terrible devastation:

> The door had been ripped off, the windows were totally crashed [*sic*], and all our furniture was out on the street, had been thrown out. The kitchen cabinets had been torn out of the walls. My mother's beautiful Limoges china, which she really saved just for her tea parties, was totally wrecked, crashed on a heap . . . We sat on the heap of broken china and crystal. My parents' painting had been destroyed with knives. And the Signac* . . . had been torn into little tiny pieces. We crawled all over the floor to find scraps of paper, which we collected and eventually my mother took to a restorer.[29]

Her mother and father returned a little later, and after allowing themselves a little recovery time they began to clear up. Their immediate neighbours rallied round, oblivious to the risks of showing kindness to Jews. On Sunday, Herr Adler went out to take

---

* Paul Signac (1863–1935), French impressionist painter.

the family's dachshund for a walk and was arrested by the Gestapo – or, as the regime would have it, 'taken into protective custody'.

Kristallnacht was everywhere, throughout what was now called the Great German Reich, from Berlin and the other great cities to villages and small towns. There did not need to be a synagogue or a business for the wreakers of destruction to get to work. It visited Germans of Jewish heritage even in what must have seemed to be the safest and most inconspicuous places.

Inge Lueg, then eleven years old, was a proud 'Bayer child'. Her father, a university-educated chemist, worked as a plant manager for the giant pharmaceutical company, which had settled at and largely created its own town, named Leverkusen. This fast-growing 'new town' lay at the confluence of the Wupper and Rhine rivers, just north of Cologne. Bayer, by that time part of the giant I.G. Farben chemicals and pharma conglomerate, was an exemplary employer of the paternalistic sort. The company provided housing, schools, a clinic, and other basic needs for its employees – in the case of Inge's family, a home in one of a large group of dwellings in the suburb of Wiesdorf, used by the British for their occupation forces after the First World War and vacated after they left in 1926. It was a 'prosperous and protected life' (*ein begütertes und behütetes Leben*) for the family of a quite senior Bayer employee, as she admitted.

Tall for her age, Inge had enough reach to open and close the heavy window shutters on the outside of the house, and took pride in doing so. On the evening of 9 November 1938, while her mother, wary of her falling out, as usual stood close behind her, she opened the windows to reach for the shutters and heard strange sounds in the neighbourhood.

> There was suddenly crashing and tinkling and shouting, a lot of screams and frightening shouting noises and the crashing went on and I said to my mother, what is that? And my mother said, oh, nothing, just quickly pull those shut. But it was something horrible. There was a Jewish family, a chemist, and the property was destroyed. We had several in the development, and some of them got away . . .[30]

She later heard from her sister that one of their Jewish neighbours had hanged himself.

The authorities themselves knew that the pretence of 'popular wrath' seemed ridiculous to many ordinary Germans. The police in Bielefeld, an industrial city of more than a hundred thousand inhabitants in mid-western-Germany, were almost brutal in the frankness of their summary. A report noted that almost nobody thought that *Kristallnacht* was spontaneous, and commented disapprovingly that in a number of cases 'school-age children were involved in breaking window panes and even the setting of fires and the destruction of furniture and similar'. It continued:

> In this context, it should further be remarked that the manner of the reporting regarding the course of these actions by the press has aroused general revulsion. Since, as has already been noted, the general populace was in almost no instances involved in the action, the continuing insistence by the press that this was the result of spontaneous popular anger appears almost ridiculous, particularly since the fact that the action was organized from above was, due to the synchronized nature of the action, scarcely capable of being misconstrued.[31]

Indeed, according to the unedited version of Goebbels's diaries, we know that on 9 November the minister himself found time to get on the phone to his long-time henchman Werner Wächter* in Berlin and request personally that the splendid synagogue on the Fasanenstrasse – to Goebbels, as a fanatical anti-Semite and for ten years Gauleiter of Berlin, a particular irritation – be given special attention by the organized gangs of thugs set loose that night; which, of course, it certainly was.[32]

Just as by no means all Germans were convinced by the lie of the spontaneous 'people's anger' (*Volkszorn*) against the Jews, so not all found the destruction of the synagogues justifiable. From

---

* Werner Wächter (1902–1945?) was a senior Propaganda Ministry official who had been Goebbels's right-hand man in Berlin since the street-fighting days before the Nazi seizure of power. He disappeared at the end of the war, believed killed.

the strongly Catholic, historic city of Paderborn, in Westphalia, the District Administrator (*Landrat*) reported that 'the predominant part of the population, which still stands under the influence of Centre [pre-Hitler Catholic Party – FT] and church circles, rejects the action against the Jews'. He continued:

> The circles that already take a fundamentally rejectionist position regarding the National Socialist State on account of their political–ecclesiastical allegiance exhibit a particularly indignant attitude towards the fact that the 'religious houses' of the Jews have been set on fire. It seems that in these circles, which still regard Jewry as merely a faith group rather than as an alien race, the scare story has spread around to the effect that later a similar action could be unleashed against the other 'confessions'.[33]

Similar observations were made in reports from Bielefeld. Even some Protestants were alarmed at the assault on the Jewish faith, fearing that attacks on Christian institutions might follow when it suited the regime.[34]

The SS Security Service's branch office in Cochem, a small, strongly Catholic town on the river Moselle west of Koblenz, discerned a subtle plot by the Catholic hierarchy to exploit the recent pogrom, with the aim of undermining the Nazi regime. The Sunday after *Kristallnacht*, so the SS reported:

> . . . in many sermons, they spoke of 'loving thy neighbour' in an unconditional way, and ordained that the precept 'to live and let live' should be followed. This form of trouble-stirring was in general well understood, even though not a word was said in commemoration of the Jews, and no mention made of them . . .[35]

From the small town of Borgentreich, midway between Paderborn and Kassel, the *Bürgermeister* reluctantly had to inform Gestapo headquarters in Bielefeld that the attacks on Jewish citizens and their properties were 'not understood':

The Jews were moreover pitied. Especially the fact that damage was done to their property and possessions and that the male Jews were taken off to a 'concentration camp'. This attitude among the local people was certainly not universal, but I would estimate that around here at least 60 per cent of the population felt this way . . .[36]

Even the young female gardener at Canstatt, a firm and usually uncritical supporter of the regime's actions against the Jews, wrote in her diary that 'Beating people up like this [*solche Prügeleien*] is not worthy of us Germans.'[37]

Of almost equal concern to many authorities was the fact that even those who had nothing against Jews being made to suffer were taken aback both at the unfettered nature of the violence and at the indiscriminate damage done to buildings, businesses and property. These material assets could, after all, have been transferred either to 'Aryan' ownership or directly to the state. This cold-eyed practical perception was particularly widespread further down the social scale.[38] It was, however, also shared by some of the elite. Göring, the man in charge of the 'Four Year Plan', though supporting the principles behind the pogrom, made clear at a ministerial meeting three days later his displeasure at the 'waste' represented by the massive wave of gratuitous destruction. This he seems to have blamed mostly on Goebbels. 'I would rather you had killed 200 Jews and not destroyed so many valuable material assets,' he told the Propaganda Minister and his accomplices with chilling candour.[39]

During the afternoon of 10 November, with the object achieved and the 'action' brutally established as a fact in the public mind, Goebbels ordered an end to the depredations. He issued a press statement that, while not condemning the 'justified' outrage of the *Volk* against the Jews, called for order:

The justifiable and understandable outrage of the German people regarding the cowardly assassination of a German diplomat in Paris found expression during last night to a comprehensive extent. In numerous towns and communities of the

Reich actions of revenge were undertaken against Jewish buildings and businesses.

A strict injunction has now been issued to the entire population to cease immediately all actions and demonstrations
against Jewry, of no matter what kind. The definitive response
to the treacherous Jewish murder in Paris will be meted out
to Jewry via the path of legislation or regulation.[40]

The announcement appeared on the front page of every newspaper in the country the next morning, 11 November, and was
broadcast on national radio. After listening to the piece being
read out over the airwaves, Erich Ebermayer weighed up his
thoughts. He briefly speculated about whether it might have been
Göring, Himmler or Hess who had issued the order, before hitting
on something like the truth:

Or it *was* Goebbels's idea, and he sees himself, now that the
precious *Volk* has joyfully seized the opportunity for gigantic
plundering, constrained to put the brake on in order to keep
the reins in his hands.

What, though, is going on with this dark threat of *legal*
measures against the Jews? I shouldn't be surprised if Hitler
and Goebbels used the welcome opportunity provided by this
murder, which should genuinely be condemned, to settle the
hash, economically and morally, of those Jews who still remain
in Germany. Everything seems to come at the right time for
this government: in February 1933 a Dutch idiot with a
Communist Party membership card in his pocket set light to
the Reichstag – which led to 'extermination' of the political
left. And now a deluded young Jew shoots an innocent German
diplomat! You have to be lucky! And these gentlemen *are* lucky.[41]

According to reports from Reinhard Heydrich, Chief of the
Security Police and of the SS Security Service and another leading
organizer of the *Kristallnacht* atrocities, 190 synagogues had been
destroyed by fire or deliberate demolition, often by dynamite,
that night (a figure soon raised to 267). Around thirty thousand

Jewish men had been arrested and for the most part incarcerated in concentration camps.[42] Final estimates by historians take the figure for destruction of Jewish synagogues and prayer houses a great deal higher, however, to over a thousand – in effect almost every Jewish place of worship in the country.[43] Seven thousand five hundred out of an estimated total of around 9,000 Jewish businesses in Germany were attacked, ransacked, and often destroyed.[44]

While Ebermayer was still pondering Goebbels's motives, Ruth Andreas-Friedrich and her partner Leo had also begun to take stock. Dr Weissmann, the Jewish lawyer friend who had appeared early on the morning after being hunted around the Kurfürstendamm by the SA, was no longer their only 'guest', as she found out when she arrived home from work on 10 November.

> The entire apartment is full of newly billeted arrivals. Levy has come to us, and Jochen Cohn. They are perched on my couch playing Écarté [a two-player trick-taking game similar to whist]. 'To take our minds off things,' says Levy apologetically. He looks exhausted and unshaven . . . Jochen Cohn rubs his forehead in embarrassment. 'To be ambushing you like this . . .'[45]

Leo was out, looking out for a friend, Dr Hirschberg, who hadn't answered his telephone and was feared to have been caught by the Gestapo. In Leo's bedroom, it turned out, were two more refuge-seekers. 'Just for one night – until the worst is over!' they stammered. Then the telephone rang. It was another friend, Franz Wolfheim. His voice was hoarse and agitated. He was just five minutes away and begged Andreas-Friedrich to open up for him downstairs. This made six house guests. 'Gradually,' she wrote in her diary, 'I am beginning to feel my whole body constricting.'

It was a feeling she would have to overcome, or at least get used to. The regime had moved from discrimination against German Jews to a policy of active persecution, heading in the direction of collective extinction, either by exile or by violence. Andreas-Friedrich and her friends would be spending the next

six and more years giving shelter and aid to their Jewish compatriots, at great risk to themselves. They would become famous,
when all could be revealed, as the 'Uncle Emil' Resistance group.

*

In the edition of the *Pommersche Zeitung* following the 9/10
November pogrom, the front-page headline screamed: 'An End
Now to the Jewish World Plague!'

All the same, for those not attending the huge anti-Semitic
demonstrations promised by the local Gauleiter, life in Stettin
went on almost as normal. The fires burning among the ruins of
the city's synagogue had been extinguished by around noon on
Thursday 10 November. The stately landmark building had stood
since 1875 in the heart of the city, a short distance up from the
main railway station, with its front facade on the bustling thoroughfare named Grüne Schanze ('Green Rampart'*). At its back
there was an administrative office and a Jewish community centre,
accessible through an entrance at 9/10 Rosengarten Strasse, a
street filled with small shops and businesses. On the corner beside
the synagogue stood the city library. The city hall was just a little
further south, a block below on Karlstrasse, and beyond that the
waterside and the port.

Demolition work began at once. As early as Friday afternoon,
less than forty-eight hours after the pogrom, demolition squads
had begun to lay explosives around the synagogue's exterior walls
to remove the 'danger to traffic'. The remains of the building
were dynamited on the afternoon of Saturday 12 November. From
that moment, the synagogue, which had for more than sixty years
served a thriving local community of some 7,000 Germans of
Jewish heritage, with room for 1,600 worshippers, effectively
ceased to exist. The trams and cars and trucks and 'Aryan' citizens
could pass freely and safely in front of the gaping ruin.[46]

Inside the *Pommersche Zeitung*, in the paper's entertainment
section, the Stettin Stadttheater (City Theatre), on the Königplatz

---

* Now in Polish *Ulica Dworcowa*, Railway Street.

about 500 metres north-east of the synagogue, offered a weekend of operetta. On Saturday evening there was *The Bird Dealer* by Carl Zeller, and on Sunday a matinee of *The Barber of Baghdad* by Peter Cornelius, with the main evening performance of Franz Lehár's *The Tsarevich* already sold out. The latter piece, ironically, had been written by Lehár specially for the internationally famous Austrian tenor Richard Tauber. Tauber was half Jewish, and had been forced to emigrate after the Nazi seizure of power, first from Germany and then, after the Anschluss in March 1938, from Austria too. A two-minute walk round the corner from the Stadttheater in Luisenstrasse was the Trocadero cabaret/variety club, with a touring show from Berlin starring Carmencita, 'the European Shirley Temple'.

The nearby Urania cinema was showing a recently re-released film from 1932, *The Blue Light*. It starred (and was directed by) the convinced Nazi Leni Riefenstahl, who before directing memorable films of the 1934 Nuremberg Rally and the 1936 Berlin Olympic Games had enjoyed a successful acting career. *The Blue Light* was the film in which Riefenstahl had first come to the attention of Hitler, who thought her looks expressed the inner spirit of the German woman. Needless to say, the names of the original writers, Carl Mayer and Bela Balázs, who were Jewish (as was the co-producer, Harry Sokal), had by this time been removed from the credits.

The grandiose new UFA-Palast film theatre, all art deco and glass, with its ground-floor bar/restaurant, stood tall on the Paradeplatz, literally just round the corner from the synagogue. Here, on Saturday 12 November, the people of Stettin could see a no-holds-barred melodrama, *Frau Sixta*. As a matinee there was a cartoon version of the fairy tale *Puss in Boots* ('Look at the cat, how he puts on boots, how he dances and sings and talks like a human!').

Anyone walking up from the main railway station to spend an hour or an evening at these theatres, or for that matter the Trocadero, could only have avoided passing what remained of the synagogue by undertaking an unfeasibly wide detour.

*

Of course, *Kristallnacht* hit the headlines in the British press. The popular right-wing papers the *Daily Express* and the *Daily Mail* seem to have totally swallowed the fiction that the excesses were the result of spontaneous popular anger against the Jews. On Friday 11 November, the front page of the *Express* carried the main headline 'Looting Mobs Defy Goebbels'. 'Synagogues and Jewish shops were looted and burned yesterday in Berlin as anti-Jewish rioters gained control of the city,' the paper told its readers. Not even Goebbels's call for an end to the pogrom could, so it claimed, 'curb the madness of the mobs'.[47] The *Daily Mail*, notorious for its favourable coverage of both Hitler's early years as dictator and the rise of the British Fascists under Sir Oswald Mosley, took a similar tack. Although it condemned the violence as an 'outrage to the name of justice', the *Mail* nonetheless described *Kristallnacht* as 'an internal affair'.

Both of these main right-wing popular papers continued with their editorial policy of opposing any relaxation of British immigration laws to accommodate persecuted German Jews.[48] Almost two weeks after *Kristallnacht*, the *Daily Express*, whose proprietor, Lord Beaverbrook, remained a stalwart supporter of Appeasement, devoted an editorial to the question. As so often, the vivid, horrified responses of *Express* reporters on the spot congealed into cold indifference when it came to actual editorial policy back at head office. It was the chief reason why Geoffrey Cox, the young journalist who had reported so movingly on the betrayal of Czechoslovakia, turned down Lord Beaverbrook's offer of a leader writer's job on the paper – he was not prepared to become his owner's mouthpiece. Cox later learned that his refusal had come within an ace of getting him the sack, for 'the Beaver' did not take kindly to such insolence.[49]

'The Jews are always in the news,' the *Express*'s anonymous leader writer began on this occasion, with evident satisfaction in hitting on a rhyme. 'Each morning we get another account of Jewish pogroms here, there, and everywhere, with tales of the sufferings of the Jewish race and stories of the disabilities now being inflicted on the Jewish people.' But he added, there was now a 'Danger Plan' being discussed in parliament. A plan to allow these persecuted Jews into Britain.

> What good purpose will it serve? Is it proposed to admit more refugees into Britain?
> That is a dangerous proposition. We have already accepted our full quota of foreign Jews. We cannot assimilate any more.[50]

It might be possible to allow Jews to settle in 'undeveloped parts' of the British Empire, of course. Except Palestine, which 'cannot take in any more of them'. Otherwise the problem was a 'purely administrative one which should be dealt with by Mr Chamberlain and his colleagues'. Under the rubric 'Least said—' the leader column concluded with matchless banality:

> The Daily Express has the greatest sympathy with the Jews. It deplores and regrets the persecution to which they have been subjected. But it cannot see that any purpose useful to the Jews or to ourselves is served by continued recriminations.
> Take counsel in the age-old saying which has now indeed become a commonplace: 'Least said, soonest mended'.

The *Daily Mirror*, though left-leaning, reported far less about the details of the riots than the *Express*, whose well-funded foreign desk delivered shocking detail, at length. On 11 November, the *Mirror* led, not with *Kristallnacht*, but with reports of a plan to end 'baby farming' – bogus adoption societies that were selling infants to childless couples – with events in Germany relegated to the far right column of the front page under the headline 'Nazi Hate Day'. The report was chilling enough, but relatively brief, and came from Vienna, where presumably the paper had a correspondent, rather than from elsewhere in Germany.

The next day, Saturday 12 November, the front page of the *Mirror* contained no mention at all of the continuing German pogrom – the banner was 'The Duke of Windsor Is Coming Home Soon'. This was accompanied by a large photograph of the Duke and Duchess meeting with his younger brother, the Duke of

Gloucester, and his Duchess, at an exclusive restaurant in Paris
for what was claimed to be their first time spent together since
the Abdication. On page 4, a one-column article headlined 'Nazis
Try to Evade Guilt of Riot Orgy' carried accusations about Jewish
persecution from the likes of Liberal leader Sir Archibald Sinclair
and a disapproving description of Goebbels's latest outpourings,
but no new details of what had happened in the country.

On the following Monday, on page 2 there was a one-column
article in the *Mirror*: 'Jews: Britain Warns Hitler' – dealing with
vague British government expressions of disapproval against
Berlin and sketchily indicating imminent further measures against
the Jews by the regime, with a fair amount of newsprint then
devoted to new anti-Catholic activities by the Nazis – and on
the back page a small one-paragraph piece, '"Hands Off Jews"
– U.S.', reporting a secret meeting between Secretary of State
Cordell Hull and the German Ambassador to Washington. Tucked
away at the bottom of page 2 there was also a report about a
founder-member of the Anglo-German Friendship League, a
Councillor H.G. Andrews of Hove, who had declared himself
appalled by the pogrom and bemoaned the 'many hundreds of
pounds' he had spent in support of close relations between the
two countries. 'I have written to German diplomats I know,' he
informed the *Mirror*, 'telling them that until they give better
treatment to these unhappy people they cannot expect friendship
from *us*.' He had cancelled three major trips to Germany planned
for the following year.

Even Lord Londonderry, former Minister for Aviation, arch-
appeaser, frequent visitor to Germany, and luminary of the
Nazi-sympathizing London set, felt moved to express disapproval
of the violence and sympathy for the Nazis' victims. This prompted
the British Union of Fascists' mouthpiece, *Action*, to express its
suspicion that Londonderry had somehow been 'got at' – after
all, it sneered, 'Surely a few broken windows in Germany cannot
account for such a conversion?'[51]

There was little editorial comment in the *Mirror*. Although it
took a kinder view on the question of accepting more Jewish
refugees, its approach tended to be coy and indirect. Under the

heading 'Choose Your Refugees', the paper's editorial never specified the race or religion of any of the people it was talking about,
but so far as the (possibly) 'not-nice' group was concerned, the
persecuted Jews of Germany were clearly meant:

> Few people (we believe) objected to receiving a few refugees
> during the last crisis or suppressed war.
>   Nice refugees, of course. Pretty little children, all winsome
> and worried. Or quite nice grown-ups. But not, odd fish from
> nowhere; destitute, dirty; lesser breeds of foreign extraction.
>   That is, in brief, the domestic refugee problem, soon to be
> raised . . . in the House of Lords. Is it – or are they – to be
> nice weekend guests or an indiscriminate billeting of bounders?
>   And what is to become of the not-nice if nobody nice will
> receive them?

A debate on the refugee question in the House of Commons
took place on 21 November on a Labour motion, also phrased
in general terms:

> That this House notes with profound concern the deplorable
> treatment suffered by certain racial, religious and political
> minorities in Europe and, in view of the growing gravity of the
> refugee problem would welcome an immediate concerted effort
> amongst the nations, including the United States of America,
> to secure a common policy.

The Labour MP Philip Noel-Baker gave a moving and detailed
description of what had happened on *Kristallnacht*, and the motion
was approved without a division.
    During the debate, Sir Samuel Hoare, the Home Secretary,
expressed his sympathy with Hitler's victims. He was, Hoare
assured the House, still a 'staunch supporter' of the Munich
Agreement and a believer in the possibility of Anglo-German
friendship. It soon became clear that his main problem was not
so much the pogrom itself but the problems it would cause in
terms of a potential increase in immigration.

I am opposed to all attempts to intervene in the domestic affairs of other countries, but the issues raised by measures against Jews in Germany, and the way in which they have been raised, force themselves on the attention of other countries.

Such an action cannot remain exclusively domestic when it involves scores of thousands of men, women and children seeking admission to other countries.

Hoare added that the problem would have to be dealt with by the thirty-two countries that had been represented at the Évian Conference in June. There was due to be a meeting in London in ten days' time. But meanwhile:

There is an underlying current of suspicion and anxiety about alien immigration on any big scale. Below the surface – and I am only telling the House the experience of the Home Office – there is the making of a definite anti-Jewish movement . . . I have to be careful to avoid anything in the nature of mass immigration that would lead to the growth of a movement that we all wish to see suppressed.[52]

Beyond vague talk of speeding up the processing of visa applications and possibly settling fugitive German Jews in remote parts of the Empire, there was no sign of an urgent rescue operation being mounted by Britain alone. It was all about administration.

The next day, the *Mirror*'s daily (and consciously folksy) 'Live Letters' discussion forum featured a letter headlined 'ARROGANT JEWS?' Written under a pseudonym from the north-east of England, it left no doubt that Hoare's remarks, though obviously self-serving, contained some truth:

I am given to understand that the *Daily Mirror* is Jew-owned and Jew-controlled.

If you are Jews and want the people of this country to like them better, appeal to the younger Jews to be less arrogant and better-behaved in public places.

I am not a Jew-hater or a Jew-baiter, but the younger Jews
are making the most tolerant lose patience.

This country is still the best in the world.

Help to keep it the land of the free by an appeal to the
younger Jews to be worthy of it.[53]

'You seem to have a large number of idiotic bees in your
bonnet,' the paper's moderators replied, concluding: 'If you're
trying to stir up bad feeling, you're doing a sloppy job of it, by
revealing yourself as a bigot, who is worthy of little else but
contempt.'

Many well-meaning people in Britain comforted themselves
with the thought – partly justified, as internal German government reports showed – that a lot of ordinary Germans had not
approved of *Kristallnacht*. The *Express*'s man in Berlin, reporting
on 14 November, told his readers that 'the pogroms have caused
such intense dissatisfaction among the masses of the people as I
have never seen during the five years Hitler has been in power'.[54]
Almost every newspaper, from the right to the left, followed this
line. When a shocked female reader wrote to 'Live Letters' a
week after the pogrom, having witnessed violent scenes against
Jews in Düsseldorf while staying with friends there, the moderators told her: 'The actions of Germany's rulers are branding the
basically decent mass of German people as insane fiends. The
danger is that the deeds of a few shall be regarded as the will of
the people they master. And that is one of the surest ways to
war.'[55] Even the firmly left-wing *Daily Herald*, part-owned by the
British Trade Union Congress and a mouthpiece for the Labour
Party, insisted that 'no one with any knowledge of the German
people will doubt for a moment that for the greater part they
will themselves feel pity and shame at such an outburst'.[56]

Soon, humanitarians of all stripes – by no means all of them
Jewish – had begun to rally in support of the persecuted German
Jews. The British establishment followed suit, though perhaps
reluctantly at times, and always keen to keep control of such
undertakings, so as not to cause diplomatic trouble with the
regime in Berlin. Even the Prime Minister betrayed the fact that,

while deploring the German horrors, he shared conventional stereotyping of all Jews as 'rich', as well as the views of some who did not want too many 'not-nice' people imported into the country. 'The persecution arose out of two motives,' he wrote to his sister Hilda some months after *Kristallnacht*:

> . . . a desire to rob the Jews of their money and a jealousy of their superior cleverness. No doubt Jews aren't a loveable people; I don't care about them myself – but that is not sufficient to explain the pogrom.[57]

In this last observation, at least, Chamberlain was right. The Nazi regime's aim in mounting the vicious pantomime of *Kristallnacht* was not simply to do violence to, and potentially to be rid of, a hated minority, and neither did it aim exclusively at large-scale confiscation ('robbing the Jews of their money') – although it did that too, for the government's addiction to deficit spending, overwhelmingly because of massive rearmament, was threatening to drive the country into bankruptcy.[58] There was also an international strategic element. That shadowy creation 'World Jewry', to which the hapless Herschel Grynszpan, and through him every individual Jew in the country, had now become inextricably linked in the mind of so many credulous Germans, was not just to be eliminated as a force in the economic and cultural life of Germany, but to be blamed for engineering the coming world conflict. Many people, including statesmen, in Britain and France might mean well, so the Nazi narrative went, but behind them lurked Jewish money and the Jewish press. These shadowy manipulators wanted to encircle and then destroy Germany, Jewry's bitterest and most formidable enemy, and were therefore propelling their Gentile political puppets in the democracies inexorably towards war.

On the evening of 10 November, Hitler had received four hundred representatives of the German press and publishing industries at the Führerbau in Munich, where the famous Agreement with Chamberlain and Daladier had been signed just weeks before. The Führer thanked them, in a forty-five-minute speech, for their efforts on the new Germany's behalf. As the Führer spoke, around a kilometre and a half away the shell of the Ohel Yaakov Synagogue was still smouldering. A recording of the speech survives which takes us beyond the harmless banality of the heavily edited version released to the press at the time. In his uncensored oration, Hitler described at length to the regime's propaganda elite the need for a 'slow preparation of the German people'. Preparation for what? He continued with an extraordinarily frank explanation. 'Circumstances,' he told his audience, 'have forced me for decades to speak almost exclusively about peace.'

> It had now become necessary to gradually reposition the German people psychologically, and to slowly make it clear that there are things which, if they cannot be achieved through peaceful means, would have to be achieved by means of force. To this end it was . . . necessary to illuminate for the people certain foreign policy events in such a way that the inner voice of the people itself slowly began to cry out for the use of force. That is, there-fore, to illuminate certain events so that in the mind of the broad mass of the people completely automatically the conviction is gradually aroused: If it is simply not possible to remedy something in a good way, then it will have to be remedied by force; things cannot be allowed to continue like this . . .[59]

Kristallnacht represented a step change in the process of radi-calizing ordinary Germans. The regime's aim was to transform, above all by propaganda means, the German people from the sceptical, distinctly pacifistic crowd that Hitler had surveyed when he looked down from the balcony of the Reich Chancellery on 27 September 1938 into a hardened, militant mass who would follow him into war. Wide sections of the German population, he told his audience that night at the Führerbau, and particularly those who considered themselves intellectuals, were just a 'bunch of chickens' (*Hühnervolk*). 'Even now,' he continued contemptu-ously, 'when we are enjoying only successes, and world-historical successes at that, they are unreliable.' This must be remedied, and the press's job was to make that happen.

'The Jews are our misfortune' (Die Juden sind unser Unglück), the prominent nationalist historian Heinrich von Treitschke had written sixty years earlier, less than a decade after Germany had been unified into a single powerful Reich. Treitschke's preferred 'solution' had been to assimilate German Jews out of existence rather than expelling or liquidating them, but his famous phrase, which had so clearly helped make anti-Semitism respectable during the years that followed, now adorned the front of the Jew-baiting Nazi scandal-sheet *Der Stürmer*. The Weimar-era composer Friedrich Holländer had satirized such slogans in his cabaret chanson 'Die Juden sind an allem schuld': The Jews are to blame for everything . 'Whether it rains or whether it hails/ Whether there's thunder or whether there's snow . . .' Holländer had written, taking anti-Semitism to its absurd limits for comic effect, at a time when it was still (just) possible to treat the subject with irony. After *Kristallnacht*, however, this was not so much satire as cold reality. The Jews were, the Hitler regime insisted ever more loudly, to blame for everything that had been, and was to come.

Wilm Hosenfeld, the provincial schoolteacher struggling with the conflict between his law-abiding Catholicism and his loyalty to the now almost entirely lawless Nazi Party, had written in his diary the weekend after *Kristallnacht*: 'Pogroms against the Jews throughout Germany. Terrible conditions in the Reich, without law and order; accompanying this, an external appearance of hypocrisy and falsehood.'[60]

Hosenfeld, and millions like him, deeply patriotic but unsettled by the direction their country was taking, would now be subjected to a relentless campaign by the regime aimed at turning them from doubters to followers, who would, if perhaps still reluctantly, nonetheless answer their Führer's call to war.

FOUR

Winter 1938/1939
'Does Conscription Mean That the Men Will Have to Go Away?'

More than two years before *Kristallnacht*, in August 1936, a 22-year-old foreign passport holder visited Berlin while the Olympic Games were being held there. The name on the Norwegian documents with which this young man travelled was 'Gunnar Gaasland', but he had been born Herbert Frahm in the German city of Lübeck. As a prominent youth activist with a Marxist splinter group, after the Nazi seizure of power he had feared arrest by the Gestapo. Working at that time for a shipping company, Frahm had organized a sea passage and fled across the Baltic to Norway, still barely nineteen years old. He returned to Germany now for the first time since then, on a genuine passport belonging to a sympathizer in Oslo but with an altered ID photograph. His task in Berlin was to inspect the state of the anti-Nazi underground and the Resistance in general after three and a half years of the Hitler dictatorship.

In tune with the dangerous times and the requirements of political exile, young Gunnar/Herbert had several aliases. He was usually known by 1936 as 'Willy Brandt', a name he adopted permanently after the war, and under which he became internationally known as a politician and statesman who played a crucial role in enabling Germany to adapt to its post-war circumstances. The young socialist firebrand of 1936, however, was not concerned with adapting to anything. He came to Berlin keen to see how the internal opposition could best hasten the (theoretically) inevitable doom of what most left-wingers considered to be a decadent end-stage of capitalism. Brandt was to be disappointed in this expectation.

Large numbers of foreigners were expected for the Olympics. Berlin was accordingly in a superficially relaxed and cosmopolitan mood, smartened up and on its best behaviour. There was suddenly little outward sign of the hitherto ever-tightening grip of the police state, and a temporary moratorium on anti-Jewish actions. The German press was told, in a reversal of the usual official attitude: 'We urgently warn against burdening reports on the Olympic Games with racial perspectives.'[1] *Der Stürmer*, Julius Streicher's anti-Semitic hate sheet, was temporarily removed from its usual public places of display.

A huge new sports complex had been built between 1934 and 1936 in the borough of Charlottenburg, to the west of the centre of Berlin, at a cost of some 55 million Reichsmarks,* in its midst a stadium for 110,000 spectators. The regime saw these games, awarded to Germany in 1931 when the Reich was still a democracy, as its great PR opportunity. People who came to Berlin from other countries would see that 'the new Germany' was progressive, efficient, successful, open to the world. Goebbels himself, addressing the world's press at a grand reception, declared the Games to be 'a festival of joy and peace' at which Germany intended to 'build a bridge with which to unite the peoples of Europe'. In the privacy of his diary, he congratulated himself on a 'major feat of propaganda'.[2]

Young Willy Brandt, meanwhile, had to report back to the comrades in Scandinavia that there was little likelihood of the internal opposition achieving anything much unless the regime began to collapse of its own volition – or, in the Marxist phrase,

---

* Approximately 210 million euros in 2017 (estimate of equivalent values at https://www.bundesbank.de).

succumb to 'internal contradictions'.[3] The fact was that, Olympics or no Olympics, the Third Reich was, on the whole, a success so far as most ordinary Germans were concerned. By this time, unemployment had been all but eliminated, 'order' had been restored, and the country's war industries and armed forces greatly enlarged. Homes, roads (including the famous *Reichsautobahnen*), and all manner of other infrastructure were being built. The factories, especially the armaments factories, were humming.

Moreover, five months before the Games, in March 1936, German troops had marched into the demilitarized Rhineland. Though most historians agree that the German army was still too feeble to resist any armed opposition, and Hitler himself saw it as his 'most tense moment', the Western Allies, who had imposed this buffer zone as a key part of the Versailles Treaty, did nothing. Germany and Italy also blatantly supported Franco's Nationalist rebels, who rose up against the elected Republican government of Spain in July 1936. Britain did nothing to help the Republic, and, despite the presence of an increasingly precarious and fragmented left-wing Popular Front government in Paris, neither did the French. Then came the annexation (Anschluss) of Austria in March 1938, again without opposition from the London/Paris axis, and finally the absorption of the Sudetenland, after the democracies' initial appearance of firm support for the Czechoslovak Republic crumbled in the face of a real possibility of European war. Now, violent anarchy had been unleashed against Germany's Jews, yet once again, all that was heard from the democracies were words, and relatively few of those.

Hitler's speech to the press on 10 November 1938, set against a chaotic background of state-sponsored anti-Semitic violence, had given the Führer the chance to congratulate himself on achieving all these things without war. At the same time, he also suggested that the German people, having benefited so greatly from his genius, were going to have to prepare themselves for the possibility – or even the probability – of war, and the sacrifices that would entail, if the full programme of national regeneration (as Hitler saw it) was to be achieved.

For the meantime, the logic of *Kristallnacht* as part of this strategy was being relentlessly promoted. While thousands of Jewish men picked up by the Gestapo in the second week of November languished in concentration camps, a swathe of new anti-Jewish laws and regulations spewed from the government machine. Most of them had been agreed at the meeting of 12 November that Göring had hosted in his spanking-new Air Ministry building.

On 11 November, the possession of firearms by Jews had been made illegal, and punishable with up to five years' hard labour.

On 12 November, the Regulation for Elimination of Jews from the Economic Life of Germany was promulgated, forcing Jews to transfer all retail businesses into 'Aryan' hands. German Jews would be required to make restitution of one billion Reichsmarks to the Reich for the damage done on *Kristallnacht*. This would be collected in the form of a special tax.

Also on 12 November, Jews were forthwith forbidden to attend theatres, concerts, art galleries and museums, or to use public swimming baths.

From 15 November, all Jewish pupils were expelled from German schools. Henceforth, they could only attend segregated Jewish schools.

From 19 November, Jews were no longer able to use the German welfare or health systems.

From 23 November, all Jewish-owned business were declared confiscated.

From 28 November, Jews were subject to curfew.

From 30 November, Jewish lawyers' right to practise was withdrawn, although they could act as 'consultants' to other Jews.

From 3 December, Jews were to surrender their drivers' licences and would no longer be allowed to own cars. This had been agreed at the 12 November meeting that Heydrich had attended, but the drafting of the law had taken a few weeks.

From 5 December, Jewish assets were frozen.

On 6 December 1938, despite *Kristallnacht*, and despite the stream of edicts designed to humiliate, terrify and intimidate German Jews, Joachim von Ribbentrop, German Foreign Minister, met Georges Bonnet, his French counterpart, in Paris. There they smiled for the cameras and signed a treaty of friendship and non-aggression. Recognizing that the two countries had no territorial claims on each other, and expressing fair words for future relations, it bore a distinct similarity to the one Chamberlain had agreed with Hitler at the end of September. In the event, it had as much (that is, as little) meaning. Although there was a brief thaw between the two countries, and hope for better economic cooperation, ultimately the French were using it to buy time. The Germans, among other things, were using it to detach France from its defensive agreements with Russia, which had been a major concern during the Sudeten Crisis. Ribbentrop, typically, later falsely claimed that in exchange for Germany's declaration of peaceful intent in the West, and promise of help in France's territorial disputes with Mussolini, France had agreed to give the Reich a free hand in Eastern Europe.[4]

From 8 December 1938, all Jews were barred from German universities.

*

In Britain, as Christmas approached, the prosperous parts of the country were beginning to loosen their purse strings. After a blip in international trade, linked to the recession that for the moment had brought the Roosevelt Recovery in America to a halt, things seemed back on a more even keel. The quickening pace of rearmament had also put more money in working-class pockets, especially in the Midlands, where the aircraft industry was an increasingly important employer of skilled and semi-skilled labour. State-supported 'shadow factories' were being hastily built. Everyone still hoped for peace, but few now dared rule out the possibility, even the probability, of war.

On 1 December, Sir John Anderson, former Chairman of the Board of the Inland Revenue, later Governor of Bengal, and now recently appointed as Lord Privy Seal, announced plans for a national register of adult British citizens. This represented a first step towards military conscription, which was being called for by many in Conservative circles, and specifically the *Daily Express*.

The register was voluntary at first, but later became compulsory.

The year 1938, with the threat of war now more or less constant, had already witnessed a change of mood among the general population; half a million Britons had answered the call to volunteer as military auxiliaries of various sorts, including applying to the territorial forces, or qualifying in first aid, or training as air-raid wardens and evacuation organizers. However, many on the left and in pacifist circles still condemned these measures as a 'remilitarization' of society. Nazi Germany, by contrast, as a genuinely (and thoroughly) militarized society, had been systematically mobilizing resources, civil and military, since the late spring of 1933, when Hermann Göring had established a centralized organization for Air Raid Protection (Luftschutzbund). Even after the boost provided by the Munich Crisis, Britain's ARP was dwarfed by the German Luftschutzbund. By 1939 the latter had 15 million members, including more than 700,000 office holders, of whom 280,000 were women.

Later in November 1938, the British government would offer £10 million in grants to help less well-off citizens install air-raid refuges in their gardens. The so-called Anderson Shelter (not named after Sir John, but after a government employee, also called Anderson, who was responsible for the design),[5] supplied in kit form, would not survive a direct hit but would protect the occupants, and any family or neighbours who might share it, from the worst effects of a near-miss. Dee Moss described the corrugated-metal-roofed, earth-covered Anderson shelter built by her father and uncle in the London suburb of Leyton after Munich:

> It was marvellous, having that air raid shelter. There was a big hole dug and then there was this sort of tin shape went in and then there was a concrete lining that went halfway up that gave you a shelf. I suppose it was about six inches deep and it went all the way round and you had a special way of rigging up blankets and things across the front. Of course, later in the war, when we grew all the food on it, we were very pleased with it . . . We painted it pink because it was supposed to be more restful.[6]

In Rushden, a prosperous town in Northamptonshire, where the main industry at that time was boot and shoe manufacturing, 27-year-old Marion Perkins was a university-educated librarian, living with her recently widowed mother. Miss Perkins had paid little attention to the international political scene in late September 1938, having been on holiday in Cornwall. She was therefore surprised when, shortly after her return home, there was a phone call from her late father's sister. Cousin Barbara would soon be arriving, her aunt informed them. Which she did, that same afternoon, suitcase and all, having been put under strict orders by her mother to flee London because of possible German bombing raids.

The next day, at the small library which Marion managed, she had a half-day free. After discussions with other council employees about the international crisis and the government's appeal for ARP volunteers, she agreed to visit houses in several streets to see which were suitable for and willing to take evacuees from the major cities. Dragging Barbara in her wake, Marion did this, rather successfully. She was a known and respected local figure because of her role at the town library, and the fact that her father had been headmaster of the local primary school. Well-educated, diligent, she was also in possession of a typewriter, which she used in her library work for cataloguing. Within a few weeks and into the next months, Marion Perkins took a major role in drawing up, typing out and distributing lists of potential households where evacuees could be billeted. She also found time to take first-aid courses and learn what to do about gas and bomb attacks. Later in the war, she would become an auxiliary nurse.[7]

During that winter following Munich, there were many thousands more volunteers like Marion Perkins. A disproportionate number were female and middle-class. Marion recalled that, though most of Rushden's working-class population were keen to help, many of both sexes were working long, rigidly structured hours in the shoe factories. While willing to accommodate evacuees in an emergency, unlike middle-class ARP volunteers they simply lacked the flexibility or the spare time needed to train, attend courses, and hold themselves available in the daytime.

All this didn't mean that the ARP's ranks were wholly filled with persons of leisure. Plenty of wardens, male or female, were able and prepared to find time despite doing busy jobs or having families to care for. Some were, naturally, more motivated than others. Reuben Hyams, a working-class man from an East End Jewish background, was one:

> By this time the rumours of what was happening in Germany to those Jewish people were very strong . . . I had to go to the doctor for a chest cold and I told him I was thinking of enlisting . . . and he said, they won't take you, and I said why? I understand he was one of the doctors who examined you before going and he said, you're far too myopic . . . I mean, short-sighted. So, I immediately volunteered for the ARP. Joining the First Aid section . . .[8]

In the autumn of 1938, Walter Togwell had just returned from fighting in the Spanish Civil War with the International Brigade. A restless soul, twenty-five years old and a convinced communist, the working-class Londoner had worked as a waiter before going off to fight for the Spanish Republic. He went back to hotel work, then managed to get himself sacked – not for the first time – for leading his fellow waiters in a protest against meagre wages at the luxurious, 426-room art deco Ocean Hotel in Brighton, which had just opened that year. Blacklisted by catering employment agencies back in London, he got a paying job with the ARP, fitting out various premises, before falling out with his employers there too. Finally, Togwell found stable employment helping to construct an anti-aircraft gun emplacement on the summit of Primrose Hill, in North London. This took him through to the outbreak of war, after which he joined the army as a fitter. It was an unusual but somehow evocative trajectory for a politicized young man of strong feelings in the immediate pre-war situation.[9]

Not all civilians were, however, convinced as yet that they could or should contribute. Nor, in fact, were all properly aware of the basic realities of what it all meant. A 'well-to-do young lady' asked a female Mass Observation reporter in Liverpool: 'Does conscription mean that the men will have to go away from home? I thought it was just sort of in the evenings. How awful.'[10] This was not an error that by 1938–39 any German would have made, no matter how sheltered his or her life.

Britain remained resolutely civilian in most of its attitudes. Even Sir John Anderson seemed unable to make the decision to introduce an element of compulsion into the country's more and more urgent national service requirements. 'To foreigners, friendly or hostile,' wrote the *Daily Mirror* in an editorial the week before Christmas, 'it appears amazing that the British people will never prepare for a crisis until it comes.'

> Years and years after the air menace became plain . . . we get a recently appointed minister, Sir John Anderson, proposing **for the first time** [bold in original] a scheme that may be called 'comprehensive'. A scheme which isn't even comprehensively national, since (rightly or wrongly) it is not compulsory.
>
> Again, we are to wait and see how this still voluntary scheme works out.
>
> If it doesn't, we are to have another review and another scheme. We are to wait and see.
>
> What shall we see while we are waiting?
>
> Rumour suggests: the revolt of certain Ministers who think that we have waited long enough and that we now ought to see results.[11]

Where something *was* being done, and with the *Daily Mirror*'s enthusiastic support, was in the area of placing refugees from Germany and Austria in the country. Child refugees mainly, it was true, but within a few weeks of *Kristallnacht* sections of the establishment had begun to take action. The former Prime Minister, Stanley (now Lord) Baldwin, continued to support the government's foreign policy, but had been appalled by the pogrom in Germany. He was persuaded to lend his name to a fund-raising exercise, the 'Earl Baldwin Fund for Refugees', which aimed to provide solid long-term financial backing for those fleeing Hitler's latest outrages. He appeared along with the Archbishop of Canterbury, the Leader of the Labour Opposition, Clement Attlee, and Lord Rothschild at the founding meeting on 7 December 1938 at the Mansion House in London. The Fund announced an initial target of a thousand displaced people to be brought to Britain in the immediate future, with many more in the longer term.

It was important to have the money ready. As the Home Secretary had made clear in the Commons debate on 21 November, the government was cagey about being seen to mollycoddle foreign Jews, thus exacerbating already widespread anti-Semitism. That refugee children should be given preferential treatment was, however, relatively uncontroversial. A precedent had been established the previous year, when almost four thousand Spanish Basque children had been allowed into Britain after the bombing of Guernica and Bilbao.

By the beginning of December 1938, the first group of Jewish children and young people was on its way to Britain, the beginning of what was to become known as the Kindertransport (German for 'children's transport'). It was a mark of desperation that so many of the children's parents agreed so quickly that they would let them go, and go alone, especially with the adults' own fates still so ominously starred. Before this could happen, however, the predominantly Jewish charities supporting the project, organized as the 'Refugee Children's Movement' (RCM), had to give the government guarantees that these new arrivals would not be a charge on the public purse. The charities were to pay the children's travel costs and provide them with foster homes, as well as putting up a bonded guarantee of £50 per head (£100 for children over sixteen but under eighteen).

The bond money, roughly the equivalent of £3,000 and £6,000 respectively in twenty-first-century values, was supposed to cover the costs of the re-emigration that would supposedly ensue after a relatively short stay in the United Kingdom. The idea of peopling the colonies with refugees was still the government's favoured option. Viscount Samuel, former High Commissioner for Palestine, leader of the Liberal Party until 1935, and, as Home Secretary in 1931–32, the first practising Jew to achieve cabinet office,* made a radio broadcast on 25 November appealing for British people – not necessarily Jewish – to take German refugee children into their homes.

The first Kindertransport reached England on 2 December 1938. Two hundred and eight children left the Hook of Holland ferry at Harwich, in Essex, and were initially put up in what the *Daily Express* described as the '£60,000 holiday camp' at the adjacent seaside resort of Dovercourt. Here, according to the *Express*'s reporter, they would be staying for a few weeks while taking English lessons and waiting to be allocated to foster parents. Most of the children, exhausted and disoriented after their shocking experiences and a long journey from Germany, were gratefully eating hearty breakfasts and sizing up their new surroundings. The reporter helpfully taught them to play darts. There were smiles, except for one sad little boy from Berlin, who said that his father was in hiding because 'he has to go in a concentration camp'. 'Why?' '*Ich weiss es nicht*' (I don't know). It was a sympathetic piece, though there was the usual stereotyping:

> A rich London Jew sent down about 300 pairs of shoes, 300 mackintoshes and 300 warm pullovers for them . . . The new clothes were still in their boxes. They were not needed.[12]

The idea that 'rich Jews' should be footing the bill for refugees from the Nazi pogrom was widespread. To a great extent, understandably, those within the Jewish community in Britain who could afford it did raise large sums to help. In the ever-reliable 'Live Letter Box' column of the *Daily Mirror*, there was nonetheless an agelessly familiar protest note:

---

* The nineteenth-century Prime Minister Benjamin Disraeli, though of Jewish heritage, had converted to Christianity at a young age. Samuel himself had actually been a convinced atheist since his youth, but for family reasons chose to remain connected to the religious community.

Why can't we place the needs of our own people before those
of the Jewish refugees for whom Earl Baldwin is appealing?

There are so many English people in this country today who
are homeless, destitute, and workless.

Can't we begin to lighten their burdens first?

Doesn't charity begin at home?[13]

The *Mirror* supported and promoted the Baldwin Fund, as did
The Times – which then suffered a lot of criticism, some of it
blatantly anti-Semitic. Even among the newspaper's staff, there
were tensions. One correspondent, recently returned from
reporting on the horrors of the Japanese invasion of China, argued
that the suffering of the Jews in Germany was 'wholly negligible'
compared with that of the Chinese.[14]

When a short filmed appeal for donations, featuring the
Archbishop of Canterbury, was shown as an accompaniment to
the main programme in many cinemas, it was careful to emphasize that not only practising Jews but also thousands of Christians
(many, of course, of Jewish heritage) would be helped by the
fund. This, as *The Times* suggested without apparent embarrassment, 'undoubtedly contributed towards a more generous
response than might otherwise have been the case'. It did not,
however, stop the British Union of Fascists from picketing cinemas
and other places of entertainment in protest at the collection of
money 'for Jews', or from distributing at least 2 million leaflets
attacking the Baldwin Fund.[15] Further bolstered in the new year
by newspaper advertising, the fund eventually raised more than
half a million pounds (well over £30 million in twenty-first-
century purchasing power).[16]

Meanwhile, as the year drew to its close, the British public
was even less confident that the Munich Agreement had 'bought
Hitler off'. More than one Mass Observation respondent voiced
a suspicion that Chamberlain was somehow 'on Hitler's side'. An
opinion poll showed that a month after Munich, 40 per cent of
voters had become unhappy with the Prime Minister, 72 per cent
wanted rearmament stepped up, and 86 per cent did not believe
Hitler's claim that he had no further territorial ambitions. This

last figure was so worrying for the government that the liberal *News Chronicle*, which had commissioned the survey, decided not to publish it, giving as its excuse that it might further excite public opinion in Germany. The same poll had the public narrowly supporting a new, anti-Munich coalition, with Sir Anthony Eden as Premier, by 40 per cent to 39.[17]

Both Eden and Winston Churchill, the most prominent critics of Chamberlain's foreign policy, were flooded with calls for them to step up and take over. Ambivalent in their attitude towards Jewish refugees many ordinary Britons might have been, but after *Kristallnacht*, few regarded the Nazi regime as anything other than barbaric and guided by unhinged personalities. Even fewer thought that Hitler was a leader that the democracies could, in Chamberlain's words, 'do business with'.

The Chamberlain government's response to criticism was to call for national unity and question the integrity of anyone who failed to fall into line. A *Daily Mirror* editorial shortly before Christmas was having none of that:

> Yesterday's Foreign Affairs debate in the House of Commons was preceded, as usual, by reproaches addressed to those who destroy 'national unity' by daring to discuss matters that affect the very existence of the nation.
>
> Those objectors seem to think that parliament ought not to intervene. Let parliament keep quiet and register decisions by Those Who Know. Like Hitler's Yes-Men in the Reichstag. This is national unity – to agree with everything done by Those Who Know.
>
> We have not yet reached that point of 'appeasement' in party politics. And this debate, like the others, showed that there is no national unity . . .[18]

As for ordinary British people, especially those of the middling classes, all they could do was to carry on, and to hope. A teenage schoolgirl from the London suburbs, daughter of a civil servant who worked for MI5, described her life just before Christmas 1938:

We were more and more occupied with end-of-term activities at school, with plays and the annual carol service. There were the usual parties, but first, of course, the examinations. I cannot remember – I was then sixteen – dwelling overmuch on the possibility of war.

I do know though that at tea-time one Saturday when the table was loaded with sandwiches and luscious cakes, Victoria jam sponge and chocolate cream sponge – which my mother baked always so excellently – that she said: 'If war does break out we shan't be sitting down to tea like this.'

The same day I had seen evacuation notices on a local school, that is instructions on how to proceed if it should come to a declaration of war.[19]

*

Kristallnacht had revealed beyond all reasonable doubt the remorseless barbarism of the Nazi state, but even in December 1938 Germany was still a place where foreign newspapers and magazines (except for left-wing ones) could be purchased, and where listening to foreign radio stations, if not encouraged, was not yet illegal. Selected foreign films could be seen. Ford cars were manufactured. Coca-Cola – first introduced to Germany in the late 1920s – was now so widely enjoyed that many Germans already seemed convinced it was actually a German product. Even a Party member joining the thousands flocking to a speech by Goebbels at the Berlin Sportpalast would have been greeted by a wall poster advertising 'ice-cold Coca-Cola'.[20]

In 1938, Maria Sommer was a teenager in Berlin, the only child of a modestly prosperous, cultured middle-class family. Her father, municipal architect to the Berlin borough of Schöneberg, was an old-fashioned nationalist. However, he also prided himself on being well informed, and regularly patronized a cafe where a selection of the international press turned up. With such refined parents, even as a child Maria Sommer knew, as she put it, 'her Baroque from her Rococo', and was well versed in the German classics of the theatre, to which she was regularly taken by her parents. That plays by Goethe, Schiller and Kleist were more common on the Nazi stage than they had been before 1933 was easily explained – many contemporary authors were in exile or barred by the Nazi government from being performed.

Tall, slender, with classic Prussian-German features, Maria Sommer had not quite reached her eleventh birthday when Hitler seized power. By the time she was fourteen, she had become active in the BDM (Bund Deutscher Mädel: League of German Girls) and an enthusiastic group leader. As such, she and her younger charges were part of the great mass of boys and girls of the Nazi Youth movement that formed such a striking feature of the opening day at the Berlin Olympics in the summer of 1936. Summoned by the Olympic bell, several thousand children entered the stadium in a vast, perfectly drilled imitation of expressive dance entitled *Kinderreigen* (literally 'children's roundelay'). The girls held skipping ropes and their moves were playful, while the boys moved in a stiffer, more military way. Forming, dissolving, reforming in time with choral music, they created ever-changing shapes visible from the high seats of the new stadium. As a finale, the children coalesced with extraordinary precision into a version of the Olympic flag. The girls, in their white dresses, made up the white background while the boys, dressed in appropriate coloured costumes, organized themselves to make up the inter-locking blue, black, yellow, green and red rings of the Games' symbol.

Sixteen years old at the time of *Kristallnacht*, Maria Sommer was, as it happened, in bed with flu while violence raged in the streets around the family home. She learned about the brutal events of the night from her mother, who had witnessed awful things. The young girl was furious. 'If only the Führer knew of this!' she exclaimed. Like many another fervent admirer of Hitler, she could not, or would not, believe that the pogrom had been ordered from the very top. But on balance, these were good times. Her parents, though not Nazi Party members, were patri-otic, and fell in with many of the regime's 'positive' achievements. And their daughter liked the BDM. She had no siblings, and it had the advantage of providing her with instant friendships and plenty to do.[21]

Further down the social scale, young Elly Luckow, coming up to her tenth birthday, belonged to a working-class family that, like so many of Berlin's poor, had never known security or stability. Her mother, a 'village beauty' (*Dorfschönheit* as the German phrase goes) from Thuringia, had been drawn to the metropolis while still in her teens. Initially employed as a nanny to a wealthy family, she had an affair with an older army officer, from which a daughter – Elly's older half-sister – resulted. Marriage had been out of the question, with such a wide social gulf between them, but the officer kept in touch and occasionally helped financially. Then her mother got married, to a working-class Berliner, Elly's father. There were two more additions to the family, a boy and a girl.

By the time Elly was six or seven, her parents had separated. Life was hard. Elly's mother worked as a domestic servant-cum-housekeeper in various parts of Berlin, in at least one case for a Jewish family. In the late 1930s, the family was living in the *Zeitungsviertel* (newspaper district), heart of the capital's printing and publishing industry. Elly had to walk quite a long distance to school and back, and found herself occasionally being waylaid by men in doorways as she made her way through the business district that surrounded their little apartment in the Kommandantenstrasse. Because her mother worked, she would often come back to an empty flat.

Elly's father died young, at around the time of the Sudeten Crisis. But, like Maria Sommer, she found the Nazi era good, at least for the moment. They had a little more money – children, seen as the basis of the Reich's glorious, ever-expanding future, were subsidized. From 1936, a family allowance (*Kinderbeihilfe*) for low-income households was introduced, payable from the fifth child onward, and from 1938 along with the third child (Elly's mother had four children). In December 1938, the *Mutterkreuz*, 'Mother's Cross', was introduced, in gold, silver and bronze. It brought the mothers of large families a medal, and social and later ration privileges, though no extra financial reward.[22] All the same, as Elly recalled, 'Things got better for us working people – and finally we got some more food on the table.'

There were sponsored treats for favoured children. The Nazi state had pretensions towards being classless, one great

Volksgemeinschaft (racial community) where social barriers should be discouraged. An attractive young girl (teenage photographs show a petite version of Ingrid Bergman), and with a scepticism of authority typical of the capital's citizens, Elly also showed that razor-sharp and often aggressive wit, notorious all over Germany as *Berliner Schnauze* ('Berlin "snout"' or 'lip'). Regardless, she was selected by the teacher at her school to spend a holiday away from the mean streets with a wealthy family in western Germany. She was put on a train to the Rhineland and picked up on arrival at the station by a chauffeur-driven car. There followed some weeks of living in a splendid country house and being only slightly patronized. The main crisis came when Elly accidentally tipped a vase from its table, only to find out that it was a valuable memento of her hostess's trip to China a few years back, but otherwise it was an unforgettable experience. And, arguably, only possible in the 'racial community' where purity of heritage (and 'Aryan' good looks) were trump cards.[23]

Beneath the rigid, outwardly puritanical surface of the Nazi state, another trump card existed, and it took the form of influence. Among the living playwrights still being performed in Germany was Erich Ebermayer, one of whose hitherto un-performed pieces was being given its premiere at the state theatre in the historic city of Oldenburg, on the north-west German plain, south of Bremen. Ebermayer had been asked to attend rehearsals and to direct the opening night. Until 1918, Oldenburg had been a Grand Duchy, and under the Weimar Republic it was a 'Free State', with its own government, on an equal basis with Prussia or Bavaria or Baden. In 1932 it achieved the dubious distinction of polling the most Nazi votes of any state in Germany, with an absolute majority in the parliament and a Nazi Premier appointed, in the shape of the veteran Gauleiter, Carl Röver, who after Hitler's seizure of power became Stadtholder of Bremen and Oldenburg.

Oldenburg was a long way from Berlin, geographically and otherwise, and Ebermayer had feared provincial boredom (not to mention the disapproval of provincial Nazis). However, he enjoyed his period there. His fellow professionals turned out to be perfectly congenial – even the General Director of the State Theatre, who was a keen Nazi and a member of the SS. There was a certain quirkiness to the place that appealed. In particular, Ebermayer was surprised when 'Herr F.', a wealthy local businessman, invited a group from the theatre, including him, to dinner at his large villa on the edge of town.

> It turned into an unforgettable and curious evening. Herr F. is a gentleman in his mid-sixties, 'Frau F.', as he blithely introduces his male companion even to newcomers, is 'only' 47, and still bears traces of past juvenile beauty – which is, moreover, confirmed by a large nude painting on the wall of the dining room. The two friends have been living together for thirty years. And *that* in Oldenburg! 'The Oldenburgers couldn't care less . . .' says Herr F., and 'Frau F.' smiles too. Even the General Director, who had brought us into this highly original house of cultivated hospitality, is all smiles. [24]

So, a very privileged gay couple could be 'out', at least to a select group of local worthies, and not be prosecuted, despite the fiercely anti-homosexual policies of the Nazi state (earlier in 1938, a decree had allowed convicted homosexuals to be sent straight to concentration camps).

The same had not, of course, been true when it came to Oldenburg's Jewish community. Some 350 Jews had been resident there in 1933. After the synagogue was burned down on 9/10 November 1938, they were all rounded up in the middle of the night and herded together on the *Pferdemarkt* (Horse Market) in the centre of town. All adult males were then placed under arrest and locked up in the toilets on the square. The next day, the men were led through the streets, in full public view, to the city station. Here they were put on a special train and transported to the concentration camp at Sachsenhausen, north of Berlin, a journey of almost 400 kilometres. [25]

*

A little more than a week before Europe celebrated the Christmas without war that many had thought it would not see, the German chemist Otto Hahn and his assistant, Fritz Strassmann, 'split' an atom of uranium in a ground-breaking experiment at the Kaiser-Wilhclm Institute in Berlin.

A few weeks later, Hahn's former close scientific associate, the Austrian physicist Lise Meitner, and her collaborator and nephew, Otto Frisch – also a leading physicist – would publish a theoretical explanation of the experiment in the British scientific magazine *Nature*. Meitner and Frisch were already living in Sweden, having been forced to flee Germany that summer because of their Jewish heritage, but she and Hahn had kept in regular contact, and so she knew all the details.

This achievement of 'nuclear fission' (a term invented by Frisch) attracted little or no public notice outside a relatively small group of specialists. It was, however, arguably the most portentous event of 1938, dwarfing the showy bigotry and land-hungry violence still dominating the international stage. Hahn's experiment opened the way to the development of the atomic bomb.

*

Much of the late autumn had been mild, well into December, but in the days before Christmas most of the Continent was overwhelmed by cold winds and snow. On 23 December 1938 the lowest temperatures were in the south-west of Germany, with Freiburg, in the Black Forest near the Swiss border and usually one of the mildest, sunniest parts of the country, registering between minus 10 and minus 15 degrees centigrade. Berlin was cloudy at minus 6–7 degrees, with 8 cm of snow.

A few days earlier, sixteen-year old Ruth Thieme, a doctor's daughter from the satellite town of Grimma, near Leipzig, had finished her semester at the commercial college where she was studying. The next day or two was spent mostly skiing with her friends. Then it was time to do her duty to the *Volk* and to those less well off than herself, while at the same time flirting a little:

On 23.12. Inge and I were at the distribution of presents by
the Winter Aid. We had to serve out coffee and perform some
songs. Raimund Winkler was also there. Inge and I walked home
with him. He showed off terribly the whole way while taking
us home. We laughed so much.[26]

The Winter Aid (*Winterhilfswerk*) was a major charity drive,
mounted to help the poor and the unemployed during the cold
months. 'None shall Starve or Freeze!' was its motto. 'WHW'
had actually been founded during the administration of Chancellor
Heinrich Brüning, almost two years before Hitler came to power,
but the Nazis had turbocharged it as the perfect expression of
classless national solidarity, and, as usual, claimed the credit for
the original idea.[27] Very soon it was an important and successful
annual event and central to the Nazi system. From October to
March every year, Hitler Youth, SA and other Nazi welfare groups
rattled their collecting tins, extracting money from citizens on
the street, in shops and bars and so on. 'One-pot Sunday' lunches
were organized, at which groups and families ate a simple stew
and donated the difference between its cost and that of a more
elaborate meal to WHW. Food, clothing and coal for heating were
distributed to deserving members of the racial community – and
presents for poor children, as at the event attended by Ruth
Thieme two days before Christmas in 1938.

Ruth Thieme's diaries reveal her as almost entirely apolitical.
Keen Nazis in her age range, however, had an even busier
Christmas holiday. Dorothea B., a fourteen-year-old girl from
Durlach, near Karlsruhe, in south-west Germany, was clearly
under the spell of the regime. Her journal lists attendance at
many strongly politicized activities in and around her home town,
as well as noting major speeches by Hitler and other events of
that sort. Like Maria Sommer, Dorothea had been trained as a
group leader in the Jungmädel, the junior wing of the BDM.

So, in December 1938 Dorothea had attended not just the
'People's Christmas Celebration' on 23 December but the 'Winter
Solstice Celebration' (*Wintersonnwendfeier*) two days earlier. The
latter event was generally preferred by committed Nazis, since

it was closer to the pagan-Germanic winter festival and therefore untainted by dubious Judeo-Christian influences. On 21 December, Dorothea attended the Jungmädel Christmas event at three in the afternoon, where presents were also distributed to the less well-off girls. 'Prima [great],' she wrote. She then went on at eight that same very cold evening to the 260-metre-high Turmberg outlook above the city, much-visited site of a half-ruined medieval tower, where the local Nazi Party was holding its official Winter Solstice Celebration. A huge bonfire was lit. This too was noted as prima.

The 'People's Christmas' at the Festival Hall in the centre of Durlach, was also a strongly politicized event. Dorothea dutifully noted how it went:

> At the beginning BDM-girls and Jungmädel sang 'High Night of the Clear Stars'.* Broadcast of the speech by City Manager Hilgenfeld. Then we sang for the beginning of the theatre piece 'The Tree of Life', the song 'Softly Flutters the Snow' and in the middle 'O Christmas Tree, O Christmas Tree, You Bear a Green Branch'. Address by Local Group Leader (Ortsgruppenleiter) Edel. The many children were treated to cocoa and cake. Then the distribution of gifts to the poor members of the racial community.[28]

The ceaseless drive of politicized events in Germany lent the life of those who were politically engaged, or at least felt obliged to appear so, a quality of permanently raucous busyness that removed the necessity of – or the opportunity for – private, individual thought. The regime had a fixed routine of things to say, and it just kept saying them in various forms, hammering home the message every day.

---

* 'Hohe Nacht der Klaren Sterne' was a very popular Nazi-era carol written in 1936, without specific religious or Christmas significance but not directly offensive to Christians. Strong on images of Winter Solstice and on obeisance to the Nazi cult of motherhood, it remained acceptable after the war and is still performed and recorded, including on a 2003 Christmas album by the veteran German singing star Heino.

The morning edition of the local newspaper in Freiburg on
23 December 1938 carried material culled straight from the
DNB's press releases, sent through from Berlin several times a
day, as it was required to do. The front page led with a story
about a proposed anti-communist pact for the Far East between
Japan, its puppet state of Manchukuo, and the Kuomintang government (with which Japan was currently at war, having occupied
huge swathes of Chinese territory) in the interests of joint suppression of communism in the region. Pure propaganda. The Japanese
were in trouble in China and wanted to drive a wedge between
the various Chinese factions resisting their invasion.*Then, underneath that, the Führer showing his popular touch by celebrating
Christmas with construction workers at his almost-completed
new Reich Chancellery building. Then Hitler again, attending the
premiere at Berlin's huge Ufa-Palast am Zoo cinema, with its
seating for more than 2,000 filmgoers, of the new blockbuster
propaganda film *Pour le Mérite*. Named after the high German
military order (known colloquially as the 'Blue Max'), the film
was a dramatization of Germany's defeat in the First World War,
the post-war humiliation of the country's heroic flying heroes,
the secret rebuilding of Germany's air force, and then the advent
of National Socialism, which triumphantly restored national pride
and strength. It ended in the present time with the four friends
from the First War reunited in the uniforms of senior Luftwaffe
officers, ready to serve their country once more. In case anyone
felt the urge to watch an American film instead, the same page
of the newspaper featured an article about how 'Hollywood is
crawling with Jews'.

To round off the front-page articles, all taken directly from
the DNB's handouts, also in the 23 December edition is an article
detailing alleged atrocities committed by British troops in Attil,

---

* In this they succeeded. Soon after, Wang Ching-wei, one of the Chinese leader
Chiang Kai-shek's lieutenants, defected into exile in French Indo-China and began
negotiations with the Japanese. He ended up as Premier of a collaborationist government, based in Nanjing. Had it not been for his death in 1944, Wang would have
been tried as a traitor after the end of the war.

a village in Palestine. It was claimed that five random civilian hostages were hooded, had their eyes gouged out, and were then shot to death *pour encourager les autres*. Other villages were looted and homes burned down. So the British, with their high-minded condemnation of *Kristallnacht*, were shown to be hypocrites (and of course allies of the ever-increasing waves of Jewish settlers in Palestine, against whom the Arab uprising was directed).

Along with frequent pieces about Jewish con men and gangsters, drawn from many different countries, day after day the Nazi press directed the minds of its readers and shaped their world view according to the regime's desired perspective. As this official version of the international situation went, innocent, well-meaning Germany, whose only desire was to rid itself of the Jewish plague and rebuild its nationhood, was surrounded by envious, hypocritical imperialistic enterprises – British, French, American – that called themselves democracies but were actually repressors of other nations. The democracies were in turn controlled by crooked Jews, whose only aim was to destroy the resurgent German Reich. This line was extremely cynical, but the problem was that, even if such reports as the ones from Palestine were exaggerated or even downright fictional (the British press, including *The Times* and the *Manchester Guardian* thought so[29]), there was an element of truth in them. Modern research reveals that the British suppression of the Palestinian uprising was an altogether more ruthless business than its government admitted in 1938.

In a regional newspaper such as the *Freiburger Zeitung*, there were usually two pages of this Goebbels-directed international and national news. Most of the rest was resolutely local and largely apolitical, little different from what it might have been ten years earlier during the era of Weimar Democracy. Some of it, however, was very political indeed.

Given the date, the 23 December edition of the paper was in a position to report on the Winter Solstice Celebrations held by the SA on the evening of 21 December, when 660 rank-and-file Storm Troopers appeared in torch-bearing ranks in the snow-bound square of the Alter Messplatz, in the east of the city, to listen to a speech by an SA Brigadeführer (roughly equivalent to a brigadier or brigadier-general in the British or American armies). A bonfire was lit in the square and its soaring, flickering flames 'cast their shimmering light over the ranks of the SA men'. The SA boss's oration may have come from a central Nazi script factory, but in their absolute nihilism and abdication of moral choice or responsibility, reported by a local newspaper, which spent some time in almost affectionate scene-setting before reproducing them for its readers, his words were somehow more terrifying than if they had come from Goebbels himself:

> Here, at the blazing pyre of flame, we remind ourselves that it was the old German manly virtues that have made us free and great and strong; the manly virtues contained within these ideas: sacred, blazing faith, uncompromising commitment to the end, loyalty to our predestined leader unto death, and the comradeship that binds us and should enclose the whole German *Volk*. So at the blazing pyre we swear to remain fighters, hard, unrelenting, simple and modest. We bear within us the sacred belief in the Führer and we vow to him at this hour to fulfil the tasks that he assigns to his SA with the fullest commitment and most complete dedication.

Four wreaths were then tossed into the fire. One for the Führer, one for fallen comrades, the third for German mothers, and the fourth, cast by a member of the Labour Front,* for German youth – 'Germany's future'. 'With the massed rendition of [the Hitler Youth song] "A Young People Rises",' wrote the reporter from the *Freiburger Zeitung*, 'this striking ceremony in this icy, silent night was brought to a conclusion.'[30]

*

In Britain, as in Germany, there was snow at Christmas 1938; in fact, in many parts the deepest and most widespread of any

---

* The German Labour Front (*Deutsche Arbeitsfront*) was the forced Nazi successor to the Weimar-Era trade union movement.

Christmas in the twentieth century. On the day itself, a ridge of high pressure lay over the snowbound country, with a bitter easterly wind bringing a few flurries but otherwise clear. As North London schoolgirl Maud Hilde recalled:

Then it was a white Christmas! A rare occurrence in London. December had started unusually mild, then on the 16th it became bitter cold with gales in the Channel, disrupting the ferries, followed by a brief thaw and hard frost again on the 23rd. On Christmas Day there were four inches of snow [around 10 cm] in Trafalgar Square, and winter sports were possible on Hampstead Heath. The roads were white and totally deserted. On the evening of Boxing Day I recall going to the front door of our house with our mother to put out the milk bottles for the delivery the following morning. Ice-cold air blew in our faces as we opened the door, and we felt happy and contented to return into the warmth of the front sitting-room with the blazing open fire. Somehow it all seemed safe and enduring, and yet there were thoughts of an uncertain future in our minds. It was still peace but no one really trusted it. It was indeed the hush before the storm.[31]

Christmas Day fell that year on a Sunday. Monday 26 December ('Boxing Day' in England) was a bank holiday, and so almost no business was done in the cities. The *Manchester Guardian*'s writer, in poetic mood, described the City of London's totally deserted financial district that evening:

The snow which had been falling since the small hours stopped, and there lay the virgin streets, paved with a commodity nearly as rare at Christmas-time as gold. A man could walk into Lombard Street like Robinson Crusoe and leave his solitary footprints on it like a conqueror.[32]

Within a few hours, as the paper then reported, temperatures rose, rain fell, and the snow began to melt. In the north and Scotland, villages remained cut off, and there was some flooding, but in general life quickly returned to its wet, wintry normal for Britain. 'Our climate,' the *Mirror* cheerfully reminded its readers, 'has made us what we are – brave and bronchial!'[33]

With Christmas over, and without the weather to talk about, the British press, in all its idiosyncratic and sometimes irritating variety, went back, in its serious moments, to the international situation. The Nationalist General Franco's rebel forces in Spain, backed by Italy and Germany, were now advancing across the river Ebro into Loyalist Catalonia, which along with the area stretching from Madrid to Valencia was one of the last remaining regions of the country to hold out for the Republic. The Munich Treaty had reverberations that went beyond Central Europe; the Anglo-French betrayal of Czechoslovakia also destroyed any last hopes of a grand alliance that might have saved the Spanish Republic at its final hour.

In a series of articles just before and just after New Year, the *Mirror*'s David Walker – released from his duties as referee of the Talking Shop column – reported from South-East Europe, first from Hungary and then from Romania, on the menace presented by growing German influence on the Danube. From still largely feudal Hungary, observing growing Fascist influence, he asked: 'Is This How You Would Behave – If Hitler Came Here?' From the Romanian capital, Bucharest, he promised 'The Truth about Hitler and Romania'. Walker tended to agree with the notion that the country, disastrously divided by warring classes and nationalities, would fall into Hitler's hands 'like a ripe plum'. Bucharest, the 'Paris of the Balkans', was a place of grim contrasts. Going with a friend out to dinner, he described seeing poverty-stricken beggars outside a luxurious nightspot:

> In the biting cold outside beggars of every age were crouched
> in the lee of office buildings, or ran along the pavement trying
> to sell shrivelled bunches of Mimosa. But inside, nobody cared.

'On Czech munitions, on Transylvanian wheat, and on Rumanian oil, Germany knows she will be self-supporting mistress of the world,' Walker added. On 3 January 1939, after the New Year break, he summed up his experiences in a piece entitled 'We Heard the Crack of Hitler's Whip', concluding that South-East Europe represented 'a wild mixture of nationalities whose fate will be decided in the next few months . . . The Blue Danube waltz! When will England realise that the romantic age is past and that at the crack of a dictator's whip this waltz will stiffen like a corpse into the hard deliberation of the goose step?'[34]

Walker's three articles represented serious reporting in a popular newspaper, and as such were rare enough. So far as the situation inside Germany itself was concerned, during these same days there was only the speculation about Goebbels's 'illness' to amuse the *Mirror*'s readers. *Kristallnacht* seemed forgotten.

On 30 December 1938, the *Mirror* ran on its front page a more typical and largely fictional story about Goebbels supposedly having been beaten up by friends of Lída Baarová's 'husband', the actor Gustav Fröhlich. The next day's front page trumpeted 'Beaten Nazi Chief Has "Relapse"' and featured an alluring photograph of Baarová. Six arrests had supposedly been made 'in film and theatre circles'. Baarová was 'in hiding' at a villa outside Berlin. By 2 January, Goebbels was 'Disgraced – Losing Jobs' and Fröhlich was 'in a concentration camp'. Almost none of this was true. Goebbels had not been beaten up, in a flat or anywhere else. Fröhlich was not Baarová's husband, though he had wanted to be, and he had not been thrown into a concentration camp. Hitler was displeased with his Minister of Propaganda, but he showed no sign of sacking him. And Goebbels would slowly but surely pull himself out of his post-affair depression.

David Walker's serious articles were the exception so far as the British popular press was concerned. In the seven weeks since the barbarism of *Kristallnacht*, reporting about the Nazi regime in mass-circulation newspapers had gone from horror story to soap opera.

The *Express*, in accordance with Lord Beaverbrook's keen support for Appeasement, refused to acknowledge that the European situation might lead to war. Farcically, just after Christmas 1938 the *Daily Express* published a set of pictures of a conference of psychics in Paris under the headline '"No War in

1939" Say French Fortune Tellers'. The only dispute, apparently, was between a M. Laffon and a Mme Luce Vidi. He predicted that Mussolini would die in 1939, she furiously disagreed, and eventually both of the bickering clairvoyants had to be escorted from the conference hall.[35]

More seriously, a few days later a leader-page article put forward the notion of no war in 1939 without reference to a crystal ball. On Monday 2 January 1939 Lord Beaverbrook's *Daily Express*, at that time Britain's best-selling newspaper, with a circulation of just under 2.5 million, published a lengthy 'New Year' op-ed piece by the writer and journalist George Malcolm Thomson. The significance of this superficially routine seasonal article was greater than might at first appear: Thomson was Beaverbrook's secretary and often acted as His Master's Voice.

Under the headline 'This Is Why You Can Sleep Soundly in 1939', Thomson declared: 'There will be no great war in 1939. There is nothing in our present situation which affords any ground to suppose that any upheaval will, or must, come.'

After some two thousand words of detailed explanation as to why precisely this was the case, the writer concluded that, however worrying recent events might appear, the dictatorships were, in fact, on the retreat:

> Look forward, then, to a year in which the bulwarks against a general war will grow in strength. Remember that war, now too costly for little States, is also growing more and more impossible for great Powers. The destruction is too great. And the peoples know it. Believe in peace – and insist that Britain must be strong in order to buttress your belief![36]

In the first weeks of 1939, the *Express* ran two campaigns. One demanded that the government stop the £10 million it had promised the Czechs after Munich. Since what was left of Czechoslovakia was rapidly turning into a dependency of the Third Reich, the money would just end up in Hitler's pocket. The other campaign called for Sir John Anderson, the Lord Privy Seal and head of the ARP, to come home from his winter holiday in Arosa, near

Davos in Switzerland, to rescue the civil defence effort, which was, it seemed, in serious trouble. The volunteers recruited and trained in the autumn and early winter were, the paper said, being left idle. The air-raid-protection trenches that had been dug so urgently in parks and open spaces at the time of the Sudeten Crisis were filling up with water from the melting snow and the subsequent rains. Ducks were swimming in them and children knocking together makeshift craft to go sailing, or tossing ARP sandbags into them to make a satisfying splash. A photograph published on 9 January showed the unfortunate Sir John awkwardly perched on a toboggan on a snowy Alpine slope. Below this, on the same page, a Mr Higgins, who had undergone ARP training and whose children were now gaily boating in just such a trench on Wimbledon Common, told the *Express* reporter: 'I passed all my tests before Christmas. I have not had a job to do yet. I have lost most of my enthusiasm. If I am not given something to do soon, I shall resign.'[37]

The *Express* reported with some satisfaction that Sir John would be arriving back at Victoria Station from Switzerland that very day and would go straight to his office to resume work.

*

Dr Hjalmar Schacht's great moment had come more than fifteen years earlier, in November 1923, when the brilliant banker, then still only in his mid-forties, had saved the Mark and ended the hyperinflation that was threatening to ruin Weimar Germany. After that, he had served democratic masters, first as Currency Commissioner and then, until 1930, as Director of the Reichsbank. Over the years, however, Schacht had moved his political stance steadily to the right, cheerleading for authoritarian nationalism and, after the Nazis came to power, accepting reappointment as Director of the Reichsbank. From August 1934 he simultaneously held the post of Economics Minister in Hitler's government.

Schacht's genius as a financier had been turned to the advantage of the Third Reich, enabling the construction of the kind of protectionist, import-averse, self-reliant autarkical economy favoured by Hitler. Schacht reduced the onerous foreign debts incurred in the 1920s by Weimar ministers and institutions through various financial sleights of hand and by negotiating a series of trade agreements that enabled Germany to pay either by barter or in Reichsmarks for its raw materials. After 1935, however, control of the economy, especially the war industries, had begun to be ceded to leading Nazis, especially Göring, whom Schacht considered, with good reason, to be more or less economically illiterate.

In November 1937, under pressure from Göring and made unpopular in the ruling circle by his constant pleas to reduce military spending and balance the budget, Schacht resigned as Minister of Economics. However, at the insistence of Hitler, who feared adverse foreign reaction to Schacht's dismissal, he remained Reichsbank Director and Minister Without Portfolio.

A 'moderate' anti-Semite, liable to make exceptions for Jewish colleagues and friends, Schacht was appalled by the violence of *Kristallnacht*. It was in this context that he approached Hitler with a plan to float an enormous loan, funnelled mostly through Jewish-influenced finance houses in London and New York. This money could be used to persuade Jews to leave Germany with a proportion (though by no means all) of their wealth. The fact that the refugees would bring money would act as an inducement to potential host countries to accept them. Germany, in its turn, would benefit to the tune of hundreds of millions of Reichsmarks. The proposal was another attempt by Schacht to 'save' Germany – and perhaps, given his problems with the regime, himself. Ultimately, it represented an offer to 'sell' Germany's Jews, thus achieving the aim of making Germany 'Jew-free', while at the same time harvesting cash and export opportunities.

So, on 14 December 1938, apparently with the Führer's approval, Schacht arrived in London to meet Montagu Norman, the Governor of the Bank of England – with whom he was on very friendly terms – and other influential British and continental bankers. His aim was to engage in what became known as the 'Schacht–Rublee Negotiations' – George Rublee was the American chair of the Inter-governmental Committee on Refugees, based in London.

Schacht returned to Berlin three days later, having fleshed out the proposals. In early January 1939 Norman travelled to Berlin, ostensibly to attend the christening of Schacht's grandson, who was to be named 'Norman' in the Bank of England Governor's honour. His other purpose was to continue the loan discussions, with Chamberlain's blessing. It was clear, however, that other members of the British elite were not so keen on buying the freedom of the German Jews. Sir Alexander Cadogan, the Foreign Office's most senior civil servant, definitely was not, and wrote a letter on the Foreign Secretary's behalf to that effect.

Cadogan had an encounter with the 'livid' Norman just before the Governor left for Germany, and came to the conclusion, first that this was a 'stunt of No. 10 [Downing Street]', and second that the negotiations were not entirely serious. He wrote in his diary that when they parted, with the Governor somewhat mollified, he said to Norman: 'Well, I hope you will let us know of any results.' Norman replied: 'There won't be any results.' To which Cadogan said: 'Tant mieux . . .' – 'All the better.'[38]

The Express, as was its habit, concentrated on the 'rich Jews' who would effectively be ransoming their poorer brethren.[39] The Times reported on the talks as details became available, while the Labour MP Hugh Dalton complained to the House of Commons that Dr Schacht had come to London 'with a plan by which we should pay the German government to allow the Jews to leave Germany. That seemed to be a pretty impudent proposal . . .'[40] The Times itself took an editorial stance shortly before Christmas in which its leader writer criticized the German government sharply, saying that 'not content with replenishing its coffers by confiscating the property of the unfortunate Jews . . . [it] . . . was endeavouring to use their suffering as a lever to wring trade concessions from other countries.'[41] The sums involved were huge, they would set a precedent – other countries with anti-Semitic governments could easily mount similar blackmail operations if this German plan succeeded – and countries such as America remained reluctant to accept the large numbers of extra refugees that the scheme would send across the Atlantic.

In any case, shortly after Mr Montagu Norman returned from his January visit to Dr Schacht, the Reichsbank Director found himself no longer in his post. On 20 January 1939, with the negotiations for the controversial loan still continuing, he was dismissed by Hitler. Walter Funk, the radical Nazi who had succeeded Schacht as Economics Minister, now took over the Reichsbank as well. Schacht retained a cabinet rank and salary, as Minister without Portfolio, a kind of human financial fig leaf. However, from now on was more or less irrelevant. In London, the day after the news became public, the *Mirror* thundered:

> How far is Nazi Germany from financial collapse?
>
> Question is in the news again, as we record the dismissal of that supreme financial juggler, Dr Schacht.
>
> Sound finance and a wild racial mania, demanding fantastic armaments, do not go together.[42]

The 'refugee loan' talks were broken off. Schacht, unknown to Hitler and the Nazi leadership, was already in contact with opposition circles. His sacking was indeed a portent of things to come. From now on, caution would be thrown to the winds. The notion of a balanced budget disappeared from government agendas in Berlin.

On 30 January, Hitler would commemorate the sixth anniversary of his seizure of power in 1933 with an address to the puppet Reichstag. The Führer's much-trailed speech was anticipated with eagerness by his followers and with trepidation by opponents inside and outside Germany. Sir Alexander Cadogan wrote a position paper on the situation, a copy of which was cabled to Washington, with Lord Halifax's signature on it, to provide talking points for the British Ambassador in his dealings with the Roosevelt administration. In the paper, Cadogan, drawing on British Intelligence sources and conversations with members of the German opposition, suggested that Hitler was planning 'a further foreign adventure for the spring of 1939':

> The economic and financial crisis with which Germany is now faced might well compel Hitler to take some action, and the choice before him is either to slow down his rearmament and to abandon his policy of expansion, or else launch into some

foreign adventure in the hope that it will both distract attention from domestic difficulties and supply him with the material resources which the country urgently requires and can no longer buy abroad. There can be little doubt that a man of Hitler's temperament may be tempted to choose the second alternative.[43]

Chamberlain had decided to have his own say, pre-emptively, using a speech he had long arranged to deliver in his home city, Birmingham, on Saturday 28 January. To the disappointment of some, the Prime Minister reaffirmed the correctness of his agreement with Hitler at Munich – he could see 'nothing to regret, nor any reason to suppose that another course would have been preferable' – and insisted that, although Britain was rearming 'for reasons of defence, not attack', he was engaged in a 'consistent, unwavering policy of peace' and still believed that there were 'no differences, however serious, that cannot be solved without recourse to war'.[44]

'Ouf!' as Chamberlain remarked immediately afterwards in a letter to Ida, the elder of his two sisters. 'Thank goodness that speech is over . . .' He insisted that the wording had been very carefully put together. Downing Street hoped that 'in spite of all rumours to the contrary' the Führer's address to the Reichstag would not take an aggressive tone against Britain. Chamberlain's Foreign Policy adviser, Sir Horace Wilson, had swiftly sent a copy of the PM's Birmingham remarks to Hitler, hoping that the Führer's own imminent speech was still at draft stage.[45]

If Wilson had hoped to influence the tone of Hitler's message to the world, he was to be disappointed. According to Goebbels, who had a meeting with Hitler on 27 January, by that time the text of the Führer's speech for 30 January was already set out for delivery.

*

They were supposed to be alone in the snowbound allotment in the woods. She was much younger than the others, but all the easier to overpower. Then the people came and interrupted him, and eventually he found himself overpowered instead.

In the freezing early morning of Sunday 29 January 1939, a man thirty-two years of age was arrested in woodland on the western outer fringe of Munich. He had attacked a pre-teenage girl in an area filled with allotments and summer houses that were near-deserted in winter, pushed her down in the snow and sexually molested her. Spotted by some passers-by, he ran off, but they pursued him, at first losing sight of him but then finding his footprints in the snow and following him to his hiding place. After that, there was no escape. Someone fetched the police.

Within hours, the newly arrested suspect had been identified as an apparently respectable family man, married and with small children, who lived nearby. His name was Johann Eichhorn, born 8 October 1906 in the Munich western outer suburb of Aubing. A qualified fitter, he had experienced periods of unemployment during the Depression, but for four years now had had a steady job working for the German State Railways at the Munich-Laim shunting yards. He commuted the 10 kilometres or so each way by bicycle. Everyone knew him as a hard-working ordinary fellow, apparently devoted to his wife Jozefa and their two small boys.

A poster distributed by the Munich police, offering a 'high reward' for more information about Eichhorn, featured a photograph of him. It showed a muscular man of average height, wearing a suit jacket, a V-necked sweater, shirt and tie, and looking every inch the respectable skilled working-class paterfamilias. He had been taken into custody on account of a sexual offence, but a number of items had been found in his possession – a polo blouse, a woman's sleeveless cardigan, a pair of opera glasses, a ring, and a comb – photographs of which were shown on the poster. Anyone recognizing these was asked to get in touch with the authorities. Police suspected that Eichhorn might have been involved in other sexual offences and robberies going back over twelve years.

The man who would become known as the 'Beast of Aubing' was at last behind bars, but he had not so far admitted very much. The story of all he had done, in its full horror, would take almost all of the new year, 1939, to unravel.

*

At eight o'clock on the evening of the next day, Monday 30 January, as Eichhorn began his second night in police custody, a ceremonial session of the now politically meaningless Reichstag was held at the Kroll Opera House in Berlin. With deputies elected from the single-list pseudo-elections staged in early December in the Sudetenland now also present, along with representatives from the Ostmark, as Austria was now officially known, the parliament had been renamed the Greater German Reichstag. This was to be the first of its very rare meetings.*

First, to some business. Göring was re-elected as President of the Reichstag, a post he had held since 1932, before the Nazi seizure of power. The Enabling Law of March 1933, which formally granted Hitler his dictatorial powers, was renewed for another four years, until 1943. Then the Führer took to the podium and spoke. For two and a half hours. Goebbels sketched all this out in his diary the next day and naturally described the speech as a 'masterwork'. The Propaganda Minister himself was still emerging from his post-Baarová slump, and the memories of 1933 made him feel sad: 'I think of the times six years go. Things were still good then. Now everything is frightful and awful.'[46]

It was not, by common consent in Germany and abroad, a warmongering speech as such. Wall Street, on a time zone six hours behind and still open for business as Hitler launched into his speech, rose healthily. True, the market closed before he had finished, but the next day stock prices in London, Paris and New York made further progress ('Stock Exchange rises on Hitler's Vagueness' as the *Manchester Guardian* expressed it).

At the Reichstag, the Führer spent a long time reminiscing about how the Nazis had come to power and what they done since. Unemployment had been conquered and, for all the difficulties of the post-war settlement and the nation's reduced living space, the country's population had been kept fed and clothed. Ninety-nine per cent of Germans, he claimed, supported the

---

* The Greater German Reichstag would meet again, briefly, only eight times until its last session in 1942, after which it effectively ceased to function, replaced by a limitless despotism.

regime. He once again repeated his assertion that Germany's aims were peaceful, that she had no more demands on Britain or France apart from the colonies, and that there was no cause for war – except for Jewish troublemaking. A long rant to this effect was perhaps directed to his domestic audience. A war would be the Jews' fault, Hitler made clear, and he went further, notoriously telling his fellow Nazis and the world:

> Again I prophesy: if international financial Jewry should succeed once more in bringing the world to the brink of war, the result would not be Bolshevism and the victory of Jewry but the destruction of the Jewish race in Europe. The peoples of the world do not want to die on the battlefield for the benefit of the Jews.[47]

At the end of his speech, he returned to this theme: 'We believe,' Hitler thundered, 'that if the Jews' international campaign by press and propaganda could be checked, good understanding could very quickly be established between the peoples.' It was a bizarre denial of a thousand years of constantly changing and constantly, violently divisive – not to mention mostly Jew-free – European great-power politics.

There was remarkably little mention, even in the liberal *Manchester Guardian*, of the genocidal threat implied in Hitler's statement that a new war would destroy the Jews in Europe (the term 'genocide' had not yet been invented). If given any attention at all, his words were underplayed as just part of the Führer's familiar repertoire of bluster, threats and blame, to which the world had somehow accustomed itself, as it does.

Chamberlain wrote to his sister Hilda in early February and, regarding the unusual but welcome lack of direct threats to his neighbours in Hitler's speech, maintained that 'at last we are getting on top of the dictators'. Borrowing a phrase from a columnist in *The Times*, he surmised that Hitler, by not swallowing the whole of Czechoslovakia the previous September, had 'missed the bus'.[48]

Inside Germany, the public mood had, apparently, been improved by Hitler's speech, which despite its many obnoxious aspects had undoubtedly been a feat of eloquence, and mostly positive in its portrayal of the domestic situation. But the mood in the country had sorely needed improvement. The *Gau* leadership in North Westphalia said in its report for January 1939:

> The Führer's powerful speech in the Greater German Reichstag at the end of the reporting month naturally improved the general mood of the entire population at a stroke. It must be said that BEFORE this event of great political importance the general mood, compared with the high-point of the liberation of the Sudeten Germans, had DETERIORATED. This observation could be made in the broad circles of industry and the middle class as well as in the countryside.
>
> The current improvement in morale due to the Führer's speech cannot therefore be a lasting one, because economic hardships and grievances in town and country are causing general difficulties.[49]

If it was really trying to persuade the German population to put 'guns before butter', the regime would have to work even harder – and provide even more spectacular successes that fed into stirring speeches by the Führer. There could be no standing still.

On 1 February 1939, Goebbels's diary tells us that he visited Hitler on the day after the speech, in which the Führer had relieved the world and its stock exchanges by declaring no new foreign initiatives. The speech was, in fact, a tactical deception. Hitler's conversation with Goebbels told the real story:

> He now intends to travel to the Mountain [Berchtesgaden] and ponder his next foreign policy measures. Perhaps it will be Czechoslovakia's turn again. Because, of course, this problem has been only half-solved. But he is not entirely clear in himself about this. Perhaps also the Ukraine . . .[50]

FIVE

Spring 1939
'It's Hitler Again: But Don't Worry!'

In the hours before dawn on the morning of 3 February 1939, terrorism had come to London.

Bombs were planted in the left-luggage offices of two London underground stations, Tottenham Court Road and Leicester Square. The first went off at 5.55 a.m. next to the downstairs glass-fronted ticket office at Tottenham Court Road. It was a very powerful explosion, blasting the door to the luggage room from its hinges and hurling it across the concourse. Joseph Eyre, a ticket collector standing by the barrier at the top of the escalator, was struck by the flying door, and left with a broken leg and lacerated arm. The ticket clerk, though suffering only minor physical injuries, went into severe shock. A large crack opened in the wall. Water began to flood the area. At Leicester Square, just a few hundred yards away, a second large bomb exploded at 6.20, also in the left-luggage area, just off the main staircase leading down from Charing Cross Road. The worst injuries were inflicted on a milkman, Albert Brice, who was in the process of placing two pint bottles outside the door to the luggage office, ready for the staff when they arrived to open up.

Fortunately, at that time in the dark February morning there were few travellers about, or there might have been many more injuries, and almost certainly some deaths. As it was, a total of seven victims were taken to hospital. The affected areas in the stations were sealed off, and within a short time something like normal service had resumed. From now on, throughout the tube and rail network, no further luggage was accepted for storage unless first opened for inspection.[1]

The culprits were assumed to belong to the Irish Republican Army. The IRA's Chief of Staff, Seán Russell, had declared his organization to be the legitimate government of the independent 'Irish Republic' (despite having just adopted a new constitution, Ireland remained a member of the British Commonwealth and the King in London still exercised certain powers). On 15 January 1939 Russell had announced a new campaign against continuing British occupation (as the nationalists saw it) of the Six Counties of Northern Ireland. The 'Sabotage' (or 'S') Campaign was intended to cause chaos and disruption on a massive scale in mainland Britain rather than great loss of life, but deaths among the British population were, of course, factored into the risk.

The 'S' Campaign continued all year long. Dozens of explosions, large and small, against power stations, telephone links, transport hubs, and in some cases commercial areas, occurred. It achieved no decisive results.

From February 1939 there were meetings, in Ireland and in Germany, between IRA representatives and German Abwehr Intelligence officials – along the lines of 'my enemy's enemy is my friend'. The main link man was the notorious Seamus (Jim) O'Donovan, a veteran IRA explosives expert (with three missing fingers to prove it) who had been a co-originator of the 'S-Plan'.[2] One of the German representatives involved in setting up this collaboration was Theo Kordt, who visited Ireland to that end.[3] This was the same London Embassy official – and friend of Ruth Andreas-Friedrich – who had been holding secret meetings with British government sources on behalf of the anti-Hitler Resistance during the Munich crisis. That Kordt could both act as a negotiator with the British government on behalf of anti-Hitler circles and at the same time set up cooperation between the Abwehr and the IRA (who were currently blowing up British citizens on the streets of London and other cities) shows the moral and practical complexity of such a figure's position.

The S-Plan, and especially the underground station bombs, did cause a certain amount of panic and anxiety. The British Empire was having to deal with another guerrilla force, too, which also put in an appearance in London in February 1939, though in talking rather than killing mode. On Tuesday 7 February 1939, Palestinian and Jewish delegates, plus representatives from neighbouring Arab countries, including Egypt, Iraq, Jordan, Yemen and Saudi Arabia, joined British officials in an attempt to put an end to the violence in Palestine. The British government urgently needed to calm things down there and in neighbouring countries, since in case of war this strategic area would have to be secured against Germany and its allies. For this reason, the Palestinians and their Arab allies found themselves in a strong negotiating position.

The conference convened amidst the grandeur of Saint James's Palace, which had been put at the delegates' disposal by the King himself. Proceedings began with an address by the Prime Minister – or rather, since the Palestinians throughout the conference refused to be in the same room as the Jewish Agency represent- atives – two addresses, one each for the Arabs and the Jews, both filled with identical pious hopes and expectations.

The Palestine Conference would last five weeks, and the argu- ments go on for a lot of the year to come. The practical result, for now, was that Jewish immigration to Palestine remained more or less banned. But under pressure of the persecution in Germany, illegal Jewish immigration continued, as did violence between Arabs and Jews.

The response in the German press to the opening of the Palestine Conference was cunning. It combined a relatively object- ive report on Chamberlain's opening speeches and the arrival of the delegates with a splash on the latest initiative from Alfred Rosenberg, the Nazis' chief ideologue.

In a speech for the benefit of the foreign press in Berlin, Rosenberg suggested for the first time in public that, with the aim now to establish a completely 'Jew-free' Germany, either Guyana in South America, or the French-ruled island of

Madagascar, off the east coast of Africa, might be suitable destinations for the inevitable wave of Jewish emigration. This would include, he made clear, Jews from the whole of Central and Eastern Europe, not just Germany, amounting ultimately to 12 to 15 million souls. Naturally, Palestine was not suitable. The area was too small, and in any case Germany was keen to present itself as a defender of Arab rights. Rosenberg portrayed the Jews as the villains in Palestine, as everywhere else, and the Palestinians as 'freedom fighters'. The idea of a Jewish state as such was in any case considered impossible, since due to the nature of the race it was bound to lead to 'mutual robbery and mutual massacres'. Instead, as the headline had it: 'No Artificial Jewish State, but Establishment of a Jewish Reservation under Police Control'.[4]

The German press's aim was clearly to expose British hypocrisy in the Middle East once more, to gather Arab support, further denigrate the Jews in Palestine and elsewhere, and to leverage the resulting influence in this most sensitive part of the British Empire for future use. The 'Madagascar Plan' would resurface at various points over the next two years or so, most conspicuously shortly in advance of the fall of France in 1940, before being abandoned in favour of a policy of extermination.

In Spain, the Republic was in its death throes. The German press gloated over the doom awaiting 'Red Spain' and 'Soviet Catalonia' and showed pictures of sturdy, ruthless-looking Loyalist troops marching into the sanctuary of France. The British press reported the end battles of the Civil War, but concentrated on the plight of refugees escaping over the Pyrenees, especially the children ('Child Refugees Lost in Mountain Blizzard for Two Days' the *Express* reported, with photograph, on 2 February).

Sir John Anderson, his tobogganing days in Arosa now a distant memory, had clearly been goaded into action on the civil defence problem, at least in the eyes of the *Express*, which reported that he had announced his decision to appoint '12 ARP Dictators' in the near future:

Sir John Anderson, ARP chief, announced at a press conference yesterday that as soon as a war is declared twelve dictators will take over supreme charge of twelve areas into which the country will be split. Sir John hopes to find the men, who will be of national standing, before early March.[5]

The paper added ominously that the system was said to be 'based . . . on methods used in Germany and Spain'.

Elsewhere in the *Daily Express*, a cartoon showed two besuited and bowler-hatted City gents strap-hanging on a commuter train. One was saying to the other: 'This year we're taking our holiday between the late spring and the early autumn crises.'[6]

*

In Germany, there were now, officially, no political jokes. Just before Hitler's Reichstag speech at the end of January, Goebbels, so his diary says, had been dictating an article – one of a series – intended to inaugurate a crackdown on what was left of satire in post-Weimar Germany. In the era to come, there would be only conformity. In his speech to the press in November 1938, Hitler had spent considerable time attacking 'intellectuals', who unlike ordinary honest Germans were constantly criticizing and warning and doubting the Führer's actions. Goebbels was determined to pursue his master's wishes.

The first victim of Goebbels's purge of the satirists was one Germany's finest, Werner Finck, then appearing at the Kabarett der Komiker (Comedians' Cabaret) in Berlin. A master of innuendo and the unfinished sentence, Finck, thirty-six years old, had been *Conférencier* (Master of Ceremonies) and part owner of Katakombe (Catacombs), a Berlin cabaret club, from 1929 to 1935. Initially tolerated by the new Nazi regime, which in its early years allowed itself a certain sheen of liberalism, Finck and his show encountered increasing surveillance. A Gestapo report from early 1935 described a performance:

The audience in the 'Katacombe' consists overwhelmingly of Jews, who reward the vulgarities and the biting, subversive critiques from the M.C., Werner Fink [sic], with fanatical applause. Fink is a typical specimen of the former Cultural-Bolshevist, who

obviously has no understanding – or does not want any understanding – of the new era and, in the style of the earlier Jewish
literati, is out to drag the ideas of National Socialism and all that
is sacred to National Socialists, into the mud . . .[7]

Katakombe was closed down later that year. Finck was inter-
rogated by the Gestapo and detained in the prison opposite their
headquarters in the Prinz-Albrecht-Strasse. On arrival in the cell
block, he was asked by a beefy SS-man with a checklist if he had
any weapons on him. Finck responded, deadpan as ever: 'Why?
Do you need some here?' He was then transferred to the
Esterwegen concentration camp, near the Dutch border in north-
western Germany.

Finck was lucky. After six weeks he was a free man again. His
unexpected release was said to have been engineered by Göring
as a tactical move in the Marshal's long-running feud with
Goebbels. Finck was then served with a year's performance ban.
Curiously, he was not, actually, especially political. He described
himself as more of a 'dyed-in-the-wool individualist' (*eingefleischter
Individualist*), which was why he found the enforced conformity
and herd mentality imposed by the regime so absurd and worthy
of mockery.

By January 1939, Finck had been performing again for more
than two years, and Goebbels had once more had enough. The
satirist was expelled from the Reich Chamber of Culture
(Reichskulturkammer), which automatically removed his licence
to perform, whether in cabaret or in film, where he had a lucrative sideline in comedy bit-parts. In an article in the Nazi organ
Völkischer Beobachter, 'Haben wir eigentlich noch Humor?' (Do
We Actually Still have Humour?), Goebbels clearly stated that
political humour was now forbidden:

Political joking-around is a remnant of liberalism. In the previous
system, one could still accomplish something with it. We are
too smart and too experienced in such matters to let them
continue on their course.[8]

The 'experience' Goebbels referred to focused on the pre-1918 satirical scene, which he saw as created by the Jews. Mockery, as Goebbels saw it, had undermined the old German state and contributed towards the loss of the First World War and that state's subsequent collapse. This must not be allowed to happen again. On 1 February 1939, as he reported in his diary, he summoned the performer and manager of the Cabaret of Comedians, Willi Schaeffers, who, although he was a Nazi sympathizer, was even more in sympathy with good jokes. They had, in Goebbels's words, 'a lengthy battle . . . I stick to my standpoint. Political jokes will be stamped out. Wiped off the map.' The Minister's conclusion made the regime's intentions absolutely clear: 'We have no wish to let useless intellectuals go on trashing our Party, our state, and our public institutions.' There might, as yet, be no war, but every aspect of life, including the right to make jokes, was to be managed as if there were:

> This nation has humour. But it follows the clear principle, learned from the Prussian Army, that the only person who has a right to mock, to complain, or even to curse once in a while, is someone who is marching in step.

Goebbels's article attacking satire was the first barrage in what became a ruthless campaign against 'intellectuals'. Its title carried a particularly ominous message for the remnants of Germany's once vocal liberal press. In particular, it was aimed directly against the *Berliner Tageblatt*. For decades an internationally recognized liberal-bourgeois newspaper of record, it had recently published a readers' poll under the rubric 'Do We Actually Have Humour?' with comments from a number of well-known comedians, including Finck. The *Tageblatt* had somehow survived into the Nazi era, with ever-diminishing traces of its old democratic, critical principles, and had run into trouble with the Nazi censors on that account. During the year in which he was banned from performing, Werner Finck had written a regular, gently barbed, satirical column for the paper. Now, with war on the horizon (Goebbels, like other members of Hitler's circle, knew by this point that conflict was all but inevitable), such holdovers from Weimar were on notice of extinction. The 31 January 1939 edition of the *Berliner Tageblatt* was its last.

The fate of the *Berliner Tageblatt* was mentioned next day in both *The Times* and, at much greater length, with an essay from its former editor, the distinguished writer Theodor Wolff, the *Manchester Guardian*. Editor of the *Tageblatt* for twenty-five years until he was forced out shortly after the Nazi seizure of power, Wolff was Jewish, and at the time the paper became defunct he was living unhappily in French exile, in Nice. He wrote among other things with bitter amusement of the 'lift boy' at the paper's offices who, on the day the Nazis won their electoral majority in 1933, suddenly appeared at work in his Storm Trooper uniform. It turned out he had been spying on the staff all along. Wolff used the lift boy's story to end his valedictory essay:

> And now this man, unless he has been advanced to some high administrative post in the official hierarchy, is conveying the gloomy figures of the last of the editorial staff down below, and unloading them there. The goods they had been supplying were mainly of the 'tied house' sort and not impeccable, but some of them may have been poor fellows of the stamp of the exciseman under James II, who had 'fourteen reasons for obeying his Majesty's commands – a wife and thirteen children'; and to these unfortunates we may well grant our forgiveness as they descend silently into the valley of oblivion.[9]

Only one other liberal paper of the pre-Nazi era now remained, the *Frankfurter Zeitung*, permitted to offer mildly critical comment from time to time. Goebbels (and also Hitler) spent years vacillating about whether to keep it going in order to maintain an illusion of press freedom, especially useful when attempting to disarm foreign criticism of the regime.[10]

Werner Finck could read the signs. He knew very well that the notoriously vindictive Goebbels was not finished with him. He tried to work out where he would be relatively safe, and with a sure satirist's eye he chose (correctly as it turned out) to join the Wehrmacht. Even before the war finally came, he was training as a radio operator with the 23rd Infantry Division and he would survive the Third Reich.

Ruth Andreas-Friedrich, in the interim, was still gainfully employed as a journalist, but her main concern as winter ended was dealing with the streams of Jewish friends who had been arrested on or just after *Kristallnacht* and were being released, often in very poor physical condition, from the regime's concentration camps. Most had been interned at Buchenwald, near Weimar, where more than 10,000 Jewish men were taken in November. They told of beatings, murders, wretched food, hundreds of captives served by only one outdoor toilet, with dysentery and other intestinal infections rife. 'Even the most patriotic Jews have had their eyes opened. Anyone who has any possibility of doing so is trying to emigrate,' as Andreas-Friedrich wrote.

The free-spirited journalist and her network were, of course, exactly the fastidious, critical, 'defeatist' 'intellectuals' that the Nazi regime was so contemptuous of – and so worried about. To the likes of Goebbels, to describe someone as a 'fanatic' was a compliment, whereas for her and her circle it was the exact opposite. While Jews of her acquaintance undertook the arduous task of getting out of Germany with their skins and at least some of their precious possessions intact, Andreas-Friedrich and Leo and her other 'Aryan' comrades did what they could to prevent their friends being picked clean by the Nazi vultures – selling furniture and dinner-sets and books on their behalf and holding on to the proceeds to keep them from sequestration by the authorities. There were by now around a quarter of a million Jews still left in Germany, urgently in need of sanctuary yet blocked and excluded wherever they turned. Andreas-Friedrich wrote in sadness and anger of their plight:

What are a quarter of a million human beings, spread through the whole world? Why does no one take pity on them? Why is not just one great power prepared to make a sacrifice for the sake of these quarter of a million lives? It is a sad kind of compassion that makes the scale of its preparedness to help dependent on how much money its object has in his or her wallet. Anyone who has no connections in the outside world, who cannot come up with some influential guarantor, has to settle for staying in this country as a burdensome alien. Everyone for himself![11]

What she and her friends were doing for the Jews was already illegal. Every pfennig was supposed to be declared so that the authorities could strip away all but a remnant before finally allowing their victims to leave the country. But it seemed like the very least a civilized person could do, and so they did it.

It was also around this same time that Ruth Adler's father was released from Dachau, where the Gestapo had finally taken him two or three weeks after his initial arrest. 'One day,' she recalled, 'my dad appeared in prison clothes.'

They had knocked out his teeth; he no longer had his teeth. They starved him, and they eventually just pushed him out of the concentration camp. It was winter, he walked along the railroad tracks to Munich, in his bare feet – Dachau is near Munich – where a soup kitchen had been established by Polish Jews to feed and to finance train rides back to people's places. They helped him get a coat over the striped pyjamas – they were just pyjamas. It was wintertime. He had no shoes.

Even while Herr Adler had been in Dachau, and no one knew if he would live or die, Ruth's mother had been working on how they could leave if and when he was freed. Even before they saw her father again, a family in New York had been found to sponsor the Adlers for American visas. Now they could begin to pack, to plan, to sort out the weary and humiliating paperwork involved in escaping Germany.[12]

Time was pressing, and everybody knew it. Although Hitler's broadly content-free 30 January speech had kept the stock markets happy, at some point the apparent breathing space would come to an end.

In March 1939 an academic friend of Ruth Andreas-Friedrich said to her with a degree of anxiety: 'Has it struck you that they're taking an unnervingly lively interest in the German minority in Czechoslovakia?'[13]

*

Since young Franz Fühmann had watched disconsolate Czech soldiers trudging down from the mountain fortifications in the early days of October 1938, on their way into the now more or less defenceless Czech-speaking interior, the state of Czecho-Slovakia (now officially hyphenated) had come increasingly to resemble that of the other German allies and satellites. On 1 February, Jewish émigrés living in the country were ordered to leave within six months. Many had already fled, along with most of the political refugees who had also sought the shelter of democratic Czechoslovakia after 1933.

Virulent anti-Semitism of the type manifested in Nazi Germany had generally been much rarer in the Czech lands. After Munich, and the forced exodus of tens of thousands of Czech-speakers from the Sudetenland, a certain new animus against Jews, especially those who had also fled the border areas, was also to be found among the Czechs. Jews in Bohemia and Moravia had, after all, historically tended to identify with the German-speakers.[14] One well-known Czech commentator wrote at the time: 'A job that goes to a German or Jewish refugee is lost to one of our people,' and he was not alone in this sentiment.

Beneš had already left for exile in London. From October 1938 both the President and the Prime Minister were from the right-of-centre Peasants' Party. The Prague government continued to insist that it would not legislate on a racist or anti-Semitic basis, and sent in police against far-right demonstrators. All the same, in light of the fact that good relations with Nazi Germany were now essential, it did take steps to ensure that refugees might be placed in other countries, to relieve the pressure. All who had settled in the country since 1914 would be encouraged to leave.

Slovakia, meanwhile, had gained a great deal of extra autonomy, and there several leading politicians and their followers were much more extreme in their anti-Semitism. Jews were boycotted, and those accused of being associated with the country's former Hungarian overlords were expropriated and deported. A battle continued through the coming winter between these groups and Slovakian leaders who, like their counterparts in Prague, disapproved of anti-Semitic extremism.

Slovakia was split down the middle, with its Jewish population subjected to sporadic exclusion and expropriation. Since Czechia and Slovakia still shared a currency, many Jewish citizens withdrew their funds from banks in Bratislava, the Slovak capital, and transferred them to Prague, where they were, for now, safe from sequestration. In general, despite growing pressure from Berlin, which expected the Czecho-Slovaks to align themselves with the Reich in the matter of dealing with the Jews, the government in Prague, and to some extent that in Bratislava, managed to maintain the rule of law and to resist attempts to impose a flood of Nazi-style anti-Semitic laws.

In the first two months of 1939, the pressure from the Germans began to gain some force, and the attitude of the Hitler government a generally menacing aspect. At a meeting between the new Czecho-Slovak Foreign Minister, František Chvalovský, and Hitler, the Führer made it brutally clear that unless the Czechs gave in to all German demands, it would be over for them.[15] Germany obviously intended to rob Czecho-Slovakia of what little freedom of movement and self-determination it had left after Munich.

Among other things, the Czech government was finally forced to ban the Communist Party and to bring in discriminatory measures against Jews in the civil service, as well as reviewing the citizenship of refugees who had been granted Czech nationality since 1933. This 'new course' recognized that, in effect, the country was at the mercy of the Germans and must at least appear to give the bully next door what it wanted. According to a Czech commentator who had been close to the deposed Beneš and had no cause to flatter those who succeeded him: 'One must concede that the post-Munich government acted moderately in the Jewish question as in other matters. It put the brake on excesses and tried to preserve at least some of the main principles of democratic policy.'[16]

There were still several hundred thousand native German-speakers living in Czecho-Slovakia after Munich, including some 30,000 (4–5 per cent) self-identifying as such out of a total of 670,000 inhabitants in the capital, Prague.[17] In the German Charles University, the city could still boast one of the oldest German-language places of learning in Europe. The father of Anton Weliminsky, the young doctor who had left the Sudetenland just before Munich, was a bacteriologist there. Anton could not find a job in the capital because of his poor Czech. Fortunately, his father had academic contacts in Britain, one of whom stood as guarantor for Anton. The young doctor left for Britain on a temporary visa. When he arrived, in February 1939, Anton found the British 'friendly . . . but they didn't realize what was going on' in Germany and Central Europe, or what they were dealing with in the case of the Nazi state. He recalled seeing a poster for the *Daily Mirror*. It advertised the story of a bride who had cancelled her wedding because she was anxious about her dog. Britain seemed like another world, inhabited by sleepers who were not yet awake but would soon have wakefulness forced upon them.[18]

At the end of February, in one among many attempts to deflect the potential wrath of its new German overlords, the Czecho-Slovak government stood the country's army down from the state of military alert that had reigned since the previous September. There was a brief pause. Then the German press started to report on unrest in Slovakia and in the so-called 'Carpatho-Ukraine' in the far east of the country, both granted wide autonomy under the Munich Agreement. The representatives of the German-speaking minority in Slovakia, which totalled about 150,000 in a nation of 2 million, were instructed by Berlin to ally themselves with the nationalist forces there, under Premier Jozef Tiso (a Catholic priest). When the ruling group of Slovak nationalists tried to declare independence, Prague moved troops and police into position in Bratislava and other important Slovak towns.

On 11 March, the tone of the German press shifted further. Fed by set-piece articles in the DNB agency handouts, suddenly stories began to appear throughout the German press not just in sympathy with the Slovaks but reporting hostile actions by the pro-Prague forces against German-speakers in and around Bratislava, the Slovak capital. Relatively minor indignities at first in the early morning edition – German Party offices occupied, a Slovak-German joint meeting baton-charged by police[19] – but by the time the evening edition came out, the propaganda machine had been cranked up. There was the story of a Czech soldier hitting a German schoolgirl in Bratislava with his rifle-butt when she failed to obey an order to halt, and a large headline about 'Czech Terror'. Franz Karmasin, a crypto-Nazi who represented the local Germans in the Slovak government, made a rousing speech to a crowd of several thousand before decamping across the Danube into the safety of German-ruled Austria:

> The methods of the Czechs have not altered in the last twenty years. Our German national group stands under the protection of the Führer, Adolf Hitler. We shall make common cause with the Slovaks to restore peace and order in the land.[20]

Within another two or three days, atrocity stories about Czech mistreatment of Germans, not just in Slovakia, but also in the Czech-ruled parts of the country, would start to flood the German newspapers, on Goebbels's orders.

The lull in the international situation, such as it was, was approaching its end.

*

In Britain, on 11 March 1939, the main news story was the sentencing of six IRA men and one woman to a total of 121 years in prison for, in the words of the trial judge, a 'diabolical conspiracy'. On 16 January, three bombs had been planted beneath manholes amongst underground cables in the centre of Manchester. Their aim had been to sabotage the city's electricity supply. However, a passing market porter had been accidentally killed by a flying manhole cover, which made the sentencing especially strict.[21]

Five young Irishmen were sentenced to twenty years' penal servitude, one to fourteen years, and a young Irish woman to seven years for their parts in the Manchester operation. There were noisy scenes in court, with those in the dock shouting slogans and their supporters in the public gallery chorusing 'Up the Republic!' The *Daily Express* described one of the ringleaders, Michael Rory Campbell, aged twenty-one, as having 'the trick of smiling with his lips, but never with his steel-cold, pale blue eyes'. Berated by the judge for his part in the death of the inno-cent passer-by, Campbell 'flushed, spoke for the first time, and shouted: "Well, it was for a good cause. I would do it again. God save Ireland!"' As he was taken down, women in the audience called out: 'Good old Rory!' Twenty-two-year-old Mary Glenn, who had been 'taught to hate England' as a child, quietly said 'God save Ireland' before being taken from the court to begin her sentence. A barmaid at the Rose of England Hotel in Manchester, she had acted as a messenger and general go-between for the IRA 'active service unit' that had planted the bombs.

Yet, with bombs exploding all over the country and Hitler menacing Czecho-Slovakia, British politicians were, it seemed, still confident that Appeasement was working. The same page of the *Express* that headlined the Manchester verdicts carried a report of a speech by Sir Samuel Hoare, the Home Secretary, in which he suggested that a five-year peace plan could bring peace to the world. If the dictators (including Stalin) and the prime ministers of Britain and France got together to restore confidence, they could 'banish a nightmare' and bring about a new golden age:

Here, indeed, is the greatest opportunity that has ever been offered to the leaders of the world. Five men in Europe, the three dictators and the Prime Ministers of Britain and France, if they worked with a singleness of purpose and a unity of action to this end, might in an incredibly short space of time transform the whole history of the world.

These five men working together in Europe, and blessed in their efforts by the President of the United States, might make themselves the eternal benefactors of the human race.

Our own Prime Minister has shown his determination to work heart and soul to such an end. I cannot believe that the other leaders of Europe will not join him in the high endeavour on which he is engaged.[22]

In line with the paper's pro-Appeasement policy, the *Express* made no negative comment on the speech. It was up to the generally liberal, high-minded *Manchester Guardian* to point out the practical flaws in Hoare's enthusiastic embrace of a new era of international cooperation. 'Again we can only hope,' its leader writer commented, 'even if it almost passes the ordinary observer's belief, that the Government has some grounds, withheld from the rest of us, for its high flights of optimism.'[23]

By the time the *Manchester Guardian* leader article appeared, on Monday 13 March 1939, the front pages of the German press were showing nothing but Czech atrocities – against Slovaks, against German-speakers, even against visitors from Germany proper. It was a 'Return to the Beneš Course', with 'Flagrant Outrages Against Slovaks and Germans'. Crowds of Czech gendarmes were chorusing 'Up With Stalin! Up With Beneš!' It was 'Terror as in the Worst Times'.[24]

The 'return to the Beneš Course', invoking the exiled ex-President's name like an evil spell, was the most sinister of the charges being made by the Goebbels-inspired press. The Prague government, desperately trying to hold what was left of its country together, had in fact only very reluctantly used any force at all against the openly mutinous nationalists in Slovakia and elsewhere. It was only too well aware how the Germans would exploit such countermeasures.

On the Continent, the ground was being prepared for something that most definitely had nothing to do with Sir Samuel Hoare's 'golden age'. By 14 March, German troops were massing on the borders of both the Czech lands and Slovakia, the press campaign inside the Reich had reached fever pitch, and Hitler had decided to make his demands on the Prague government – demands which in practice would take away the last vestiges of the country's integrity and independence.

Slovakia would be independent, Ruthenia in the far east of the country also, and what Hitler contemptuously referred to in conversation as the 'Rump Czechia' (*Rest-Tschechei*) would be . . . what would it be, and what would it even be called? The *Express*'s man in Prague wasn't sure, but he knew that in the cafes and bars you could order 'a pair of the best Prague sausages with mashed potato and sauerkraut for 3½d'. You could also get a good-quality suit for a song, because although the country's textile-manufacturing areas, in what had been the Sudetenland, were now in Germany, the old contracts had some time to run, which meant that for now clothing was artificially cheap. All the same, as he observed:

> Gloom hangs over the Praguers today. They congregate in the cafes of Wenceslas-square asking each other questions.
>
> The breakaway of Slovakia means the end of the state of Czech-Slovakia [*sic*] founded by the Allies after the war. It is as though we in London heard suddenly that Scotland had walked out on us, and then the Welsh, and made an alliance with a great enemy power.
>
> They ask each other, what will our country be called? For with Slovakia gone, you can't just call the rest Czech. We have no longer even a name.[25]

Opposite this report on the leader page – separated by a lengthy article (with picture) about the mostly disappointing fates of the four young women who had been selected by the film tycoon Sir Alexander Korda as his company's 'stars of the future' in 1936 – the Opinion column had no good news for the Czechs either:

> This is an intolerable and wretched attempt to impose on them a political system that they certainly do not want, even though the Slovaks and the Ruthenians may.
>
> But it is not the responsibility of the British government to defend these countries.
>
> There will be no war on this account. There will be no September crisis atmosphere this March; no autumn jitters in the spring.

The issue of war was settled at Munich when the Sudeten territory was conceded to the Germans.

And it had been obvious for many months that Czecho-Slovakia had been a vassal state of Germany.

There were bound to be disturbances among the different races of this miniature League of Nations.

Yet we promised to defend it after Munich with its Czechs, its Slovaks, its Croats [*sic*]* and its Magyars. That promise was absurd . . .

Even before Hitler's army had started to move, not only Lord Beaverbrook's Appeasement-preaching mouthpiece but the British government had made it clear that what had seemed like a guarantee given to the Czechs at Munich was actually nothing of the kind. The front page of the *Express* summed it all up for its 2 million-plus readers in one cosy text-box headed: 'It's Hitler again. BUT DON'T WORRY!' The bullet-pointed list linked to its page 10 Opinion piece, which went on to remind readers that the government had already forsworn action in defence of the Czechs, and then cited a speech the previous evening by Lord Halifax, the Foreign Secretary:

Lord Halifax . . . warned the public against seeing a crisis in every event:

'It is not surprising in these times that many nerves are taut and overstrained; and strained nerves and calm judgment go ill together.

'Almost every week events occur in some part of Europe which are represented as a crisis.

'The air is constantly filled with sensational rumours of what is going to happen, and some of us take little trouble to distinguish between fact and fiction.

---

* This is a puzzling reference, though not as such wholly incorrect. There were actually small Croat-speaking minorities in both Slovakia and Czechia – remnants of the migrant populations of the old Austro-Hungarian Empire – but at a few thousand altogether their numbers were tiny compared with, say, the Ukrainian speakers of Ruthenia, who do not merit a mention here.

'The Government's actions will not be deflected by these unsupported speculations.'

At four on the afternoon of that same day, President Emil Hácha and his Foreign Minister left by train from Prague for the German capital to meet with Hitler and his paladins. According to the public protocol, the meeting was purely at the request of the Czecho-Slovak government, but, though this may have been technically true, in fact the train was provided by the Germans. Berlin had been waiting and planning for this moment, as Goebbels gloated in his diary entry for that day.[26] In any case, it represented a last attempt on the part of the Czechs to salvage some shred of hope for their country from the German-engineered crisis that their supposed friends and protectors in the West refused to recognize as such.

*

The German press, of course, presented the humiliation of the representatives of 'Rump-Czechia' during the night of 14/15 March 1939 as a gracious solution to the problems presented by the Czech state's inherently chaotic nature. The early edition of the *Freiburger Zeitung* on 15 March was still all mayhem and reports of anti-German atrocities. It carried only a brief mention of the Czech President Hácha's arrival at the Anhalter Station in Berlin at 10.40 p.m., after an almost seven-hour journey from Prague.

Hácha was given a full head-of-state reception, with a military band and a troop inspection. Once he had arrived at the Reich Chancellery, however, he was kept waiting while Hitler finished watching a popular film in his private cinema, reportedly the newly released romantic comedy *A Hopeless Case* (*Ein hoffnungsloser Fall*). It starred the Austrian actress Jenny Jugo, who was actually present at the screening. She later told Erich Ebermayer that, when the Führer had finished watching the film, he and she left the room together. As they parted, Hitler smiled, jerked his head in the direction of the door behind which the Czech President was still waiting and joked: '*Another* hopeless case!'[27]

Hácha and Foreign Minister Chvalovský were finally ushered into the presence of the Führer and his henchmen around one-thirty in the morning. The diminutive Czech President, in his sixty-seventh year and suffering from heart problems, was about to experience the pitiless methods of the German criminal state at first hand.

The later edition of the Freiburg paper that Wednesday announced the entry of German troops into Bohemia and Moravia. The reports of violence disappeared completely, turned off like gas from a tap. Instead there were three full pages of triumph and joy. 'Lösung und Erlösung durch Gross-Deutschland' (Resolution and Salvation Through Greater Germany) was the front-page headline. Swastika flags were fluttering above Prague. After talks in the early morning hours, the Czech delegation had supposedly requested that their country give up pretensions to independence, and the Führer had agreed. 'The Decisive Hour. The Führer takes the Czech People under the Protection of the German Reich', said the page 2 headline.

There was, of course, no mention of the relentless barrage of threats that had caused the Czechs to surrender. Göring, who had returned from his spring break on the Italian Riviera just that evening, on Hitler's orders, was at the Chancellery and joined in the festival of intimidation. The Marshal made it clear that unless the Czech leaders gave in and signed the order to place their country under German 'protection', his Luftwaffe would reduce historic Prague to rubble. Hácha held out for two and a half hours of remorseless bullying, reportedly suffering a minor heart attack and kept going with the aid of injections from the physicians Hitler had thoughtfully placed on hand. Shortly before four in the morning, Hácha and his Foreign Minister appended their signatures to the document the Germans had prepared. They were then escorted to a suite at the Hotel Adlon, in the bitter knowledge that their country had, indeed, ceased to exist and that most of their compatriots would forever view them as traitors.

'I shall enter history as the greatest German of them all,' Hitler boasted to his secretaries on emerging from his victorious confrontation with the Czechs.

About two hours later, at 6 a.m., the Wehrmacht moved over

the border into Bohemia and Moravia. By nine o'clock that morning, German troops had entered Prague.[28]

The declaration issued by the Führer to justify this long-prepared invasion is an example par excellence of how to justify an attack against a neighbouring country. Eighty years later, Hitler's playbook remains one from which his successors in aggression neither want nor need to deviate in any significant way:

To the German People!

Just a few months ago, Germany was forced to take her racial comrades, living in cohesive areas of settlement and subjected to the intolerable terroristic regime of Czecho-Slovakia, under its protection. In the last weeks similar occurrences have once again become increasingly apparent.

As a reaction to these new attacks against the freedom and existence of these racial groups, they have now broken loose from Prague. Czecho-Slovakia has thus now ceased to exist.

Since Sunday, wild excesses have been taking place in many locations, to which now, once again, many Germans have fallen victim. A stream of refugees, robbed of their property and possessions, has once more begun to flow out of the populous linguistic enclaves that last autumn were, by the generosity of Germany, left as part of Czecho-Slovakia.

A continuation of these conditions must inevitably lead to the destruction of all order in a region where Germany has existentially important interests, since it belonged for over a thousand years to the German Reich.

In order now to bring a definitive end to this threat to peace, and to create the preconditions for the requisite reordering of things in this living-space, on this day I have made the decision for German troops to march into Bohemia and Moravia. They will disarm the terrorist gangs and the Czech combat forces that are supporting them, take the lives of all threatened people under their protection, and thereby secure the basic conditions for the introduction of a thoroughgoing regulation of affairs that will do justice to the spirit of a thousand-year history and to the practical needs of the German and Czech peoples.[29]

Not once did Hitler bother to repeat the story that the Czech President, Hácha, had 'voluntarily' put his country under the 'protection' of Germany. The language of the Führer's proclamation was purely one of conquest, utterly belying the supposed legal justification of the action.

Accompanying the regular troops were, naturally, SS and Gestapo units, operating – just as they had in the newly occupied Sudeten areas the previous October – according to a long-prepared plan to neutralize any opposition and to lay hands on any enemies of the regime who had not had the foresight to leave Prague. Under this scheme, known as Operation Railings (*Aktion 'Gitter'*), some 450 arrests were made within forty-eight hours in the city alone. Over the next weeks the figure for Prague would rise to about 2,500, including Czech and German refugees and oppositionists.[30] The twilight of Czech democracy quickly shaded into totalitarian night.

There had been late-season and in parts heavy snow in the border lands and even in Prague itself, though there a slight thaw had just set in. Käthe Strenitz had fled with her Jewish family from the Sudetenland the previous year and was now studying and enjoying Prague's artistic scene. She would recall the German army's entry into the ancient Bohemian capital, watched by sullen groups of Czechs lining the streets:

> It was slushy weather. I remember them moving slowly in, all the armoured vehicles and things. There was a feeling, you know, one had the feeling of doom, but I wasn't really scared until towards the end when I left; I wasn't particularly scared, I was scared for my mother and my brother and my father, because there didn't seem to be any way of them coming out. And that was the case.[31]

A precocious sixteen-year-old, Käthe Strenitz would soon become one of the older participants in the Kindertransport. Her mother would not let her younger brother go because she could not bear to part with him.

Hitler followed his troops to Prague later that same day, spending the night at the Hradschin castle above the old city, for the past twenty years seat of the Czech government, finalizing arrangements for how his new 'protectorate' was to be ruled and enjoying his moment of mastery.

While all this was happening, Major Helmuth Groscurth, the oppositional Abwehr officer who had been intimately involved both in helping foment the disturbances before the Munich Agreement and also in making plans for a coup should the resulting Sudeten Crisis lead to war, was still trapped by routine duties in Breslau. To his chagrin, in fact, on the afternoon of 13 March 1939 he had been left in charge of headquarters while the rest of the regiment moved out of barracks and headed south for the Czech border in what was obviously a prearranged invasion. A protest to his superiors in Berlin was of no avail. He was still kicking his heels in Breslau when troops from his regiment advanced into Prague with the main body of the Wehrmacht on 15 March.[32]

By now, Groscurth was seething with frustration. An urgent telegram to his once close collaborator in mischief, the Sudeten Gauleiter, Henlein, and a note to his commanding general in Berlin, asking to be given something suitable to do, were left unanswered. However, on 17 March Groscurth reported in his diary a trip with Captain Dingler, head of the Abwehr in Breslau, south over the border, through the eastern fringe of the Sudeten *Gau* and into the newly occupied parts of Moravia around the old city of Olmütz (Olomouc in Czech). From there, Groscurth reported:

> Life goes on completely normally, as if nothing had happened. The shops are open, the population is reserved or approachable, nowhere hostile. Czech soldiers and officers stroll around the streets and make friends with us. An astonishing business.

It all contrasted with the activities of the SS, who were now, to Groscurth's disgust, temporarily lodged at the barracks of the 49th Infantry Regiment in Breslau – those same SS units who, Groscurth said, had 'comported themselves like vandals' in the Sudetenland and were now being transferred to Slovakia.

Groscurth, back from his excursion into 'Rump-Czechia' – now to be known as the 'Protectorate of Bohemia and Moravia' – was also more and more appalled by the international reaction to the German seizure of these overwhelmingly Slavic territories, contrary to all Hitler's public pronouncements of wanting only to liberate German minorities ('I want no Czechs', he had told the democracies at Munich). Chamberlain, Britain's architect of Appeasement, was horrified, too. On 17 March, he had given a speech making his reaction clear. 'Chamberlain's speech was devastating,' Groscurth wrote in his private diary:

> Who, indeed, is supposed to believe us, after we have put aside all agreements and completely tossed out the principle of nationality?[33]

The infuriating thing was, as Groscurth remarked, that the 'solution of the Polish question would be much more important'. This latest, greatest, and surely unignorable betrayal would only make this problem worse.

Poland had participated in the dismemberment of Czechoslovakia in the autumn of 1938, and in the early months of 1939 had appeared willing to improve trade and political relations with Germany, but now the Warsaw high command had to think about defending itself. No more trust, just more rearmament, and the democracies wholly on the defensive.

In the small town near Hanover in which he lived, Wilhelm Sölter, a 36-year-old legal clerk at the local prosecutor's office and aspiring author, wrote in his diary, as he did most days. He expressed genuine delight at the invasion of Czechia – Sölter was a keen admirer of the Führer – but also, perhaps, a hint of foreboding:

> Yesterday evening Hitler moved into the Hradschin. A real Imperial Duke! Now the old, glorious time has returned.
> Went for a walk with Busser [his small son]. One can go on good walks with him. He asked me how you steer an aeroplane.
> In the evening there was a blackout practice.[34]

*

Sir Cuthbert Headlam, a Conservative grandee in the north-east
of England and a slightly sceptical supporter of Chamberlain, had
no doubt what the occupation of Prague meant for Britain and
the Prime Minister. 'I fear that this will be the death-knell of
poor Neville's policy of appeasement,' he wrote in his diary on
15 March 1939, 'and equally, of course, all his opponents will
say "I told you so!"' He continued gloomily:

> It is also the end, I should imagine, of any further dealing with
> Hitler – the man henceforward should be treated as outside
> the pale – and when we are strong enough should be fought.

On 18 March, after Chamberlain's 'fine' speech, Headlam was
even more generally glum, despairing of the nation's follies since
the end of the previous war:

> We are to blame for Hitlerism – there's no doubt about that
> – and by we I mean the English nation, and its cranks, faddists,
> fools and futilities who have misled it and deceived it since the
> Armistice.

Chamberlain's speech the previous evening had been made not
in the House of Commons but, as was so often the case with his
most important statements, in his native Birmingham. He and
those around him were fully aware of its importance. The address
– as Chamberlain coyly reminded his audience, made on the eve
of his seventieth birthday – was broadcast on the main 'National'
radio service of the BBC and throughout the British Commonwealth
and the United States. It was also transmitted in full in German
translation at 10.50 that same evening.

The speech contained a lot of sorrow, some anger, some self-
justification, and a touch (as was typical with Chamberlain) of
hedging of bets, just in case peace could, despite everything that
had happened, be preserved.

The Prime Minister told his audience that the hopes of
everyone in Europe that the Munich settlement would usher in
a new era of peace and prosperity had now been 'wantonly

shattered' by the German seizure of Bohemia and Moravia. Chamberlain defended himself against critics (chief among them, of course, Churchill) who traced the origins of this latest outrage back to the signing of the Munich Agreement. Once again, the superficially polite elderly gentleman with the umbrella and the old-fashioned taste in clothes revealed a hidden but no less fierce egotism. Chamberlain rarely admitted he was wrong, and this evening was no exception. In this new version, he and Daladier, the French Prime Minister, had made a deal six months previously because the alternative was war – and a futile one at that, for (so Chamberlain ventured) nothing could actually have been done to save Czechoslovakia by military intervention from the West. He repeated the assurances Hitler had given in September 1938 that after the Sudetenland 'I have no more territorial problems in Europe' and that 'I shall not be interested in the Czech state any more and I can guarantee it.' Chamberlain's anger at the Führer's blatant bad faith was certainly genuine.

The Prime Minister exposed this as the key point. Hitler had inflicted a 'series of unpleasant surprises' on the world – the Rhineland occupation, the annexations of Austria and the Sudetenland. Yet these had at least claimed some justification in justice and national self-determination – 'however much we might take exception to the methods which were adopted'. This was a new situation:

> The events which have taken place this week, in complete disregard of the principles laid down by the German Government itself, seem to fall into a different category, and they must cause us all to be asking ourselves: 'Is this the end of an old adventure or the beginning of a new? Is this the last attack upon a small state, or is it to be followed by others? Is this, in fact, a step in the direction of an attempt to dominate the world by force?'[35]

He pleaded with those members of the public who had not yet volunteered to reconsider the government's call to national service. There was now talk of possible armed resistance to Hitler, but still none of compulsion when it came to providing the means. At the end, Chamberlain expressed himself with his innate caution:

> I feel bound to repeat that while I am not prepared to engage this country by new unspecified commitments operating under conditions which cannot now be foreseen, yet no greater mistake could be made than to suppose that because it believes war to be a senseless and cruel thing this nation has so lost its fibre that it will not take part to the utmost of its power in resisting such a challenge if it were ever made.

The response of his Conservative audience was nonetheless a lengthy ovation and a chorus of 'For he's a jolly good fellow'. A resolution was passed expressing 'unabated confidence in his leadership'. The Prime Minister replied briefly before the evening was wound up:

> We need not be downhearted. This is a great and powerful nation – far more powerful than we were even six months ago – and acts of violence and injustice bring with them sooner or later their own reward. Every one of these incursions raises up fresh dangers for Germany in the future, and I venture to prophesy that in the end she will bitterly regret what her Government has done.

Chamberlain had justified Munich, justified rearmament, covered his back, at least for the moment, in assuring his audience that there would be no more guarantees such as he had given to Czechoslovakia the previous year (and reneged on). Tucked into the speech was even the hope that Hitler's seizure of Prague was somehow 'the end of the adventure' and not the beginning of further aggression.

*

The British Ambassador, Sir Nevile Henderson, was temporarily withdrawn from Berlin. France and Britain delivered protest notes to the German Foreign Ministry, which State Secretary von Weizsäcker, in loyal Hitlerite guise, refused to accept. Goebbels, like his Führer, had become accustomed to the West's readiness to bark but reluctance to bite. He wrote in his diary on 19 March 1939:

> In the afternoon, a sharp official declaration came from London. The Munich Agreement had been broken. England did not recognize the new order in Bohemia and Moravia. But that is likely all theatre-thunder. What do these democracies propose to do other than protest? It's just hysterical screaming after the fact, and it leaves us completely cold. Contempt is the only suitable reaction.[36]

Outside of the Nazi elite, actually, the doings of 15 March had not been greeted with universal approval. For all the loudly proclaimed official notion that the restoring of a medieval imperial relationship amounted somehow to a national renewal, a lot of Germans knew what it actually meant: a policy of bringing Germans 'back to the Reich' had now turned into one of conquest of other peoples. In other words, they understood Chamberlain's point perfectly. Many suspected that this made war a serious possibility, even inevitable.[37] Major Groscurth was one. Erich Ebermayer was another. The high-living literary gadabout had listened to excerpts from Chamberlain's speech the previous evening on Radio Beromünster, the Swiss radio station whose powerful AM signal, reaching far into Germany, provided one of the few sources of independent German-language news and information.

Ebermayer grasped at once that no one would trust Germany from now on, that this was 'cold, naked law-breaking'. Henceforth neighbouring countries could only either submit – or fight.

> Chamberlain has evidently used the first opportunity offered to express himself following the shock of Hitler's invasion of Czechoslovakia. His speech blazes with outrage, bitterness, disappointment. The English may cultivate coolness in times of

adversity and danger – but this time the flames of anger and
hatred burn in the English leader's words attacking the man
who has betrayed him, the all-too trusting gentleman, in such
a primitive, brutal way.[38]

Coincidentally, or not, Ebermayer had, just a few days earlier,
made an offer on a tumbledown castle outside Bayreuth, in
northern Bavaria. It was owned by an elderly doctor. A believer
in natural healing and vegetarianism, the vendor was a Nazi Party
member with a 'gold party badge' (i.e., an early recruit to the
cause), but along with his aristocratic wife, he was beginning to
find the property unmanageable. Ebermayer had been born and
had spent his childhood in this region. It was safe and comfort-
ingly rural, as well as accessible from the new Berlin–Munich
Autobahn. The idea of acquiring a country retreat had occurred
to Ebermayer during the Sudeten Crisis, when, amid rumours
of surprise air attacks, he had experienced a feeling of 'physical
danger' in Berlin.

Whatever his chief motivation, with the Czech invasion out of
the way and Germany surrounded by distrustful and angry foreign
powers, Ebermayer had little confidence that peace would
continue to reign. His offer was eventually accepted, and in the
spring of 1939 Ebermayer became the owner of a medieval semi-
ruin on top of a hill in Upper Franconia. Such a quaint second
home, suitably renovated, provided a bolthole of the kind that
was not available to the vast majority of his fellow Germans, war
or no war. In the turbulent months and years to come its new
owner would make good use of it.

Among the mass of the German people, not just among intellectuals like Ebermayer and soldier-scholars like Groscurth, there
were doubters too, or at least plenty who could not quite
summon the enthusiasm that had greeted the Führer's earlier
territorial coups. There were uncritical Hitler supporters like
Wilhelm Sölter, of course, but others – even Party members
– whose hearts had beaten uncomfortably fast until the 15 March
invasion had been successfully concluded. To their relief, it
became apparent that, once again, neither the Czechs nor the

Allies were going to fight. Everything had happened a great deal quicker than in the Sudeten Crisis, which had dragged on for months of rising tension, tortuous negotiation, and ever-increasing general anxiety. In March 1939 there was a brief, hysterical propaganda campaign, and then a few days later the Czechs surrendered and the Wehrmacht occupied Prague. Good or bad? No one was sure.

The Sopade reports, now produced from the Social Democratic Party in Exile's new base in Paris but still founded on a wide network of informants inside Germany, reflected this ambiguity. One report reluctantly admitted that the invasion of Czecho-Slovakia represented a 'new, big prestige success' for Hitler, which had done something to quiet the discontent that had been simmering under the surface during the late winter:

> There are no arguments against the kind of successes that Hitler can boast of – not even the argument that Czecho-Slovakia has been attacked and that Hitler has committed an illegal act. Of course many people ponder the question whether this goes against Hitler's declaration that he wanted no foreign peoples [in the Reich]. But even calm, objective-minded people have allowed themselves to be influenced by the massive propaganda campaign that Hitler had to unleash in order to keep things calm. Gradually, it is true, more news is filtering through from abroad, especially from the English radio stations broadcasting to Germany, but as a result of years of isolation the ability of people – except for a small educated class – to think independently has suffered a severe decline.[39]

Another report told a somewhat different story. In private, it said, people would be more frank and speak less to the regime's liking. One told the informant: 'Everything will go on as before. These "successes" do not interest me.' Another 'bolder' respondent said: 'I think we should have left the Czechs in peace and to themselves. This won't end well.' Yet another gave a short historical lecture, followed by a very contemporary consumer report:

We had another time when we were constantly victorious and things came to a bad end. Even Napoleon had to learn that one cannot always win and that even the most wonderful successes do no good after a certain stage. We should stop this now and come to an understanding with the others. Since coffee is down to 65 grams [per week], the butter ration is getting smaller all the time, and loaves of bread still don't look the way they used to, improvements in these areas would be of much greater interest.[40]

In Upper Silesia, hundreds of kilometres to the east, a coal and steel area bordering the newly created 'Protectorate' of Bohemia and Moravia to the south and Poland to the east, Sopade reporters summed up the mood as: 'Where is this madness leading us?' Even Nazis – outside the highly visible Party elite – were privately prepared to express their misgivings. 'Politically educated' workers (that is, those who had not yet succumbed to the Nazis' blandishments) thought that 'economic and financial difficulties had by now reached such a pass that the only way out of them was through war. Once preparation for war had gone this far, there was no way back.' The lower middle class and self-employed expected to be taxed even more; even the capitalists were worried at the growing radicalization of the regime, whose policies – typified by *Kristallnacht* – had, so they believed, started to resemble the very Bolshevist menace that the Nazis were supposed to be protecting them against. Only among school-age children and the Hitler Youth, subjected by now to more than six years of indoctrination, and the younger Storm Troopers, was there any real euphoria to be found.[41]

In fact, cause for unalloyed satisfaction came for most people in Germany only the week after the seizure of Czecho-Slovakia. On 22 March, the Baltic state of Lithuania, until 1918 part of the Russian Empire, with a population of just over 2 million to Germany's 80 million, was forced to hand over the strategic port of Memel (Lithuanian: Klaipėda), at the northern coastal tip of East Prussia. A Prussian city for four hundred years, under the Versailles Treaty Memel had been placed under international control. It had then been seized by Lithuanian irregulars in early

1923, a fait accompli that its predominantly German population and the then beleaguered government in Berlin were forced to accept. However, neither intercommunal nor international tensions went away. In 1938, a 'United German List' of candidates won 87 per cent of the votes in elections held under Lithuanian government auspices. As in the case of Danzig, the city was now, in practice, Nazi-controlled.

A few days after the occupation of Prague, Ribbentrop formally demanded that Memel be returned to Germany. Squeezed between an aggressive Germany and Russia, the Lithuanians had little choice but to agree. Amid scenes of rejoicing in Memel and the Reich, the city 'went home'. Minna von Alten, eighty years old, wrote from Braunschweig in Germany to her granddaughter in Utrecht, Holland: 'My dear child, I just hung out the flag for Memel, which since last night belongs to us. We live in wonderful times, hopefully it is all for the best . . .'[42] Erich Ebermayer, who had been so disturbed by the invasion of Rump-Czechia, made a mildly cynical note in his diary which amounted to the written equivalent of a shrug:

> The Memel Territory has now been united with the German Reich by a 'state treaty'. The Memel Territory is being evacuated by the Lithuanian military and police. Memel will become a free port. We are used to such a lot of things that are even worse and even more contrary to the law, that this reincorporation of a territory which was detached by the Versailles Treaty does not seem to upset anyone any more.[43]

Again, it was an essentially German place returning to Germany. But a precedent had been set. As Sopade pointed out in a subsequent report from the free city of Danzig, like Memel created by the Versailles Treaty: 'After the occupation of the Memel Territory, there is a general feeling in Danzig that Danzig will now be definitively annexed by Germany.'

However, Poland had started to bring in army reinforcements around the city, and to make other preparations against any sudden German action. The message was that the Poles would not tolerate any coup in this strategic city, and according to Sopade the message was received and understood in local Nazi circles.[44] Poland, with its 35 million people and large army, was not Lithuania. The question was, did Hitler realize this? And if so, did he care?

The day after Chamberlain's Birmingham speech, the British cabinet also, for the first time, discussed offering assurances to Poland in case of German aggression.

*

Five days after the German entry into Prague, and two days after Chamberlain's speech, a Mass Observation reporter heard two Yorkshire mill workers on a train. Their conversation expressed something of the mercurial and sometimes bizarre mixture of feelings and opinions many ordinary British experienced in the wake of the collapse of Appeasement:

 — Hitler has gone as far as he can.
 — He doesn't care a damn.
 — He must have told lies all along.
 — Air warfare is terrible. That is why our government held back. They want to let them settle their own affairs. It is a shame we have to be mixed up in it.
 — We always get mixed up with these affairs.
 — Our air force is better than Germany because we have the best material.
 — We should take them [Germany] under our government and settle them for good.
 — They want to get on top of us.
 — We ought to be able to manage without getting into wars.
[at this point they got out so I heard no more][45]

Many British considered themselves pacific, and yet were also proud of holding down an empire by force and (like the mill worker in the conversation) fancying their country able to 'take them under our government'. What most did seem to want was some increased element of national unity in the face of the Hitler threat. Sir Anthony Eden, within two days of the seizure of

Czechoslovakia, had called for something of the sort, naturally enough criticizing the failure of Appeasement, though not actually attacking Chamberlain's continuing role as Prime Minister, When there was no immediate positive response to that in parliamentary circles – after all, the country was already ruled by a coalition with an overwhelming majority and had been since 1931 – Eden then proposed something along the lines of a 'Foreign Policy Council' that would provide a forum for all parties to hammer out a way of handling the dictators.

On 18 March, the *Daily Mirror* – which in the absence of a coherent replacement for Appeasement supported both some kind of conscription and the idea of a more broadly based government – carried out one of the opinion round-ups of which it had grown increasingly fond, under the title 'The Way the Wind Blows'. It found, so it said, most of its five apparently random interviewees more or less firmly in favour of something resembling Sir Anthony Eden's suggestion:

> – I agree that something should be done to stop what will undoubtedly come to us.
> – Our Premier's weak policy has given Hitler false courage, but a combined Party, strong in its convictions, should stop this terrible state of affairs.
> – If we are to keep our prestige, it's essential for all parties to combine under a strong leader to fight foreign aggression.
> – I think that what we need is two or three strong right-hand men to help Mr Chamberlain in his arduous duties.

Only one of those asked, a male accountant, stood firm in a kind of bellicose isolationism. Britain should not become mixed up in continental affairs. 'I don't consider that a single English life should be risked until Hitler attacks us directly,' he told the *Mirror*'s reporter. 'Government or no Government, he would then see what England is made of.'[46]

In the same issue, proving that celebrity trumps all else, the *Mirror* also gave over a whole page to a pro-German article by 24-year-old Unity Mitford. A fanatical Nazi supporter and friend of Hitler, she was one of the six glamorous and aristocratic Mitford sisters, daughters of Lord and Lady Redesdale. Her elder sister, Diana, was married to the British Fascist leader Sir Oswald Mosley, while her younger sister, Jessica, had become a dedicated communist. Unity Mitford claimed that the British and Germans, as Nordic races, had everything in common and no real clashes of interest, and that, of course, Hitler himself was pro-British. The two countries should become allies, not enemies. The *Mirror* was keen to proclaim its opposition to her views and solicit its readers' responses ('We Don't Agree with Her and the Editor Asks What You Think!'). More than a thousand wrote in and, with a handful of exceptions, all of them hated her. One of the pro-Mitford correspondents took refuge behind the pen-name of 'Indignant of Birmingham':

> Good luck to Miss Mitford for having the pluck to say what I am sure all thinking people believe to-day.
>
> It is rubbish to say that entering Czechoslovakia was aggression when actually Hitler marched in to pacify the country and stop it from falling to anarchy.
>
> There is no time for sloppiness and sentiment nowadays.
>
> Germany is the strongest power in Europe and it is up to us to recognize it and make a full alliance with her.
>
> Together we would be strong enough to impose our will on all the world.[47]

Mass Observation recorded one or two similar views, including: 'I think Hitler is fine. We want someone like him over here' (Male Railway Clerk, 45: 'identified as a known fascist who had written to the *Liverpool Daily Post* at the time of Munich to call for a general public holiday in celebration').[48]

In general, however, the British public seemed persuaded that Hitler could now definitely not be trusted and that he intended to continue steamrollering through Eastern and South-Eastern Europe, scooping up not just German-speakers but also many millions of non-Germans. Romania, Poland, Hungary were all on his list. Not that this necessarily meant Britain should fight him:

Hitler? What he does isn't bothering me very much. So long as he doesn't bother us; and I don't think he will, you know, so why should we trouble? In any case, some of those European countries are nothing but sources of trouble. They could do with a strong hand, I think.

[asked if there would be a war]

No – as I say, I don't think old Hitler or old Muss [Mussolini] 'll bother us.[49]

And on 20 March, one middle-aged woman in Burnley, Lancashire, was startlingly clear that the whole international situation was a conspiracy:

Housewife . . . thinks there will be no war. The financiers and armaments firms are having a good time. They are the powers behind the scene and no need for war – they are in clover. Hitler will slow down – he has not enough money to start a war. So inclined to be cynical and thinks whole affair may have been engineered . . . Wonders which the 'master' and which the 'puppets'—Hitler & Co. or Chamberlain & Daladier – or are both lots puppets in some unseen hands?

[asked if planned to volunteer]

No interest in ARP or national service.[50]

There were also those who believed that the powers that be were preparing to use the danger of war as a way of introducing authoritarian rule by the back door. A commercial artist (thirty-three) told a Mass Observation reporter in Northampton:

Almost certain no war in Europe between major powers for a number of years. Reactionary elements inside democratic countries are using a period of scares to introduce a form of fascism on the peoples.

ARP and national Register regarded as leading to conscription, involving industrial conscription and loss of bargaining powers of trade unions.[51]

It is possible to over-emphasize the civilian nature of British society in the 1930s. Millions of British men, still in middle age, had experience of military training and combat during the First World War, often as conscripted soldiers, and – as George Orwell pointed out in his sceptical essay 'Democracy in the British Army', written during the middle of 1939 when the national debate about conscription was in full swing – thousands of middle-class British, more especially English, boys who attended elite, fee-paying schools experienced some form of military training:

> A fact not always appreciated by Socialists is that in England the whole of the bourgeoisie is to some extent militarized. Nearly every boy who has been to a public school has passed through the O.T.C. [Officers' Training Corps] (theoretically voluntary but in practice compulsory), and though this training is done between the ages of 13 and 18, it ought not to be despised.[52]

Although every organ of opinion in the country, barring far-right publications such as *Action*, agreed that Hitler had finally lost the political fig leaf provided to his programme of conquest by his 'Germans only' claim, there was still no unity about what Britain's course of action should be. Whereas the German press, under the regime's firm control, began to move in lockstep into a campaign vilifying Britain's supposed policy of 'encirclement', across the Channel, individual as well as press opinions remained varied and often downright eccentric.

The *Daily Express*, as usual, provided some excellent on-the-spot coverage of the invasion of Bohemia and Moravia from its committed and well-resourced reporters. However, in line with its (or rather its proprietor's) determined anti-war stance, the paper awkwardly combined purse-lipped disapproval of Hitler's betrayal over Czecho-Slovakia with a firm defence of the British right, alleged guarantee or no alleged guarantee, not to get involved:

> Mr Chamberlain took a wise course in making the Munich bargain. He is under no necessity of defending that bargain.

But he is also under no necessity of defending Hitler, who has broken the bargain.

Conscription – or 'Compulsion' as the *Express* called it – was the answer, in the paper's view. It went against British peacetime traditions and would act as a signal to the dictators of the country's national determination.

> Will Mr Chamberlain give it to us?
> Twice before he had had the opportunity of an occasion when the people were stirred to their depths. Once when Austria fell. Once again in the Munich Days.
> Now opportunity knocks a third time at Number Ten. Once more the Prime Minister finds the nation waiting responsive, ready, eager to be led. And knowing, too, that if the need was great last September, it is greater by far today.
> Will Mr Chamberlain answer the knock? Will he recognize the summons?[53]

The Prime Minister's public response to Hitler's betrayal on the evening of that same day was gratefully received. Though mildly apprehensive that Chamberlain had not actually mentioned 'Compulsion' in his Birmingham speech, the paper gratefully returned to its well-worn theme of 'no war':

> We make this prediction:-
> Out of the Prime Minister's strong words will come a realisation of the situation in those quarters where that realisation is most urgently needed. And on that account a new term of peace will come to a troubled world.[54]

A bizarre comment by one respondent to Mass Observation's 'March Crisis' on 18 March 1939 may, in its way, have summed up the true feelings of many in the United Kingdom of the time. Britain was privileged to be an offshore island nation of overwhelming linguistic homogeneity, and its people at times showed a spectacular lack of understanding of the problems of continental peoples struggling to navigate in a sometimes chaotic wilderness of nationalities and cultures, without the protection of natural borders. When asked what might be done about the international situation, the woman concerned, forty-eight years old, unmarried, and a Girl Guide commissioner, confessed to her interviewer in obvious exasperation that: 'You really don't know what to say, on what's going to happen next':

> The only thing I can suggest is for every German on Czechoslovakian soil to be stricken suddenly with some fatal disease.[55]

SIX

April/May 1939
'We All Love Him Very, Very Much'

On the morning of Thursday, 20 April 1939, the weather in Berlin was cloudy and cool. By midday, the temperature had nudged up towards 14 centigrade, with occasional spells of sunshine. There was a light wind.

Unspectacular as the weather might have been, the day would bear witness to the grandest military parade since the end of the First World War. It was Adolf Hitler's fiftieth birthday. From the Baltic to the Danube, from the banks of the Rhine to the mouth of the Vistula, millions upon millions of his subjects hung out flags and cheered. Or most of them did.

In Berlin, where Hitler was spending the day being feted and reviewing a giant parade, the event also counted as a kind of opening ceremony for the first section of the planned great 'East–West Axis' which lay at the heart of Hitler's (and his protégé Albert Speer's) dream of transforming Berlin into a 'world capital' renamed Germania. The idea was that this Autobahn-sized highway (50 metres wide in total, with east- and west-heading lanes each 14.5 metres wide) would, within a few years, stretch for 50 kilometres, from Westermark, 30 kilometres west of Berlin, eastward through the city's western suburbs and Charlottenburg, past the Charlottenburg Technical College (now the Technical

University of Berlin), along the Charlottenburger Chaussee (now the Strasse des 17. Juni) to the Brandenburg Gate, and from there on into the historic east-central part of the city, ending at the eastern extremity of the Frankfurter Allee.

The first stretch of the Speer-directed project, opening to coincide with Hitler's significant birthday, was 7 kilometres long, extending westward from the Brandenburg Gate. The 60-metre-high Siegessäule (Victory Column), topped by an 8-metre-high, 35-ton gilded bronze statue of 'Victoria', was moved 1.6 kilometres westward, just about the entire length of the Grosser Tiergarten, to a massive plinth on the Grosser Stern (Great Star) road junction.

The highway had actually been inaugurated by Hitler the previous evening, with an illuminated ceremony in front of an enormous crowd. The Swiss newspaper *Neue Zürcher Zeitung* described it:

> Shouts of 'Heil!' and applause arose from the densely packed rows of spectators as the lengthy convoy of automobiles bearing Hitler and his entourage drove past. At the beginning of the ceremony all the bells sounded from the surrounding churches, which were bedecked with swastika banners.[1]

'There was no question of getting through the crowd,' wrote Ruth Andreas-Friedrich in her diary. She and her partner, out for the evening in central Berlin, found themselves struggling to make their way through the 'laughing, chattering, thrill-seeking' throng that ebbed and flowed around the area. They heard distant choruses of 'Heil! Heil!', gradually coming closer, and realized that Hitler's motorcade was approaching. '"Damn! The Führer!" Leo murmured.'

> [He] forces me with all his might into a side street. Behind us, the crowd is stretching full out to deliver the 'German salute'. 'Sieg Heil! Sieg Heil!' Anyone who doesn't raise their arm will be arrested. When we look around us, we see some fifteen to twenty other people who have likewise wriggled out from the crowd and taken refuge in the quiet side street. 'Good evening',

we greet them in passing. – 'Good evening', is the friendly response. One man, touched by the situation, even smiles and raises his hat.[2]

On the birthday morning itself, there was a reception at the Reich Chancellery that included representatives from twenty-four countries, among them the Papal Nuncio, Monsignor Orsenigo. Orsenigo, a Fascist sympathizer, had been instructed by the new Pope, Pius XII, to offer Hitler the Vatican's warmest congratulations.[3] Other special guests were the newly appointed 'Reich Protector' of Bohemia and Moravia, Konstantin von Neurath, accompanied by the powerless President Hachá ('He does not play a happy role', as Goebbels commented sarcastically), Father Tiso, now Prime Minister of Slovakia, and the Romanian Foreign Minister, Grigore Gafencu. The Burgomaster and Nazi Gauleiter of Danzig, Albert Forster, presented Hitler with a document conferring upon him honorary citizenship of the city.

Just before midday, the Führer and his courtiers were transferred by car 2 kilometres or so to a massive dais in front of the Charlottenburg Technical College. Seated on a throne-like chair surrounded by his aides, Hitler appeared to the German people and the world not just as a successful statesman but, in a new and awe-inspiring way, as warlord and commander-in-chief of a mighty military power. It was a clear message. *We have won a lot without war but we can fight if we must.*

The film historian Fritz Terveen summarized the scene before the huge march past:

It is not just a proud celebratory parade that is beginning here, but a well-calculated spectacle and act of power of absolutely specific domestic and foreign policy significance. Since Munich, Hitler had known only too well that among wide swathes of the population readiness for war was lacking . . . now it could do nothing but good to convey to the people a concentrated vision of the military strength that the Reich had in the meantime achieved, designed to limit any tendency to 'defeatism'.[4]

The seemingly never-ending parade involved some 50,000 troops and took four and a half hours to pass the Führer's vantage point. It was a spectacle designed to thrill the German public – and intimidate foreign observers. Hitler had reportedly told Ribbentrop to ensure that among the invited foreign guests there should be 'as many cowardly civilians and democrats as possible'. Squadrons of new Luftwaffe aircraft roared overhead. The foreign dignitaries did, for the most part, look impressed. Only the Russian military attaché, judging from when the newsreel camera settled on him for an instant, seemed able to maintain an impressive poker face.

The entire parade route was once more thronged with cheering, saluting crowds. Goebbels, the master of these fearsome revels, seemed half-crazed with the glory of it all when he wrote next day in his diary:

> A dazzling image of German might and strength. Our heaviest artillery is shown for the first time. Everyone is immeasurably astonished and stunned. Storms of applause. The Führer is celebrated by the people as no other mortal being has ever before been. This is where we stand. The Goddess of Victory shimmers in the glittering sunlight. A miraculous portent. The public goes wild with delight. I have never seen our people like this before.[5]

On the Propaganda Minister's instructions, a special twenty-minute edition of the Weekly Newsreel had been prepared, in Goebbels's words, 'in order to project an atmosphere of discipline and concentrated power' upon the German public. Twelve specially chosen camera operators had shot nine to ten thousand feet of film[*] from various vantage points during the parade, of which one-twentieth was finally used. This huge amount of material – for a weekly newsreel – was edited together to fit in with carefully selected, dramatic, mostly military music before being quickly released in cinemas throughout the land.[6]

---

[*]　i.e. something between 90 and 100 minutes' running time.

Away from the parade, the entire city was festooned with flags and banners. The atmosphere was fervid, almost religious.

In every shop window stands a photograph of Hitler, framed with laurel leaves. Oversized Hitler pictures hang on the facades of commercial buildings. The highway from the Brandenburg Gate through the Tiergarten and through Charlottenburg . . . is lined with huge gold-bordered flags, monumental pylons and altar-like constructions, on which are enthroned black and gold eagles.[7]

Naturally, the broadcasting network was devoted exclusively to the Führer's birthday, and the press all over Germany brought out illustrated supplements, special articles, and artistic and literary tributes. 'German Peace through the Führer' read one headline. 'To the Greatest Son of Our People' was another. Then (Adolf Hitler's Name – A Programme for the World) and (We Believe in Him). And finally, just simply: 'Wir haben ihn alle sehr, sehr lieb!' (We All Love Him Very, Very, Much!)[8] A doggerel poem printed in the SS newspaper the *Schwarze Korps* was not by any means the only literary tribute to find its way into the public sphere at this point, but it was more or less typical of the general trend:

Führer

We once swore an oath to thee.
We are thine forever.
We lose ourselves eternally,
Like streams into your river.

Even when we cannot comprehend,
We'll trust and follow thee.
You'll let us grasp clear in the end,
The visions you foresee.

Our hearts surround you loyally
Like bronze-cast shields so bold.
To us, it is as if through thee
That God preserves his world.[9]*

Reich Press Chief Otto Dietrich compared Hitler with Julius Caesar, who on his fiftieth birthday had crossed the Rubicon to seize power in Rome, as well as with Charlemagne and Frederick the Great (Hitler's birthday present from the Party had been fifty original letters written by the eighteenth-century Prussian king). Dietrich put him above Alexander the Great and Napoleon 'because the founder of the Greater German Reich did not have the luck of battle and the results of chance to thank for his success, but had proved himself to be a political master-builder of genius'.[10]

Erich Ebermayer, just back in Berlin from a spring visit to Venice, gave the event a cynical but oddly elegiac commentary:

Today Hitler has his 50th birthday. The famous sea of flags waves across the city. And everywhere parades of troops. He's no longer such a youngster . . . as one finds oneself thinking. In general, one imagines him as actually 'ageless'. A robot without the attributes of life. It's altogether impossible to imagine him at 60 or 70. The mild, wise elderly gentleman up on the Berghof, the *pater patriae* [father of the country] – 'no chance of that', as the Berliner would say.[11]

The next day, the London *Times* acknowledged the display as a 'formidable sample of German military might', noting – as had Goebbels – the large-calibre artillery, especially the 5.2-inch anti-aircraft guns (said to be able to hit enemy bombers at a height of up to 35,000 feet), the first appearance of airborne troops in the march past, and the unusually large proportion of motorized vehicles in the parade. This last aspect led the paper's Berlin correspondent to remark rather snidely that the modern military parade had little glamour about it, being 'a monotonously efficient

* Author's free translation.

procession of vehicles and engines of destruction . . . the spirits of the crowd obviously rose when an occasional squadron of dashing cavalry made an appearance'.[12]

The *Daily Express*'s correspondent emphasized the fact that after his return to the Reich Chancellery following the parade, Hitler was prevented from attending a planned visit to a performance of the opera *The Merry Widow* by the crowd's demands that he show himself again and again on the balcony outside. It also ran a piece underneath the headline 'London Nazis Toast Hitler. Guard at Restaurant' which described how 150 members of the London German Club had attended a dinner in honour of the Führer's birthday at the Florence, a venerable Italian restaurant in Rupert Street, Soho. A telegram of congratulations was dispatched by the diners to the great man in Berlin. These festivities were presided over, the article mentions, by none other than Embassy Secretary Theo Kordt, the diplomat with German Resistance connections, whose private opinions of Hitler were, in fact, anything but celebratory.[13]

According to Sopade reports from Germany at this time, the apparently universal ecstasy, though mostly genuine, was in some ways misleading, for 'above all the flag-waving pomp and the celebratory din loomed the paralysing pressure of fear of war'.[14] That Hitler had his millions, and his tens of millions, of admirers, was undoubtedly true. The general populace was certainly convinced that the Nazi leader was a clever politician and a cunning, in fact almost genius, statesman. However, 'it is conceivable that respect for Hitler, the politician, will soon be lost once he experiences a failure in his foreign policy.'[15]

In the industrial areas of Silesia, the same report noted that local Nazi officials had been going from house to house in the working-class districts. Residents were required to sign an assurance indicating they were aware that between 19 and 21 April, inclusive, all windows were to be festooned with flags, and to certify that they were in possession of the appropriate flag:

The display of paper flags was forbidden, and cloth flags had to be displayed in courtyards as well. Anyone who did not possess any flags and was unable to equip themselves with such before the appointed time had to make a note of this on the list, and they would then be provided with flags and pennants on a loan basis by the block supervisor. These instructions were accompanied by a warning that anyone who did not hang out flags on this occasion would be reported to the police as an enemy of the state and would furthermore lose their employment.[16]

In Prague, after just over a month of German occupation, local Nazis and civilians and soldiers of the occupation administration held their own parades for Hitler's birthday. Meanwhile, a rumour spread among the Czechs that flowers were being laid on the Jan Hus Memorial on the Old Square in the city. The great fourteenth-century Bohemian religious reformer's martyrdom in 1415 at the hands of the Catholic authorities had unleashed a great revolt against the Roman Church in the Czech lands and initiated the 'Hussite' golden age in the national history. This had lasted for nearly two hundred years, ending with the imposition of Catholic, German-speaking Austrian rule.

According to the Prague correspondent of *The Times*, by 7 p.m. on the evening of 20 April 1939, as, hundreds of kilometres to the north, noisy crowds were still thronging outside the Reich Chancellery in Berlin, at the foot of the steps leading up to the Hus Monument some 30,000 bunches of primroses had been placed, generally in prayerful silence, by ordinary Czech citizens. At the front of the Monument, foot-high floral lettering spelled out the abbreviated version of one of Hus's most famous pronouncements, which had been adopted as its motto by the post-1918 Czechoslovak Republic: *Pravda Vitezi* ('Truth Prevails').[17]

*

There had been plenty of guns in evidence around Berlin that April, but not so much butter. True, Germany now enjoyed full employment – so conclusively, said the SD's report on economic affairs, that with a mere 140,000 German males jobless at the end of March 1939 the authorities had decided not to publish employment figures in future. To do so would, it was claimed, indicate mostly just natural turnover in the labour market rather than actual shortage of work, and thereby give a false impression.[18]

However, wages remained low compared with those in other advanced industrial countries, especially for industrial workers. The Nazi Party could and did remind the labouring population constantly of the terror of unemployment, which had now been banished. There was nonetheless widespread ill-feeling, as even jargon-laden Party reports admitted, about the fact that 'the population has concerns, which have their origins not at all in honourable commitment in case of war, but in worries about social and nutritional-political questions'.[19] There were emerging serious shortages of basic foodstuffs, with one report from the Ruhr complaining of the fact that wholesalers were going to the central market in Essen, the largest local city, and finding little available. 'Mostly the merchants return with empty trucks, without receiving any allocation of vegetables. The population's anger at this is very great.'[20] Many items were price-controlled and their availability therefore vulnerable to black-market-like tactics:

> There was no kale to be had anywhere at the market, until somewhat late in the day a merchant arrived with a large basket of it. By the time the women came to buy, he had already established that he alone in the entire market had kale. He loaded it back on his cart and said: 'Looking at the way these females are flocking round the kale, I'd be better off taking it back home and eating it myself.' Probably he could make more money selling it [i.e. on the black market] in his own neighbourhood. Given the proverbial insolence of the merchants and their own anxiety not to get involved in a scene, the women unfortunately did not pluck up the courage to report this disgraceful attitude to the Trading Standards Police.[21]

Shortages of items like coffee – actual, subtropically grown coffee rather than malt or chicory or other home-grown vegetable substitutes – were becoming a considerable problem, especially for the middle classes. People liked their real coffee, but the Nazi regime's autarkical economic policies meant that priority for foreign currency expenditure was given to essential materials and minerals for armaments production rather than to 'luxury' imported items.

In January 1939, a Party report for the *Gau* leadership in Westphalia specifically mentioned 'coffee hoarding' (*Kaffeehamsterei*) as a problem, especially in the cities and among 'the better-situated classes'. In the wealthier districts of Berlin, for instance, women queued outside specialist shops and snapped up supplies immediately they became available. 'Here we must intervene with drastic methods in such circumstances, so as to make such "coffee-patriots" ridiculous in the public eye. And as and where it occurs!' the report declared.[22] Goebbels himself was stirred to write an article in the *Völkischer Beobachter* attacking the '*Kaffeetanten*' (literally: 'coffee aunts') who were making fools of themselves by scrambling to get supplies of what was, after all, an exotic luxury beverage too expensive for the broad masses to enjoy on a regular basis. Anyway, coffee was not especially salubrious. In fact, Goebbels sniffed, 'A shortage [of coffee] is extremely conducive to general family health.'[23]

The fact was that the standard of living in the country was not (and arguably never had been) as high as that in, say, America, or even Britain. Hitler had stated in an interview: 'I have the ambition to make the German people rich and Germany beautiful. I want to see the living standard of the individual raised.' However, as the economic historian Adam Tooze has pointed out, 'By the standards of the day, let alone by the standards of the later twentieth century, Germany in the 1920s and 1930s was not an affluent society.' Income per head – a basic measure of comparative standards of living in Germany – was exactly half that in the United States during this period and no more than two-thirds of that in Britain.[24]

There is no question that between 1933 and 1939 the German economy recovered and expanded, but at no time did the national investment in consumer industries regain anything like the level it had reached before the Depression. The overwhelming majority of the increase went into armaments, aircraft and shipbuilding, and various forms of war-related infrastructure, as well as hugely expensive developments of synthetic fuel capacity and rubber, designed to make Germany self-sufficient in case of war.

Real incomes for most Germans also lagged behind those enjoyed in the later years of the Weimar Republic, even though Gross National Product had increased by 31 per cent since the Nazis took power. Taxes had been sharply increased, and there were dues to be paid to the Nazi Party and its institutions that had not existed in democratic times. Josepha von Koskull, a single working woman in her late thirties in Berlin, remembered the more problematic side of the Nazi 'miracle':

> With each salary adjustment, of which there were several after the 'seizure of power', I had my salary reduced, because I was, of course, not a Party member. As a librarian in the end I was receiving a salary less than that of the secretaries. My little flat became almost too expensive for me. Long before Hermann Göring offered us guns instead of butter, I was buying margarine instead of butter and was forced to do without coffee, cake on a Sunday, and much else besides.
>
> Out of my small salary I had to pay contributions to the Labour Front, the People's Welfare, and the Air Raid Protection. One could not avoid belonging to these three organizations if one was employed in the Third Reich. During the half-year of winter one also had the contributions to the Winter Aid. Those few Marks all added up.[25]

In Westphalia, at around the time of Munich, a whole section of the *Gau* Inspector's report was devoted to growing unrest among the region's miners, whose situation was 'almost catastrophic'. Wages remained low, piecework targets were constantly being screwed higher and longer hours imposed. The Party's plea for productivity increases was falling on deaf ears. Sons, the report noted, were not following their fathers down the mines. 'In general,' it observed, 'there exists in the working population a fundamental aversion to becoming a miner,' and continued:

The worker is aware that every mining company is currently operating at a profit, and is therefore surprised that heavy industry makes so few concessions when it comes to shaping workers' free time, especially making vacation times more attractive through 'Strength Through Joy' etc., as, fortunately, other enterprises do.

'Anchoring the National Socialist world view here,' the reporter advised, 'would be easier at the moment if these hard-working people were granted the standard of living they deserve.'[26]

Observing similar accounts of workers' complaints from its informants inside Germany, the socialist exile Sopade reports did not, naturally enough, attempt to gild the lily of exploitation in the way that Nazi sources, however sympathetic on a human level to workers' grievances, were bound to do. For the Sopade, exploitation was exploitation, and only to be expected under fascism. Although, technically, Germany was still subject to the eight-hour-day law introduced under the Weimar Republic, in fact normal working days for adult males (women's and juveniles' workdays were still quite strictly regulated) were between nine and ten hours – for which overtime rates were not paid – and productivity targets were constantly being increased. Exhaustion was common, and productivity therefore suffered, as even some of the tame industrial press was beginning to point out. Young workers were deserting mining and agriculture for better-paid, cleaner, less onerous work in modern factories. This was growing so problematic that in March 1939 an order regarding 'Restriction of Changing Jobs' was promulgated, requiring official permission to move jobs if the change took workers out of branches of industry deemed crucial to the nation, including agriculture, forestry, mining, and iron and steel.[27] According to figures from the German Labour Front, by late spring 1939 there was a shortage of 50,000 miners in Germany.[28]

Everything was being subordinated to what the socialist exiles called the 'crazy tempo' of rearmament. The proportion of German national income spent on consumer goods in 1928 had been 71 per cent; by 1938 it had fallen to 59 per cent. Defence and armaments expenditure amounted to 23 per cent of total national spending. Again, this stood in sharp contrast to Britain, where during those same years, to some extent aided by cheap imports, consumption of consumer goods continued to increase at a brisk pace.[29] Britain continued, it was true, to be a grossly unequal place, and unemployment remained relatively high. German newspapers regularly reported (at Goebbels's direction) with great glee about British jobless figures. There was a demonstration just before Christmas 1938 by unemployed workers in London at the Ritz Hotel's Grill Room. Some forty-five protesters marched in and ordered tea (which they said they were prepared to pay for) but were not served. Police eventually persuaded them to leave.

The Ritz incident was seized upon eagerly ('Unusual Guests at the Ritz') by Goebbels's German News Agency, illustrating as it did the failure of Europe's greatest democracy to provide work for its citizens. At the same time, the story usefully highlighted the still-prevalent snobbery and hypocrisy at the heart of British society, which compared badly with the supposedly egalitarian 'racial community' of proudly non-democratic Nazi Germany. However, the Ritz Grill Room was actually closed at the time the National Association of Unemployed Workers mounted its stunt, a fact that the British press mentioned but the German News Agency did not.[30]

*

In 1939 Britain had roughly double the number of private cars on the road – about 2 million – compared with Germany, even though one of Hitler's first acts had been to reduce the tax on new automobile sales. The problem lay in the general purchasing power (or relative lack of it) in Germany, even among the supposedly well-off middle class.

The disparity in absolute ownership levels – two to one – was even greater, since Britain had only 47 million people compared with Germany's 67 million (79 million after the annexations of Austria, the Sudetenland and Memel). One in twenty-five Britons owned a car as against one German in sixty. Car ownership in the United States, home of Ford and General Motors, massively exceeded that in any other advanced society. In 1939 there were more than 26 million registered private vehicles in the country, which meant one car for every five Americans out of a population of 131 million.[31]

In 1937, the German Labour Front conducted a survey which calculated the average wage in Germany at 182 Reichsmarks a month. Of this, rent, heating, food and clothing took up 85 per cent. What little was left over allowed 4 Reichsmarks for furniture and housewares, 6 Reichsmarks for education, entertainment and leisure, 2 Reichsmarks for transport, and a meagre 80 pfennigs for vacations and excursions. Another study in 1938 showed that, for a family of four, on an annual income of 2,300 Reichsmarks, after allowing for food, housing and utility bills, owning even a modest vehicle running 10,000 kilometres a year would consume their entire disposable income.[32]

For all that the country still lagged behind other industrial nations, between 1933 and 1939 the number of privately owned cars in Germany had trebled. By the mid-1930s, Inge Lueg's father, a manager at the chemical concern Bayer, had bought a car, a little Opel, which meant that this well-to-do middle-class family could cut a dash in the neighbourhood and take quite wide-ranging holidays, venturing up to the Baltic coast and visiting relations on the way back to their home in the Rhineland.[33]

Erich Ebermayer also owned a car. He had been heading back to where he had parked it in central Berlin on *Kristallnacht*, when he found himself forced to watch the Fasanenstrasse synagogue burning down. More happily, the mobility provided by the car allowed him to buy his derelict castle near Bayreuth.

Victor Klemperer, the academic and diarist, had bought a second-hand Opel in March 1936. He was both thrilled and intimidated by the experience. First, he had to pass his driving test. Then, a garage had to be built onto the front of his house in Dölzschen, on the outskirts of Dresden. It all cost a lot of money and worry. Also, for a man who had just been forced out of his teaching post at the Technical University because of his

Jewish heritage, the price of this new freedom of movement represented a considerable financial risk. At the time he wrote:

> The car was bought on 2 March. 850M – but 19M a month tax on top of that. Opel 32 hp, 6 cylinders, built 1932, completely open . . . I can only drive it once the papers have been obtained from Brandenburg district. Will I be able to drive? How will my nerves, how will my money bear up? 19M tax, 33M insurance a month! The whole thing a desperado adventure . . .[34]

Although he did not actually drive, the Führer was well known as a keen car fan, who enjoyed being chauffeured around at speed. Beginning in the early 1920s, Hitler had been consistently preaching the virtues of a 'motorized Germany'. After seizing power, he kept giving impatient speeches, especially at motor shows, urging manufacturers to make cheaper cars that would open up the freedom of the road to ordinary members of the 'racial community'.

Finally, largely at Hitler's insistence, the state intervened. The brilliant automobile designer Ferdinand Porsche was charged with creating the famous Volkswagen or 'People's Car'. The term Volkswagen, incidentally, was not new. It had been used frequently to describe affordable personal transport for at least a decade previously in German car manufacturers' advertisements and promotions – so much so that the term had to be trademarked in the mid-1930s in order to prevent their continuing to use it.[35]

Hitler had also ordered that the cheap, efficient personal runabout must be sold for less than a thousand Reichsmarks. Germany's hitherto most affordable car, the Opel P4, produced by the American General Motors' German subsidiary, remained stuck at a showroom sale price of 1,450 Reichsmarks, despite extensive cost savings through advanced production-line techniques imported from Detroit.

Since, for propaganda reasons, the cost of the proposed car was below just about any conceivable market-based price, the Volkswagen project was heavily subsidized. The project provided yet another state-enforced distortion in a German economy already warped almost beyond bearing by a bloated rearmament effort carried out against a background of autarky, crazy over-spending, and serious foreign currency shortages. The idea being that the Volkswagen would be sold to blue-collar German workers, the project was handed over to the German Labour Front, to be run as a non-profit enterprise.

The car would not be for sale in the usual manner, through dealerships, but only as the end product of a savings scheme organized by the Labour Front via its leisure and travel subsidiary, 'Strength Through Joy' (*Kraft durch Freude* = KdF). The would-be owner was expected to make a weekly deposit of at least 5 Reichsmarks. It was promised that when the account reached 750 Reichsmarks the saver was entitled to an order number and delivery date for the car. On delivery the owner would be required to take out a two-year insurance policy costing 200 Reichsmarks, in itself a considerable sum. Membership of a Party organization was required.

The Labour Front was supposed to subsidize the project by liquidating assets it had 'inherited' from the pre-Nazi trade unions when these assets were seized in 1933. Porsche had typically ambitious plans to build a motor-manufacturing complex at Fallersleben in mid-Germany (later renamed Wolfsburg), with 450,000 vehicles a year to be produced in the first phase. It would eventually have the capacity to build 1.5 million units of the KdF-Wagen annually. This would make Fallersleben larger than Henry Ford's massive River Rouge plant at Dearborn, Michigan, until then the biggest car-production facility in the world.

According to the Sopade reports from inside Germany, the initial announcement led to a rush on the KdF sales offices, whose staff had not yet received proper training. There was a delay before proper paperwork became available, and even then, in their haste the designers of the application form had forgotten the all-important loyalty question for purchasers: 'Are You a Member of the National Socialist Welfare?'[36]

The vehicle was certainly competently designed. Two adults could fit in the front and three children in the back. Its rear-mounted 995cc engine exerted 23 horsepower. It could cruise at 100 kilometres an hour (just over 60 mph), the speed needed to keep traffic flowing on the new *Reichsautobahnen*. It used petrol – which was expensive – at the rate of 7 litres per 100 km (39 miles to the British imperial gallon). Its shape, rounded and shell-like, led it to be given the nickname *Käfer* (beetle). The car was characterful, modern, and seemed to presage a more prosperous future. Even the Sopade agents had to admit that the KdF-Wagen counted as a propaganda triumph for the regime:

> For a large number of Germans, the announcement of the People's Car is a great and happy surprise. A real Strength-Through-Joy car-psychosis developed. For a long time the car was a main topic of conversation in all sections of the population in Germany. All other pressing problems, whether of domestic or foreign policy, were pushed into the background for the moment. The grey German everyday was forgotten under the impression of this music of the future. Wherever the test models of the new Strength-Through-Joy construction are seen in Germany, crowds gather around them. The politician who promises a car for everyone is the man of the masses if the masses believe his promises. And as far as the Strength-Through-Joy car is concerned, the German people do believe in Hitler's promises.[37]

It may or may not have been coincidence that a quite prominent article taken from a Labour Front press release, entitled 'How Does One Quickly Get to a KdF-Wagen?', appeared in the *Pommersche Zeitung* on 12 November 1938. The rest of the paper was filled with the brutal aftermath of *Kristallnacht*, with reports on the 'Jewish plot' behind the murder of vom Rath in Paris, on the brutal new restrictions on Jews, and on huge anti-Semitic hate rallies being addressed by the local Stettin Gauleiter.[38] Thinking about the KdF-Wagen – a reliable 'good-news story' – may have helped give the readers a little essential light relief.

By the end of 1939, 270,000 Germans had signed up, putting 170 million Reichsmarks into an escrow account of the Labour

Front, without a single private individual taking possession of a car. Jokes were made about the cunning of the government and of Hitler himself, in persuading ordinary people to pay up front in this way. 'Adolf has a head on his shoulders,' Sopade reported one contact commenting. 'Builds the biggest factory in the world without having to use a pfennig of his own capital.' Another added a dark pay-off suitable for the times:

> Has there ever in the world been such a canny stunt? To get paid for a product when the factory that's supposed to make it has only just started to be built. Even the smartest Jew couldn't match you in that.[39]

In total, some 370,000 savers had paid into KdF-Wagen accounts by the end of 1940. However, compared with the initial enthusiasm, and the numbers bandied about in 1937–8, this was disappointing.

The SS Security Service was altogether less impressed than Sopade, perhaps because it had inside access to the stark financial facts of the matter. Its report did not mince words. Despite a huge sales campaign by the KdF organization, 'the people' did not seem willing or able to buy 'the People's Car':

> The orders for the KdF-Wagen have not so far corresponded to expectations, so that the first year's production has not yet been sold. The participation of the working population is reckoned at 3 to 4 per cent.[40]

In other words, the cheap car for the masses was mostly being bought by those who could have afforded one of the other models available before the KdF-Wagen was put on offer. A further government survey would show that the average KdF-Wagen saver had a very comfortable income of 4,000 Reichsmarks a year, about twice the typical worker's salary.[41] Moreover, a third of them did, in fact, already own a car.

The most widely purchased petrol-driven vehicle bought by actual workers remained the motorcycle, which cost as little as

250 Reichsmarks, but the most popular system for private transport in general remained the one based on pedal power. There
were some 20 million bicycles in the Germany of the time.

Especially against the background of frantic expenditure on
armaments, the average German consumer was simply too *poor*
to support a universal car culture, and would remain so for
another twenty or more years. Nonetheless, from 1937 onwards,
until war intervened, the KdF-Wagen project was relentlessly
pushed ahead, as if by wishing Germany to become America,
Hitler and his underlings could make it so. The German post
office even released a postage stamp with the car's image on it.
It was a perfect example of the regime's 'blend of propaganda
and illusionary politics'.[42]

*

The Führer's dream of a car that would turn Germany into a
motorized society akin to America's was just that: a dream. Not
for the first or the last time, the regime's grandiose plans did not
correspond to the country's capacity to achieve them. The German
word for this syndrome is *Machbarkeitswahn* – a manic delusion
of feasibility, of the world inevitably bending to the will, if that
will – and, in particular, the supposedly biologically superior
German will – just wants it enough. The next few years would
show that this problem did not apply only in the relatively harmless realm of consumer goods.

The addition of the prefix *Volks-* ('People's') to almost any
basic commercially available item was common in the Nazi era.
It implied affordability, made possible by standardization, mass
production and state approval. Its subtext was a promise, however
pale, of the glittering mass consumer society that would surely
follow the current time of austerity, once Germany's needs for
raw materials for armaments and territory for expansion had
been fulfilled.

After the Volkswagen, the most successful of such products
was the Volksëmpfänger, or 'People's Radio Receiver'. There were
already more than 4 million licensed radio sets in Germany in
January 1933, but Goebbels, aware of the propaganda advantage

that a Nazi-controlled radio would give the regime, had urged
the design of a cheap universal radio set for the masses almost
from the moment the Nazis seized power.

A prototype of just such a basic, no-frills radio was displayed
at the Berlin Radio Exhibition later in 1933. Selling at
76 Reichsmarks, its cost represented just less than two weeks'
wages for the average worker. The official radio licence fee added
another 2 Reichsmarks per month. By 1937, the radio set's price
was down to 65 Reichsmarks. A smaller, even more basic receiver
sold for 35 Reichsmarks. Its larger sibling had sold 2.8 million
by 1938, while the small receiver, which eventually sold
2.5 million units, was given the semi-affectionate nickname
Goebbelsschnauze ('Goebbels-Gob') by the general populace.
Goebbels's association with these cheap radio sets was one of
his proudest achievements, and he mentioned it often. In the
same chilling diary entry (10 November 1938) in which he
rejoiced at *Kristallnacht* in Munich, he found time to record with
delight the fact that the ten-millionth German radio set had now
been licensed.

The radio was for Goebbels perhaps his most successful and
subtle propaganda instrument. He knew better than to fill the
broadcasting days with tedious, obvious propaganda. Günter
Hätte, a teenager in Hamburg at the time, recalled:

> The so-called 'little people' could at last afford a radio. The
> 'Goebbels-Gob' made it possible. That was the general public's
> word for the cheap subsidized receiver. Of course, the Reich
> Propaganda Minister had his own motives for this. National
> Socialist ideology could now be spread into every family, skil-
> fully packaged between entertaining music programmes.
> Anyway, from now on merry tunes, folk songs, and above all
> marching music resounded in almost every household. I can
> still well recall the Saturday afternoons when the folksy enter-
> tainment programmes were broadcast . . . At those times people
> would gather by the radio, as they do now in front of the
> television set.[43]

Whether government promotion of the 'People's Radio' played a role in the rapid expansion of listener numbers is a matter for debate. Other countries, where there was no government subsidy, developed just as quickly. In Britain in 1939, 66 per cent of households had access to a radio as against Germany's 46 per cent. In America the proportion was almost 90 per cent.[44]

Television had been inaugurated on 22 March 1935, transmitting from a studio in Berlin-Witzleben, a district of Charlottenburg. It was claimed to be the first public television station in the world. Eugen Hadamovsky, the head of German Radio, declared that: 'In this hour, broadcasting is called to its greatest and most sacred mission: to implant the image of the Führer indelibly into all German hearts.'[45]

In Britain, the BBC would not begin its own television service until the next year, but when it did, it provided a high-definition 405-line picture, and soon the ability to reach thousands of homes. The German system was technically inferior, using mechanical cameras and giving only a 180-line picture. It seemed that, in fact, the main object of the exercise was to be 'first' at all costs, ahead of the British. However, by 1937, with early electronic cameras in use, the picture quality at 441 lines was slightly superior to that provided by the BBC.

The most telling difference between television broadcasting in the two countries lay in the number of private television sets. In Germany, the method used to reach the general population was through public *Fernsehstuben* (television rooms). Despite the small screens of the sets, these at first attracted considerable crowds, drawn to the novel and thrilling notion of 'live' images. The television rooms were initially available only in Berlin, then in Potsdam and in Leipzig and later Hamburg. A few hundred receivers were distributed to prominent Nazis, including Goebbels and Göring, and to senior media and arts functionaries.

One hundred and sixty thousand enthusiastic viewers were said to have watched the continuous broadcasts from the 1936 Olympic Games, running for eight hours a day. For the Games, the number of these rooms was increased in both number and size, so that some could hold up to 400 viewers. The still-tiny image, roughly the size of an A4 sheet of paper, was sometimes captured and projected onto a screen for these larger audiences. Another favourite in the rooms, perhaps not surprising in a police state, was *Die Kriminalpolizei Warnt!* (*The Criminal Police Warns!*), the earliest version of the still perennially popular viewers-help-with-unsolved-crimes show.

Otherwise, much of the programming was boring and repetitive, and the images not always of best quality, so that after the excitement of the Olympics audiences generally slackened off. There are indications that for some Berliners the television rooms were prized, in the winter, mainly as a 'cheap source of warmth'.[46] Until picture quality improved and screens got bigger, there was also a widespread feeling that, compared with radio or cinema, television could limit as much as enhance personal horizons. Four years after the first broadcasts, a German journalist specializing in broadcasting could still write uneasily:

> On a fine summer evening, it is true that one gladly listens to radio music out on the balcony, but one goes only reluctantly from the warmth and light into a room to sit, in an oppressively airless, closed space, to look at images.[47]

It was not until 1939 that the sale of a specially designed television receiver for the German general public was announced, under some pressure from the manufacturers, who had invested so much in developing the technology. The set, a sort of televisual equivalent of the People's Radio Receiver, would carry a price tag of 650 Reichsmarks – more than four months of the average wage and two-thirds of the price of a KdF-Wagen – and consequently constituted another miracle of technology reserved, during the foreseeable future, for the middle and upper classes rather than the masses. A mere 10,000 were due to be produced.

Perhaps it was too much to prefix such a costly item with '*Volks-*'. Introduced to the public at the Berlin Radio Exhibition on 28 July 1939 in the presence of Minister Goebbels, it was given the title of E1 Einheits-Fernseher (E1 Uniform-Television Set). The entire apparatus, including separate speaker, measured

25.5″ long by 14.5″ high by 15″ deep. The screen, with a clear 441-line picture, was 7.7″ by 8.6″. The proposed release date was Christmas 1939.

Television in Germany was a joint project between the Reich Post Office, the Ministry of Propaganda, and Göring's Air Ministry. Apart from the technology's obvious use in air defence, there was also the thought that orders might one day be instantly shareable with geographically distant military commanders via a special, secret Wehrmacht television network. This three-way collaboration led to vicious inter-ministerial conflicts, but also to lavish funding, especially in view of the potential military appli-cations, which guaranteed high priority.[48]

In Britain, by contrast, BBC television was still a poor relation of radio, with a budget of only £400,000 a year to radio's £3 million. All the same, by 1939 some 20,000 British owners of TV sets could watch programmes in their own homes, mostly within 20 miles of the BBC transmitter at Alexandra Palace, in North London. The number of sets sold had doubled in the previous year alone. Total regular audiences were reckoned at around 100,000.[49] And audiences did not share the mixed feelings that seemed to bedevil television watching in collectivized, tightly controlled Germany. There were plans to reach 25 million poten-tial viewers through regional transmitters, beginning in 1940 with Birmingham, which was already linked to London by a high-capacity GPO cable.

In November 1938, the BBC undertook its first direct broad-cast of a West End play. A performance of J.B. Priestley's comedy *When We Are Married* at St Martin's Theatre was fed through to the Alexandra Palace transmitter via a GPO coaxial cable that had been installed through central London. Major sporting events were also shown, as a result of triangular deals between cinema chains, sports promoters and the BBC. In February 1939, the Corporation achieved a world 'first' when it televised the British lightweight title fight at Harringay Arena, between Eric 'Boy' Boon from the Fenlands and Arthur Danahar from Bethnal Green, London. It went to fourteen punishing rounds, and the success of the broadcast led to a new surge in demand for television sets.

As a result of the deal between the cash-strapped BBC, the National Sporting Club and the fight promoters, the latter were granted rights to run a live feed of the BBC broadcast to a selection of cinemas, where paying audiences had the thrill of watching the sell-out fight as it happened. As John Macadam of the *Daily Express* proclaimed, the Boon–Danahar fight 'put a new industry on the map':

> The thing bristles with possibilities. There is fighting – the new television combination is prepared to do business with all boxing promoters, including Wembley and Harringay, who stage the Harvey–Gains fight shortly – there is professional tennis, there is the Boat-race, the Cup Final, Test matches. Why, there is just everything that the sporting world can offer.[50]

Macadam, one of the most distinguished sports journalists of his day, correctly predicted that the days were gone of boxers laboriously making careers from fighting in provincial halls until, if they were lucky, they got a major fight in front of a decent-sized crowd. 'Now,' he wrote, 'with television and cine-television forcing him on the public he can jump into stardom overnight. And when he is a star, he can command more money from one fight than he could have from a dozen before.' This would be true of other sports, too, but boxing was the prototype for this kind of path to success.

The next month, the day after Hitler invaded Czecho-Slovakia, Cornish heavyweight Len Harvey fought Larry Gains of Canada for the British Empire title, and won. James Agate, the legendary journalist and critic, watched on his set at home ('I saw the fight by television'), reporting drily that the fight ended when Harvey 'opened up some wild country above Gains's left eye'.[51]

In Britain, television was unquestionably regarded optimistically by the mass and the elite alike. The *Express* led a campaign calling for the expansion of a service that everyone seemed to want: 'More money should be spent. Television should be relayed to the whole country.'[52] It was the wave of the future. *Express* readers' thoughts were already turning in truly prophetic directions. 'But oh,' wrote one, 'how nice it will be when we can shop by television!'[53]

Television technology was progressing with impressive speed. Even though, as the *Express* reminded its readers, it was 'only as old now as was radio in the age of the "cat's whisker", technically it is already far ahead.' This was true in both Britain and Germany.

If the chief ground for delays in the expansion of the television service in Britain was bureaucratic parsimony, in Germany there may have been a more hidden, in fact quite sinister, reasoning behind the slowness of its spread. The regime was fascinated by technology of all kinds, and television was no exception, but it also liked government control over publicly available media to be as complete as possible. Television was overwhelmingly a live medium, the effect of its intimate-feeling images could not be predicted with certainty, and people experiencing it in the privacy of their own homes had the freedom to react as they wished. The regime's decision-makers, even the propaganda wizards at Goebbels's ministry, were not quite sure what to do with it – apart from celebrating the technological miracle that television represented.

One unignorable problem was, what if Goebbels or Hitler or some other key Nazi figure had appeared on television looking less than perfect, and perhaps stumbling over his or her script? What if – unthinkable for a Nazi propagandist – Hitler himself came into your home via television and *you switched him off*?[54] As one German film magazine of the time suggested:

> In television broadcasting one cannot edit something out after-wards or insert it in, if from time to time an image does not correspond with the way it had been imagined. If such a thing sneaks into the camera tube, it then races as quickly as a thought through the ether and into the television picture of the receiver; and once that has happened no one can charm it out of existence again.[55]

In fact, none of the Nazi leaders ever broadcast directly to the public through television. Scenes from the Nazis' Nuremberg congresses were transmitted in September 1937 and September 1938, but most of the material was in long shot, it seems.

Radio was, in any case, much easier to control. The authorities knew how to use it. During the first four years of television in Germany, home reception was therefore confined to trusted members of the Party and media elites, with general, unrestricted access occurring only in the public 'television rooms'. Here, as in cinemas, the environment as well as the content could be controlled and policed.

The '*Volks-*' craze went on. There were even to be *Volkswohnungen* ('People's Flats' – cheap apartments made possible by generous government aid and mass-produced building components) that would solve the severe housing shortage. Given the need to keep rents low, the designs ended up limiting electricity supply to lighting only, and having only communal bathrooms, as well as offering a claustrophobically small amount of living space.[56]

Whether the *Volkswohnungen* would have been a longer-term success is hard to say. The regime might boast that it cared for its citizens' everyday needs and lives, but war, or the possibility of war, took priority over everything else. There seems little doubt that the chief problem in making the *Volkswohnungen* scheme work, as in other areas of life-improvement for the average German, lay in the fact that even in the pre-war period the armaments industry took absolute precedence. It ate up almost all the materials, labour and financial subsidies that would, in a more civilian-oriented – a more 'normal' – society, have gone into general, peaceable, human needs.

The Third Reich was still a capitalist society, but altogether more heavily regulated and directed by government than Britain or the USA (even taking into account the rush of government intervention following Roosevelt's election and the 'New Deal'). The primacy of rearmament trumped all normal business calculations.

Nor, unlike contemporary Britain or America, could the Reich be called a 'consumer society'. This was the case despite full employment, aspects of a welfare state, a superficial sheen of prosperity – 'The beautiful illusion of the Third Reich' as the historian Peter Reichel called it – and the simulation of plenty encouraged by all the various 'people's' products. In fact, few of these actually succeeded (the *Volkskühlschrank* or 'People's Refrigerator', for instance, got no further than the drawing board). There was no real play of supply and demand.

Ultimately, Nazism was a firmly collectivist philosophy. It was willing to harness individual and corporate enterprise, but – in contrast with Britain's Baldwin and Chamberlain and most of their ministers – the instincts of its leadership were those not of the merchant but of the warrior chief. It was no coincidence that one of the advertisements encouraging saving for the KdF-Wagen showed a small boy outside his house, admiring the new family vehicle parked at the front gate. Behind him he is trailing a toy replica of a field gun.

*

By the end of April 1939, Johann Eichhorn had been held in Munich's Stadelheim Prison for three months. He had from the beginning undertaken a strategy of systematic denial, conceding only two previous sexual assaults committed in 1928. He was actually guilty of dozens of rapes and sexual assaults, going back to the late 1920s. Finally forced to concede others after being identified by a series of survivors, he was charged with thirty-four counts of rape, to some of which he eventually confessed.

The Munich Kripo (Criminal Police) had by now learned something of Eichhorn's modus operandi and character, and harboured suspicions that he might have been involved in unsolved murders of women in the Munich region. Eichhorn, though he conceded the non-capital sexual offences, continued to deny killing anyone.

Then, on 25 April 1939, the corpse of Maria Jörg was discovered by chance in her shallow grave in the Forstenrieder Park. The gunshot wound to the head and the terrible genital mutilations were similar to those inflicted on previous murder victims. Items found in Eichhorn's possession, and his known past ownership of a gun, pointed clearly to his involvement.

However, Johann Eichhorn still stubbornly denied having killed women, and without a confession the police would have difficulty getting convictions. All the same, the trial for the rapes was postponed, clearly so as not to impede possible indictments on the murder charges.[57]

*

Out in the great world, following the last in the wave of annexations, and then the grand climax of the Führer's fiftieth birthday, everyone seemed to take stock.

What next? Where next? Until the invasion of Czecho-Slovakia, the British had appeared ready to accept German hegemony in Central and South-East Europe as the price for avoiding a possible attack by the Axis powers on their Empire. After Hitler's armies occupied Prague, however, it had grown clear even to the most Appeasement-fixated members of the British elite that the Führer had finally abandoned the world of international order and agreements.

Talk of guarantees for his next most likely target, Poland – though not, as yet, any concrete or binding suggestions as to how these might be framed – had begun to fill the British press and transform the mood-music of the political world. It was now all about deterrence. Above all, the notion that Britain might, for the first time in its history, introduce peacetime military conscription was beginning to find widespread public acceptance.

Alone of all the European powers, Britain imposed no compulsory military service on its male population. With an army of only 180,000 men (spread in great part over large swathes of the Empire) and a territorial army of 130,000, all the rearmament in the world would not give the country a force able to face the combined strengths of Germany, Italy and the other Axis satellites – not to mention the threat of Japan, in the Far East. On 27 April 1939, Leslie Hore-Belisha, Secretary of State for War (and, because of his Jewish heritage, a favourite target for Nazi propagandists), announced a draft conscription law.

The legislation, known as the Military Training Act, passed parliament on 26 May. It was not really comparable with the continental model. All able-bodied males of twenty and twenty-one

– a total of some 200,000 men – would be called up, not for formal service in the armed forces, but – as the name of the legislation implied – for a period of six months' training.

The trainees would be known as 'Militiamen' to distinguish them clearly from professional soldiers. Each would receive not only a uniform and equipment but also, in a nicely unmilitaristic, almost Wodehousian, touch, a civilian 'walking out' suit. Registration would begin on 3 June, via the labour exchanges, further underlining the civilian status of the participants.

As Janet Flanner, Paris-based correspondent of the *New Yorker*, commented, the British were 'still moving with all their traditional majesty'. She hoped that 'Herr Hitler doesn't mind waiting for them'.[58]

The traditionally anti-militarist Labour Party opposed the bill at first. Its leader, Clement Attlee, argued that it would 'divide the country' (and especially vex Labour's allies, the trade unions, who were anxious it might be followed by industrial conscription, undermining workers' rights and wages). However, in the end Labour agreed not to vote against it, provided the government agreed to amendments guaranteeing that men would get their jobs back at the end of the training period, their dependants would be provided for, and conscientious objectors protected.[59]

Chamberlain all but apologized for the entire unfortunate necessity. As for the novelty of peacetime conscription:

We are not at war now, but when every country is straining all its resources to be ready for war, when confidence in the main-tenance of peace is being undermined, and everyone knows that if war were to come we might pass into it in a matter, not of weeks, but of hours, no one can pretend that this is peace-time in any sense in which the term could fairly be used.[60]

Winston Churchill, from within the anti-Appeasement group in the Prime Minister's own party, attacked the plan for not going far enough. 'To imagine,' he thundered in the House of Commons, 'that our European problems can be solved by calling up 200,000 youths is a delusion.'[61]

There was a shift taking place. Erich Ebermayer, watching from Berlin, saw it. 'Great things are happening in Great Britain!' he wrote in his diary. 'The sacrifice involved in general conscription is a genuine sacrifice on the part of the island, for there people don't go willingly and gladly to be soldiers, as we do. The fact that the English are prepared to sacrifice their freedom and their cult of individuality in this way is an interesting symptom.'[62]

The reactions of the young British men affected by the new conscription law varied. The first batch of 'trainees' was due to report to barracks on 15 July. A young pit worker from Northumberland, earning a below-average wage, disliking his job, and feeling stuck in the village where he had grown up, saw six months' Military Training as a break, even a release of sorts. 'Why?' as Tony Cameron, then twenty, put the rhetorical question before filling in the answer with some passion:

> Because I'm having six months out of the bloody coal hole – slavery work – and for the money we were getting struggling backward and forward with those tubs . . . it was slavery . . . and anyway it was the one chance I'd ever get of getting further away from that village and having a look at the rest of the world . . .[63]

Albert Davies, from Shropshire, was earning a good wage in the building trade, but felt tyrannized by a father who dictated everything from his haircut to what he did for a living, and who allowed him only sixpence a week 'pocket money'. Davies was delighted to get away, if only for six months, and even more pleased to know his father could do nothing to stop him. He might get only a shilling a day in the Militia, but it was more than he was allowed at home. Catching the train into Shrewsbury to report for duty, he found it full of other young men, all the same age, doing the same thing, and that was a pleasure too.[64]

Those who didn't much like the idea tended to be white-collar and middle-class. The Military Training Act did indeed have egalitarian implications. Since the same basic training would apply to all, regardless of background, this was perhaps the first time in

British history that more privileged young men had not been offered the option of going for a commission. To do that, they would have to join the regular army or the Territorials, which would entail a real commitment rather than simply six months out of their career paths.

James Plant, who had left school at sixteen and had a clerical job with an export company, ignored the original summons and only registered at his local labour exchange, as required, after being threatened with legal sanctions. Erich Ebermayer had been right. Britain was still a civilian, individualistic society – certainly compared with Germany, where such an attitude would have been asking for something a lot worse than a rude letter from the authorities. 'Well, I suppose [it was] just awkwardness,' Plant confessed years later:

> Because at that time we just couldn't understand why they would suddenly want you just because you're twenty-one, so you've got to leave your work and job and join the army. I suppose I was just a little bolshie, I don't know.[65]

Almost all the reluctant 'Militia' recruits consoled themselves with the fact that it was just a six-month break. The attitude was, get it over with, it might even be an interesting experience, and then it will be time to get back to the job or career. Most of them, like Ivan Daunt from Chatham, read the international news and could see why all this was happening, but they were enjoying their young lives. As for the prospect of war, in Daunt's words, they 'somehow couldn't visualize it'.[66]

*

Following the occupation of Bohemia and Moravia, and the British commitment to further rearmament, the Nazi regime had already begun to promote the notion of the 'Encirclement' of the Reich as the new danger. On 1 April, speaking in Wilhelmshaven at the launch of the 35,000-ton battleship *Von Tirpitz*, Hitler attacked British interference in Germany's affairs and resurrected the old idea, fashionable at the time of the First

World War – a favourite theme of the Kaiser, in fact – of
cunning, long-laid British plans to surround Germany with
enemies, thereby keeping her weak:

> In spite of the fact that . . . Germany was for decades the surest
> guarantor of peace and devoted herself only to her own peaceful
> business, other nations, and particularly their statesmen, could
> not refrain from persecuting this regeneration with envy and
> hate and finally answering it with a war.
>
> We know today from historical records how the encirclement
> policy of that time had been systematically pursued by England.
> We know from numerous established facts and publications that
> in that land people were imbued with the conception that it
> was necessary to crush Germany militarily because its annihi-
> lation would assure to every British citizen a larger measure of
> this world's goods.
>
> Certainly Germany at that time committed errors. Its worst
> error was to see this encirclement and to take no steps in time
> to avoid it. The only reproach which we can level at the regime
> of that day is the fact that it had full knowledge of the devilish
> plan for a surprise attack on the Reich, and even so was unable
> to make up its mind in time to avoid such an attack, but allowed
> this encirclement to mature right up to the outbreak of the
> catastrophe.
>
> The result was the World War.[67]

At the time of the Führer's Wilhelmshaven speech, Goebbels
was in Athens, on a private tour undertaken with Hitler's consent.
Beginning in Budapest, then on briefly to Belgrade and Athens,
his trip culminated in a two-week holiday on the island of Rhodes,
at that time under Italian occupation. The Minister had earned
his break. His wife Magda was off on a six-week trip to Italy
looking at Greek and Roman architecture along with various
other prominent Nazi culture fans, including the Speers, Dr Karl
Brandt (Hitler's personal physician) and Frau Brandt, and the
sculptor Arno Breker and his wife. 'Peace again at last,' as Goebbels
could not help but remark.[68]

Neither in Athens nor, for a much longer time – broken only by a swift tourist trip to Egypt – on Rhodes, could Goebbels be in contact with Hitler's office. He seems to have relied on the newspapers being flown in daily to gain an idea of what was going on in the world – an unusual situation for the usually super-informed Minister of Propaganda.

Colonel Beck, the Polish Foreign Minister, had gone to London on 2 April. Two days later, Chamberlain announced that Britain would stand guarantor for the Poles against outside attacks. It was a situation where, normally, Goebbels would have leapt into the breach to set the propaganda tone for whatever countermeasures Hitler deemed necessary, but he was not there. He had also not been there when Hitler, probably on 1 April 1939, instructed General Wilhelm Keitel, Chief of the Wehrmacht High Command, to prepare a plan for an attack on Poland, codenamed 'Case White' (*Fall Weiss*), 'that . . . can be carried through at any time after 1 September 1939'.[69]

For months, Hitler and Ribbentrop had been trying to get some movement from the Poles on the thorny issue of Danzig and the Corridor. This was not a simple black–white contest. At the beginning of 1939, Poland's status in Europe was ambiguous. Poland had leapt in without hesitation to carve slices off the stricken carcass of Czechoslovakia in October 1938. Many in the West would have regarded the Poles at this point as friends, if not allies, of Germany. The standoff at the beginning of November over the Polish Jews at the frontier had caused bad blood between Berlin and Warsaw. Ultimately, it led to the horror of *Kristallnacht*. However, in practical terms these events represented a dance between two neighbouring powers whose governments espoused anti-Semitic policies of varying force and toxicity, neither of which wanted to be burdened with thousands of stateless Jews when the music stopped. Had not his parents' fate led Herschel Grynszpan to shoot Ernst vom Rath, the *Polenaktion* would probably have gone down as an unpleasant incident between two fairly unattractive regimes, without, at least in the short term, further direct import.

In January, Beck had visited Hitler at Berchtesgaden. The encounter had appeared fairly amicable. Having failed in his

strategy of building up a 'Third Europe', a counterbalance to
Germany on one side and the Soviet Union on the other, the
Polish Foreign Minister was seeking to mend fences with Germany.
The two countries had signed a mutual non-aggression pact in
1934, while Poland's veteran military strongman, Marshal
Pilsudski, had still been alive. It was time to refresh this. There
had already been discussions with Germany about Poland taking
a more decisively anti-Russian attitude, perhaps even joining the
so-called 'Anti-Comintern Pact' (Germany, Japan, Italy and
Francoist Spain), in exchange for which Germany would guarantee
Poland's borders. A strong Poland, the Germans said, was in their
interest, given the Nazi regime's undying enmity with the Soviet
Union.[70]

There was, however, a problem. The borders Hitler was
prepared to guarantee would have to concede Danzig to
Germany and permit an extraterritorial section of the German
Autobahn around a hundred kilometres long and an uncontrolled
rail line linking Germany proper with East Prussia via the
Corridor. East Prussia had suffered serious economic damage
from being cut off from the rest of the Reich since 1918. These
links would reconnect the historic province to the Reich by a
land route.

Germany would, Hitler told Beck, naturally guarantee Polish
use of Danzig, at the mouth of the river Vistula, and the Polish
port of Gdynia (created after 1918 just along the coast), through
which a total of 77 per cent of Polish exports flowed. However,
from the Polish point of view the highway would provide an
attack route into Poland for the German army, and also the ability
to cut off the otherwise landlocked country from what was left
of its coastline any time Germany chose. To most Poles, and to
their government, this was unacceptable. The meeting at the
Berghof ended without agreement.

A trip by Ribbentrop to Warsaw at the end of January also
failed to bring progress. Despite this, in his speech to the Reichstag
on 30 January, Hitler spared kind words for Poland and insisted
that good relations with Warsaw formed a cornerstone of his
policy ('in the course of the tense months last year, German–

Polish friendship became a reassuring factor in the otherwise troubled political life in Europe').

The occupation six weeks later of Bohemia and Moravia, and the creation of an independent Slovakia – which quickly forged a formal alliance with Germany, whose troops would be stationed on Slovak territory – represented a radical change in the relationship between Berlin and Warsaw. Poland now faced the Wehrmacht on three sides. Ribbentrop repeated the offer made to Poland in January – only this time with a strong hint of threat. Poland had come into being during the First War only with German aid,* he told Beck and his aides. Poland depended on friendly relations with Germany for her very existence.[71]

Neither the promises of January nor the threats of March persuaded the Poles to give way over Danzig or the Corridor. Within days, Colonel Beck was on his way to London to confirm that the British would stand by Poland if those German threats became immediate. He arrived at Victoria Station in London, to the bemusement of the British press, wearing, not a military uniform or a formal top hat and tails, like his reception committee, but a camel-hair overcoat, a brown striped suit, and a slouch hat, looking 'like a man off on a motoring holiday'.[72] Beck was nevertheless an impressive figure. He was as tall as the six feet five inch, lanky Lord Halifax, who met him at the station, and of more powerful build, with a determined mien. He stayed in London until 8 April, and agreements were arrived at.

By the time a sun-blessed Goebbels returned from the Mediterranean to Berlin in mid-April 1939, a few days before Hitler's birthday celebrations, the die was all but cast. Beck had secured a preliminary agreement with the British, and the French had also expressed their support for Poland in case of German aggression. The question was, how binding should the guarantee

---

* A shrunken puppet 'kingdom' of Poland was indeed set up by the Germans in former Russian Poland in the autumn of 1917. It attracted little popular support, and even the 'regency council' installed by the Germans lost no time in declaring a fully independent Polish republic when it became clear that the Reich was losing the war.

be? The talk was of Britain coming to Poland's aid if Warsaw felt its independence to be threatened. Who was to be the judge of that? Or was Britain going to provide an open-ended commitment?

The *Daily Express*, though recognizing the increasingly aggressive tone of German policy, was not convinced that Britain should provide a guarantee or become involved in any kind of collective security arrangement. On 4 April, after formal government statements about negotiations with Poland, in a slightly woolly article on the editorial page ('The Public Have Changed the Policy of the Government. But the Public Are not Always Right'), proprietor Lord Beaverbrook's mouthpiece, George Malcolm Thomson, stood out against the Polish guarantee. Britain should not bind itself by treaty to the needs of another country, even when that country was under threat. To do so was to sacrifice national sovereignty and the future of the Empire.

The *Express* was alone in its opposition to the change in British government policy. The rest of the British press unanimously approved the guarantee – except, in the far left corner, the communist *Daily Worker* ('Chamberlain is behind the plot to keep out the Soviet Union. The Chamberlain government has encouraged Colonel Beck and other pro-Nazis in Poland to carry through this plot'), and on the far right, briefly and brutally, the fascist newspaper, *Action* ('Poland Mortgaged to Jewry').

The House of Commons, too, lent overwhelming support. The *Manchester Guardian* told its readers: 'Not since 1914 has the House of Commons been so united on foreign policy as today.' It was, in its way, an ominous reference, given the slaughter which followed that unity a quarter of a century earlier.[73]

It was true that, had it not been for the insoluble problem of Danzig and the Corridor, and the resulting permanent tension with Berlin, the authoritarian regime in Poland might have continued to have as much, if not more, in common with Germany and Italy than with the Western democracies. Apart from seeking British loans to bolster Poland's military strength, Beck came looking for British help with resettling his country's 'surplus Jews' in suitable parts of the British Empire.[74] It was a curious, faintly disturbing combination of needs. Nothing would be done for the 'surplus Jews', however, and the loan negotiations would prove difficult and embittering for both sides.*

On 28 April, in response to a note from President Roosevelt, asking for guarantees against Germany's using force in international affairs, Hitler gave a speech to the Reichstag in Berlin. In what most observers agreed was a skilful oration, cunningly argued and peppered with real wit, he once more rehearsed, at great length, the sufferings of the German people after 1918, his desire nonetheless for peace, despite arming Germany to the teeth, and his supposedly justified demands. Here they were expressed for the first time fully in public. Warsaw must agree to the return of Danzig to Germany and to extraterritorial German access to East Prussia via the so-called Corridor, thus all but blocking Polish access to the sea. And there was a full-blooded attack on the British for their 'encirclement' policy, of course. In light of this, the Führer abrogated the Anglo-German Naval Agreement of 1935, which had limited the size of the German navy. Even more ominously, he declared the 1934 German–Polish Friendship and Non-Aggression Pact at an end. Hitler claimed that the Poles had themselves nullified this treaty by arranging the British Guarantee at the beginning of the month.

Unlike his power-play against Czecho-Slovakia, about which many Germans had mixed feelings, Hitler's demand for Danzig and extraterritorial access to East Prussia was almost universally popular at home. The amputation of Danzig, an old German trading city, and the truncation of eastern Germany through the imposition of Poland's corridor to the sea, were crucial, always visible elements in the Versailles humiliation that had followed the First World War. Even Erich Ebermayer, in a burst of optimism earlier in the year, had admitted that on this issue, at least, the Führer had a point:

---

* The British press had predicted a £25 million loan, while the Poles had asked for £60 million. The negotiations dragged on through the summer and remained bogged down at about £5 million, which Warsaw rejected as derisory. No money flowed to Poland until the war had actually begun.

The difficult thing for us opponents of the regime is that in this question, similarly as with German-Austria, somewhat less similarly as with the Sudetens, reason speaks for Hitler's demands. The cutting off of Danzig from the Reich, the 'Corridor' – drawn with a ruler – is and remains unacceptable. Anyone who has just once travelled in a car through this Corridor, who has experienced this Versailles absurdity, can understand that a re-strengthened Germany desires an adjustment here. Hitler's demand: Danzig German, extraterritorial link – that is, without need for a visa or customs checks – to East Prussia, seems not unjustified . . .[75]

Ebermayer had consigned these thoughts to his diary back in January 1939, after returning from a relaxing winter break in democratic Switzerland. He had hoped, as he went on to write in this same diary entry, that 'clever' Colonel Beck – then on a 'friendly' visit to Berchtesgaden – was in a mood not to provoke conflict with Germany over this matter and might even be willing to make genuine concessions.

Ebermayer's hopes of peace were soon dashed. After the events of April 1939 – and especially, after Hitler's speech of 28 April – the Polish Foreign Minister's and the Polish public's position hardened. In a speech to the Polish parliament, the Sejm, on 5 May, Beck was polite but firm:

Peace is a precious and a desirable thing. Our generation, bloodied in wars, certainly deserves peace. But peace, like almost all things of this world, has its price, a high but a measurable one. We in Poland do not know the concept of peace at any price. There is only one thing in the lives of men, nations and countries that is without price. That thing is honour.[76]

By the evening of that same day, just as it had the previous year during the Sudeten Crisis, the DNB was busily pumping out atrocity reports to the German press, only this time accusing Poles, not Czechs, of persecuting the German minority in their country. It spoke of a 'Stream of German Refugees as a Consequence of Polish Terror' in the district in and surrounding Thorn (Polish: Toruń), the largest town in the 'Corridor'.[77] The next morning, the *Ostdeutsche Morgenpost* (East German Morning Post), published in the Upper Silesian border city of Beuthen, carried the screaming headline: 'What Do You Say to This, Herr Beck? Poles Demand Breslau – Hitler to the Gallows'. Other headlines included 'Poles Demand March on Berlin'.[78] Scores more articles of similar tone followed, fed by instructions from the Ministry of Propaganda. Hans Fritzsche, a well-known radio commentator and very senior official at the Propaganda Ministry, admitted after the war that at the Propaganda Ministry meetings during this time the possibility of a German attack on Poland was openly assumed. The resulting press campaign was simply a 'propaganda weapon', a companion to the tanks, aircraft, shells and bullets that would decide the physical conflict.[79]

As for the British, despite their pledge of support, whether Polish honour alone would provide a reason for them to go war on Warsaw's side was, and remained, doubtful. In private, Chamberlain's government was still encouraging the Poles to keep negotiating with the Germans. After Beck's 'Honour' speech, the head of the British Foreign Office, Cadogan, put considerable effort into 'trying to restrain Beck from going off at the deep end at once if Danzig declares for the Reich', suggesting to him that he might begin by 'quarantining' the Free City.[80]

The British Prime Minister had made his commitment to Poland to assuage public opinion and his critics inside the Tory Party. After the German occupation of Prague, there had been calls for a restructuring of the government, possibly under a new leader. Chamberlain also hoped that both Hitler and his own domestic naysayers would be further deterred by his new law on 'compulsory military training' and the general boost to the British armed forces.

Hore-Belisha clearly thought that Chamberlain would backslide if he could. He told an acquaintance that the PM seemed to think 'an occasional bold speech was enough in itself', that 'he had no intention of doing anything' if Hitler persisted, and that, in any case, 'Neville [Chamberlain] still thinks he can control Hitler and Mussolini and that they need him'.[81]

Moreover, when it came to soft-pedalling criticism of Germany, the government was still behaving as it had during the height of the Appeasement era. One of the Prime Minister's aides told the BBC that it was 'definitely undesirable that, at times like the present, issues of foreign policy should be discussed in a controversial spirit on the air'. By contrast, the impeccably connected anti-Appeasement MP, writer and diplomat Harold Nicolson warned in May in the *Spectator* magazine: 'The public are not being informed of the extent or imminence of our immediate danger. I believe that at this moment the country *ought* to be alarmed and *ought* to be disquieted.'[82]

From the practical aspect, Danzig was, in all but detail – a Polish post office, some Polish customs officers in the port (Danzig was in customs union with Poland), and, technically, subordination to Poland in matters of foreign policy – thoroughly German. By 1939, it was also every bit as thoroughly Nazified – political repression, one-party state, racial laws, Gestapo, and all. According to a Sopade informant, reporting to Paris in April 1939, there were even Hitler supporters in Danzig who had doubts whether it was worth risking war over the future of their in many ways favourably placed city state. Apart from fear of their home town turning into a Polish–German battleground in case of a forced incorporation into Germany, one Nazi also pointed out that, while Danzig remained technically independent, they were exempt from the austerity regime that Reich Germans had to put up with:

I sat one evening with a few SA leaders in a Danzig restaurant and for the whole evening the subject was, of course, 'The War'. A Sturmführer, whom I know well to be an old Nazi, declared, among other things: 'I don't rightly understand the Führer, really. Actually, Danzig is anyway as good as German. What difference is there between us and the Reich? Doesn't the German population here live well? The League of Nations has had no say in things here for a long time, and Poland, in actual fact, also none.' The other five listened to what he said, without any contradicting him. On the contrary, another Sturmführer later added: 'If things get going here, we'll have nothing to laugh about! Everyone has always believed that things will be based around the Poles going at us first, and now it is starting off here. It would be much better to deal with the others [countries] one by one and afterwards it would be the Poles' turn.' And a third, who, it is true, talked not of war but of 'annexation', said: 'Well, if we become part of the Reich, then it's all over with butter and pork – we'll all be drinking chicory.'[83]

At the same time, there was no question that Berlin's presence in Danzig was being constantly increased. In May 1939 the Sopade reported:

The Danzig Political Police has been reinforced with Reich-German Gestapo. About 350 men are being lodged at the Hotel Reichshof, most of them coming here from Memel. In mid-May, something like a company of East Prussian SS moved into the Danzig Police Headquarters in full combat array. The [Nazi] Party formations are also still being held in a state of constant alert.[84]

An armed Nazi coup in Danzig was, during these weeks, a real possibility. According to socialist informants, one strong rumour had it that this would happen on 13 May 1939, but in the end, though on that day some SS and Party units had staged a march through the city, it came to no more than that. The Poles, so word had it, threatened to take action if an uprising occurred.[85]

As Hitler's intimates and senior military planners now knew, of course, August was the month when Danzig's, and Europe's, fate was due to be decided by force. Barring some deviation from that plan, the rest was just psychological warfare and background noise, designed to prepare Germans for war.

SEVEN

June/July 1939
'Fine, Fine, Fine. Blue and
Sunshine Everywhere'

The muffled but insistent rumours of war over Danzig did not seem to harm bookings for the German Labour Front's KdF ('Strength Through Joy') tours, home or abroad, in the first half of 1939. After more than a year of hysterical propaganda, tension and fear, followed then by peaceful victory for the Führer, Hitler's people had grown somewhat inured to danger. Germans had, perhaps, come to assume that the wizard in the Reich Chancellery would always manage to pull off another stroke of magic and gain yet more territory for the country without provoking a new apocalypse.

Over the course of 1939, 140,000 'racial comrades' were privileged to take part in KdF's programme of overseas cruises. Many millions more went on subsidized domestic trips of various kinds – to the seaside, the forests, the mountains, to picturesque towns and villages; the list of possibilities was long. Just a few years earlier, trips away from home had been, for millions, an improbable dream; in the Weimar era, there was no legal minimum entitlement to paid annual leave, which had accordingly varied, sometimes dramatically, from workplace to workplace. A survey in 1933 of the 42,000 workers at Siemens's giant plants in the capital revealed that 70 per cent had never spent any of their free time outside Berlin.[1] When the Nazi regime declared that German workers would be entitled to two to three weeks' paid *Erholungsurlaub* (relaxation leave), the way was all at once open for the recently founded (November 1933) leisure subdivision of the German Labour Front, KdF, to start offering travel and vacation possibilities alongside its other 'after-work' activities such as sports clubs, popular libraries, keep-fit clubs and the like.

Both the new paid vacation ordinances and the regime's sponsorship of mass tourism were shrewd propaganda moves, compensating as they did for the loss of trade union and collective bargaining rights under the repressive labour laws introduced early in 1934. The KdF vacation offerings were a good part of the reason why, whatever their initial hostile attitudes and continuing gripes about low pay and long hours, millions of workers gradually found themselves inclined to reach an accommodation with the Nazi system. Even in the Sopade reports, the balance was more than positive for the regime when it came to KdF. 'Yes, the state never offered us things like this before, in those days we never got out of our old neighbourhoods,' said one respondent. Another: 'Today you can see what use our trade union dues are put to.' 'Women especially,' another reporter observed, 'talk for months about the wonderful trips and thereby spread enthusiasm to those around them.'[2]

Then a teenager in Berlin, Rudolf Urbahn later admitted that KdF *had* worked its magic on him:

> After Hitler's seizure of power, at first we got the pleasant sides of it. After three years there was near-full employment instead of mass unemployment, which probably all of us thought the most important thing. Seen as a particular achievement was the organization 'Strength through Joy', KdF for short (a subsidiary organization of the German Labour Front, the successor to the forcibly dissolved trades unions). With this the little man could possibly afford a sea cruise. 'Up and Away to Madeira' was the motto, or 'Off to the Norwegian fjords'.

For me personally, there's the joyful memory of the fact that as a nineteen-year-old I could go on vacation for the first time. Until then, it was always Berlin to Leipzig to stay with the grandparents, but now my friend and I travelled with a KdF special train to spend ten days in Fischbach-on-Inn, in Bavaria. The whole thing cost, with travel, full board and two bus excursions, 49.50 Reichsmarks, and even for those days that was a real gift.[3]

The regime's policy was to accommodate the domestic mass-tourist participants in small boarding houses and inns, cottages and farmhouses in the countryside. It fitted the Nazis' ideological dislike of large enterprises, supplied reliable extra income for those who offered hospitality in their spare rooms, often in economically depressed rural areas, and, of course, helped keep prices down. Broadly, it helped bring Germans together.

Where, however, KdF tour participants found themselves alongside regular, non-subsidized guests at larger inns and hotels, the contrast could lead to trouble. One case reported was of a KdF group in the Harz mountains, whose members noticed that the private customers got a dinner of several courses, whereas they had to make do with a one-pot meal. In the course of the subsequent argument, accusations of unpatriotic discrimination against deserving 'racial comrades' were tossed about. Since the full-price diners were not prepared to settle for humbler fare, the altercation finally resulted in the landlord's being forced, on this occasion, to serve relatively lavish dinners to KdF guests as well. Discrimination of this sort, expressing itself in less high-quality food and drink, cramped accommodation and inferior facilities, or simply snobbish attitudes on the part of staff towards KdF groups, was quite widespread.[4]

The KdF offered a varied range of trips. The most popular numerically were weekend tours to relatively local sites of interest, which reached their high-water mark in 1937 with 6.8 million before declining somewhat in 1938/39. The same rise and decline also applied to the hiking groups, which were a separate category, and to the longer tours, lasting up to fifteen

days, which rose to 1.4 million a year, again by 1937, but declined
to 1 million or so by 1939. This last was in good part due to
competition for transport from the increasingly war-alert military,
which block-booked rail passenger allocations.[5]

The foreign trips, mostly on cruise liners, were the most
glamorous. By 1939, KdF had a fleet of twelve ships, eight of
them purchased outright by the organization, two of them – the
Monte Olivia and the *Dresden* – under charter from the Hamburg-
South America Line and the North-German Lloyd Bremen
respectively. Two were actually purpose-built for the KdF. The
first was the *Wilhelm Gustloff*, named after the Swiss Nazi leader
assassinated by a Jewish student in 1936. Then there was the
Robert Ley, a 27,000 gross-register-tonnage tribute to the German
Labour Front leader's lack of personal modesty. Built in Hamburg
and launched in March 1939 in the presence of the Führer, the
Robert Ley was immediately designated flagship of the KdF fleet.
Carrying 1,750 people, including the crew and service personnel,
it boasted a two-storey theatre/cinema, 5,000 square feet of deck
space, a gymnasium, and a swimming pool painted with mermaids
riding frolicking dolphins.[6]

The total numbers of participants in the KdF cruises were
relatively small, but sufficient to offer a symbol for the egalitarian
'racial community' that the Nazi regime claimed to have established. The press was full of pictures of happy, apparently classless
participants enjoying what were for most Germans unimaginably
luxurious facilities. Lots were supposedly drawn for cabin allocations, although there is evidence that on the chartered ships,
where the accommodation was still laid out along highly discriminatory commercial lines, civil servants and white-collar employees
tended nonetheless to end up in first- and second-class cabins.
On the purpose-built ships, the cabins were all of the same modest
but acceptably comfortable size, so the problem did not arise.[7]

Privilege nevertheless found almost grotesque expression when
genuine Nazi big shots were involved. Karl Brandt, Hitler's
personal physician, took a cruise to the Mediterranean and Adriatic
towards the end of 1938 with his wife and the wife of Jakob
Werlin, a car dealer who had sold Hitler his first Mercedes and

later became an intimate of the Führer and a director of the
Volkswagen Company. From the outset, the Brandt group separated themselves from the other tourists, demanding the best
table for meals and monopolizing the attentions of the ship's
captain and senior officers. They also obtained private transport
for onshore trips, while the mass of participants either walked
or were packed into buses. 'That this kind of preferential treatment in a KdF ship contributed nothing to elevating the mood
of the vacationers is understandable,' as the SD agent reporting
on the cruise observed, showing that it was not just resentful
socialist exiles who disapproved of the Nazi elite's well-developed
sense of entitlement.[8]

The destinations available ranged from the Norwegian fjords
to Madeira, Italy, the Adriatic Coast, Istanbul, the Black Sea, and
North Africa, including the Italian colony of Libya, where
Mussolini's fascist forces had finally succeeded in suppressing a
long-standing local rebellion against foreign rule. Apart from the
exotic and interesting experiences offered, there were also politically useful lessons in the poverty suffered by ordinary people
in other countries, by contrast with which the KdF traveller,
however humble, was enabled to appreciate the privilege of
belonging to the efficient and caring German racial community.[9]
When they were visiting fascist or otherwise friendly countries
(Italy, Portugal, and even Greece under the dictator Metaxas),
tour groups going ashore were often greeted by local political
and labour activists, and patriotic songs were sung. So, although
peaceful, the KdF cruises also served to emphasize the increased
German presence at sea – an impression further underlined by
the fact that German naval vessels would put on pride-inducing
displays for KdF cruise ships en route.

The ethos on the cruises, as throughout the KdF empire, was
communitarian. The day began early with a trumpet blast at 6.30
or 7 a.m., followed by callisthenics until breakfast, and subsequently
a flag parade, featuring patriotic music from the ship's orchestra
and a chorus of the KdF anthem, 'Freut euch des Lebens' ('Enjoy
Life'). Only then was the traveller free to choose among the ship-
board or onshore activities. Snobbish behaviour or conspicuous

spending was frowned upon, as was one-upmanship expressed through expensive clothes and ornamentation.

In short, discipline was expected of the 'racial comrades' when on voyage. Naturally enough, given the availability of alcohol and the fact that many of the vacationers were alone, either single or released from the ties of marriage for the duration, this sometimes broke down. Bad behaviour of a timeless, universal sort was by no means uncommon. Nazi officials, who if 'on business' tended to travel without their families, were particularly liable to take advantage. As one Sopade informant noted, such men:

> . . . welcome the opportunity, beyond the reach of their wives, to relieve themselves of some of the stress of their difficult official duties. Each of them can bring home a little intimate experience for which he can thank the Führer, who also satisfies the sexual fantasies of his faithful followers in this manner.[10]

The officials and guides aboard were expected to complete reports on any problems that had occurred on voyages, and, of course, there were always SD agents, keeping an eye out for dissident behaviour. One problem was that quite large groups of predominately male passengers from different parts of Germany could find themselves on the same voyage, and they did not necessarily share the solidarity between Germans of all classes and regions that the cruises were supposed to typify. On one trip, a group from Silesia and another from the Rhineland experienced a serious falling-out that led to their refusal to be in the same room with each other. On another, the situation took an even more serious turn. A group from Silesia and one from Westphalia actually got involved in drink-fuelled fisticuffs, when the Westphalians contemptuously called the easterners 'Polacks' and 'Polish pigs'. In the end they had to be forcibly separated by crew members.[11] Both incidents occurred on the chartered liner *Dresden*, where the nature of the accommodation tended to encourage envy and resentment and exacerbate class and tribal differences.

The gigantism that clearly affected KdF's cruise offerings was not confined to sea trips. Going somewhat against its previous policy of favouring small hospitality providers, the Labour Front decided to construct the largest complex of tourist accommodation in the world at the Prora resort, on the Baltic island of Rügen.

Eight huge blocks, stretching for 5 kilometres along the shore, would house 10,000 small, and by modern standards underfurnished apartments (showers, bathrooms and toilets were communal). Dining and entertainment would also be firmly mass, shared experiences. The design won a Grand Prix at the 1937 Paris World Exposition. Thousands of workers were engaged on the massive project. Just as no one took delivery of a KdF-Wagen, however, no one ever spent a vacation at Prora. The events of September 1939 ensured that it was never completed, and what had already been built was turned over to war use.[12]

Advertising and press coverage of the KdF beach vacations and sea trips generally featured good-looking, healthy, Aryan-looking men and women – the latter not heavily made up – wearing modern leisure clothes or even swimwear, depending on the context. Especially for the women, the usual pose was attractive, sporty, but not overtly or provocatively sexy, in line with the Nazi regime's public preference for modesty and subtle indication of female fitness and therefore fecundity. The presentation of how Germany and Germans should be – built on 'joy' but not self-indulgence, 'strength' not hedonism – expressed itself almost perfectly in KdF's visions. For the most part, it worked extremely well as a tool to counteract the people's resentment at constantly delayed gratification in other spheres of life and to promote obedience, consent and contentment.

*

As the behaviour of Karl Brandt and his companions on that notorious KdF cruise showed, the Reich's elite was a law to itself. No classlessness for them. Its members might be photographed *en famille* eating austere Sunday 'one-pot' (*Eintopf*) meals for the Winter Aid – usually some variation of pea or lentil soup, with ham or sausage – but otherwise – as the majority of ordinary

Germans knew — most of the Party's leadership lived a life of luxury and indulgence.

During these pre-war months, for instance, Erich Ebermayer was invited to a ball at the residence of the Minister for Church Affairs. It was a glamorous, mixed crowd of Party, theatre and film people — dancing, a cold buffet, a lot of gossip — with, according to Ebermayer, one of the chief subjects of discussion being whether Frau Lutze, wife of SA Chief of Staff Viktor Lutze, should indeed have hazarded giving the Hitler salute on entering the room, despite wearing a strapless designer evening gown.

The debate broadened out until it was agreed that only 'gold badge' Party members — Frau Lutze, like her husband, had joined the NSDAP in its early days — needed to do this. She told Ebermayer, as they later took a turn on the dance floor, that she herself had been shopping 'for knickerbockers for her son' earlier that same day in Hannover, 300 miles west of Berlin, where her husband used to be Gauleiter. They had flown from Berlin aboard the SA leader's personal private aircraft. Rather than ask his successor as Party boss in Hannover to lend him a car, Lutze had commanded official limousines from Berlin to drive all the way to Hannover, so as to be at the airfield in time to collect the family, take them on their shopping expedition, and then return them to board the aeroplane that transported them back to the capital. All this, presumably, in time for Frau Lutze to change into her strapless gown and make it in time for the Minister's ball. High life, Nazi style.

With regard to the more general, non-privileged run of womanhood, the press often took a much sterner view. In the *Freiburger Zeitung*, in the section 'Voices from the Country Folk', claiming to channel the views of truc (that is, 'blood and soil') German womanhood, fashionable females came under direct fire:

That sort of 'modern' woman, who often simply out of convenience, or even on account of keeping a 'girlishly slim' shape, doesn't want children, should follow the example of our old-fashioned Black Forest peasant woman.

The Germany of today needs mothers and working people
and not fashion dolls, who are just playthings for the men and
so far as the *Volk* is concerned are just duds![13]

Ruth Andreas-Friedrich, divorced and with just one teenage
daughter, and undeniably slim and elegant, might have seemed
to belong to the category of 'fashion dolls' of which such moral
guardians of the regime were so suspicious. Even her job at a
woman's magazine, *Die junge Dame* (*The Young Lady*), which
included health, cosmetics, and relationship advice for younger
women, was potentially superfluous and conceivably harmful.

The regime's guard dogs had no idea that Andreas-Friedrich
and her circle were more than just attractive but more or less
irrelevant cultural ornaments. Nevertheless, the magazine she
worked for did come in for criticism from the official press. The
SS newspaper, *Das Schwarze Korps*, described *Die junge Dame* as an
'impudence' (*eine Frechheit*), since it promoted 'elegance, painted
nails and a movie-star smile'. This makes it sound as if Ruth
Andreas-Friedrich's contributions to the magazine attracted
particular attention, and that through her work her detractors
may have picked up on something really subversive about her
without – fortunately – grasping exactly what.[14]

It was not that Germany in the first months of 1939 was bereft
of frivolity, more that it could be bizarrely inconsistent in its
approach. Female stars of film and stage such as Zarah Leander,
Ilse Werner, Kristina Söderbaum and the ill-fated Lída Baarová were
always heavily made up and expensively dressed. On an everyday
level, the newspapers carried advertisements for local clothing
stores' new summer fashion lines, showing sylph-like women in
the latest dresses, coats and hats, here and there accompanied by
(for some reason, usually moustachioed) men in elegant clothing.
The wares on show were not so different from the kind of desirable
apparel offered – to those who could afford it – in the British press.
But there was another element in the German media, particularly
as regards women's permitted desires, that showed, yet again, how
Nazi Germany could not settle on what it wanted. The national

mission, expressed in a constant obsession with war and its needs, defeated the simple, apparently non-essential pleasures.

Heinrich Himmler, the race- and purity-obsessed SS leader, seems to have been genuine in his promotion of the earthy, plaits-and-dirndl female ideal, as was Walter Darré, extreme 'blood and soil' racial theorist, *Reichsbauernführer* (Reich Farmers' Leader) and since 1933 Minister of Food and Agriculture. Darré went so far as to advocate dividing the female population into those who were *zuchtwert* (valuable for breeding) or *zuchtunwert* (worthless for breeding).

The Führer himself in reality preferred glamorous, well-dressed women. 'In his Munich private apartment,' as historian of the Third Reich Hans-Ulrich Thamer recounts, 'Hitler kept a special folder with photographs of women he held a torch for – mostly film actresses, dancers or female athletes. It contained not one of those plaited BdM-girls with whom the official propaganda machine liked to photograph him.'[15] Göring had married the well-known (and very fashionable) actress Emmy Sonnemann, after the death of his Swedish first wife, Karin. Frau Lutze, wife of the SA Chief of Staff, who flew 300 miles to go shopping, was by her own unashamed admission a high-maintenance individual. Goebbels may have stayed married to the mother of his children and symbol of wholesome German womanhood, Magda, but meanwhile he indulged in a string of liaisons with beautiful actresses, including Baarová, who was actually a Slavic Czech and not German at all.

The most senior female Nazi official was Gertrud Scholtz-Klink, head of the Party's women's organization, the NS-Frauenschaft (NSF). Scholtz-Klink resembled more the Himmler/Darré image of femininity. Thirty-six years old, and the mother of four children, although personally highly energetic and ambitious, she preached the approved cult of motherhood and natural inequality between men and women, insisting that 'the German woman must work and work, physically and mentally she must renounce luxury and pleasure'.

Scholtz-Klink had visited Britain in March 1939 at the invitation of the Anglo-German Fellowship and the Women's League of Health and Beauty, led by Lady Prunella Douglas-Hamilton, née Stack. The Fellowship, a superficially non-political organization promoting understanding between the two countries, was actually a stronghold of stubborn appeasers and in some cases outright pro-fascists. Lady Douglas-Hamilton, twenty-five, had acquired her title by lately marrying a son of the Duke of Hamilton. The Women's League of Health and Beauty (an organization founded by her late mother, Mrs Mary Bagot Stack) had, at its peak in 1936, more than 100,000 members, although this had declined by early 1939, in part because of women diverting their free time from keep-fit sessions to first-aid training and ARP duties. Lady Douglas-Hamilton had visited Germany the previous summer, while the Munich Crisis was still simmering, and while there had been hosted by Scholtz-Klink. She was simultaneously impressed and unnerved by the 'Strength through Joy' ethos.[16]

Frau Scholtz-Klink's aim was supposedly 'to study social conditions', according to the *Daily Mirror*, which called her 'Hitler's Perfect Nazi Woman'.[17] Her visit aroused some protests from communists and anti-fascists, including an incident at Croydon Airport during her arrival, on 7 March, where one of the tyres on her car seems to have been deliberately punctured. However, it was in many other ways a last hurrah for the Appeasement era. There was a lavish dinner at Claridge's in London, attended by members of the Anglo-German Fellowship, as well as by many prominent London women, among them Lady Halifax, wife of the Foreign Secretary. Also present were representatives of the German community in London, leading members of British women's organizations, and, of course, staff from the German Embassy, including the ubiquitous Theo Kordt. The next day, Frau Scholtz-Klink watched the 'ladies' of the Women's League going through their flexibility and fitness exercises in their uniform of sleeveless blouse and blue satin knickers.

No particular prominence was given to Frau Scholtz-Klink's visit in the German press, which contained bland, routine references to her being in Britain to 'correct misunderstandings' between the nations.[18] The press in Britain was more cutting, and unfairly picked on the visitor's supposed dowdy and dour appearance. Next to Lady Douglas-Hamilton, a younger woman and a renowned beauty, the leader of the NSF, although only a little more than a decade her senior, could be appraised unfavourably, and this she certainly was. Richard Baxter, a British journalist who would later write a breathtakingly misogynistic book attacking the allegedly subversive role of British women in the Appeasement story (entitled, in deliberate imitation of the famous book *Guilty Men* by 'Cato', *Guilty Women*), described Scholtz-Klink as possessing 'the biggest pair of feet I had ever seen on a woman'.[19] The London *Evening Standard* was less crude, but unflattering all the same:

> Germany's woman Führer wears no make-up. She stepped from the airliner which had brought her from Berlin wearing clothes of the kind that Herr Hitler thinks Nazi women should wear. She had on simple black shoes, dark stockings, a black cape of silky material, a black tailored suit, with white shirt and tartan tie. On the lapels of her suit she wore a Nazi badge . . . She has fair hair which she wears in plaits wound around her head. Her face is freckled and her eyebrows are unplucked.[20]

While, as photographs show, Frau Scholtz-Klink was neither conventionally beautiful nor possessed of any special capacity to charm, and, unlike the wives of many male Nazi bosses, a stranger to strapless gowns, she was efficient, a competent speaker, quite tall and slender, with 'classic' German features, as one commentator put it. She was also prepared to smile if she saw something she approved of, as evidenced by a photograph in the *Daily Express* of her watching Lady Douglas-Hamilton's ladies going through their callisthenic paces. Another photograph in the *Manchester Guardian* showed her beaming at a baby during a visit to the 'Mothercraft Training School' at Highgate, in North London. According to a reporter who had interviewed her in 1937 for the *New York Times* she was a 'friendly woman in her middle thirties, blonde, blue-eyed, regular featured, slender', who exuded 'gentle femininity'.[21] At least one historian who met her after the war saw her as not at all dour, though certainly still chillingly fanatical in her political beliefs, and described her appearance as 'smiling . . . proud, athletic and trim'.[22]

Frau Scholtz-Klink's visit to London saw stereotype colliding with stereotype, and the British press and much of the country's establishment were just as guilty as their counterparts in Germany of imposing such labels on individuals they (understandably, in this case) did not like. More genuine and valid were the demonstrations against her, largely by left-wing and anti-Nazi British women, in her capacity as representative of and collaborator with a brutal regime that also oppressed its own female population. Slogans such as 'Clear Out Scholtz-Klink' and 'No Nazi Klink for British Women' graced placards hoisted by women demonstrating on the last day of her visit outside the German Embassy, where she was staying. They would have applied even if the Nazi women's leader had resembled Zarah Leander rather than the popular British imagining of a straitlaced German *Hausfrau*. Some on the right also remained unseduced. Even the Conservative MP and arch-appeaser Lady Nancy Astor, who had, admittedly, by now begun to calibrate her support of Chamberlain's policy, spoke out against Scholtz-Klink on feminist grounds and refused to meet her.

The Nazi state, which the *Frauenführerin* supported so loyally, was indeed aggressively sexist. Its basic ideology stipulated that women were biologically destined to stay home to look after their men's needs and have the hordes of children who would populate the much-expanded *Lebensraum* to which the German race was entitled. The notion of equality of the sexes, like the existence of homosexuality, was dismissed as 'Jewish' and decadent.

Women were expelled from government roles after 1933. During the early years of the Third Reich, women were also excluded from positions as judges and public prosecutors and from almost all university positions. Because women could not 'think logically or reason objectively' (in Hitler's words) they were no longer allowed to serve on juries. High school education for women was reorganized so as to make it difficult for young women to go to university. Men had been allowed to apply for permanent tenure in the civil service from the age of twenty-six, while for women the age was raised to thirty-five, and it was made clear that any such appointments would be unusual. Married women were no longer permitted to practise as doctors, and from 1935 unmarried female physicians could no longer receive payments from the state-supported health-insurance system.[23] In order to encourage marriage and breeding children, couples were offered quite generous marriage loans from 1933 onwards – on condition that the women did not work.[24]

In the end, as was perhaps inevitable, economic imperatives defeated, or at least, severely undermined, ideology. Meanwhile, Frau Scholtz-Klink had radically modified her stance. Working women were no longer betraying the racial community by not staying home to care for ever-increasing broods, but were 'Heroines of the Everyday'. With headlong rearmament sucking in now-scarce male workers, labour shortages had grown so acute that the regime found itself tweaking its own rules, first mildly, then more forcefully. The stipulation that women could only qualify for marriage loans if they undertook not to work was rescinded. At the beginning of 1938, under another government order, the *Dienstpflichtgesetz* (Service Duty Law), women under twenty-five intent on entering the labour market as office workers or light-industrial operatives had first to undertake a year of agricultural work or domestic service. These were spheres in which workers in general were both poorly paid and often subject to the whims of oppressive employers, and in which there were, as a consequence, serious shortages.[25]

However, even though there were almost a million non-working but employable single women of that age, and more than 5 million similarly placed but childless married women in Germany, such dictatorial powers over the female workforce never came close to being fully applied in peacetime. Perhaps the sexist ruling attitude made male officials reluctant to press 'ladies' into such service. Before the autumn of 1939, in any case, only 50,000 or so young women were affected by the law.[26] Up to 1937, the share of women in the labour market had declined from 37 to 31 per cent, but by 1939 the proportion had risen once more to 33 per cent, including traditional areas of activity such as agriculture and domestic service but also, increasingly, clerical and secretarial work in both the private and state sectors. In any case,

the whole Nazi propaganda myth of the saintly, home-loving
German *Hausfrau* never fitted the facts. In Germany, throughout
this entire period, significantly more women were employed than
in Britain or America, where in both cases they made up only a
little more than a quarter of the workforce.[27]

Ironically, by the time the first 'Mother's Cross' awards were
presented, in May 1939, in absolute numerical terms more women
were working than ever before in the history of Nazi-ruled
Germany. Some may have done their supposed duty and had
three, four or more children (like Frau Scholtz-Klink). The state
did not ban birth control, but it put substantial barriers in its
way. However, despite strenuous propaganda by the regime in
favour of large families, after a rise in birth rates during the early
to mid-Thirties (which also occurred in other industrialized countries as the end of the Depression enabled couples to afford to
have children again), by the end of the decade the average number
of children per family in Germany had settled down to a modest
1.8 – barely replacement rate.[28] Low male wages and high prices
may have had more to do with limiting the size of German families than any amount of coils or condoms.

Between the two main women's organizations, the NSF and
the Deutsches Frauenwerk, some 4 million women – mostly
middle- rather than working-class – were organized in the service
of the regime, although only 30 per cent of these were actually
members of the Nazi Party. In terms of full-time employees, the
NSF itself was exceeded only by the German Labour Front and
the Nazi Party-affiliated Reich Federation of Civil Servants.[29]

'Even though our only weapon is the soup ladle, its impact should
be as great as that of other weapons,' as Frau Scholtz-Klink declared
in a perfect mix of bathos and grandiosity at the 1937 Nuremberg
Rally. Her empire's vast and busy programme encompassed domestic
and cookery advice, dietary instruction (especially, tackling the problems of feeding a family from the limited range of foods available
due to restrictions on imports), and organizing courses covering
pregnancy, birth and motherhood, as well as training for marriage.

The political influence of these organizations on the women
who joined them was often indirect, but no less insistent and

effective for that. After all, as the historian Claudia Koonz pointed out: 'They were the ones who incrementally brought Nazism home. They indoctrinated their children in anti-Semitism. They were the ones who would tell their children to stop playing with the Jewish children down the block.'[30] It was also the millions of members of the NSF and its affiliates who, even while cooking and sewing, caring for their men and tenderly nurturing children, were often the Gestapo's most diligent informers, and who famously comprised so many of the most enthusiastic, not to say fanatical, supporters of the Führer and his plans for Germany and the world.

*

Relations between Britain and Germany were already deteriorating at the time of Gertrud Scholtz-Klink's visit in March 1939, and by June they had slid even further. Mr Chamberlain, however, remained surprisingly optimistic about the prospects for peace.

Even six weeks after Hitler's occupation of Prague, and Hitler's 'encirclement' speech at the end of April, the Prime Minister could write: 'I don't take . . . a gloomy view myself. I believe every month that passes without war makes war more unlikely and although I expect to have periods of acute anxiety yet in cold blood I cannot see Hitler starting a world war for Danzig.'[31]

A month later – incidentally the second anniversary of his taking office as Prime Minister – Chamberlain again wrote to his sister, Hilda: 'All our information goes to show that we need not expect any coup at present but that preparations are being made to effect one (in Danzig) when a favourable moment arrives. We are therefore still in the danger zone, but I myself still believe that Hitler missed the bus last September and that his generals won't let him risk a major war now.' He added rather tastelessly: 'But I can't see yet how the détente is to come about as long as the Jews obstinately go on refusing to shoot Hitler!'[32]

By June, the Premier was somewhat more on edge, worrying about the effect of the guarantee to Poland and musing that 'the Poles haven't done anything they shouldn't, yet they keep us in a state of anxiety', adding: 'Only the Germans remain quiet and that is the most ominous of all.'[33] Still, at least by 25 June Chamberlain could comfort himself with the fact that while on a tour of Labour-supporting South Wales ('always regarded . . . as an enemy stronghold') he found the crowds shouting 'good old Neville' and 'God Bless You'. According to the Prime Minister, Sir Robert Webber, proprietor of the regional newspaper the *Western Mail*, had told Mrs Chamberlain that '80 or 90 per cent of the people were solidly behind me and it certainly looked like it. Women, children, shopkeepers, engine drivers, porters, factory hands and navvies all grinned and took their caps off & I never heard a solitary boo'.[34] His own break from these responsibilities was due in August, when he would spend some weeks pursuing his favourite recreation, fly-fishing in the Highlands of Scotland.

The British summer holiday season was indeed about to begin. There was a clear contrast between the highly organized activities offered to the German population by the KdF and the more individualistic choices made in Britain. In 1937, the nearest equivalent to KdF, the Workers' Travel Association, supported by the trade unions and the Cooperative Movement, organized trips and holidays for 61,000 participants, but its aims were much more earnest and educational, to do with broadening experience of other societies and learning languages – in 1924, for instance, it had taken a group on the first tourist visit to Russia since the revolution.[35] The Cooperative Society also ran holiday camps for members, as did some trade unions.

Far more numerous were the private enterprises providing mass leisure opportunities – though still nowhere near as mass as KdF. In 1936 Billy Butlin, already a successful showman and amusement-park owner, had started up his first 'holiday camp' at Skegness, on the coast of Lincolnshire, in mid-north-east England. Convenient for the industrial areas of Nottinghamshire and Derbyshire and Leicestershire, and possibly further afield as well, it was, as the resort's advertisements euphemistically expressed it, 'bracing', even in the summer. However, the beaches were good, the family-friendly 'chalets' comfortable, and there was a lively provision of meals – three a day – and free entertainment, supplied by energetic 'Redcoats' to keep the vacationing masses from becoming bored. A second, at Dovercourt in Essex, near the ferry port of Harwich, was requisitioned in order to provide shelter for the Kindertransport refugee children, but there was soon also a third, at Clacton-on-Sea in Essex, a traditional leisure destination for Londoners.

Hiking or staying in the countryside was not unpopular in Britain, though by no means as general as in Germany. The tradition of making for the coast as soon as a few days' or even hours' leisure made it possible was by the 1930s deeply rooted in the British working class. The profusion of seaside resorts in Britain reflected the huge amount of coastline surrounding the island nation – most of it within easy reach of England's major industrial conurbations, with the landlocked Midlands the main exception. Manchester and the surrounding industrial towns fed into the Lancashire resorts, above all Blackpool; there were Scarborough and Bridlington and Whitby for Yorkshire and the industrial north-east; the Essex and Kent resorts were easily reachable by rail from London in an hour or two, as were south coast beach destinations such as the Blackpool of the south: Brighton.

The weather in Britain in June began unusually warm. London saw a temperature of 90 degrees Fahrenheit (32 centigrade) on 7 June, and high temperatures were enjoyed as far north as Glasgow. Then, in the second week, low pressure spread east from Ireland and the weather remained unsettled for the rest of the month, with periods of sunshine but generally cooler and wetter. The weather in July was even worse. The Meteorological Office's report described the weather throughout as 'dull; cool; excessive rainfall, especially in Scotland; frequent and widespread thunderstorms'.[36]

Nothing – neither weather nor worries about Danzig and the Corridor – stopped the British exodus to the seaside. In the north, Blackpool was preparing for its most successful summer ever (visitor numbers would be up by a fifth on the previous record). Development at Britain's most popular resort was frantic. The almost 3,000-seater modernized Opera House ('Europe's Most Modern and Beautiful Theatre') had just reopened. Its first

1. Left to right: Mussolini, Hitler, Daladier and Chamberlain begin talks at the Führer Building in Munich, 29 September 1938.

2. Construction of 'Anderson' bomb shelters in British families' back gardens began after the Munich Crisis.

3. BBC television cameras cover the England–Scotland game, 1938. It was the first football match broadcast in its entirety. Scotland won 1–0.

4. An eager tobogganer on Hampstead Heath, London, during the snowy Christmas season of 1938.

5. 'Like a film star', as one impressionable observer saw him.
The dashing anti-appeasement politician in his trademark Homburg hat,
known as the 'Anthony Eden'.

ROBERT
DONAT

THE BEST
PICTURE
OF ANY
YEAR

GOODBYE
MR. CHIPS

with **GREER GARSON**

A SAM WOOD PRODUCTION
SCREEN PLAY BY R.C. SHERRIFF,
CLAUDINE WEST and ERIC MASCHWITZ
PRODUCED BY VICTOR SAVILLE

A METRO-Goldwyn-MAYER PICTURE

COUNTRY OF ORIGIN U.S.A

"This year we're taking
our holiday between the
late spring and early
autumn crises."

OPPOSITE

6. (*above left*) A poster for the Oscar-winning weepy, *Goodbye, Mr Chips*.

7. (*above right*) A crisis-weary cartoon in the *Daily Express*, Britain's largest-circulation newspaper, 9 February 1939.

8. (*below*) A deputation of British unemployed men attempt to have lunch at London's Ritz Hotel, 21 March 1939, much to the glee of Goebbels' propagandists.

THIS PAGE

9. (*right*) Pre-war BBC television's first female announcers, Elizabeth Cowell (*left*) and Jasmine Bligh (*right*) outside Broadcasting House.

10. (*below*) A fascist anti-war rally in the East End of London, May 1939.

11. Sir Oswald Mosley addressing a fascist meeting.

12. Leslie Hore-Belisha, the British Secretary of State for War, addresses
the first intake of 'Militiamen' near Guildford, Surrey, in July 1939.
The unmilitary appearance of the young conscripts is striking.

13. (*right*) English singer, actor and comedian George Formby (1904–1961) with his trademark ukulele, circa 1938.

14. (*below*) A 1939 publicity shot from the working-class Lancashire seaside resort of Blackpool contrives to make it look like a glamorous Mediterranean playground.

15. (*above*) An overdressed beach-goer in Brighton scans the paper for crisis news while his companion catches up on sleep, August 1939.

16. (*right*) Late August 1939. Defying the imminent threat of world war, an enterprising bus company tries to keep holiday bookings coming in.

17. The balcony to the New Reich Chancellery where Hitler appraised the popular mood on 27 September 1938. This picture shows his appearance the previous January on the regime's fifth anniversary.

18. (*above*) Nazi women's leader Gertrud Scholtz-Klink attends a banquet organized by the Anglo-German Fellowship in London, March 1939.

19. (*below*) A commemorative postcard issued to celebrate the Munich Agreement featuring Chamberlain, Daladier, Mussolini and Hitler. Postmarked 'in the liberated Sudetenland'.

20. (*above*) German troops greeted enthusiastically in the industrial town of Aussig (Ústí nad Labem) in the Sudetenland, early October 1938.

21. (*below*) The smashed display window of a Jewish-owned shop, 10 November 1938, after *Kristallnacht*. Some passers-by seem pleased by the destruction.

Zur historischen Begegnung

29. Septbr. 1938 in München

22. (*above left*) Serial
killer and rapist Johann
Eichhorn, the 'Beast of
Aubing', photographed after
his arrest, January 1939.

23. (*above right*) Lída
Baarová, the Czech-born
film actress who became
Goebbels' mistress.

24. (*left*) Johannes Gottschalk,
the 'German Clark Gable',
tand Brigitte Horney,
his co-star in the romantic
desert epic *Uproar in
Damascus*, filmed during
the winter of 1938/39.

25. A German family gathers around their new 'people's radio'
in its place of honour on the kitchen table.

26. A public 'television room' in Berlin, operated by the Reich Post Office, late 1930s.

27. (*above left*) Stars from the Tobis Film Studios in Munich celebrate the arrival of the New Year, 1939.

28. (*above right*) The 'Strength Through Joy' organization offers members of the racial community cruises to Italy, winter 1938/39.

29. (*below*) Hitler watches the military parade in Berlin on his fiftieth birthday, April 1939. To his left the hapless Czech President, Emil Hácha (in top hat), displayed like a captured barbarian chief at a Roman triumph.

30. Hitler Youth in gas masks taking part in a realistic air-raid drill, late 1930s.

Der Innenlenker

31. Superficially peaceful advertising for the Volkswagen 'Beetle' (or KdF-Wagen). Note the little boy is dragging behind him a toy field gun.

32. Reading the news at the lakeside bathing beach of Wannsee, Berlin, late August 1939. The anti-Polish propaganda headline screams: 'Kidnap camps for captured hostages. Places of horror for 30,000 Germans'.

production, the review *Turned Out Nice Again*, starred 'the world's most expensive star attraction', the Lancashire singer/comedian and film star George Formby, whose annual earnings in those years of his greatest success were reckoned at around £100,000 (equivalent eighty years later to £5–6 million by a straight inflation calculation, considerably more by more sophisticated measures).[37] Also opening for the first time this year were the 1,800-seat Odeon cinema, the Casino at the Pleasure Beach, and a smart new bus station. Along with the fun fairs, the pier, the 500-feet-high Blackpool Tower (constructed in 1894 in imitation of the Eiffel Tower in Paris), and of course the beach, the town was a huge factory complex for fun in all weathers (vital to success in a British resort, given the unreliable climate) and at all prices.

The British 'holiday', often embarked upon during the two weeks in the summer when factories would close down, was a typical mixture of communality with individualism. Not for British 'holidaymakers' the huge apartment complexes that were being built for their German counterparts by KdF at Prora. Just as at home most British people lived in houses rather than blocks of flats, so it was with their vacation spaces. This was expressed in life at the new 'holiday camps' that started to proliferate even before the war when the success of Butlin's became apparent. Mass accommodation, yes, and a certain amount of regimentation, but with freedom of choice and a touch of privacy. And no patriotic songs or saluting the flag. A young woman from a Lancashire industrial town described such a holiday with her widowed father at Blackpool's clean-and-basic Squire's Gate Holiday Camp:

> There is only my father and I and we wish to spend our holidays together so I think we can't improve upon our choice of the last two years, namely a Holiday Camp. Here we can both enjoy ourselves in our own way and make friends suitable to our different ages. The tennis, swimming, putting and dancing (all available within the camp-grounds at any well-organized camp) appeal to me while the whist drives and the motor coach drives and the general sociability appeal to my father. We both like the good fellowship and the utter absence of any snobbishness

we have always found in these camps, whilst the separated chalets provide the privacy and comfort without losing the freedom and open air life of ordinary camping. The food, well served and cooked, whilst plain, is varied and wholesome, and the homeliness of the Dining Hall makes meals a real pleasure. This holiday is also quite reasonable (£2), well within the reach of most working-class people.[38]

As the summer season in Britain got under way, however, at the very beginning of June 1939 there had come a reminder that the sea could be a source of life and pleasure, or it could be a graveyard.

*

On 1 June 1939, the newly launched British naval submarine *Thetis* (named after an ancient Greek sea deity, mother of the hero Achilles) sank in Liverpool Bay. It happened 12 miles offshore from the seaside resort of Llandudno, while the vessel was undertaking a final series of test dives to complete her sea trials and qualify her for service.

The bizarre accident seems to have arisen from a faulty torpedo tube in the bow, which flooded when opened as part of routine pre-dive checks. The weight of water that rushed into the nearby chambers dragged *Thetis* down, submerging the 275-foot vessel, bow first, though leaving a small section of the stern showing above water.

Four men managed to save themselves from the submarine by using the escape hatch, but this then failed, trapping the remaining men in the overcrowded vessel, which for this special, celebratory occasion was carrying twice its usual complement. There were attempts to keep the stern above the surface with the aid of a wire hawser connected to a salvage vessel, but eventually this snapped, and *Thetis* sank to the bottom of the bay.

With a small horde of rescue boats circling helplessly around her, all those left on board the *Thetis* died, mostly of asphyxiation. The disaster cost the lives of 99 men, the death toll made up of 51 crew, 26 employees of Cammell Laird, the firm that had built her (including some of the company's top submarine designers), a harbour pilot, and a number of Admiralty inspectors and civil servants. Two employees of a catering company, who had remained on board to serve celebratory drinks and snacks after the dive, also perished.[39] A member of the crew of HMS *Bedouin*, which put the four survivors ashore at the Prince's Wharf in Liverpool, recalled witnessing the 'heart-breaking' vigil on the dock of friends and relatives waiting for news. 'We couldn't tell them anything. We just backed away and went out to sea again.'[40]

In the words of one junior officer whose ship had been present when she sank, the fate of the *Thetis* 'cast great gloom over the fleet'.[41] It also did little to increase public confidence in the powers that be. The *Daily Mirror* reported that the Prime Minister had 'tears in his eyes' when addressing parliament about the tragedy on 6 June, but the next day, on its hard-hitting 'Live Letters' page, under the headline 'Thetis! Widespread Criticism', the paper reprinted a selection of readers' comments out of hundreds submitted. None of them was flattering for the government. 'Public confidence has been badly shaken by the handling of this disaster,' one letter said, after detailing all the alleged mistakes made when the navy attempted to raise the vessel.[42] The *Express* papers also devoted several opinion pieces to the disaster, and with a similar reading of the public mood. On 3 June, in an opinion column headed 'Grim Drama', the *Daily Express* asked: 'Is this the end?' before continuing:

> Yet it was hard to conceive that the vessel could be located, seen, assisted by every contrivance that the ingenuity of men could devise, and yet still be lost.
>
> There were hours when we said: 'Ah, now that they have started to come out, it will not be long now!'
>
> With dismay and bewilderment we have seen that early confidence dissipated.
>
> What happened?[43]

The failed rescue operation had been fraught with delays and errors, as even contemporaries realized. It is possible to infer from hints in documents not available until long after the war that there was a cost-related reason why the stern of the vessel had not been cut open while it was still above water and the trapped men released. It had been feared that this would weaken the hull such that, even if repaired, the costly and technically advanced ship would become unviable in war conditions. The government, misjudging the situation, and still believing that the men could be got out without such drastic action, held off until it was too late.[44]

It happened that a submarine of the United States Navy, the USS *Squalus*, had also flooded and sunk during a test dive just a week previously, on 23 May 1939. In contrast to the *Thetis*, it was the subject of a successful rescue operation. Although 26 crewmen died in the initial inrush of water, 33 sailors who survived in another section of the vessel were saved in a timely and efficient operation involving navy divers. No expense or effort was spared by the American authorities to recover the survivors, drawing a grim contrast with the delays and bungling on the British side.

Meanwhile, eager for some positive news, the public had, in fact, directed its eyes on America, though for a different reason. Britain was following, via radio, press and newsreels, King George VI and his Queen, Elizabeth, in their month-long progress through Canada and, at the personal invitation of President Franklin D. Roosevelt, the USA (for five days, from 7 to 12 June). It was the first time that a reigning British monarch had set foot on United States soil.

Transatlantic relations had recently been languishing somewhat, due to still-strong isolationist feeling in parts of America and in the US Congress. There was a perception, in the wake of Munich – even at the fervently anti-Hitler White House – that Chamberlain's government was devious and cowardly, liable to change course at any moment in pursuit of the interests of the British financial elite. On the British side, there had been those in the Foreign Office who had feared that, rather than improving things, the royal side-trip to the United States might backfire. The visit would run the risk of being seen as an attempt by the old colonial power to bounce America into supporting it in a coming European war.

Fortunately, the royal couple's American visit turned out to be a great success. The King's surprising ability, during a cookout at Hyde Park on the Hudson in the company of President and Mrs Eleanor Roosevelt, to eat a hot dog ('as popular on Coney Island as winkles at Southend' as the *Mirror* explained helpfully to its British readers)[45] in front of the news cameras with a reasonable degree of dignity and competence (that is, without recourse to knife and fork) went down particularly well. There were favourable headlines on both sides of the Atlantic. The *Express* was particularly excited by the comments attributed to 'the famous columnist Walter Winchell':

Queen Elizabeth reminds you of queens you read about in fairy tales – yes, she does.

His Majesty seems to be unlike other Englishmen you meet in Noel Coward's reviews. He seems alive, natural, and free from the 'Dash it all, bai jove' type.

*

William Strang, head of the British Foreign Office's Central Department, who had accompanied Chamberlain in his negotiations with Hitler the previous year, had departed for Moscow on 14 June. Strang was, according to the *Daily Express,* a man 'you would take . . . for an ordinary suburban commuter', as witness his house called 'Treetops' in Northwood, Middlesex, and the host of rose bushes, tended by Mrs Strang, in its 'small' garden.[46]

Strang's task during his trip was to hasten the slow-moving Anglo-French alliance negotiations with the USSR, which were supposed to complement the democracies' rather nervous guarantees to the Poles. An extra deterrent in case the Germans really decided to blow hot over Danzig and the Corridor again. The German press was prompting a simmering level of anti-Polish propaganda very similar to the campaign mounted against Czechoslovakia in the summer of '38, ready to be brought to the boil if more drastic political and military action was called for. On the day that in Britain the *Mirror* and the *Express* were printing stories about the royals in America, the *Freiburger Zeitung* carried two lengthy anti-Polish articles on page 2: 'Insolent Polish Threats against Danzig' (alleged excessive numbers of and overbearing acts by Polish customs officials) and 'New Murder of Ethnic German. Polish Criminals Get Off Scot Free' (unemployed member of German minority in Poland shot crossing the border looking for a job in the Reich).[47]

However, Mr Strang and his colleagues faced worse difficulties than they knew. On 15 June 1939, the Soviet Chargé d'Affaires in Berlin had met the Ambassador of Bulgaria, a German ally. In the course of their conversation, he casually asked the Bulgarian's advice on the possibility of a German-Soviet Non-Aggression Pact. The Soviets' hope was that their conversation would be reported to the German Foreign Office. This duly occurred. The first piece was being set in place for what the historian A.J.P. Taylor would call 'the greatest set-back for British diplomacy in the Twentieth Century'.

On 16 June 1939, under a new banking law, although Hjalmar Schacht's successor Wilhelm Frick remained its president, the German Reichsbank was placed under the direct control of the Führer and Reich Chancellor, Adolf Hitler. There would be no more arguments about where all the money for the war was going to come from.

*

At the beginning of June the British-MGM film *Goodbye, Mr Chips*, starring the already famous Robert Donat and the newly discovered Greer Garson (who had made her first acting appearances on BBC television during its experimental period), was premiered in London at the Empire, Leicester Square. It would become a hit on both sides of the Atlantic, and Donat would win an Oscar for his performance.

Covering the half-century between the 1870s and the 1920s, the film told the sentimental story of Charles Chipping, a master at a fictional British public school, of his long and loyal teaching service, and of his late (and ultimately tragic) marriage. One of the extraordinary features of the film was how successfully Donat, in real life just approaching his mid-thirties, 'aged' in the part.

A key subplot showed his pre-war friendship with Max Staefel, a German master at the school (played by the exiled Austrian actor Paul Henreid, soon to gain international fame as the heroic anti-Nazi Resistance leader Victor Laszlo in *Casablanca*). Staefel returns to Germany just before the outbreak of war and is killed while fighting for his country. In a moving scene towards the end of the film, 'Mr Chips', recalled from retirement to become acting headmaster during the First World War, includes the name of Staefel along with those of all other staff and pupils recently lost, not mentioning that he fought on the German side, only that he was 'killed on the Western Front a few weeks ago'.

Goodbye, Mr Chips was shot in England in the winter of 1938/1939, but the scene itself originated in James Hilton's novel, first published in the more optimistic mid-1930s. Its continued inclusion in the film places it firmly within the late flowering of the hope for peace and reconciliation that followed the Munich Pact.

One of the most successful German film dramas of the time, *Aufruhr in Damaskus* (*Tumult in Damascus*), set mostly in the Middle East during the First World War, also shot during the winter and released in the spring of 1939, likewise carried a message of reconciliation between Germany and Britain. The film focused on a German military unit, led by Hauptmann Schultz (Hans Nielsen) with his second-in-command and actual hero of the film, Leutnant Keller (Joachim Gottschalk – 'Germany's Clark Gable'[48]), sent to reinforce the collapsing Turkish Army in Syria in the autumn of 1918, just before the final surrender. Love interest was provided by a German nurse, played by the versatile and popular actress Brigitte Horney.

The action of the film was supposed to play out mostly in the citadel of the Syrian town of Dara'a, 90 kilometres south of Damascus at the foot of the Golan Heights, where historically just such a German unit was stationed during the time concerned. There the realism ended. Dara'a was shown as a desert town. However, it is not situated in a desert area at all but in a green, fertile agricultural region well inland from the Mediterranean. The film was actually shot in the Italian colony of Libya, in the medina of the coastal city of Tripoli, on the edge of the Sahara, which is actually as far from Damascus as Damascus is from Berlin. The architecture is North African. Local characters are dressed in the manner of North Africans rather than Syrians, and when they occasionally speak in their own language the dialect is Libyan.[49]

The film opened with a quotation from T.E. Lawrence's auto-biography, *Seven Pillars of Wisdom*, praising the courage and resilience of these German troops. During the action, the British military was shown protecting wounded Germans against the brutality of Arab insurgents after they take Damascus.[50] Apart from the pro-British elements, the film also glorified German grit and the ability to 'fight to the end'. It was classified as 'polit-ically valuable' by the Reich Ministry of Propaganda.

Neither Robert Donat (himself of Polish-German descent) nor Greer Garson was known for political engagement. Not so, Gottschalk and Horney, the German stars. It was forced upon them. Gottschalk's wife, Meta Wolff, a successful actress before being banned by the Nazis, was Jewish, and their young son, Michael, was therefore classified as mixed-race 'in the first degree', or *Mischling ersten Grades*. During *Kristallnacht*, Gottschalk had been on the other side of the Mediterranean, filming *Tumult* in Libya, leaving his terrified wife trapped in their central Berlin apartment and dependent on the kindness of friends.

Somehow, protected by important people in the theatre and film world – including Brigitte Horney, who made no secret of her anti-Nazi opinions in private – and with his wife half hidden from view, Gottschalk had managed to avoid the usual official 'solution' to such a problem – which was that the Jewish spouse must be divorced. So he managed to continue working as a major stage and screen actor. The reckoning would come eventually, but not until after September.

*

The last traces of Appeasement were slowly fading from the British political scene, but one odd and unpleasant British phenom-enon was about to make a last, in its way spectacular and explosive reappearance: Sir Oswald Mosley and his Fascists.

A strikingly handsome man, and the wealthy heir to a baron-etcy, the 42-year-old Mosley had been a considerable orator and competent minister during his early political career. First elected as a Conservative in 1918, he had defected from the Tory Party to Labour, and then, at the height of the economic crisis, to the so-called 'New Party', of which he was a key co-founder. It proposed a state-directed Keynesian expansionism, combined with high tariff walls, in order to bring Britain out of the Depression.

The New Party had originally recruited from all the mainstream parties. Despite some authoritarian traits (considered key to the defeat of unemployment and industrial stagnation), it was rela-tively conventional in its ambitions. However, the New Party failed to win any appreciable electoral support, and by early 1932, after a European tour that included a meeting with Mussolini, Mosley had converted to fascism. He spent the summer of 1932 writing a manifesto, 'The Greater Britain', and in the autumn of that year founded the British Union of Fascists (BUF).

'Monster' rallies, street-level provocations, paramilitary organ-ization and incendiary rhetoric marked the BUF's operational style, as they had that of the Fascists in Italy and the Nazis in Germany on their roads to power. The party's symbol was a lightning bolt within a dark-blue circle against a red background. No Fascist candidates were put forward in the 1935 General Election, though Mosley promised that they would stand at the next one after that. For the first two years of its existence, the BUF was supported by Viscount Rothermere's *Daily Mail* (with its infamous headline 'Hurrah for the Blackshirts!'). Membership reached a maximum of about 50,000 until some violent street clashes, brutal intimidation of opponents at BUF rallies, and increasingly anti-Semitic tendencies alienated many respectable, above all middle-class, supporters. After 1936, when the so-called Cable Street disturbances in the East End of London (a stronghold of the BUF, but also of its opponents) led to police and legal action against the party, Mosley's movement declined to less than half its previous strength.

Notwithstanding its problems, and a failure to make a mark in most of the by-elections and council elections it contested, the

BUF was still capable of staging a monster rally if it needed to. In the summer of 1939, with war once more on the horizon, and the loosening of immigration restrictions on refugees from Germany reawakening xenophobia in some quarters, that is what it did.

Earls Court Arena, in West London, had already housed several huge rallies addressed by Mosley. The one planned for Sunday 16 July 1939 was the largest, as well as the last, of such performances. The theme was 'Britain First', and the object was to mobilize against any involvement with continental opposition to the Nazis.

By July 1939, perhaps sensitive to association with an increasingly unpopular Hitler, Mosley's organization had changed its name to simply 'British Union'. All the same, at the rally there were banners and pseudo-uniforms aplenty. Mosley entered in a similar way to Hitler, surrounded by a praetorian guard and speaking, black-shirted, from a podium 20 feet high. There were, according to the *Manchester Guardian*, upwards of 20,000 in the audience out of a maximum capacity for the Arena of 30,000. As most reports agreed, not all who were there had bought tickets, since, once the paying customers had been admitted, the Mosleyite officials had offered seats to the crowd outside for free. This was nonetheless said to have amounted to the largest indoor political gathering in British history.[51]

Mosley's party claimed to have toned down the anti-Semitic content of its programme by this point, but the leader's speech showed little sign of it. 'A million Britons shall not die in your Jews' quarrel!' he bellowed, to great applause. The crowd booed and hissed when he attacked Churchill's attitude towards Germany. Mosley insisted that Britain should have nothing to do with Eastern and South-Eastern Europe. Let Hitler have it, if he wanted it. There could then be general disarmament in the West, because Hitler was not interested in expanding westward:

> They want to build houses in Berlin; we want to build houses
> in Britain. What folly to use the resources that can be spent in
> building houses for our people in arming against each other
> when we have nothing in the world to fight about. [Cheers.]

And I am as certain as I stand here tonight that if we said to Germany: 'We won't interfere on your Eastern borders and you leave us alone in the British Empire and in the West of Europe,' I could immediately get a disarmament conference relieving the stricken people of Europe, not only from the threat of war, but lifting from their backs for our time and beyond it the crushing burden and fear of arms for war. [Cheers.]

Towards the end of his eloquent and undoubtedly powerful two-hour oration, Mosley also launched a venomous attack on 'the open door', which he (falsely) claimed characterized the government's policy on immigration. Without mentioning Jewish refugees specifically, Mosley painted their arrival in Britain in apocalyptic terms:

Not only are their goods coming in, but they are coming in themselves, thousands of them; thousands of them coming in, not only undermining our standard of life, not only debauching our commercial practices, not only swelling the practices of criminal lawyers, not only changing the commercial outlook and morality of the British to the detriment of our simple and honest people; not only that, my friends; this policy of the open door, this universal entry of alien standards and alien life if permitted to continue, is going to change the whole character of English life and English people, and is to complete the work which a century of capitalist production began, uprooting the English from the soil of their own native land and changing forever the life of our people. [Cheers.][52]

The *Daily Mirror*'s star columnist, 'Cassandra' (William Connor), was strangely impressed, acknowledging Mosley's oratorical skills and the fact that his arguments about the rich cabal controlling the world might prove effective 'when you bear in mind that ninety percent of the people in this country earn less than four pounds a week'. 'Blackshirt Caesar!' ran the headline. 'Can Mosley Succeed? Is Fascism on the Way Up?' And in July 1939 'Cassandra' thought he might be:

Each reverse of the National Government helps Fascism.

Mr Chamberlain's tragic hesitancy brings recruits to Mosley's creed.

This strange young man, with his violent remedies and his uncompromising courage, may yet serve to rock the smug conservatism that acts like a drug on our political life.

If so, he deserves a place in history.

But his wares, dolled up with all the theatrical display of a stage Caesar, will sell better only when Englishmen are nearer desperation and farther from sanity. [bold in original][53]

As might be expected, the massive pro-Hitler meeting was given far more attention in the German press than in Britain. 'A London Sensation,' the main front-page headline in the *Freiburger Zeitung* proclaimed, 'Massive Rally of the Mosley Party – A Reckoning with the Encirclers – "We Want No War"'.

*

On 20 July 1939, sixteen-year-old Ruth Thieme wrote in her diary that she had travelled into Leipzig with her father from their home in suburban Grimma. She reported casually that they had gone to some 'Jews', 'to look at the dog that we are supposed to be getting. It is a toy spaniel named Sonja.' On the same trip, her father also brought her a tennis racket, which seemed to Ruth equally, if not more, exciting, and was reported in exactly the same tone. There was no indication of why the Jewish people they went to see were parting with their dog. It was not yet illegal for them to keep pets, though one day it would be. Perhaps they were emigrating. Just in time.[54]

By the summer, some 70,000 Jewish refugees from Germany and Austria had managed to reach the safety of British soil. Most had been guaranteed by friends or relatives, or in some cases by Jewish and Quaker charities, as the London government required. A few could afford to guarantee themselves.

Not all the new arrivals were welcome. If anything, despite the horrific tales coming out of Germany and Central Europe,

there was a certain stiffening of opposition to continuing acceptance of foreigners, and especially Jews, as the attendance at Sir
Oswald Mosley's supposed 'Peace Rally' showed.

The *Daily Express* continued its policy of claiming that Britain
was 'full' and that the only possible policy was to accommodate
Jews in backward parts of the Empire. The paper commented
after Britain agreed to accept almost 300 desperate refugees from
the steamer *St Louis*, with 900 German Jews on board, which
had been refused entry to Cuba, the United States and Canada,
and forced to return to Europe:

> This example must not set a precedent. There is no room for
> any more refugees in this country. But there are underpopulated
> parts of the Empire which need settlers. There are lands to be
> developed by pioneers beginning a new life.
>
> If we give refugees a home in this country they become a
> burden and a grievance. We should give them the chance to
> make homes for themselves overseas, and the proud work of
> Empire-building.[55]

Earlier in the same month, a testy exchange on the *Mirror*'s Live
Letter Box page bore witness that even on a left-wing paper, which
had broadly supported a policy of acceptance for political and racial
refugees during the previous months, tempers could fray if the
newcomers were considered ungrateful. A correspondent with a
Jewish surname had written in to complain that Britain was not
taking so many refugees as France, to which the *Mirror* replied:

> Refugees are taking advantage of the hospitality of this country
> and should be grateful for it.
>
> They should also be thankful for our armed forces built up
> and being paid for by British taxpayers, that keep continental
> threats at bay.
>
> Hundreds of millions a year of our money are being spent
> to deflect the terror from which these people have just escaped.
>
> They have made and are making no contribution to this end.
> Let them keep a civil tongue in their heads.[56]

Fritz Lustig, just turned twenty years old in the early summer of 1939, had arrived in Britain in mid-April from Hamburg, via Le Havre, aboard an American ocean liner, the *President Roosevelt*. Coming by liner had been, apparently, a ruse to take advantage of a loophole. The émigré was allowed to take a little more cash on such a voyage, and a little more cash on top of that if booked into a first-class cabin. Fritz, son of a modestly prosperous, educated middle-class family from Berlin (his father had a business selling bicycle parts to wholesalers), had obtained a visa, after a number of delays and hitches, though the Quaker Refugee Committee. However, the precious document was only valid for twelve months, after which he would have to apply to emigrate again, to Australia or New Zealand, or possibly Canada.

Fritz had wanted to study music – he was already an accomplished cellist, and had brought his much-loved instrument with him to Britain – but was unable to do so in Germany, because of the Nazi racial laws. His family was liberal, highly educated, Jewish only in ancestry (Fritz was confirmed as a Lutheran at fourteen, after which he became an agnostic). But, as they were all well aware, people such as them were no less endangered than if they had been conspicuously orthodox in dress and religion.

While waiting for his visa, Fritz had taken a boring job as a clerk at a dental equipment firm in Berlin. He had few regrets at being sacked towards the end of 1938 during a purge of Jewish employees, although it meant a loss of income. Fritz and his family knew there was no future for him in the Germany the Nazis were making, and he was keen to start again somewhere else. Naturally, there had been some tugging of the heartstrings when he said farewell to his parents on the dockside at Hamburg.

It was at Le Havre, where the passengers had almost a whole day ashore before continuing to Southampton, that the young Berliner felt the first, and perhaps deepest, impact of leaving an oppressive dictatorship for life in a democracy. There was suddenly no fear of being followed, or of saying a wrong, dangerous thing; no threatening uniforms or signs saying 'Jews Not Welcome'. 'This feeling of having an almost unbearably heavy burden lifted from one's whole being can probably not be imagined by anyone who has not experienced it,' he wrote many years later.[57]

Fritz had, actually, already spent a summer in Britain. In 1937, he had stayed with an English family, the Francises, at Britain's first 'garden city', Letchworth, in Hertfordshire. There he had honed his English and made lasting friends, but immediate help now came from an established émigré couple, the Kuttners – Mrs Kuttner was an old friend of Fritz's much older sister. Richard Kuttner picked up Fritz and his cello at Waterloo Station, crammed him and the sizeable instrument into his small car, and took him home to North London, where the young Berliner would spend the next few days. Fritz was then due to go to Letchworth, where he would wait with the Francises for information from the Quaker refugee charity that had sponsored him. Helpers were trying to organize a building apprenticeship for him, so that he would have a marketable skill for his new life.

Fritz Lustig was the first to admit that his story, while involving the tribulations of involuntary exile, and some anxious moments, was a relatively fortunate one (he would title his memoirs *My Lucky Life*). The Quaker committee duly found him an apprenticeship with a builder just outside Cambridge, and he was encouraged to enrol in evening classes in 'building science' at a technical college. He also benefited from membership of a large, close family network. An émigré uncle, a physicist, was an academic in Cambridge, and he and his wife were happy to offer Fritz house room. Having passable English language skills was obviously an additional help. The only time young Lustig appeared to really feel his foreignness was when the builder he was working with insisted on not addressing him as 'Fritz' but by the British equivalent name, Fred.

Käthe Strenitz had an altogether more difficult time, at least initially. She was sixteen in the late spring of 1939 when, courtesy of the Zionist youth organization Aliyah, she got a place on a Kindertransport train to England. The atmosphere in Prague was turning ominous, and so she felt relieved to be going, though sad to leave her parents and younger brother (none of whom would survive the war).

On arrival in London, Käthe was met by the brother of a friend from Prague's artistic circle, and spent some time in the British capital. Her host was kind, and did his best, but he had no money and neither did she, not having been allowed to bring more than a pittance with her when she left Prague. Matters took a turn for the worse when, thinking it would be good for her to go to the countryside, where there would at least be work and food, he sent her to a flower farm in Hampshire. This, given the imminent threat of war, was being turned over to massive green-house cultivation of tomatoes.

Käthe was then subjected to a fate not much better than slave labour. She slept in the farmhouse on the landing, never having a room of her own, and worked from early in the morning until late at night in the glasshouses, or cleaning the house, or heaving huge tubs of washing down to the river meadow. There was not enough to eat. She could not remember ever being paid. One day she was discovered eating an apple she had picked up from the lawn by the house and forced to parade in front of the other workers and confess to being a 'thief'.[58]

Käthe was a little too old to be taken into the education system (Quaker schools had an especially heroic record in taking in Jewish refugee children, many of whom in later life made distinguished contributions to Britain in the arts, sciences, industry and the professions).[59] Arriving in 'tolerant' Britain without the protection of family or powerful connections – such as Fritz Lustig enjoyed – could be a bruising experience for a refugee. For a girl of her age there was little protection against exploitation and abuse.

*

On Saturday 15 July 1939, the first intake of almost 34,000 twenty- and twenty-one-year-old males reported for duty with the new Militia units and began their six months' training.

The popular press besieged the camps. With the King and Queen not due back from Canada until the following week, Queen Mary, widow of George V, appeared at Shorncliffe Camp, near Folkestone, to witness the arrival of several hundred young men in their only partially military uniforms. Mr Hore-Belisha visited the barracks at Stoughton in Guildford. The regular army sergeant commanding the reception party at the station was reported by the *Sunday Express* to have told each new arrival: 'You are going to have a lovely time.' The Secretary of State himself addressed the officers in their mess. The Militiamen had, he said, been 'welcomed as friends'; from his chats with them he was 'convinced that although the scheme only covered a period of three years, young men after that would demand the right to undergo the same experience'. Each recruit had been issued, the *Express* reported, with a picture postcard of the barracks on which they could write home to announce their safe arrival.[60]

There were hosts of 'human interest' Militia stories. There was the trainee who was less than 5 feet tall and who couldn't be fitted with a uniform; the trainee who weighed 21 stone (almost 300 lb); the newly married Militiaman who turned up to report and brought his bride with him; and the young man from a wealthy family who arrived at the approach to the barracks in a chauffeur-driven car before transferring to a lorry with the rest of the 'boys'. And so on.

The generally amused tone of the coverage fitted easily with the notion of a new 'democratic' army suitable for the times. The *Express*, especially, having enthusiastically promoted conscription over the past year or so, devoted a great deal of attention to the process. During July, it appealed for material sent in by readers relating to the Militia call-up. Especially desired were 'stories and pictures of humour' and 'stories with pathos thrill or a romantic angle will be welcomed also'. Ten shillings and sixpence would be paid for any contributions used. And used they were. From the first day, the *Express* had a paid contributor from among the ranks of the conscripts, 'Gunner Ronald Savage', twenty-one, a city clerk from London ('I am looking forward to it. When you have been a clerk in the city for five years you need some excitement').[61] A week later, he was still feeling optimistic, though missing certain things ('I've had permission to send home for my ukulele').[62]

There was also a lot of reporting in the 'quality' press. The *Manchester Guardian* described the father of one recruit accompanying his son to the barracks and being given a tour by an officer. Having described the accommodation as 'wonderful', he was shown the menu for one of the evening meals:

> Hors d'oeuvres: tomato soup: fried fillet of fish: roast joint: new potatoes: roast potatoes: green peas: jelly and blancmange: tea or coffee.

The concerned parent, seemingly concerned no longer, remarked: 'They will be feeding better than I shall while they are here.'[63] The authorities were clearly eager to show that crude militarism was not part of their scheme so far as these young quasi-civilians were concerned.

The *Observer* had reported the army's insistence that there would be 'no bullying'. 'The boys of the New Brigade will find themselves in a New Army,' the paper said. There were pictures of the trainees in their suits and ties and jaunty dark-blue berets, a last-minute addition to the 'walking-out' kit.

> They will find instructors schooled into avoiding any suggestions of the Music Hall sergeant-major style. 'No rudeness, bullying or sarcasm' are the instructors' special orders. Employment of militiamen on fatigues will be restricted as far as practicable.[64]

The *Daily Worker*, organ of the Communist Party of Great Britain, would have none of that. Hore-Belisha's claim, shared by most of the press, that this was some kind of 'marvellous example of democracy' amounted, the paper claimed, to a cruel sham:

> To some of the sob [*sic*] writers the idea that a duke's son should really serve six months in the army, learning to defend the country in which and on which he lives appears to be too democratic for words.
>
> But before we get lyrical over the democratic virtues of the militia we must ask who is running the show. And the answer is quite clear. It is that the professional officers selected from a very narrow upper layer of the British people and in the main

notoriously anti-Labour and anti-democratic are running the show.

Under these circumstances it is humbug for Mr Hore-Belisha to suggest that service in the present class-ridden fighting forces is a 'great democratic experience'.[65]

All in all, though, barring these predictably negative comments, the politically delicate first intake of Militiamen counted as a successful public relations exercise for the government.

One of the middle-class recruits, who had got his papers just after completing his examination for the Civil Service, recalled many years later: 'Of course we were the first to be conscripted in peacetime. The press were watching everything and I mean the day I was called up in 1939 all the press were there to see us and see what happened to us. But of course it was very well organized and I think ninety-nine and a half per cent of us were perfectly happy with our treatment.'[66]

*

The entire – as it turned out, short-lived – Militia episode had a somewhat comical, unreal atmosphere about it. Fear ruled in the early summer, with the rumblings in Eastern Europe and the seemingly endless talk of alliances with Poland, Russia, France, and all the rest, to try to rein in Germany. But life went on for tens of millions, and the prospect of war, despite the news head-lines, continued to seem oddly distant.

In Patrick Hamilton's novel *Hangover Square*, written in 1940 when this time was fresh in the author's memory, the entire bewildering year following Munich serves as an ironic counter-point to the petty personal tragedies suffered by the characters.

The novel's needy, down-at-heel middle-class anti-hero, George Harvey Bone, lives in a seedy part of the London suburb of Earls Court, surviving off a modest legacy. A shambling, well-meaning alcoholic, victim of false 'friends' who manipulate him into funding their drinking bouts, Bone is more and more subject to schizophrenic episodes in which he feels drawn to murder. He also suffers from a sexual obsession with one of this

circle, a beautiful, faithless (and talentless) actress named Netta
Longdon. Netta exploits his generosity, toys with his emotions
while more or less openly sleeping with one of the other drinkers,
a Fascist sympathizer, and attempts to use Bone's old school
friend Johnnie, who works for a powerful theatrical agent, to
further her career. One fine day in July 1939, Johnnie has lunch
with Bone in the West End, then heads back to his Soho office.
This is a glimpse of London in its last days of peace:

> When they had parted Johnnie strolled back through Leicester
> Square towards the office . . . In the middle of the Square the
> effigy of Shakespeare stared greyly out in the direction of the
> Empire Cinema with its bright advertisements of 'Good-bye,
> Mr Chips', with Robert Donat and Greer Garson. A pigeon
> had alighted on the head of the poet, who seemed to be watching
> the red coat (like an old-fashioned golfer's coat, yet giving a
> touch of hot exotic colour to the whole scene) of the man who
> cleaned shoes on top of the Men's Lavatories. Fine, fine, fine . . .
> Blue and sunshine everywhere.
>   Fine for the King and Queen in Canada . . .
>   Fine for the salvaging of the *Thetis* . . .
>   Fine for the West Indian team . . .
>   Fine for the I.R.A. and their cloakrooms . . .
>   Fine for Hitler in Czechoslovakia . . .
>   Fine for Mr Strang in Moscow . . .
>   Fine for Mr Chamberlain, who believed it was peace in our
> time – his umbrella a parasol! . . .
>   You couldn't believe it would ever break, that the bombs had
> to fall.[67]

EIGHT

1–22 August 1939
'To Die for Danzig?'

On 2 August 1939, the exiled German physicist Albert Einstein signed a letter warning President Roosevelt that Germany might be developing an atomic bomb. Since the crucial nuclear-fission experiment using uranium, carried out by Otto Hahn and Fritz Strassmann at the Kaiser Wilhelm Institute in Berlin the previous December, other physicists in America, Britain and elsewhere had been evaluating this experiment's significance, tying it in with their own research on nuclear reactions.

Léo Szilárd, a forty-year-old Hungarian-born physicist, had worked with Einstein on various projects in Germany in the 1920s. Now also living in the United States, Szilárd was the prime mover behind this activity. One of his reasons for suspecting that the Third Reich might be trying to develop an 'atomic' weapon was that, after Germany had taken over the Sudetenland, it had abruptly stopped exporting uranium produced in mines situated there. He had therefore approached Einstein earlier that summer, as a famous figure who might help him get the government's attention.

A first visit to the discoverer of relativity's rented summer beach house at Nassau Point, near Cutchogue, on Long Island's unfashionable North Fork, had piqued Einstein's interest. On 2 August, during a second visit, Einstein dictated a letter in German based on Szilárd's suggestions. The Hungarian and his companion on the visit, Edward Teller – also a distinguished physicist – translated it into English. The letter drew President Roosevelt's attention to the recent developments and urgently suggested that the US government become directly involved in securing supplies of uranium (available from mines in Canada and the then Belgian Congo) and endeavour to 'speed the experimental work'. The military implications were not explicitly stated, but clear, especially as the final paragraph emphasized the German government's official interest in the work going on in Berlin. The Germans might be developing a bomb based on nuclear fission, and their team included the son of the State Secretary at the Foreign Ministry, von Weizsäcker.*

Current calculations estimated that to make such a devastating weapon would take several hundred pounds of uranium, and so the Szilárd/Einstein warning letter posited the danger of a ship carrying this enormous payload being sailed into a harbour and detonated, thus destroying the town and the surrounding countryside.[1] Only some time later did further experiments show that, in fact, a mere 10 kilograms (about 20 lb) would suffice, enabling the weapon to be delivered by an aircraft.

It would take two months and a huge change in the world's circumstances until Roosevelt was able to receive and react to the physicists' letter, but the President would act promptly. By then the German research had already been placed under the control of the Army Armaments Office (Heereswaffenamt). The deeply secret race to develop what would be known as the atomic bomb had begun.

*

Four thousand miles east of Cutchogue, the tectonic plates of European geopolitics were beginning to shift. Germany was courting the Russians.

---

* Carl Friedrich von Weizsäcker (1912–2007) was a brilliant theoretical physicist. A group of German scientists informally calling themselves 'The Uranium Club' (*Uranverein*) had begun work on potential military applications in the spring of 1939, building on Hahn's and Strassmann's discovery.

The notion of a rapprochement between Nazi Germany and Soviet Russia, political opposites and arch-enemies, unthinkable as it might have seemed just a short while earlier, had in fact been a serious prospect for some time before the summer of 1939. As the alliance negotiations between the Western democracies and the Soviets dragged on, despite Mr Strang of the Foreign Office's willingness to desert his roses and the tranquil streets of Northwood for as long as it took, diplomatic activity between the Hitler and Stalin regimes began to ratchet up.

Stalin, a connoisseur of raw power if ever there was one, had watched the West betray Czechoslovakia, to which the Soviet Union had been tied by alliance along with the French, leaving Russia isolated. Stalin was now faced with a direct border between the German sphere of influence and his own territory, enabling the possibility of direct invasion. Moreover, after the Munich Agreement, first Britain and then France had signed 'friendship treaties' with Hitler, raising, if one worried about such things, a possibility of their joining with Germany against Russia (Chamberlain, in particular, was a passionate anti-Communist). A Soviet arrangement with the Nazi state started to look like a rational course of action for Stalin.

As Europe's two main 'black sheep', Germany and Soviet Russia had been keen trading partners immediately after the First World War, as well as political and military collaborators. Under secret clauses of the Treaties of Rapallo and then Berlin between the two countries in 1922 and 1926, Weimar Germany had built up extra military forces forbidden under the Treaty of Versailles, trained a clandestine air force (likewise forbidden), and even experimented with chemical weapons, on Soviet soil before 1933.

Trade between Russia and Germany continued to be brisk until the virulently anti-communist Nazis came to power. In 1932, 46 per cent of the Soviet Union's imports of industrial machinery had originated from Germany; by 1938, that figure was down to 4.7 per cent, with German goods replaced by American and British products.[2] However, by 1938 the Soviets wanted German technology and weaponry, and the Nazis needed raw materials, which Russia had in plentiful supply. And then there was Poland.

The slow-burning campaign in the German press began to crackle more fiercely by the beginning of August 1939.

On 26 July 1939, Karl Schnurre, a Russia expert working for the Third Reich, had met with a senior Soviet diplomat, Georgei Astakhov, for dinner in a private room at Ewest, an old-established and exclusive Berlin restaurant just off the Friedrichstrasse that was often used by high German government officials. Each brought a junior colleague with him for confirmation's sake. Exploratory talks, led by Schnurre, about increased economic cooperation (German manufactured goods for Russian raw materials, as usual) had already progressed quite well. Now Schnurre upped the stakes. He had a three-stage deal prepared for the Russians – one that reportedly stunned the young German colleague he had brought with him to the dinner, who had no idea what was going to be discussed. Schnurre made the following suggestions:

Stage One: The reestablishment of collaboration in economic affairs through the credit and commercial treaty which was to be concluded.

Stage Two: the normalization and improvement of political relations.

Stage Three: The re-establishment of good political relations, either a return to what had been in existence before (i.e. the Berlin Treaty*) or a new arrangement which took account of the vital political interests of both parties.

'This stage three,' Schnurre said, 'appeared to me within reach.'[3]

On 1 August, the two men met again. Astakhov set two preconditions before political talks could begin: all anti-Soviet reports in the German press must cease, and there should be agreement on an economic treaty. The Germans assented. On 4 August, the German Ambassador in Moscow, Friedrich-Werner von der Schulenburg, met with Vyacheslav Molotov, Stalin's new

---

* Signed in 1926 and providing for neutrality if either Germany or Russia was attacked by a third party. The Berlin Treaty was perceived as a joint potential threat against Poland, the most likely 'third party' to be involved in any such conflict.

Commissar for External Affairs, who had replaced the pro-Western Litvinov in May. Schulenburg reported that the Soviet representative 'abandoned his usual reserve and appeared unusually open'.[4]

*

Hitler had already earmarked 26 August as the date for his attack on Poland. All the talk of British aggression and the German will for peace was therefore mere window-dressing, but the Führer as peace-lover was the line taken in the German press, under Goebbels's direction, during the first part of August.

The 'encirclement' idea was constantly hammered home: Britain, France and Poland and any other Eastern European countries they could persuade or bribe to join them were planning to intimidate Germany into giving up its justified claims – or, if Germany would not back down, to attack from multiple directions. Paranoid rhetoric along these lines filled the German press throughout the summer. The press also criticized the British and the French (but particularly the British) for hypocrisy in preaching democracy and the rule of law while actually possessing huge empires inhabited by subject peoples who enjoyed none of these things. And in this, at least, the Germans had a point.

In July 1939, the novelist and essayist George Orwell analysed the problem in a review of a book by the American journalist and internationalist Clarence K. Streit, a well-meaning and largely sensible writer. Streit wished, as did many others at the time, to unite the democracies – including their 'dependencies' (i.e. colonies) – against fascism. Orwell, who had his own experiences as a colonial police official in British-ruled Burma to fall back on, indicated the flaw in this idea:

> Look again at his list of sheep and goats. No need to boggle at the goats (Germany, Italy and Japan), they are goats right enough, and billies at that. But look at the sheep! Perhaps the USA will pass inspection if one does not look too closely. But what about France? What about England? What about even Belgium and Holland? Like everyone of his school of thought,

Mr Streit has coolly lumped the huge British and French empires
– in essence nothing but mechanisms for exploiting cheap
coloured labour – under the heading of democracies![5]

According to Orwell, the unspoken exception for most writers
in the democracies was that black and brown people did not
count in the moral equation. 'What we always forget,' he argued,
'is that the overwhelming bulk of the British proletariat does not
live in Britain, but in Asia and Africa.' He continued:

> It is not in Hitler's power, for instance, to make a penny an
> hour a normal industrial wage; it is perfectly normal in India,
> and we are at great pains to keep it so. One gets some idea of
> the real relationship of England and India when one reflects
> that the *per capita* annual income in England is something over
> £80, and in India about £7. It is quite common for an Indian
> coolie's leg to be thinner than the average Englishman's arm.
> And there is nothing racial in this, for well-fed members of the
> same races are of normal physique; it is due to simple starvation.
> This is the system which we all live on and which we denounce
> when there seems to be no danger of its being altered. Of late,
> however, it has become the first duty of a 'good anti-Fascist' to
> lie about it and help keep it in being.

It was not, of course, that Nazi Germany intended to behave any
differently if it got back the colonies it had lost after the First World
War – or when it came to the non-German lands in Europe that it
had already taken possession of or planned to conquer. However,
the hypocrisy of Chamberlain, Churchill, Halifax and company in
complaining about these things while their own subject races and
nations laboured under the British yoke was a handy weapon for
German propaganda. Palestine, of course, was especially useful,
since emotive articles listing the travails of the natives there (again,
to a large extent justifiably) served the useful dual purpose of simultaneously discrediting the British occupiers and the Zionist Jews.

The DNB digests for the German press in July were again
full of 'encirclement', the treachery and iniquity of the British

ruling class, and especially – in the latter regard – about the duel of ideas between Goebbels and British former naval officer, writer and broadcaster Commander Stephen King-Hall. King-Hall, then a well-known public figure, published a liberal-internationalist Newsletter that attracted subscribers in the tens of thousands.

The Commander had visited Germany and the Sudetenland that spring and been appalled at how easily ordinary Germans seemed to have been convinced by their government's anti-Czech and anti-Polish propaganda. In consequence, he had roused a group of fellow London clubmen and financed a scheme whereby, he was convinced, progress could be made towards encouraging influential Germans to see the British point of view. It was difficult. Germany was, after all, a closed society compared with Britain. King-Hall sought to solve this problem by writing a letter, in effect a leaflet, claiming to place the 'facts' of the Nazi government's bad intentions before the German public. 'Your leaders – at least, Ribbentrop, Goebbels, and Himmler – are quite impossible persons,' the letter proclaimed. It emphasized the determination of the British government and people to resist aggression, and warned of the dire consequences that would follow another war (the fate of a defeated Germany would make the Versailles Treaty look like 'child's play').[6] This was then mailed to 50,000 individuals, mainly businessmen, inside Germany.

King-Hall's initiative, which evidenced a certain clever, even brilliant, simplicity, outraged the German leadership. It even provoked a personal response from Goebbels – a six-page article for the Nazi Party newspaper the *Völkischer Beobachter*, which was then cited in every German paper. Hitler himself approved the text.

Their line ran, naturally, that King-Hall was not acting as a private individual, as he claimed, but was simply a propaganda tool of the British Foreign Office. In this clandestine capacity, King-Hall was supposedly working to divide the German people from its leaders on behalf of the notorious 'Lords' who would do anything to keep their empire – its evils described in the usual grisly detail in the article – and aiming to stop Germany from achieving her divinely ordained position in the world. The ex-naval man's 'letter' was nothing but a swindler's trick disguised by the apparently bluff, honest manner of an 'old sea dog'.[7]

The 'private war' between Goebbels and King-Hall continued into August, with mass mailings of another four letters to Germany. 'I shall certainly continue to send the letters,' King-Hall told the British press, continuing rather disingenuously, 'I do not know why the German Government is making so much fuss over purely private letters sent from an Englishman to German people. Goebbels in his news broadcasts is distorting the contents of my letters. He is even putting in words I have never written.'[8]

In response to German government complaints that their refutations of King-Hall's 'libels' were not being given their due in the British press, the Commander helpfully arranged, at his own expense, for excerpts from Goebbels's tirade to be printed in British daily newspapers, suggesting at the same time that perhaps the German government might, in return, publish some of his work in their own press outlets. Predictably, the latter request remained unanswered.[9] Instead, Goebbels ordered English translations of excerpts from his attack on King-Hall to be mailed to addresses in the United Kingdom.[10]

Goebbels's counterblast had been uncharacteristically clumsy as well as disproportionate. The time and space devoted to his response to King-Hall seemed to indicate discomfort on the Nazi regime's part.[11] According to the Sopade reports from their Silesian informants, it was only because of Goebbels's thunderous article that most locals had even heard about the King-Hall letter. There was mostly a certain wry admiration for the British publicist's brainwave among Germans who took an unfavourable view of the regime, but predictable outrage among Hitler's keen supporters.[12]

On the plus side, although Goebbels's response might have been judged excessive, it did to some extent neutralize King-Hall's effect on the pro-regime majority. It also provided an opportunity to keep the anti-British wave in full spate without the Propaganda Minister's needing to repeat himself. At the beginning of July, Hitler had impressed on Goebbels how important it was to 'stir up hatred against England. The German people must recognize that country as the heart of the resistance against us.' As for the enemy to the east, the Führer told the Propaganda Minister: 'We have to wear away at the Poles with our further silent preparations. They will lose their nerve at the decisive hour. England will be softened up by incessant propaganda.'[13]

The German press had been relatively kind to Chamberlain after the Munich Agreement. It was only following the Nazi occupation of Prague, and the change in the Prime Minister's rhetoric to a more critical tone, that German propaganda became more aggressive. Even then, the Goebbels-controlled press tended to concentrate on the 'warmongers' such as Churchill, Duff Cooper or Eden. By the summer, however, *Der Angriff,* organ of the Berlin Gauleiter (which is to say Goebbels himself), was quoted in the British press as transforming the British Prime Minister from the kindly peace-loving old gentleman who had flown to Godesberg and Munich into Britain's hypocrite-in-chief:

> This 'good old man' flew the Channel for the first time to Cologne. Naturally, he only undertook this journey 'in the cause of peace'. He was consequently feted in England and even in Germany, because a few fools really believed in this apostle of peace.[14]

In response to this relentless campaign of vilification, the British government did not, in fact, whip up the press against Germany. Rather, Sir Nevile Henderson, British Ambassador in Berlin, publicly requested that, given the delicate situation in Europe, King-Hall and his colleagues cease provoking the Germans. 'It is significant,' wrote the *Daily Mirror*, 'that according to a statement made yesterday, Sir Nevile considers it dangerous to "irritate" the Nazis, and that the withdrawal of Commander King-Hall's newsletters from circulation in Germany is indispensable to an improvement in Anglo-German relations.'[15]

Sure enough, a week later, Lord Beaverbrook's pro-Chamberlain *Express* called for the Commander to give up his campaign:

Commander King-Hall should stop sending his letters to
Germany. The only result has been that Goebbels has started
sending letters here. And we can be sure that the commander's
propaganda has no more effect on the Germans than Goebbels's
has on us. Such letters—if they serve any purpose at all—only
increase the tension between Germany and this country.[16]

King-Hall's letters had patently cut the Reich to the quick.
When Sir Nevile Henderson received his very last communication
from the German Foreign Minister, a few fatal weeks later, King-
Hall was mentioned by name and promoted to official spokesman
of the British government:

The intention communicated to us by order of the British
Government by Mr King Hall, of carrying the destruction of
the German people even further than was done through
the Versailles Treaty is taken note of by us, and we shall therefore answer any aggressive action on the part of England with
the same weapons and in the same form.[17]

Like most modern dictators and their servants, Hitler found
it impossible to believe that his government had been subjected
to extreme embarrassment not by some dastardly envoy of a
foreign power but by an eccentric independent commentator
who followed his instincts and wrote what he liked. Such people,
after all, had not existed in Germany since the very earliest
weeks of 1933.

*

The German press campaign during the early summer had concentrated less on direct anti-Polish propaganda than on the alleged
British 'encirclement' in which Poland, vulnerable to the bribes
and manipulations of the ever-cunning London string-pullers and
their Jewish financiers, had become implicated, arguably almost
against its will. Yes, there had been provocative material in the
German press about Polish interference in Danzig, but as yet no
rabid terror propaganda.

However, keeping the main thrust of German resentment within these boundaries had been something of a tactical choice. In July and early August, Hitler and the Danzig Gauleiter Albert Forster had systematically raised the stakes on this issue. The Führer's aim at this point, it seemed, was to engineer a crisis over the issue of Danzig's status which would give him, as the city's self-appointed protector, legitimate grounds to intervene, first diplomatically and then militarily, on its behalf. Before the Western allies knew it, Germany and Poland would be at war over what, on the face of it, was a relatively obscure technical matter. Within weeks, while the world was still puzzling as to the rights and wrongs of the argument, Poland would be defeated. Britain and France would be faced with 'facts on the ground' – facts over which, Hitler believed, they would not be prepared to plunge the entire Continent into war.[18]

The British assurance to Poland, after all, only pledged to defend the country's 'independence'; it did not guarantee its borders. In the past few weeks, the Chamberlain government had been pursuing a dual strategy, pursuing rearmament and conscription while at the same time trying to reopen negotiations with Germany, which might conceivably involve the Poles' agreeing to a territorial compromise regarding Danzig. Hence the government's pleas to the likes of Commander King-Hall not to provoke the Nazis.

At the beginning of August, the German press was still dealing with the ongoing dispute over the role of Polish customs officials in the city. Within a week there were more and more stories of Polish bureaucratic persecution of the German minority in the Corridor – German-owned bakeries and dairies closed down for hygienic reasons, groups of Polish thugs harassing Germans in church or at social events. Then, in the second week of the month, the dam began to crack. Even in the *Freiburger Zeitung*, in the far south-west of the country and hundreds of miles from Poland, there were dramatic headlines about the threat to Danzig and the prospect of mass violence against 'ethnic Germans' (*Volksdeutsche*) in Poland.

None of this was a coincidence. Between 7 and 9 August, Gauleiter Forster had been Hitler's guest at Berchtesgaden. He flew back to Danzig and at once made an incendiary speech, calling for the city to return to Germany. From then on, his demands would grow deliberately more extreme. Just as Henlein, the leader of the Sudeten Germans, had been ordered to make demands that the Czech government could not possibly fulfil, so now the Danzig Nazi leader began to provoke the Poles into breaking off negotiations or engaging in various border reprisals, and thus providing a case for war.

Between 10 and 13 August, Count Ciano, the Italian Foreign Minister, was in Germany. He met with Ribbentrop, his German counterpart, in Salzburg, and with Hitler at nearby Berchtesgaden. Ciano conveyed Mussolini's concerns about launching a war over Poland, but Ribbentrop and Hitler were implacable: Germany must attack and defeat Poland. The British and French would not go to war because of it. The democracies would ultimately put up with a localized war in the east for the sake of general peace.[19]

The indications were there that war was all but inevitable. On 11 August, according to Goebbels's diary, Hitler had ordered that the propaganda campaign against Poland be turned up to '80 per cent volume', and four days later would come the 'final spurt'.[20] In the early edition of the *Freiburger Zeitung* the next day, Saturday 12 August, in accordance with the new orders, a headline screamed 'War Against Germandom. 204 Attacks Accuse Poland'. In the past five weeks, it claimed, more than two hundred serious assaults on 'ethnic Germans' in Poland had been carried out, leading to six deaths and twenty-one cases of serious injury. It was a 'consciously targeted campaign for the extinction of Germandom in Poland', carried out with the open support of the Polish authorities:

> The patience with which the Reich has stood by and observed the shameless agitation and the megalomaniacal threats and power claims of Poland has found its limits . . . It seems that in the pro-Polish countries no one has yet realized that Polish megalomania has, through unleashing persecution of Germans in Poland, already begun that war at the prospect of which the democracies tremble.[21]

The British Foreign Office had, in fact, some idea of Hitler's timing. On 12 August Sir Alexander Cadogan wrote in his diary that Hitler had 'decreed *Spannung* [tension]' for 15 August, which meant the beginning of the 'battle of nerves'.[22]

The German press, meanwhile, was insisting that Germany and Italy were as one in their intentions, mocking British insinuations of disagreement between the Axis allies. These were just more mischief-making by the devious London 'Lords', who could have no idea what Ciano had discussed on his visit to Germany. As it happened, this last assertion was not true. Erich Kordt, the Resistance's man in Ribbentrop's entourage, had been in Salzburg that week, where he had heard about Italy's concerns from Ciano himself. Kordt had promptly made a coded telephone call to his brother Theo at the German Embassy in London, detailing the Italians' explicit disapproval of Hitler's warlike intentions. Within hours, the veteran Foreign Officer adviser Robert Vansittart had been fully informed in a meeting at a safe house, both of the disagreements between Italy and Germany, and of the time-window during which the attack on Poland would take place (25 to 28 August). The information was passed on to Lord Halifax. Halifax in turn wrote a long letter to the Prime Minister, who was still on his summer fly-fishing holiday in the Highlands of Scotland.[23]

Meanwhile, to complement the growing tide of stories about Polish madness and mayhem, there were articles in the German press boasting of the might of the Wehrmacht and the unshakeable unity of the German people, contrasted with tales of British anxiety and disorder. The *Freiburger Zeitung* for 14 August told of fears in London government circles that the country would starve in case of war, as it almost had in 1917; strikes among workers on military construction sites on Salisbury Plain; and disastrous failures during a recent British air defence exercise.[24]

The German propaganda offensive was carefully calibrated. Lurid accounts of Polish atrocities and persecution of 'ethnic Germans', of Danzig's determination to be German, and repeated assurances that the Reich's 80 million population and 'the best and most modern army in the world' would spring to the defence of their fellow Germans in the face of the Polish threat were counterbalanced by constant protestations of peaceful intent.

The next Nazi Party Congress (*Reichsparteitag*), due to be staged in Nuremberg from 2 to 11 September 1939 was, after all, officially titled 'The Party Congress of Peace'. Seven hundred thousand Party members had attended the 1938 Congress, titled 'Congress of Greater Germany' in celebration of the Austrian Anschluss. It was an impressive spectacle, and whatever reservations they might at some stage have harboured about the dictatorship, most Germans ended up duly impressed. Nineteen thirty-nine promised to be even more grandiose.

The press described the party congress grounds (*Reichsparteitagsgelände*) extending over 16.5 square kilometres on the outskirts of the city, as the 'Biggest Construction Site in the World'.[25] The gigantic Congress Hall, intended to seat up to 50,000 Party members, was still unfinished, as was the 'German Stadium', the 'biggest stadium in the world', as Speer described it, which would hold more than 400,000 spectators for the sporting events – including competitions in combat skills such as grenade-throwing – that the regime planned to stage there. Construction of the *Märzfeld* (Field of Mars) had only just begun, but it was intended to be a huge parade ground in which 250,000 spectators at future Party Congresses would be able to admire large-scale manoeuvres by the Wehrmacht.

Whether deliberately or otherwise, the 'Party Congress of Peace', with its seductively calming name, became a kind of totem for many at home and abroad. The more ominous things became, as the month of August wore on, the more stories about the Party Congress appeared in the press. If we could just get to the *Reichsparteitag*, there might be hope, the optimists surmised – the *Express*'s man in Berlin quoted Germans as saying: 'You see, nothing is going to happen – at least not until after the Party Congress.'[26]

By the middle of the month, however, it was becoming clear that the seemingly endless talks in Moscow between the French and British and Stalin's representatives were still not going well. Concrete discussions had begun about potential military cooperation. The Soviets had accordingly demanded a categorical agreement from Warsaw that the Red Army be granted free passage through Polish territory in case of war with Germany. The distrustful Poles, with several hundred years' history of foreigners entering their territory and refusing to leave, were holding out against any such assurance.

As for the talks between Germany and the Soviet Union, the details for an economic agreement were all but finalized. This would guarantee, from the Soviet side, raw materials, fuel, grain – all the supplies that would ensure Germany could sustain a major war. And, of course, since these materials would be coming from the east, mostly by land, Germany would not be threatened by a British naval blockade. The Nazi leadership was obsessed with avoiding a repeat of Germany's sufferings during the First World War, when such blockades had caused mass hunger and played a crucial role in bringing the Reich to its knees in 1918, amid riot and revolution.

*

'Don't Mind Hitler. Take Your Holiday. Book Here,' ran a poster outside a London travel agency in the summer of 1939.

The *Daily Mirror* was also eager to cheer up the British masses. More money was in circulation than ever before, and unemployment was down to about a million, the lowest for many years. Much of this inflation – for that was what it was – resulted from the rearmament boom, with reasons far from cheerful. On 5 August, the Saturday of the summer bank holiday weekend, the paper's opinion page nevertheless declared all this as cause for celebration under the headline 'There – And Back':

> You are going on a peace-time evacuation of happiness notwithstanding a year of hideous alarms. You have come cheerfully through the Nazi battle of nerves. John Bull is considerably stronger in armament biceps than he was this time last year.
>
> This is not to say that we are by any means complacent about the world situation, but common sense demands that we make holiday occasionally as a necessary physical and spiritual mobilization.

In Germany, though, it was not just holiday but also harvest time. Getting the harvest safely in is a key priority when war impends. Crops were being gathered in at fever pitch. With the continuing leakage of native agricultural labour from country to city, temporary labour from outside had to be conscripted on a massive scale in order to complete this key task. The Reichsarbeitsdienst (Reich Labour Service) was, as ever, drafted in to help. Certain classes of young childless women had also recently been declared liable to a year's conscription to work on the land before being released to find more congenial employ-ment. Members of the NS-Frauenschaft volunteered to do so – although not as many as the regime would have liked. Even the Wehrmacht in East Prussia, the 'granary of the Reich', was sent into the cornfields, with portions of it staying there despite the Führer's mobilization deadline of 26 August. And large numbers of adolescent members of the Hitler Youth, then on their summer school break, were drafted into rural areas, where makeshift work camps had been set up.

One such young draftee was shocked by the primitive condi-tions he endured in the countryside. Kurt Elfering, from Schwerte, a middling industrial town near Dortmund, had signed up for what he thought was a two-week camping trip with the local Hitler Youth group to Silesia, 800 kilometres to the east, not far from the border with Poland. It was only when they arrived in Breslau, Silesia's largest city (now Wroclaw), early next morning that they realized this was not just a leisure trip. At the station, they were told that before they could start their vacation they must spend a week doing farm work. They were loaded onto farm carts and transported to an agricultural estate outside Ohlau (Polish Olawa), 25 kilometres south-east of the city.

The boys' introduction to rural life was not a heartening experience. The farm itself looked dreary and the atmosphere was oppressive and feudal:

> Low cottage-like buildings lay on one side of the square. The
> first of these was where we were to be lodged. The dwellings
> were single-storeyed, with just an attic above them. On the

ground floor lived the cottagers (so far as we were concerned, these people were almost serfs of the estate). The floors of the dwellings were no more than trampled mud. There was just one door. The inner 'doors' were hung with sackcloth curtains. The beds had been crudely nailed together from boards and the mattresses were straw sacks. Compared with this, the miners' houses in the Ruhr region were luxury apartments.[27]

The Hitler Youth boys were put up in the attics, reachable via a steep wooden staircase. Straw was spread on both sides of the loft floor, leaving a narrow path down the middle. They laid the fly sheets from their tents over the straw and their blankets over the sheets to make rudimentary beds. They got to know the cottagers, all labourers on the estate, and a generous one-pot stew for lunch, served on a long table set up in the courtyard, further served to compensate a little for their gloomy first encounter with life on the land.

The boys were not due to start work until the next day, so there was a chance to look around. The landowner, whose status could only be described as feudal, lived nearby in an impressive mansion. He was something important with the government. His children played behind high hedges, supervised by nannies; the boys from Schwerte glimpsed them when the swings on which the children were amusing themselves rose high enough to be visible above the shrubbery. Kurt had relatives who farmed in the countryside near his home town, but they were prosperous independent farmers who owned their own houses and land. The medieval conditions here in the east were a revelation.

The next day, the boys were up at six to help with the harvest, along with the 'serfs'; they all followed a horse-drawn reaping machine supervised by a farm manager who patrolled on horseback and carried a short whip. A bell sounded to tell them when to start work and when to break. They were taught to bind the cut stalks, and over the next few days they were also put to work pulling turnips and digging potatoes, in intense heat. Nostalgia for 'the good old days' would never be an option for Kurt after that week on the farm in Silesia.

August 1939 had started out mostly damp, causing great concern about the fate of the ripening crops. After the middle of the month, however, the weather turned fine, and it stayed that way for the rest of the month. In the end, the harvest of 1939 in Germany was, along with that of 1938, the most successful of the 1930s. In that final year of peace, the country, in line with the autarky enforced by the regime, and despite the relative backwardness of German agriculture in general, managed to supply a record amount of its own basic food requirements – 83 per cent, compared with 68 per cent in 1928. By the autumn of 1939, the Reich had 8.8 million tonnes of grain in store, representing four times the reserve in 1937 and sufficient to supply the population with bread for a year even if the entire next year's harvest failed.[28]

Britain had plentiful foreign currency reserves, of course, plus established worldwide trading links, and an empire to call upon. Autarky was not the British way. Though the August weather had at first been wet, much as on the Continent – 'it has rained and rained and rained', as the *Daily Express* glumly informed its readers – there was no urgent conscription for the harvest.[29] By contrast with the Reich, and despite the recent introduction of agricultural subsidies to improve self-sufficiency, in 1939 the United Kingdom imported 70 per cent of its basic food requirements.[30] But as in Germany, a year's grain reserve had been built up, in Britain's case largely by discreet mass buying of wheat from abroad, along with large quantities of frozen meat shipped over from Australasia and the Americas. This fact was publicized as the international crisis worsened, perhaps to reassure the British public – mostly used to a more varied diet, enriched by plentiful imports, including tropical fruits, coffee, chocolate, and similar items generally in short supply for ordinary German consumers by this time – that in case of war they would not face starvation.[31]

Little more than twenty years after the end of the Great War that had brought disease, hunger, mass slaughter and destruction to Europe, the Continent's peoples found themselves facing another conflict, remembering the suffering the previous one had caused, grimly calculating what pain was yet to come, and how it might be borne.

Even some of those involved with the harvest in remote parts
of Germany gradually became aware of the impending crisis. Kurt
Elfering, for instance, cutting rye and digging potatoes for twelve
hours a day with the other boys from Schwerte, recalled:

> Not far from the farm ran the Autobahn to Upper Silesia.* From
> a nearby road bridge we could follow what was happening on
> the Autobahn. Since it was August 1939, and there were already
> indications of the coming European war, it was no wonder that
> on the Autobahn huge military transports were in motion,
> heading towards Upper Silesia. But at the time we hadn't quite
> realized the full significance of these events.[32]

Shortly after, the boys set off for their week's camping in the
mountains. By the time their chartered train arrived back in
Dortmund, the world was forever changed.

*

In the second week of August, the writer Erich Ebermayer finally
returned to Berlin from his recently acquired country retreat at
Kaibitz, near Bayreuth. Soon afterwards, he met with Hans
Schweikart, the director of his latest film, *Liberated Hands* (*Befreite
Hände*), in the bar of the Eden Hotel in the Budapester Straße, a
popular meeting place for Berlin's cultural elite. Everyone loved
Ebermayer's script, Schweikart assured him, and it was 'becoming,
toi-toi-toi, a great thing'. Brigitte Horney, who starred in *Aufruhr
in Damaskus*, had been signed for the lead role, playing a woman
who discovers her talent for sculpture and struggles to escape
dull everyday life and devote herself to art. Ebermayer took a
cynical view of people in the self-referential Berlin film world:

> No matter whom you talk to in Berlin – no one believes in a
> serious crisis this autumn, let alone the possibility of war. I hold
> my tongue as best I can. But it is strange how seriously even

---

* Until the First War a province of Prussia, after a disputed plebiscite in 1920,
mostly part of Poland – to many ordinary Germans' disgust.

clever people are afflicted with blindness. They don't *want* a crisis – so none is coming. Why should it? Everything is so wonderful, after all! Everywhere, things are on the up! Everyone is earning splendid money. The weather is good. So, why worry?[33]

But worry did start to come, slowly, even to the privileged, as August ran its anxious course. Travel began to be restricted. In Britain too, people began to return from trips abroad earlier than they had planned. Just in case.

Meanwhile, tolerance for the British friends of Hitler's Germany was wearing thin. Sixty-year-old Admiral Sir Barry Domvile KBE CB CMG, former chief of Naval Intelligence and Chairman of 'The Link', a pro-Nazi, anti-Semitic organization opposed to war with Hitler under any circumstances, was accused by the Home Secretary, Sir Samuel Hoare, of functioning as a propaganda arm of Germany and accepting money from Berlin. The Admiral was a frequent visitor to Germany and had been an official guest at the 1936 and 1937 Nuremberg Rallies. A reporter visiting Domvile's mock-Tudor West London home in August spotted a signed photograph of Hitler and snaps of Himmler and Hess on the walls in the living room, as well as a cased medal commemorating his attendance at Nuremberg. The Admiral, an English eccentric of the less appealing sort, denied being anti-patriotic and appeared to lie outright about his Nazi sympathies:

'I am non-party. I hold no political views,' said Sir Barry. 'I was a guest of the Nazi authorities at the Nuremberg Conferences of 1936 and 1937. Last year I could not go because my wife was ill. This year I hope to go because, although it is tiring, it is a magnificent spectacle . . .'[34]

As the attendance at Mosley's Earls Court rally in July had shown, there remained a sizeable and vocal minority in Britain that opposed any military response to Hitler's expansionist plans. The majority seems to have instinctively supported Chamberlain's new policy of rearmament and support for threatened small countries, especially Poland, though there was often a distinct vagueness when appraising what was actually going on in Europe. A report for Mass Observation in the late spring of 1939, after the Nazi occupation of Prague had all but destroyed public support for Appeasement, stated that exactly the same percentage of the public was satisfied with the Prime Minister's foreign policy (28 per cent) as had favoured his (quite different) foreign policy the previous year. What had increased, however, quite substantially, were the numbers who expressed themselves as 'vague, doubtful or bewildered' regarding which policy to approve. Respondents taking refuge in this last option had risen from 40 per cent to 55 per cent of the total. As the MO report stated, 'for those millions who do not understand maps and have no passport, the whole thing seems merely crazy'.[35]

At least in Britain opinions could be publicly expressed, even when they did not agree with the government's approved course of action. Guesses – educated or uneducated – could be made as to what was going on in the world and what to do about it.

Some three dozen by-elections in the time between Munich and the final crisis with Poland did not give a clear idea of general public opinion on foreign policy matters. There was a general trend towards Labour, but although the leftward drift was not decisive, it was sufficient to persuade Conservative Party strategists to discourage Chamberlain from calling an early general election to exploit his supposed popularity after Munich.[36] As the sporadic tests of public opinion via the ballot box continued into 1939, participation levels dropped, while the swing towards Labour and anti-Chamberlain candidates steadied, and if anything slowed. Indifferent – or perhaps bewildered – as many British citizens may have been, the public debate was both constant and lively, and to some extent it influenced government strategy. Whenever Chamberlain was tempted to renege on his post-Prague promises to toughen up, public opinion kept him at least partly in line.

In Germany, however, the state was now omnipresent and Hitler's power untrammelled. Schacht had been pushed out of the Reichsbank earlier that year, giving Hitler total control of the nation's finances, and since von Blomberg's forced resignation in January 1938 the Führer was his own War Minister as well. Given this situation, and whatever their private political convictions, Ebermayer's artistic friends' deliberate refusal to acknowledge the gravity of the international situation almost begins to look like a rational choice. Barring involvement in the illegal Resistance, opposition to Hitler's decisions could not be expressed in public – or even in private, unless the speaker was sure of the discretion of the hearer. Moreover, even among those who felt disquiet about what the Nazis were doing to their country, there was not, on the whole, a commitment to the rules-based model of international behaviour, or to the institutions such as the League of Nations that embodied those rules, which still influenced people in the Western democracies.

What most Germans saw as the wretched fate of their country in the 1920s and early 1930s, when the Reich had – it seemed to them – agreed to 'play by the rules' and suffered for it, hardly encouraged belief in anything beyond pursuit of the country's immediate interests. Looked at in this way, Germany's interests to a great extent consisted not of supporting the international order but of disrupting it. Such narrow national priorities were the only aims that Hitler's ideology recognized, and so far, from the remilitarization of the Rhineland to the Anschluss, the annexation of the Sudetenland, and in the past spring the occupation of the rump Czecho-Slovakia, he had got away with his ruthless and spectacularly disruptive pursuit of those priorities.

Might he not get away with it again, this time retrieving Danzig and the Corridor for Germany without a major war? And if things came to it, a 'little war' of border revision against Poland, correcting the last serious injustice inflicted by the Treaty of Versailles, might be a tolerable prospect, not worth the spoiling of a fine summer over.

Somehow, the Führer's constant assurances that he was a man of peace had sunk into the national consciousness. By 1939, ordinary Germans for the most part believed him. They were not to know that, in private with his intimates and senior officers, Hitler had during the past months and even years made no secret of his ambitions to expand Germany, especially to the east, by force. As he had already admitted to the Reich's loyal journalists in Munich the evening after *Kristallnacht*, the Führer's 'love of peace' was fakery for public consumption, a pretence that could be abandoned when he was sufficiently confident in Germany's military power to act as he wished.[37]

NINE

23–31 August 1939
'Grandmother Is Dead'

At the end of the third week of August 1939, Hitler pulled off his most brilliant and unexpected trick of disruption yet. In the evening edition of the *Freiburger Zeitung* on 22 August, a banner headline proclaimed: 'Greater Germany's Diplomacy Has Presented the Outside World with a Sensation. Event of World-Historical Importance'.[1]

The announcement of a Non-Aggression Pact between Germany and the Soviet Union was indeed a worldwide sensation, but it was something even more radical than that to the majority of Germans. They had been told for six and a half years now that Moscow was the fount of all evil, a backward, Asiatic, Jew-dominated peril to the world. Unease ensued. As a report for the Party leadership in Westphalia put it, although most people saw the military logic of the new relationship with Russia, 'politically or philosophically one often encounters a considerable sense of uncertainty, even in the ranks of Party comrades'.[2]

Even as Ribbentrop boarded his aircraft to fly to Moscow for the signature ceremony, British, French and Polish military representatives remained in Moscow, still hoping to conclude discussions with the Soviet government about an alliance to defend Poland. The announcement was received by government, press and public in Britain with stunned disbelief. Just the previous day, reporting on the trade treaty between Russia and Germany, the *Express* had assured its readers that 'the conclusion of the pact has no political significance. The Russians take the view that trade relations are completely divorced from political relations.'[3]

Although the possibility – thought to be, on balance, relatively slight – of a Russian–German agreement had been casually discussed over the past weeks,[4] it seems from the Foreign Office mandarin Sir Alexander Cadogan's diary that the British government had only learned early that morning that the pact was imminent. The American government, apparently well-informed about the German–Russian talks, had actually sent a telegram to London on 17 August providing an update, but it carried no priority marking and had not been received by the Foreign Office's Central Department until 22 August.[5] R.A. Butler, Minister of State at the Foreign Office, found himself under attack in the House of Commons, accused of being unprepared for the Moscow surprise, and plaintively told Cadogan that 'last night everyone was asking me what "our intelligence" is up to'.[6]

For the moment, the government decided that it must tough things out. On 23 August, the *Express*'s banner headline was that Britain would stand by Poland and that a new Defence of the Realm Act (DORA), similar to that passed in 1914 and giving the government emergency war powers, would be introduced within the week.[7] A note delivered by the British Ambassador to Hitler at Berchtesgaden warned that the new accord with Russia would make no difference to Britain's commitment to Poland ('no greater mistake could be made' than to think so). The effect of Chamberlain's stern words for Hitler was, however, slightly blunted by the addition of extra remarks at the end of the note in which he appealed to the Führer to seek a peaceful solution to his differences with Poland and promised that Britain would cooperate with any such efforts.[8] That evening, Cadogan wrote wearily in his diary: 'These crises are really too tiresome. We can't go on living like this in Europe.'[9]

The Foreign Office was using every means at its disposal to read behind the sound and fury of the German preparations.

There were rumours of frayed relations between the German railways authorities and the Reich leadership. The officials responsible for making the trains run in these unpredictable August days had made it clear that they could manage either a mobilization of the Wehrmacht or travel arrangements for the Party Rally in Nuremberg due in the first week of September (the latter the largest single transport challenge of any given year), but they could not do both. Which would the powers that be choose? Cadogan wrote on 20 August:

> The first information is to the effect that he had chosen the Nuremberg Rally, but I understand that both the Admiral[*] and Van's[†] sources are now disposed to be of one mind in the sense of thinking that the Nuremberg Rally will be, in comparison with previous gatherings, symbolic – the railways being absorbed by troop transport and the meeting being only for those who can get there on foot or by car.

On 23 August, Cadogan reported 'all German military preparations going forward' but, despite information from the German opposition that the attack on Poland was planned for the end of that same week, he was still not prepared to see it as necessarily more than part of the 'war of nerves'.

The next day, 24 August, was a 'black day'. The Foreign Office nonetheless began to hatch a scheme to have Mussolini put a brake on Hitler. Cadogan told Halifax, the Foreign Secretary, that 'only one thing to do was to say to Musso: "We can't urge Poles to agree to Danzig's incorporation in Reich. *If* Hitler will agree (a) that Polish rights must be safeguarded and (b) that settlement must be internationally guaranteed, that would give us a basis on which we might approach the Poles."' Chamberlain agreed to this and a telegram was sent off to Rome.[10]

Meanwhile, early on the afternoon of 25 August, Hitler had

---

[*] Admiral Sir Hugh Sinclair, the head of MI6.

[†] Sir Robert Vansittart.

actually issued the directive for 'Case White' (the plan for the invasion of Poland). German forces began to mass at the frontier. The attack was due to be launched before dawn on 26 August.

At around the same time on 25 August, however, Britain, reacting with unaccustomed speed to the Nazi–Soviet Pact, had agreed a formal Treaty of Mutual Assistance with Poland. And also that afternoon, the Italians did finally tell Hitler that they could not mobilize along with their German ally: Mussolini was not ready. For the last time, the Führer hesitated. That night, he halted his army's movements towards the frontier with Poland, though these were already well advanced, especially in Pomerania and East Prussia.

On Saturday 26 August, the 1939 Nuremberg 'Rally of Peace' was officially cancelled. Later that same day, Hitler, apparently regaining his nerve, reissued the 'Case White' directive. The date for the invasion of Poland was now set for Friday 1 September.

On 27 August, Sunday, it was announced in Berlin that ration cards would be introduced for many everyday items. If this was indeed, as Cadogan surmised, part of some clever German campaign to unnerve its enemies, an imitation of war, then it was getting terrifyingly close to the real thing.

*

The extremism of the propaganda campaign mounted against Poland in the latter half of August is hard to exaggerate. To read through the articles published day after day in the various DNB handouts, pressed onto every editor of every newspaper in Germany, is to suffer a rage, a haunted invention, which almost defies description. Every measure introduced by the Polish government during these crisis days was picked up, pulled apart and malevolently interpreted, every act of the Polish authorities with regard to the German minority in the country likewise, and every clash between Polish- and German-speakers, especially in Danzig or the Corridor, portrayed as an anti-German atrocity or at the very least a provocation. The wilder shores of Poland's lively ultra-nationalist fringe were trawled for violently anti-German and pro-war pronouncements, which were presented as official Polish policy.

During the decades before the First World War, governments

in Berlin had aggressively encouraged German settlement in the formerly Polish provinces annexed at the end of the eighteenth century by Prussia. After 1918, when Poland became independent once more, and these areas were returned to the new state, the process went into reverse. The previously substantial German population in the 'Corridor', in what had been 'West Prussia' (around Poznań) and in Polish Upper Silesia, declined sharply, owing to forced departure or voluntary emigration. That there was discrimination against the remaining German minority in Poland – totalling around three-quarters of a million, or 2.3 per cent of the population according to the 1931 census – there can be no doubt. The policy of the Warsaw government during those years towards its Germans was one of strong pressure to assimilate or leave. It was appreciably more intolerant in that regard than the Czechoslovak state. However, it was not genocidal.

Until early 1939, the Hitler regime had underplayed the injustices inflicted on ethnic Germans by the Warsaw government. Hitler, seeking stability while building up his military strength, had, after all, signed a treaty of friendship and non-aggression with Poland in 1934. Only when the Sudetenland had been digested and Prague gobbled up, and the regime began to look further east for new acquisitions, did Goebbels and his propaganda machine discover how especially foul the Poles were to 'their' Germans. As late as Hitler's speech to the Reichstag on 30 January 1939, he had referred to the friendship between Poland and Germany as 'a reassuring factor in Europe's otherwise troubled political life'.

In his speech on 1 April at Wilhelmshaven, in which he had launched his campaign against Britain for its allegedly treacherous 'encirclement' strategy, Hitler had not mentioned Poland by name at all – even though he had, that same day, given orders for the Wehrmacht to be prepared for an invasion at any time after 1 September 1939. That deadline was now fast approaching, and hence the flood of anti-German atrocity stories. It was a tried and trusted technique for attracting sympathy from the foreign press and governments, and above all for persuading the German people itself of the urgent need for military intervention. A sample of headlines in one single-page handout dated 18 August 1939 is typical:

**Mistreatment of political leaders of the Foreign
Organization* in Poland**
('In the last 24 hours, the brutalities of the Polish authorities
against racial Germans have reached unsurpassable levels. The
bestiality with which German women and girls are mistreated
shows the complete moral inferiority of the Poles.')
**Panic Atmosphere in Upper Silesia
Polish troops abuse the Germans of Pomerelia†
100 Germans arrested again
Germans in Polish prisons beaten to death
Danzig railwaymen arrested in Poland
Poland: England's colony on the Vistula**[11]

A week later, the headlines stepped up a level, moving from
atrocity reporting to accusations of Polish warmongering:

**Poland plans surprise attack on German territory
Monstrous Polish mass murder at Lodz
Prices on heads of Germans
Poles smuggle explosives to Danzig
State Secretary Stuckart‡ shot at by Poles**[12]

The *Freiburger Zeitung*'s front page on 25 August accordingly ran
a headline about 'aggressive Polish mobilization' plus an equally
prominent version of the 'surprise attack' piece from the DNB (in
this version, 'Threat of Polish Attack. Gdingen and Eastern Upper
Silesia an Army Camp – Strongest Threat to German Territory').
Several other stories from the same edition of the DNB were
used in the following day's paper (26 August), with the front two

---

* 'AO' (*Ausland-Organisation*) of the Nazi Party, open to all racial Germans outside
the territory of the Reich.

† The official name for the 'Polish Corridor'.

‡ Wilhelm Stuckart was a Nazi lawyer and State Secretary at the Interior Ministry,
responsible for among other things framing anti-Semitic legislation. His aircraft was
fired at by Polish anti-aircraft artillery as he returned to Berlin from a conference
in Danzig.

pages taken over almost exclusively with articles detailing Polish aggression, threats, or atrocities, including the Stuckart story, the 'mass murder at Lodz' story, and rumours of Polish preparations to invade German Silesia, including production of street and station signs in Polish to replace the current German ones.

Two articles also moved away from the specifics of the dispute with Poland and into the area of psychological preparation of the population for the coming conflict. On the front page there was a piece entitled 'The Hour of Liberation Is Coming. Germany Will Not Allow Itself to Be Betrayed by Phrases Again', attacking President Roosevelt's appeal for a peaceful solution. It reminded German readers of how the Americans, with their apparently idealistic 'Fourteen Points' at the end of the First World War, had promised peace and democracy but inflicted only pain on the defeated Reich. This too was taken from the previous day's DNB, amounting to a lightly rewritten version of a boilerplate article entitled 'Sanctimonious Peace Slogans Like 1918'.[13] Page 4, after a quick round-up of local news, then went on to reproduce a half-page condemnation of young people in Poland, their idleness, drunkenness, criminality and lack of proper hygiene or education ('Degenerate Polish youth'). Seventy per cent of Poles, the article claimed, suffered from tuberculosis or trachoma, and one in five had syphilis. And so on and on, hammering home the regime's message that Germany's neighbours were filthy and degenerate and criminal; in the final analysis, little more than vermin.[14]

This was the language of systematic dehumanization. The German people was being primed not, as Hitler continued to claim for international consumption, to wage a righteous war to redraw unjust borders, but rather to eliminate a nation, Poland, that in his eyes had no moral or even biological right to exist. Hitler had already vouchsafed this in a two- to two-and-a-half-hour speech at a secret meeting with his most senior military commanders on 22 August in the meeting hall at the Obersalzberg. They had been driven to the conference in civilian clothes to avert suspicion, with Göring appearing in old hunting tweeds.

In his address, the Führer revealed his plans to crush Poland as an independent political entity. No authorized transcript exists, but several of the participants thought his remarks sufficiently important – and perhaps chilling enough – to create a record. According to shorthand notes jotted down by Colonel General Franz Halder, who was present, Hitler did not his mince his words when informing his commanders of their task as he envisaged it and the ruthlessness he expected in its execution. First urging his generals to 'stay hard' even if Germany was attacked by Britain and France, the Führer became chillingly specific about the nature of the coming campaign in the East:

2) Goal: Annihilation of Poland – destruction of active power. We are not setting out just to reach a specific line or establish a new frontier, but rather we seek the annihilation of the enemy, which we must pursue in ever new ways.

3) Means to this end: It does not matter what they are. The victor is never called on to vindicate his actions. The question is not one of the justice of our cause, but exclusively of achieving victory.

4) Execution: Harsh and remorseless. We must all steel ourselves against humanitarian reasoning![15]

Hitler's address to his paladins was reportedly an unbuttoned affair. According to at least two separate accounts, he described the democratic politicians he had encountered at Munich as 'little worms', and expressed his determination to go to war this time. His only fear, he said, was that (as in September 1938) 'some *Schweinehund* will put forward a mediation plan'.[16]

There were, actually, some potential mediators around. Mussolini, of course. And a Swedish businessman acquaintance of Göring, Birger Dahlerus, who spoke excellent English and had extensive business contacts in England. At the Reich Marshal's behest, Dahlerus – whose actual sympathies were not entirely clear – undertook some amateur shuttle diplomacy over the next few days. The British were prepared to encourage Warsaw to compromise over Danzig, but (correctly) saw German demands for the Corridor, even with a plebiscite attached, as something the proud and stubborn Poles were extremely unlikely to stomach.[17]

There was a great deal of activity over the next days, but agreement proved fatally elusive. The only recourse for ordinary people was to follow the news on the radio and in the newspapers and, especially in Germany, to observe at close quarters the massive mobilization of the armed forces that was now in seemingly unstoppable progress.

*

Ruth Andreas-Friedrich and her partner, the Russian-German conductor Leo Borchard, were in Stockholm on 22 August when the news of the Nazi–Soviet Pact hit the world's headlines 'like a bomb'. Borchard returned from the city with a pile of newspapers and said gravely: 'It looks like the time has come. I fear we shall have to be on our way.'

Andreas-Friedrich and her circle had known since 1933 that sooner or later Hitler's policy would mean a war – one they thought Germany would lose. She felt a stab of guilt at the fact that defeat for her country might be the only way to rid it of the totalitarian evil, but 'an end with terror would almost be more bearable than this terror without end'.[18]

By late on Saturday 26 August, she and Leo were back in Berlin. During their return journey, the streets, station platforms and waiting rooms along the line swarmed with reservists carrying rucksacks and cardboard boxes of belongings, heading to report to their units. 'Their anxious faces said: "We don't want a war,"' Andreas-Friedrich reported. When they finally arrived at Berlin's Stettin Station, the situation was chaotically crowded. They secured a porter to carry their luggage, and were surprised that he spoke freely about the crisis, without obvious fear of the Gestapo: 'First day of mobilization. They've sent the kids home from school and summoned the Reichstag. The craziness is supposed to get going tomorrow.'

On arriving back at her flat, a travel-weary Andreas-Friedrich found a note from her friend Susy Simonis, who had close contact within the government elite though her cousin, Erich Kordt, requesting that she call her immediately. This Andreas-Friedrich did. Susy had intended to warn her that rationing was about to be introduced, but now it was too late to do anything. The shops were closed and wouldn't be open again until Monday, by which time the restrictions would be in place.

Out in the real world, where people did not have government contacts, the foreshadowings of war – mobilization and the issuing of ration cards – were received with mixed feelings. There was still general reluctance to go to war, but the feeling that the government had things in hand provided some comfort. All the same, German women, at least according to the Party's eyes and ears in the Westphalian city of Bielefeld, were especially vulnerable to concerns about their men being called up:

> Among the female part of the population, which judges things more from the emotional side, one can ascertain a certain nervousness. More especially, the thought is widespread that a war for DANZIG is an act of madness, for it would be irresponsible to sacrifice millions of human beings for the sake of one town. It might perhaps be appropriate to enlighten the people about this to the effect that quite other things are at stake here, that this is a matter of the existence or non-existence of the German people.[19]

The report went on:

> The most outstanding indication of the general popular mood seems to be fear of a war, which frequently conceals itself behind the assertion that one does not believe that it will come to war. But this is just a manner of speaking, because people hope that it will not. In reality they all reckon with a war, one with which no one – apart from a few young people – has the slightest sympathy. It is not that people fear the others' superior strength, but that they are still too much influenced by the experience of the previous war.

On the positive side, for the regime, the trust of the public in the Führer was 'unshakeable, and the people will follow him whatever happens'.

The last point was generally true. The continuing faith of the masses in Hitler was, ultimately, what the survival of the dictatorship would depend on if, despite the people's anxieties and lack of enthusiasm, the country went to war. The report's appraisal of the younger generation's attitude also seems to have been accurate. Almost seven years of insistent propaganda had exerted their effect on a cohort born in the early to mid-1920s, with no memory, however faint, of the previous war. 'Oh yes,' as one woman, then a teenage girl and enthusiastic member of the BDM would recall. Her generation's self-belief had been total. 'There was a certain euphoria'[20] In Bielefeld, the authorities found themselves on the receiving end of complaints from the young at being blocked from joining up:

> Younger people in many cases complain bitterly that there is no possibility for them to enlist voluntarily, as many would like to do. I know that the recruitment squad is only planning to take on volunteers after the mobilization is complete.[21]

Certainly, serious anxiety (perhaps not all that different from the 'bewilderment' felt in Britain) was not confined to those who opposed the regime. As Erich Ebermayer pointed out, the locals in the area where he had bought his castle were overwhelmingly enthusiastic Hitler supporters, but, during the days of mobilization and tension, no less despondent for that. 'The mood in the district capital, Kemnath, is suddenly very flat,' he wrote on 28 August:

> All these Party members – I don't believe that, apart from the priest, there are any who are not! – are almost visibly hang-dog to look at. The bicycle dealer* and his wife are totally depressed. It is as if these simple people, who have never before bothered with politics – our Führer will sort everything out! – have suddenly awoken from a whirl of big slogans and seen reality in front of their eyes. Poor German people![22]

---

* Ebermayer had just bought a bike, in response to the rationing of petrol and anticipating all the local cycle shop's stocks being commandeered by the military.

Ruth Andreas-Friedrich had written about the frantic atmosphere on the city streets, and at the railway stations. In remoter
parts, the atmosphere was a little different – more thoughtful,
even elegiac. A nineteen-year-old diarist, son of a farming family
near Lindau, on Lake Constance, described being woken at 2
a.m. on 28 August. A mobilization official had arrived in his village
by car and roused the local reservists – older men familiar to
him since childhood – from their beds:

> The neighbours who have been called up are almost all married,
> and an oppressive mood of departure hangs over the whole
> village.
>   Feeling the chill, I sit at the window. A cool night wind is
> blowing, and I listen to the discussions these men are conducting
> in the small hours. The final sentence of all these conversations
> is: 'War is coming.' By the way they speak I think I can discern
> what these veterans of the previous war are not willing to put
> into words: 'So, is killing to be our duty again? Are the bloody
> years of 1914–18 going to be repeated once more?'[23]

Germany waited. War was now just a matter of a final order
from Berlin; an order that, after almost seven years of dictatorship, depended wholly on the decision of a single, near-enough
omnipotent man who, unknown to his people, had all but made
his mind up to attack.

*

By the last week in August 1939, in Britain, the Militia conscripts,
six weeks into their training, had been set to work guarding
bridges and tunnels – not against possible German parachutists
but against the IRA, whose campaign had stepped up since the
first bombs in Manchester and London and was about to become,
if briefly, bloodier still.
    On Friday 25 August 1939 at 2.32 in the afternoon, a 5 lb
bomb exploded in the carrier of a tradesman's bicycle parked
against the kerb outside Astley's, a hardware store in Coventry's
main shopping street, Broadgate. Friday was the local market day,

and the streets in the centre of the Midlands industrial city were busy. Five passers-by were killed, twelve seriously injured, and forty or more needed treatment.[24] Two of the victims were shop assistants on their lunch breaks. One of the other dead, 21-year-old Elsie Ansell, had been so terribly injured as to be identifiable only by her engagement ring. She had been due to marry in September. John Arnott, at sixteen the youngest of those killed, worked as a sales assistant at a nearby branch of W.H. Smith, the newsagent. He was, by all accounts, a cheery young man. Newspaper reports described him as a 'curly-headed lad who wore glasses and must have served thousands of Coventry people with their papers and magazines'. Rex Gentle, thirty-three, one of a pair of identical twins from mid-Wales, had been in Coventry just two weeks, also working at W.H. Smith on a summer holiday relief basis. He too was engaged to be married. Gwilym Rowland, fifty, a street sweeper for the city council, happened to be doing his job in Broadgate when the bomb went off. The oldest victim, James Clay, was a spry 81-year-old who still worked part-time as an accountant. He had been lunching with an old business colleague at a cafe but had left early because he felt unwell. After the explosion, the friend told reporters that this was the first time, in six years of regular lunch dates, that he and Mr Clay had not left the cafe together.[25]

It was assumed at once, and rightly, that the attack had been mounted by the Irish Republican Army. Dozens of IRA 'actions' had been carried out all over Britain during the first eight months of the year, mostly to no great effect.[26] Counting minor transgressions such as wire cutting or small incendiary attacks, Coventry had already experienced a couple of dozen incidents that were probably part of the campaign. In June 1939, an unexploded bomb was found near a petrol dump in the city. At the beginning of July 1939 there was an explosion in the cloakroom of Coventry Station. One person was actually killed by a similar bomb at King's Cross Station in London towards the end of that month. On 13 August an explosion destroyed an allotment shed occupying waste ground behind some suburban houses in Coventry. Police suspected an accident at an IRA arms dump.

So it cannot have come as a particular surprise to the authorities when a bomb went off in Coventry less than two weeks later, on 25 August. What may have been genuinely unexpected was the fact that it was set to explode in a much-frequented public place and cause inevitable loss of life. Until now, no bombs of such destructive power had been laid. Indeed, the IRA had publicly announced earlier in the year that it intended no deliberate civilian casualties.

Although the timer-controlled explosion had blown off the entire front end of the bicycle, scattering fragments hundreds of feet into the air, forensic experts rapidly started to make sense of the mess. The bicycle, it seemed, had been left, parked directly behind a car, for up to an hour before the detonation.

The hunt for more evidence soon revealed not just traces of the timing device but also a registration number on the frame of the bicycle, which proved that it had been bought at a shop in Coventry three days previously. The purchaser, an Irishman who gave his surname as Norman, handed over £5 to reserve the item, the balance to be paid on collection. However, it was a different Irishman who had appeared three days later, at around noon on 25 August, handed over the rest of the money due, and ridden the bike away. Less than two hours later, its carrier now packed with a home-made explosive charge of potassium chlorate, the bicycle exploded. The address its original purchaser had given was a false one, as was his name.

It was the existence of a parallel plot in London that led to the unravelling of the mystery. Also on 25 August, Special Branch police raided a flat in Leinster Gardens, Paddington. The Irish tenants had been observed taking possession of a tradesman's tricycle in the East End and having other tradesmen's cycles at the address. After a chase across the local rooftops, four were arrested and the flat searched. Explosives were found. A timer clock was set for 2.31 that afternoon (one minute before the Coventry bomb's setting). Questioning revealed that Scotland Yard, Westminster Abbey and the Bank of England had been their intended targets, using the cycles currently parked outside the address.

That evening, an Irishman named Peter Barnes was arrested at his nearby lodgings. Barnes was an IRA transport officer, suspected of having couriered the explosives from Liverpool to London and – as evidence in his room indicated – to Coventry also. Police also found an incriminating letter, unposted but addressed to a certain 'Jim Kelly' in Ireland, which strongly implied Barnes's role in and expectation of an imminent IRA 'spectacular' bombing. When asked by an officer to confirm if he had visited Coventry recently, Barnes replied: 'I have been to Coventry, but coincidences can happen, can't they?'[27]

The attack caused a wave of anti-Irish feeling in Coventry, which had a large Irish population, including recent arrivals attracted by the jobs available in its booming aircraft and armaments factories. The *Daily Mirror* described the overwrought scenes that had followed the explosion:

> Five people – three men who ran from a public house and entered a car, a woman and a youth – were taken to the police station for protection.
>
> The youth, aged about fourteen, was crying as he was placed in the police van.
>
> As the police made their way with them through the crowd, the crowd shouted 'lynch them!'. Police had difficulty in protecting the men.
>
> One of them was knocked unconscious by a hammer blow to the head.
>
> Later all five were released. The police were satisfied that they were not connected with the outrage.
>
> At one time, the crowd became hysterical, and Irish people in it were roughly treated. The police restored order.[28]

The incident might well have attracted more attention if the crisis between Germany and Poland had not dominated the headlines. There were more anti-Irish incidents in Coventry over the following days. On the Monday after the outrage, some 2,000 workers from the Armstrong Whitworth aircraft works at

Baginton, on the city's outskirts, left their work and marched into the centre to protest against having to 'cooperate with Irish labour'. Outside the Council House (as Coventry Town Hall is known), they were addressed by their chief shop steward and then by the city's Mayor, Sidney Stringer. Stringer, a strong Labour man, reminded the protesters that the overwhelming majority of their fellow citizens of Irish heritage were equally appalled by the atrocity.

The crowds eventually dispersed, but it took some time for feelings to ease. Threats were made against Irishmen lodging in the city, and many left, at least temporarily.[29] The city's Chief Constable, Captain S.A. Hector, felt forced to issue a bizarre statement disclaiming suspicions about his own background:

> Stupid rumours have reached me that I am of Irish extraction. I am a Somerset man. I am not Irish, and had had no Irish connections, and I have never even been in Ireland.[30]

*

The Coventry bombing represented, in the end, the last major 'mission' undertaken on the British mainland by the IRA during its 1939 campaign, but the emergency kept the half-trained Militiamen busy. It also headed off some of the gentle mockery that had come their way over the past weeks. Earlier in August, there had been stories of recruits refusing to eat tinned salmon because it was rumoured to be of Japanese origin, in protest at the Japanese blockade of the British concession in the Chinese port of Tientsin, which had begun in June and was still being enforced in mid-August.

The *Sunday Express* came to the conclusion that the Militiamen simply didn't like tinned salmon:

> Now most of our Militiamen are splendid fellows. It is only a very small minority of them who fill the newspapers each day with squawks and squeals.
>
> The time has come to crack down on this troublesome lot. Men who served in the trenches twenty-one years ago laugh

at the grievances brought forward today. They know that old soldiers never die, and certainly not from eating tinned salmon, whichever country it comes from.

The fact is that the Militiamen were over-publicised from the start. Altogether too much attention has been paid to their complaints. We do not want an army of caviar and champagne soldiers.[31]

Continuing with the theme of pampered 'mama's-boy' Militiamen, the *Mirror* also had some fun with an announcement from a 1,200-strong Militia camp near Taunton in Somerset. According to the report, the young men's families would be invited to visit on a set day in the near future, an event that the paper headlined as 'Parents' Day for Militia'. The camp commander was keen to prove that he was 'really taking an interest in the Militiamen's welfare', and the jolly event was planned for 2 September.[32]

In the meantime, a concern was creeping into the consciousness of British newspaper readers that doesn't seem to have occurred to their equivalents in Germany. What to do with domestic animals in case of war? In an article entitled 'Is There a Pet in Your House?', the *Mirror* writer Susan Day tackled the problems presented by the possibilities of bombing, gas, and evacuation, for pets and their owners:

You must ask yourself if you will be able to have them evacuated with you, if you are going away.

You must wonder if you will be able to get enough food for them to eat.

You must ask yourself: 'How will I calm their fears in an air raid, and how shall I protect them from gas attacks?'.

Of course, you want to spare them all the pain and terror that you can, and you do not want to have them painlessly destroyed unless it is absolutely essential for their comfort.[33]

The last possibility — euthanasia — was not purely academic. Later in the article, it was mentioned as an unfortunate necessity

with which the National ARP Animals Committee could help
in extremis, if you could not find a country-dwelling person
willing to take your dog or cat, or could not afford suitable
kennel or cattery accommodation. As a last resort, of course.
After all, 'If there should be no war, you would feel terribly
upset afterwards to think that you had parted with your little
friend for no reason.'

There had, in fact, been a spate of anxious pet lovers taking
their animal companions to vets to be euthanized during the
Munich Crisis, perhaps amounting to several thousand in all. The
National Canine Defence League had been forced to refuse a
wave of requests for help with 'putting to sleep' pet dogs, advising
owners to await the outcome of the Hitler/Chamberlain talks
before taking such drastic decisions. It was an experience which
meant, a year later, that the NCDL (and its equivalent for cats,
the CPL) had built lists of potential homes for city pets threatened
by possible enemy action.[34] Perhaps it saved some.

The rising panic among a nation of supposed 'animal lovers'
was clear in the days during the end of August 1939 when the
crisis reached its climax. Another article on 30 August notified
readers of advice from the National ARP Animals Committee to
'Guard Your Pets' and 'not hand them over to unauthorized people
for evacuation or destruction'.[35] A day later, on the *Mirror*'s 'Live
Letter Box' page, a representative of the NCDL told readers that
in event of war and evacuation animal clinics would be open 'day
and night' for those who felt the need to 'dispose of' their pets.[36]

As August moved to a close, and there was no sign of the
crisis being settled, the numbers of British tourists returning
from the Continent increased from a trickle to a flow and began
threatening to turn into a flood. In the last week of the month,
the society columnist of the *Daily Mirror*, Ivor Lambe, reported
seeing more of the society crowd out and about around Park
Lane, in London, than was usual at this time of the year, when
they would usually be in Le Touquet or Juan-Les-Pins. Indeed,
he bumped into Lord and Lady de Broke emerging from the
Dorchester and found that their summer plans had also been
frustrated by the international situation. This aristocratic couple,

both qualified pilots, had taken off from the private airfield at their stately home and headed across the Channel, only to find themselves facing a flying ban over France, imposed in case of possible German air incursions.[37]

On 26 August 1939, Croydon Aerodrome, south of London, experienced its heaviest day of traffic ever, with a record 1,500 passengers arriving by air from the Continent. The 22- and 27-seater airliners were flying empty to Paris and then returning full. Passenger aircraft leaving Germany were also packed.[38] At Harwich and Folkestone, many thousands of anxious travellers arrived back daily from the Continent on overcrowded steamers, including the families of British Embassy staff from Berlin. All trains and planes from the South of France were fully booked, leaving many tourists unable to leave the region. Ocean liners heading for America were also overcrowded. The film star Douglas Fairbanks Jr and his wife, Edna Best, bedded down on mattresses in a children's playroom on the Dutch-owned transatlantic liner the *Nieuw Amsterdam*, along with other notables, so eager were they to reach the safety of New York.[39]

The newspapers were filling up with articles about how to mask your car headlights, how to act in the blackout, and what to buy so as to ensure that you and your family could outlast temporary shortages – corned beef was especially popular. But still, in the *Express*, the columnist 'William Hickey' pushed on with the paper's long-established line: 'My tip: no war this crisis'.[40]

More serious was the government order to start evacuating children from the cities. Irene Naylor, forty-one, had been expecting this for some days. On Thursday 25 August, Miss Naylor, a social worker resident in the London suburb of Chiswick, had found herself attending a summer school in folk-dancing in Stratford-upon Avon, 90 miles or so north of the capital. 'Unlike some of the students,' she recorded in her report for Mass Observation, 'I read the paper every day and am not unprepared for the development of the crisis.'[41]

Sure enough, that same evening Miss Naylor received a telegram from her office instructing her to 'report for duty'.

She nevertheless decided to stay for the evening's dancing and leave on the early train the next morning. Back in London, she deposited her suitcase at the Paddington Station left-luggage office ('after being searched for possible bombs') and by shortly after 10 a.m. was at her office. There she found colleagues drinking tea and talking. Others had not yet returned from holiday, including her boss, who arrived from Wales around lunchtime.

Miss Naylor's first task was to go to County Hall, the London County Council's headquarters on the South Bank, and there interview and register voluntary helpers for evacuation work. At 8 p.m. she and her colleagues were sent home. The next day, Saturday (in 1939 still a working day), she was once more in her usual office, where there was 'very little doing', with some colleagues still returning from France and reporting in. Dismissed at 4.30 p.m., she had her hair shampooed and set, 'not knowing when there will be another opportunity'. The next day, Sunday 27 August, she stayed at her lodgings, writing letters and 'doing odd jobs such as washing, mending, etc., while there is still time'.

On Monday 28 August, Miss Naylor was sent with six social-worker colleagues to the Divisional Dispersals Officer's office in Kensington. There they handled paperwork and interviewed volunteers applying to escort mothers and babies to the safety of the countryside. Tuesday was similar. She and a friend from work lunched at a restaurant in Kensington High Street, thinking how normal everything looked, with women still in their summer frocks and appearing calm. 'Somehow,' she noted, 'the thought of war seems very far away, and we joke about the evacuation, saying what a waste of work it will be if it never comes off.' But there were rumours that the order for the mass evacuation would come very soon.

Amidst the worry, there was still room for the joyful trivia of daily life. On 29 August in the conservative cathedral city of Armagh, Northern Ireland, nineteen-year-old student S.J.C. Harrison had just returned, with some difficulty, 'after two days' wild and hectic travelling', from a holiday in France. He had, as he put it, 'a great time telling my experiences as a "refugee"' to his large middle-class family. However, the appeal of this topic was, for the moment at least, limited:

> The chief subject of conversation in our house today was not the crisis but the slacks, which my sister Helen (13) had borrowed – or rather hired for 6d a week from my sister Gladys (14). She (Helen) caused quite a sensation when she went through the town in them – you've no idea how 1923 this place is – especially among the country people here for the market. The Rector laughed at her rudely, and pointed at her with his stick. They suit her very well – Gladys is too fat for them – and it took some nerve to wear them here . . .[42]

By the next day, however, the conversation was almost all war, even when he and his friends went to an Italian cafe to 'drown our sorrows in ice-cream'. They were all of an age where military service was more or less inevitable if war came. 'I started to feel very heavy inside,' young Mr Harrison wrote, 'and begged the others to stop talking about war. They did so, but the conversation soon went back to it. Sammy and I decided we wouldn't go until "they" came to fetch us, but Harry said he'd go at once. 2 school-girls humming "South of the Border" in the next cubicle began to get on my nerves. I nearly poured ice-cream down their necks to stop them . . .'

That same evening, the diarist got home and found that a former school friend of his elder sister and her boyfriend were visiting. 'I heard merry laughter,' he wrote, 'significant of fun and games . . . when I went in I found the family (all except Gladys, who was in bed) and the visitors sitting around in Bacchanalian attitudes sipping from little glasses of sherry. This was a very unusual sight as we never drink in our house and I didn't know there was any sherry in the house. War was mentioned once or twice in this way: "I'll do so and so – unless there's a war" . . .'

*

On Monday 28 August, schools normally still closed in this last week of the summer holidays* were temporarily reopened so that nearly 2 million parents and children could rehearse procedures for (voluntary) mass evacuation from vulnerable towns and cities in case of war. This represented a massive logistical challenge, blithely codenamed by the government 'Operation Pied Piper' (the original fairy tale was, after all, German and did not end well for the children concerned). Up to 900 schools in London were involved, while 80,000 children took part in Manchester alone. Other large towns and cities chosen included Leeds, Sheffield, Gateshead, Newcastle, Portsmouth, Southampton, Birmingham, Edinburgh and Glasgow. Their destinations would be foster homes in rural areas and small towns deemed safe from bombing.

If we are to believe the *Daily Mirror*, despite all the natural anxiety the atmosphere at what it dubbed 'the big dress-rehearsal' was surprisingly playful. There was a photo-spread showing children merrily playing together, keenly examining each other's gas-masks, and munching on chocolate 'rations' provided by parents. 'MOTHERS' BRAVE FRONT HELPS' ran one headline, along with 'A GOOD TIME WAS HAD BY ALL', and looming over it all the only partially convincing claim that 'IT WAS A GRAND DAY OUT FOR THE CHILDREN'.[43] The *Express*, in a piece from its star female reporter, Hilde Marchant, took a less upbeat tack. Weeping mothers had to be consoled by husbands, policemen, and other male authority figures. In such cases, the women were not encouraged to accompany their children into the classrooms for the rehearsal proper ('it would only add to the confusion').[44]

The children had to carry a specified number of items, which they brought with them in a bag or backpack, or in some cases just a paper parcel tied up with string. A Ministry of Health leaflet

---

* In 1971 the official August Monday Bank Holiday was moved from the first Monday of the month (as it had been for the past hundred years) to the last. Therefore, on 28 August 1939 most schools were still on holiday for another week, but it was not a day off for the adult working population.

outlined what this kit should contain: 'a handbag or case containing the child's gas mask, a change of under-clothing, night clothes, house shoes or plimsolls, spare stockings or socks, a toothbrush, a comb, towel, soap and face cloth, handkerchiefs; and, if possible, a warm coat or mackintosh. Each child should bring a packet of food for the day'. Especially in deprived areas, not every child could manage all these things. Hilde Marchant described a distraught inner-London mother confessing to a teacher that her three children had never used or possessed a toothbrush, and she could not possibly afford one for each of them; luckily the school was able to supply these and other hygienic necessities. Every child had a luggage label pinned to their coat on which was written their name, school and evacuation authority.

For a country that was far less thoroughly militarized than its prospective opponent, Germany, Britain's relatively hasty formation of an ARP organization and related civilian-staffed but quasi-military organizations in the span of less than a year between Munich and the Polish crisis was a considerable feat.

The German equivalent of ARP, the Luftschutzbund, now involved some 15 million 'racial comrades' and hundreds of thousands of functionaries. The kind of largely improvised activity that, say, council-employed social workers such as Irene Naylor quickly embarked on as the threat of war drew near would not have been necessary in Germany. By 1939, something like an entire 'shadow society' existed there, based around the Nazi Party, its welfare and women's and youth organizations.

*

Curiously, in spite of almost an excess of organizational power being available, in Germany nothing like 'Operation Pied Piper' was mounted during these days at the end of August. There were camps for refugees claiming persecution in Poland, and safe billets in the interior of the Reich were arranged for several hundred thousand civilians from areas bordering France. However, there were no plans for systematic evacuation of children, or any other vulnerable groups, including pregnant women and the infirm, from the nation's cities, as there were in Britain.

In the First World War, the majority of casualties by Allied air raids had been in border cities such as Karlsruhe and Mainz, and also Freiburg, which due to its closeness to the Alsace section of the Front – the fighting in the Vosges mountains was audible from the city – had been bombed on twenty-five occasions between December 1914 and October 1918 by the French and British air forces. The raids had caused more than a hundred casualties, including thirty-one deaths, and a great deal of damage and panic.[45]

Compared with the air-raid preparations in Britain, however, things were kept low-key, even in a town where experiences of being bombed over twenty years earlier were still vivid in many citizens' memories. In August 1939, proud, in fact bombastic, articles assured the readers of the *Freiburger Zeitung* of the superiority of German air defences and the cruel fate that would await any enemy bomber that dared cross the Rhine:

> German spirit, tenacious will and courage, and the skill of our gunners and fliers, supported by German technology, will condemn any attacks to miserable failure, in fact to complete annihilation.[46]

A full blackout rehearsal took place in the town on the night of 30 August 1939. 'In any case, the blackout had nothing depressing, or even mood-affecting, about it,' wrote a local reporter next day in an article cosily entitled 'Freiburg – Only by Moonlight', 'on the contrary it gave one a sense of being secure, such as we are usually wont to feel only in our little bedchambers after we put out the light.'[47]

But then, not long afterwards, Reich Marshal Göring, commander of the Luftwaffe, would boast with typical arrogance that if 'a single English aircraft' overcame his air defences and bombed Berlin, then 'you can call me Meier' (*'dann will ich Meier heißen'*).

As notes hurtled back and forth and between the various protagonists in Berlin, Paris, London and (as supposed peace-broker), Rome, the tone in the German press was carefully controlled. The Third Reich, Germans read in their newspapers, was reasonable, peace-loving, calm, and confident, desiring only to solve the questions of Danzig and the Corridor. The French and the British were encouraging the crazed Poles by their foolish pledge of unconditional support for that upstart country's megalomaniac pretensions.

The stream of atrocity stories gushed on, fed by the propaganda machine. Not only were there repeated provocations from Warsaw, but there was the one-sided, threatening mobilization of the Polish army. The German press remained, naturally, almost completely silent about Germany's own military preparations, and its aggressive behaviour in Danzig. Pro-Berlin forces in the city had been heavily armed and reinforced with regular units, and on 23 August the city's Nazi-controlled Senate had passed a motion proclaiming its intention to become part of Germany. Gauleiter Forster was declared its Head of State, effectively deposing the League of Nations High Commissioner who had overseen the governance of the city since 1920.

The constant horror propaganda was key to Berlin's strategy. As such, the narrative went, the Polish state's aggression and unreason could be borne. But . . . the suffering of the 'racially German' minority in Poland, combined with incessant border provocations, meant that Germany's patience must be severely limited. The readers of the *Freiburger Zeitung* were told unequivocally on 30 August:

> The intransigence, brutality and power-political fantasies in which the Poles indulge themselves would, as such, leave us cold – were it not for the thousands of German people who are falling victim to this bloody terror. These victims determine the tempo of the decision, and prohibit our waiting any longer in expectation that the irresponsible guarantors of these Polish power pretensions might perhaps finally realize what a catastrophic position they are steering themselves and the whole of Europe into with their calamitous policy of encirclement.[48]

As all sides were aware, by this stage of the endgame around Poland, the chief aim was to deflect blame for the near-inevitable conflict. Hitler had told his commanders at Berchtesgaden that it 'did not matter' what means were used to provide a cause for war, since the victor does not, retrospectively, require vindication. However, he and his propaganda chiefs were aware that it was not just the international public that needed to be provided with some justification, but the German domestic audience as well – perhaps even *especially*, given the nation's general reluctance in September 1938 to go to war over the Sudetenland. Hence the ever more shocking claims of outrages against German-speakers in Poland, and hence also, as the end of the month approached, some sudden initiatives from the German side that seemed, on the surface of it, surprisingly conciliatory.

Hitler had postponed the assault on Poland originally planned for 26 August. However, he had not halted the mobilization process or the preparations, including massive movements of forces into border areas adjoining Polish territory. In their communication of 28 August, the British had made it clear that they would not be persuaded, by any German promises, to let their new Polish allies down. There would be no new Munich:

> They could not, for any advantage offered to Great Britain, acquiesce to a settlement which put in jeopardy the independence of a state to whom they have given their guarantee . . . the next step should be the institution of direct discussions between the German and Polish Governments on a basis which would include the principles stated above, namely, the safeguarding of Poland's essential interests and the securing of the settlement by an international guarantee.[49]

When Sir Nevile Henderson delivered this message to Hitler, the Führer promptly announced that Germany must have Danzig, the whole Corridor, and adjustments in Silesia. It was a tense encounter. Henderson told him that he must choose between moderation, and thereby an understanding with Britain, or war. Hitler emphasized that he was not bluffing; Henderson told him that the British were not bluffing either.

On 29 August, Hitler made a formal reply, including proposals which the British were to pass on to the Poles. The Führer was

prepared, for the sake of peace – so, at least, runs his implication
– to undertake direct talks with the Poles about the fate of
Danzig and the Corridor, including a possible plebiscite in the
latter. However, this would not happen on neutral ground or at
a peace conference à la Munich. Hitler demanded, rather, that
the Poles send a plenipotentiary negotiator to Berlin within
twenty-four hours, empowered to make an immediate and
binding agreement.

At heart, Hitler's plan was now to present Britain, Poland and
the world with proposals that, on the face of it, appeared moderate
and reasonable – so moderate and reasonable that, even at this
late stage, they might just weaken British resolve and detach them
from their commitment to the, by contrast, unreasonable Poles.
There were, however, 'hooks' attached to the offer, as the German
phrase goes. Danzig would definitely become part of Germany.
The Corridor plebiscite would take place within twelve months
under international supervision, but there would be restrictions
on those qualified to vote. German-speaking residents who had
remained there after 1918 could vote. Germans born or formerly
resident there who had left or been expelled from the Corridor
after 1918 (potentially amounting to several hundred thousand)
would also be permitted to return there to vote. Polish speakers
and their descendants resident in the Corridor who had been
born there before January 1918 could vote, but 'Congress Poles'*
– those born in the Corridor since 1918 or who had moved there
after 1918 – would have no voting rights in the plebiscite. And
then, perhaps even more crucially, there was the stipulation that
a Polish plenipotentiary must appear in Berlin within twenty-four
hours.

However superficially reasonable the German negotiating position might seem, the schedule was near-impossibly tight, the
conditions likewise. Everyone in Warsaw was aware that less than

---

* 'Congress Poles' was the name informally given to Poles who were originally
from what was regarded as the nation's heartland, the Grand Duchy set up after
1815, with its capital in Warsaw. This did not include the Corridor and similar areas
such as West Prussia that were at the time part of Prussia.

six months earlier, in mid-March, the Czecho-Slovakian President had also entered the lions' den of Berlin under similar circumstances, to be held hostage and bullied into signing away his country's freedom. Colonel Beck said at once that he had no intention of going to Berlin under such circumstances as 'he had no intention of being treated like President Hácha'. Lord Halifax also conveyed to the Germans via Dahlerus, Göring's Swedish middle-man, that Britain was only prepared to become involved if it was really a matter of 'negotiation and not dictation on the Czech-Slovak model'.[50]

It is impossible to entirely dismiss the idea that Hitler thought he could in fact win Danzig and the Corridor without having to fight the British and the French. As late as 29 August he reportedly told his adjutant, Major Engel, that he wanted his own 'First Silesian War' – a reference to the rich province that Frederick the Great of Prussia had seized by force from Austria in 1740, thus greatly expanding the wealth and power of his kingdom. So, a limited regional conflict with Poland alone. But he was also, by this stage, prepared if necessary to go to war with Poland's allies, Britain and France. Such a war would be their responsibility, Hitler claimed.[51] Another contemporary account, also from 29 August, tells a less ambiguous story. In his diary (in form more like daily rough notes), General Halder, present while these decisions were being discussed, described the naked cynicism of Hitler's 'offer':

Today: Poland directed by British to go to *Berlin*, as requested by Germans – Fuhrer wants to have them come tomorrow.

Strategy: Keep up a barrage of demographic and democratic demands. Ask for plebiscite within six months, under international supervision. Anyone opting for Germany must remain German citizens, and conversely the Poles. Poles will not want Germans in their territory. – The Poles will come to Berlin on 30 August. On 31 August the negotiations will blow up [*zerplatzen*]. On 1 September start to use force.[52]

Indeed, no Polish plenipotentiary came to Berlin on 30 August. Late that night, Sir Nevile Henderson saw Ribbentrop. According to Cadogan, Hitler's Foreign Minister 'read out at top speed' the full list of demands that would have been presented to any Polish emissary before asserting that it was too late anyway because there had been no response from Warsaw. He refused the British Ambassador a copy of the proposal. With the German and Polish armies mobilized and figuratively glaring at each other across their borders, it was a desperate situation. Afterwards, Henderson wrote gloomily to Cadogan:

> The Poles must put themselves in the right by making a gesture of some kind, or else we must all fight. Perhaps the second would be the best, but the responsibility is too great for me to encourage the idea.[53]

Hitler would soon enough admit that the offer, which became notorious as the 'Sixteen-Point Plan', was intended mainly for popular consumption inside Germany. 'I needed an alibi, above all in the face of the German people,' he later told his official interpreter, Paul Schmidt.[54]

Erich Ebermayer, writing in his diary during the night of 29–30 August, had thought Hitler's offer 'astoundingly conciliatory'. He was disappointed when, the next morning, the British government's reply seemed 'cool', since surely the Führer had come up with a 'satisfactory' proposal. However, on reflection Ebermayer was forced to conclude: 'Unfortunately, one has the feeling that the two adversaries, England and Germany alike, are each working hard, in case of war, to foist the historical blame onto the other.'[55]

*

On 26 August 1939, the day Hitler had originally planned to start his war for Danzig and the Corridor, the Munich Criminal Police held a press conference. It was reported in some detail the next day on a back page devoted to crime reports in the Sunday edition of the *Freiburger Zeitung* under the sensational headline 'A Dangerous Criminal in Custody. One of the Biggest Sex Offenders of All Time'.[56]

Johann Eichhorn had been persuaded to confess not only to a total of thirty-seven cases of rape in suburban Munich over a period

of around ten years, but also, finally, to two murders, that of a
seamstress, Rosa Eigelein, on 31 August 1937, and on 29 September
1938 of the housemaid Maria Jörg – in both cases knocking them
from their bicycles in lonely places, then shooting, raping and
mutilating them (in fact, he had killed five young women in all, as
he would eventually admit).

As the summer began, the 'Beast of Aubing' had found himself
sharing a cell with a fraudster, Schneider by name. Eichhorn had
apparently already admitted the rapes and murder to Schneider,
who was actually a police stool-pigeon. In his confession, Eichhorn
blamed these appalling crimes on his ungovernable appetites. In
a garbled, handwritten personal testimonial, Eichhorn, who was
clearly only sketchily literate, further claimed to have no recollection of the actual deeds:

> It's not possible that my sex drive is normal or that I am normal
> in other ways either, or I could not have done such terrible
> things, for despite everything I am a human being and I would
> give someone my last pair of pants or I could not do anything
> to an animal or even a human being I often don't even know
> myself any more . . .[57]

There seems good reason to believe that Schneider had played a
part in persuading Eichhorn that he might get away with a diminished responsibility plea – which would avoid the death penalty
– in order to coax a confession out of him.[58]

The timing of this dramatic article was odd. Eichhorn was not
Jewish, or a foreigner, or politically suspect – in fact, some years
previously he had attempted to become active within the Nazi
movement, but in the end had been excluded on account of
'neglect of duty'.[59] Even odder was the fact that, even with the
spin put on the narrative by the police spokesman ('tireless work'
to achieve a success that 'deserves the highest recognition from
the public and is calculated to strengthen the trust in the Criminal
Police to the highest degree'), just the bald facts, as stated in the
article, make the reader question why it took them ten years to
catch the killer. After all, he was operating under their noses in

a smallish area of suburban Munich. Eichhorn had finally been caught, as the police also admitted, not as a result of their detective work but 'owing to the presence of mind of a young girl'. There was talk of the crimes being carried out 'at dusk and in the dark' and of the women being so terrified that they had 'quite different pictures of the perpetrator' than the reality. In all, the police remarks contained more than a whiff of embarrassed self-justification.

Then the story disappeared again. Perhaps the existence of the likes of the impeccably 'Aryan' Johann Eichhorn just didn't match the required national image, especially now that war was on the horizon, of a pure and loyal racial community united against its brutal foreign foe. Moreover, with blackout rehearsals under way, the tale of a killer and mass defiler of women committing atrocities for years with impunity in darkness and half-light was deemed unsuitable for broad distribution.

It would be three months before Eichhorn was heard of again.

*

The Polish Ambassador in Berlin, Józef Lipski, did finally deliver a reply to the German government. On the evening of 31 August, having received instructions from Warsaw, he telephoned Ribbentrop to ask if they might discuss the basis for negotiations over Danzig and the Corridor. Asked if he had full powers, as Hitler had demanded, Lipski answered No. Ribbentrop promptly ended the conversation.

Within a short time of this exchange, the 'Sixteen Points' had been broadcast over the German radio, with a clear message that the Führer had made a generous offer to the Poles, but they had refused to engage. 'Heard . . . Germans had broadcast their offer to Poles, which *looks* very good,' Cadogan wrote in his diary that evening. 'They add the lie that Poles have known of this for 2 days and not answered, which can be taken as rejection! Told Peake* to kill this lie (11.30) . . .'

*

* Charles (later Sir Charles) Peake, head of the Foreign Office's News Department.

In the background, the Nazi regime's plans to manufacture a plausible and specific reason for war had already reached a very advanced stage. The rival intelligence services, the SD (under Heydrich) and the Abwehr (military intelligence) under Canaris, were closely involved, intimate rivals in the matter.

Projects involving the use of irregular forces, in civilian clothes or enemy uniforms, had been developed as far back as the time of the Sudeten Crisis. The Abwehr chief, Admiral Canaris, and his underlings, including Major Groscurth, then head of Department II (Sabotage and Subversion), had played a key role in liaising with Sudeten German activists. Through the summer of 1938 the Abwehr and its allies had helped create the chaotic circumstances in the Sudeten territories required to justify Hitler's annexation plans, as well as developing irregular commando groups that would have operated behind the Czech lines if it had come to war.[60] In August 1939, similar operations had been prepared for 'Case White', the invasion of Poland.

*

The invasion Hitler had first ordered to begin before dawn on Saturday 26 August was postponed at almost the last minute (around 7.45 p.m., less than nine hours before the attack was due). All the same, at least one military operation did take place that night. A group of thirty or so trained German irregulars, under the command of an Abwehr officer, Lieutenant Herzner, had set off on 25 August through a remote wooded area on the border between Slovakia (now a reliable German satellite) and Poland. Their goal was the Jablunka (Polish Jabłonków) Pass, where a railway tunnel provided a key link north through the Carpathian mountains into southern Poland, a route vital to any German invading force coming up from Slovakia. Their aim was to seize it and the nearby railway station at Mosty, so preventing the Poles – who had wired the tunnel for destruction earlier in the summer – from blowing it up in case of war.

Because of the nature of their mission, particularly the need to pre-empt Polish countermeasures, the commandos had been instructed to attack even before the scheduled invasion began.

When the invasion was called off, however, it proved impossible to contact Herzner by radio. The commandos crossed the densely forested border in darkness into Poland sometime after 3 a.m., Soon machine-gun fire was heard from the area round the Jablunka tunnel.

The Germans captured the railway station and even took some prisoners – a bemused group of Polish labourers who had been waiting for an early-morning train to their nearby place of work. They managed to enter the tunnel and, though accounts differ, perhaps even to defuse the explosive charges. Then, at 8.30 a.m., radio contact was finally re-established between Herzner and his superiors. He and his men, carrying with them two wounded, duly began to pull out, and finally managed to withdraw into the safety of Slovakia, under Polish fire, at around midday.[61] The commander of the German 14th Army, stationed in that part of Slovakia, is said to have sent a deputation of German officers over the border to apologize to the Poles for the incident, 'which had been caused by an unbalanced individual'.[62]

The following Monday, in its early morning edition, the DNB included a sly little reference which was reprinted elsewhere in the German press:

Near Reichwaldau [Czech Rychwald] it was possible to discern drunken hordes of this new Polish 'police', which is not uniformed, who were firing with blind fury into the crowds.

According to mutually corroborating observations, in the night leading into Saturday an extraordinarily powerful explosion occurred in the area of Jablunka, so that the detonation of the tunnel through the Jablunka Pass is supposed. In consequence of the complete sealing of the border, it was not possible, however, to obtain confirmation of this news.[63]

The piece is a fine example of cunningly misleading propaganda. It provides an improvised alibi of sorts for the Herzner Commando fiasco, in case any news got out, while libelling the Polish author-ities, implying (without actually affirming) that drunken Polish auxiliary police (carefully noted as non-uniformed) might have been responsible. Jablunka, though some hundred kilometres to the west of Reichwaldau, was in the same part of formerly Czech Silesia that Poland seized in October 1938, and similar Polish auxiliaries would have been potentially active in the area.

However, even more blatant deceptions were very soon on their way. The new deadline for the German attack on Poland was 4.45 on the morning of 1 September. This time there were to be no delays and no mistakes. The Abwehr was once again involved in some fakery and commando operations, but the crucial job now went to the SD. Heydrich's dirty-tricks team brought to its task a lack of moral boundaries, a ruthlessness and cunning that Canaris's honourable soldiers could not rival. The Abwehr, like all intelligence organizations, involved itself in sabotage and deception, but it did not pride itself on cold-blooded murder.

*

The substantial Upper Silesian town of Gleiwitz (Polish Glewice), then very close to the Polish border, was one of the targets for the SD's deception operations. Sturmbannführer Alfred Naujocks, at twenty-seven a seasoned SD operative, had been ordered to the town by Heydrich in person in mid-August. He had since been resident at the Hotel Haus Oberschlesien there, making plans and awaiting the order for a project known as 'Operation Grandmother is Dead'. According to this plan, Naujocks and a group of other SD men, posing as Polish insurgents, would carry out a fake attack on the German radio transmitter in Gleiwitz. One of their number, an ethnic German from the area who spoke both languages, would broadcast a proclamation in Polish over the airwaves, calling for local Poles to rise up against German rule. As Heydrich explained it: 'An actual proof of Polish encroach-ments is necessary for the foreign press and for German propaganda.'[64]

There were also conversations with the Gestapo chief, Heinrich Müller (known as 'Gestapo Müller'), who mentioned having a store of concentration-camp inmates who could be used in case of 'false-flag' operations, and promised Naujocks one of them. On 31 August, as the group prepared for their operation, an agricultural machinery salesman by the name of Franz Honiok, who had been arrested for pro-Polish activities, was delivered over to the conspirators.

At 4 p.m. on 31 August, Heydrich telephoned Naujocks with the coded message 'Grandmother is Dead'. Shortly before eight in the evening, the Sturmbannführer and his heavily armed squad approached the radio station, an imposing structure with a tall mast. They burst in. Shots were fired into the ceiling. The terri- fied technicians and staff were herded into the cellar. It was then that the attackers realized they had attacked the wrong building. Here no original programmes were made; it was merely a relay for the main transmitter. They did, however, find a microphone reserved for making urgent emergency announcements (the so-called 'storm microphone'), which when needed could be hooked up to the radio network, interrupting the main broad- casting programme. The Polish-speaker used it for his proclamation. This began: '*Achtung! Achtung!* Here is Gleiwitz. The transmitter is in Polish hands . . . the Hour of Freedom has struck . . .'

The transmission went on for three to four minutes, ending with a call to arms: 'Long Live Poland!' Shortly afterwards, the raiders fled the building. A body – dressed similarly to the departed false-flag agents – was found left outside, bearing gunshot wounds to the head. The corpse was that of Franz Honiok. It is thought he had been rendered unconscious by injection, delivered in that state to the site by a separate group of conspirators, and then killed to look like the victim of a gun battle with German police.

Honiok had been chosen because he was known to have taken up arms on the Polish side in 1921 during the dispute over the area, so when his body was found a feasible account could be cooked up. There were several other false-flag operations at points in German Silesia close to the border that night, however, all likewise staged at Heydrich's behest and under his close super- vision. At Pitschen (Polish Byczyna) a forester's house was attacked and shot up by SD operatives, some in Polish uniforms and some clad like Polish irregulars. This occurred just a little while after the Gleiwitz attack. At Hochlinden (Polish Stodoły) a customs

post was attacked in the small hours by a similar group. There
was a staged shoot-out (the 'customs officials' present were also
SD operatives), substantial damage was done to the building and
its contents, and then the intruders vanished again, supposedly
back across the border into Poland.

At Hochlinden, however, the SD operatives left behind six
bodies in Polish uniforms, all supposedly killed in an exchange
of fire with gallant German defenders of the customs house. These
were the notorious 'canned goods' (*Konserven*), the codename by
which they were known to Heydrich, 'Gestapo' Müller and the
other directors of the conspiracy. The callous humour of the
codename tells its own story. The pockets of their uniforms were
filled with Polish pay books, tram tickets, cinema tickets and so
on, but the corpses were those of German political prisoners,
selected from the concentration camp at Sachsenhausen and transported to Silesia. There, like the unfortunate Honiok, they were
knocked out by injection, carried to the site of the attack, and
murdered on the spot.[65]

The Abwehr had known of Heydrich's plans, and especially his
intention of murdering concentration-camp prisoners in order
to provide 'evidence' in the form of bodies in Polish uniforms.
They did not approve. Major Groscurth commented in his diary
on 24 August that Canaris had resisted the scheme and refused
to supply the Polish uniforms until ordered to do so by Hitler
himself (the operations had originally been prepared for 26
August, then postponed when Hitler's order to invade was
rescinded). The regime's propagandists were also closely involved,
since the propaganda barrage that would follow these 'incursions'
and would rouse the German people in support of the war had
to be carefully organized. Goebbels, in his diaries, noted coyly
in his entry for 31 August 1939: 'The SS gets special orders for
the night.'

*

The faked attack on the Gleiwitz transmitter was included in the
late-night bulletin on German radio at 10.30 p.m. Six hours later,
as the last of Heydrich's undercover operations was coming to

an end, the German pocket battleship *Schleswig-Holstein*, which for the past six days had been anchored off Danzig on a 'friendship' visit, swung its four 11-inch guns around to face the shore. Its target was a military site – technically an ammunition store – on the Westerplatte peninsula, situated on a spit of land within the city of Danzig. Since the early 1920s, it had been permitted by the League of Nations to house a small Polish garrison. The local Germans had always seen this as an offensive reminder of their dependent status, and since the Nazis had taken over the city it had been a source of constant friction.

At 4.38 on Friday, 1 September 1939, shortly before sunrise, the *Schleswig-Holstein* opened fire and began to shell the Westerplatte. Minutes later, German troops began to move across the land border into Danzig. German aircraft appeared in the skies. Over hundreds more miles of frontier, from the Baltic in the north to the Tatra mountains in the south, some 2 million soldiers of Hitler's Wehrmacht began to smash their way into Poland.

There would never be a declaration of war. Crowning a relentless, months-long propaganda narrative of Polish aggression, after last night's phoney incursions Hitler could and did plead to the world that his invasion was a defensive action, pure and simple, forced on him by his supposedly lunatic neighbour to the east. Germany was, as he would put it, merely 'returning fire'.

All this might suffice to convince a reluctant German people that, under such circumstances, war was their only option. The real question, though, was a different one: could the German regime persuade Poland's allies, even at this late stage, that their protégé was actually to blame? Would this conflict therefore be accepted as just a 'police action' against Poland, or must it mean a world war? The German people certainly hoped for the former, and perhaps their Führer somehow still did too.

The next hours and days would decide.

TEN

1–3 September 1939
'So the Madness Unfolds'

All over the Continent, and in Britain too, the first days of war were accompanied mostly by fine, calm weather.

Sybil Falkenberg, née Bannister, was a thirty-year-old Englishwoman who had married a German doctor and gone to live in Danzig. By now she had been glued to the radio for days, alternating between the German and English news. Her husband, she said, was sure that everything would turn out well. She was less convinced. 'Well, well, folks,' she wrote in a letter to her family in Uckfield, Sussex, on 28 August 1939, 'it's just a case of keeping your pecker up.'[1] It would be the last direct communication she would have with them for six years. As she wrote in the diary she kept during these years:

> About five o'clock in the morning on 1 September 1939 I was suddenly awakened by the roaring of guns which seemed to be firing on top of us. 'This is the end,' I thought. I leapt out of bed and dressed as quickly as I could, trembling so violently from head to foot that I could scarcely grasp my clothes or stand on my shaking legs.

The intrusion of war into a formerly peaceful life was particularly shocking, since Sybil Falkenberg was very heavily pregnant (her son would be born just a week later) and alone. Her husband Kurt had been called up as a medical officer with the Luftwaffe and was with the forces when the war broke out.

At 5 a.m., a mere fifteen minutes after the first shells had hit the Westerplatte, Gauleiter Forster declared Danzig reunited with the German Reich. Mrs Falkenberg's maid never appeared for work that day – she later telephoned to explain that the streets were full of military personnel and vehicles. Thus, despite the fine weather, the mistress of the house stayed indoors with only her Siamese cat for company. She dared not go out for fear of bursting into tears, so distressed did the situation make her, especially as it might involve her native and her adopted country facing each other, for the second time in this century, in war.

The German forces, supported by the Danzig local militia (Heimwehr), took over the city within a few hours, with the exception of the Westerplatte garrison – it would hold out with astonishing courage for almost seven days – and the Polish post office in the city, which under the 1920 treaty enjoyed extra-territorial status.

At the post office, the Polish staff, who were mostly army reservists, had stored weapons in the building. They resisted the overwhelming force of the paramilitary Danzig police, the SA and the SS for fifteen hours before, as Sybil Falkenberg put it, being 'smoked out like vermin'. A number of the defenders were killed in the siege, others shot while trying to surrender, and the rest executed as 'illegal combatants' some weeks later. A handful escaped.

German aircraft had already started bombing and strafing Polish troop concentrations and towns. Even before the *Schleswig-Holstein*'s guns opened up on the Westerplatte, twenty-nine Stuka dive-bombers of the Luftwaffe's 76 Squadron, commanded by Captain Walter Sigel, had already swooped down, their sirens (known as 'Jericho trumpets') screaming, on the small, strategically unimportant Polish town of Wieluń. They must actually have left their base at Nieder-Ellguth (now Ligota Dolna) in German

Silesia shortly after 4 a.m. They arrived over the town about half an hour later, and probably started bombing at about 4.35, ten minutes before the recognized beginning of the war.

In this first wave, which hit the western part of the town, twenty-nine 500-kilo high-explosive bombs and a hundred and twelve 50-kilo bombs were dropped. Among the many buildings severely damaged or destroyed was the main complex of the All Saints Hospital, even though it had a red cross painted on its roof. Like most of the townspeople, Sygmunt Patryn, a doctor at the hospital, had been asleep when the Stukas began their attack. He was wrenched into wakefulness by the sound of their sirens:

> Suddenly there was an explosion within the hospital grounds. There was the tinkling crash of breaking window panes, and shards of glass fell onto my bed. I jumped up, grabbed my clothes, and ran outside. At that moment the building behind me collapsed. A bomb tore such a huge crater in the garden that half a house could have fitted into it. Two nuns, four nurses, and twenty-six patients were killed in the raid.[2]

By 5 a.m., Sigel's bombers had begun to arrive back at base. The captain would note in his mission report: 'Target obliterated. Fires observed.' There were two more bombing waves of similar size during the course of the morning, one shortly after Sigel's, the next around 9 a.m., led by Major Oskar Dinort. Later, in a Nazi propaganda publication entitled *The Hell-Birds* (*Die Höllenvögel*), Dinort would recall with satisfaction dropping the most powerful single bomb of the raid 'directly onto the market place'.

As an eight-year-old boy, Józef Musta stood with his sister on the edge of town and watched the mayhem. He recalled:

> There were big grey aircraft with black crosses. Many people were running from the town. After the attack, we went into the centre to see what had happened there. It was very badly destroyed. Everywhere there were bodies and blown-off body parts. Arms, legs. A head.

Expert opinions differ on the total numbers of casualties from the Wieluń bombing. The most conservative estimate is 127, based on the meagre official statistics (the German forces that took over the town had little interest in such matters), but other authorities, including the distinguished historian of Poland Norman Davies, and the Eastern Europe expert Timothy Snyder, believe that more than 1,200 civilians – almost 10 per cent of the population – were killed.[3] It is agreed that some 70 per cent of Wieluń's built-up area was destroyed, including the hospital, the synagogue and the Catholic church; and of the tightly packed old streets of the town centre, 90 per cent. The town's only industry was a sugar factory, it contained no vital transport links, and while a cavalry unit had been based there some years before, there was no military presence in 1939. Sigel also wrote in his mission report: 'No particular observation of enemy'.

Both Davies and Snyder believe that Wieluń was deliberately selected exactly because of its insignificance, to test what bombing could do to a small town and its population. 'The Germans had chosen a locality bereft of military significance as the site of a lethal experiment,' as Snyder wrote. 'Could a modern air force terrorize a civilian population by deliberate bombing?'[4]

The attack on Wieluń was ordered by Luftwaffe Major-General Wolfram von Richthofen, attached to the German Tenth Army as 'Flier Leader for Special Deployment'. As commander of the German 'volunteer' Condor Legion that fought alongside the Francoist forces in the Spanish Civil War, von Richthofen had also been responsible for the notorious attack on the historic Basque town of Guernica in April 1937. He had written in his war diary at the time:

A town of 5,000 literally razed to the ground. Bomb craters still visible, simply terrific [*einfach toll*].[5]

*

The earliest of the DNB's press releases on 1 September 1939 still prioritized the 'Sixteen Points' story, boasting of a 'generous proposal to Poland' to which the Poles had allegedly refused to respond. A report of the fake raid on the Gleiwitz Radio Transmitter made up the second lead. Then, within an hour or two, it was war. Hitler's prepared proclamation to the Wehrmacht led the mid-morning edition:

> The Polish state has refused the peaceful regulation of our neighbourly relations that I have striven for; instead, she has called upon force of arms.
>
> The Germans in Poland are being persecuted with bloody terror and driven from their homes and lands. A series of border violations, unacceptable to a great power, proves that the Poles are no longer willing to respect the Reich's border. To put an end to these insane machinations, I have no alternative from now on but to match force with force.
>
> The German Wehrmacht will carry out the struggle for the honour and existential rights of the resurgent German people with hard determination.
>
> I expect that every soldier, mindful of the traditions of eternal German soldierly service, will fulfil his duty to the last.
>
> Always remain aware in all situations that you are the representatives of the National Socialist Greater Germany.
>
> Long live our people and our Reich![6]

At 10.07 a.m., according to the official press release, the Führer arrived at the Reichstag. It was already crammed with Nazi deputies, most of them in uniform, as well as a full complement of ministers and senior military chiefs, including Goebbels, Ribbentrop, Admiral Raeder, Frick, and Deputy Führer Rudolf Hess. Hitler was greeted with 'a storm of *Heil* salutes and clapping . . . enthusiasm such as has never been witnessed before . . . an expression of the profound trust of the German people in the decision of the Führer, especially in this grave and proud hour'. After a brief introduction by Göring, President of the Reichstag, Hitler launched into his big speech. It contained the habitual protestations of peaceful intent destroyed on the rocks of Polish aggression and arrogance, the usual accusations of atrocities and injustice and theft of German lands, going back to the Versailles

Treaty, and a re-stating of the narrative of last-minute Polish rejection of Germany's 'generous offer'.[7]

Here was all the crowd-pleasing self-justification that might have been expected, and, as ever, skilfully delivered. But some of Hitler's remarks clearly targeted not just domestic opinion but also Britain and France, on the chance that their leaders might still be weighing up whether to intervene on Poland's behalf. Women and children would be protected, Hitler said, and only military targets bombed. As well as securing Danzig and the Corridor, he said, he wanted 'thirdly, to ensure that in the German relations with Poland a change ensues that secures a peaceful coexistence'. To this end, Hitler expressed his determination to 'fight until the current Polish government is inclined to bring about such a situation, or until another Polish government will do so'. There was no actual declaration of war, just the formulation, in the words of the official Reichstag record: 'For the first time, today, Poland has also employed regular soldiers to open fire on our territory. [storm of booing] Since 5.45[*] this morning fire is now being answered with fire. [thunderous applause] And from now on bomb will be avenged with bomb. [renewed roars of applause].'

Hitler's public utterances, at least during this crucial weekend, still promised a limited war with limited aims, as well as 'gentlemanly conduct' (although the destruction of Wieluń by the Luftwaffe had been completed just an hour or two earlier). It even left open the possibility that Poland, though losing Danzig and the Corridor, would continue to exist (the British had, after all, guaranteed not Poland's borders but only her independence), not to mention a Poland that might, by some astonishing feat of forgiveness, be prepared to live in friendship and peace with the same Germany that had just attacked her. It was a bold – and shameless – attempt to neutralize both domestic and foreign opposition.

Major Groscurth, currently in Berlin and anxiously monitoring the commando operations that were supposed to secure

---

[*] Actually 4.45.

the Wehrmacht's advance, heard the Führer's speech on the radio ('terrible impression everywhere'). Soon after, he received the disappointing news that the seizure of the key road and rail bridge over the Vistula at Dirschau (Polish Tczew), some 30 kilometres south of Danzig – along with the securing of the Jablunka tunnel, the other main commando operation of the first day – had failed. The Poles had managed to blow up the bridges, blocking the route through which the High Command had hoped to funnel its armour in the attack on the Polish interior.

Groscurth wrote of giving a pep-talk to his officers, 'ensuring good morale and impeccable attitude', but he had already expressed his true feelings about the war the previous evening after the order to invade had been given, confiding to his diary simply: 'So the madness unfolds' (*So rollt der Wahnsinn ab*).[8]

*

Even before Hitler set his armies in motion, in Britain the evacuation of city children had finally begun. Newspapers early on the morning of 1 September led with the evacuation story, or the German 'Sixteen Points' proposal, which they seem to have taken seriously right up to the last moment. The actual outbreak of war came too late for Fleet Street's first editions, though there was time for the Gleiwitz 'incident' and its co-conspiracies to find a place ('Poles accused of radio raid in Germany'). There was still desperate hope, during those last few hours, that peace could be preserved.

After lunch on 31 August, Irene Naylor, the social worker who had been pressed into service on the evacuation plans, found a note on her desk informing her that the evacuation would start the next day. She was to report at 7.15 the following morning at East Acton station, where she would be Assistant Marshal. Arriving back at her lodgings after work, however, she found that her landlady, with whom she was on amicable terms, had decided to go and stay with friends in Somerset, accompanied by her grown-up son, to escape the danger of bombing. Since Miss Naylor had no desire to remain in the house alone, they arranged for her to stay with people down the street, whom she knew and liked. She spent the evening helping the would-be evacuees to pack, then moved her things over to her new 'quarters' at about 11 p.m. At midnight she heard voices calling from beneath her window. It was the landlady and her son, who were about to start their long drive down to Somerset and wanted to say goodbye. They held their cat up in his basket to complete the farewell ritual.

Early the next morning, Miss Naylor joined a team of three marshals at East Acton. The regular commuter train service ceased at eight, and after that there would be only the evacuee transports. Children started to arrive, with their teachers. Miss Naylor, whose regular job was at a nearby health clinic, incidentally noticed quite a lot of ex-patients.

> They march up in good order, accompanied by teachers and helpers and all carrying kit and gas-masks. Some of the mothers and fathers come to see them off, but have to say good-bye at the station entrance as there is no spare room on the small platform. All are looking cheerful – hardly any in tears – but I feel rather a lump in my throat myself at seeing them all going off so cheerily. The ticket collector makes a remark about the 'fine spirit of the London kids' and I agree . . . There is a general feeling that they are all coming back next week, and everybody is bright and cheerful.[9]

In Armagh, Northern Ireland, young Mr Harrison heard the war news from one of his sisters:

> At 10.35 a.m. I was sitting here in my room, when Peg came in with the news that Danzig had been taken and Germany and Poland were fighting. Peggy tragic as usual, Gladys making me laugh at her, and Flo and Helen rather annoyed as everyone had said there would be no war. Dad holding a long-faced conference outside with the three clerks from the office. Peggy has gone down to join them. She would. I still don't feel in the slightest alarmed or nervous. This is worse than last September but I

still haven't got that horrid numbed feeling I had then. I am
going down now for a haircut.[10]

Things began to seem a bit more real when he got to the barber's
shop, which was usually the most talkative of places, and 'hardly
a word was said except "thank-you"'.

Douglas Mannion, studying medicine in London, 'woke at 9.30
and dressed leisurely, had a mouthful of breakfast, and went down
to buy papers (Telegraph and Evening Standard (!)). Read them;
Invasion of Poland, Germany bombed, etc. Listened to 11 o'clock
news on radio. Decided that war had come at last.'

At Guy's, Mannion's teaching hospital, the students were
advised to leave London and await instructions. He decided to
head down to Surrey, where his prosperous family lived. His
father was on business in America, and as the only other adult
male in the family he saw himself called upon to deputize as 'head
of the household'. After collecting his things – noticing that the
barrage balloon near Lambeth Palace was now inflated – Mannion
bade farewell to his fellow students: 'The casual "Cheerio, and
good luck", with which we took leave of one another – words
which we have used on countless occasions, mostly unimportant
– took on a new significance.'[11]

Elizabeth Crowfoot, the young actor who had recorded her
fellow thespians' thoughts on the Munich Crisis almost a year
earlier, was at her own family home near Beccles, in Suffolk.
There she was closely involved in air-raid preparations, as well
as arrangements for a group of child evacuees and their teachers
who were expected any time. The locality was 'in uproar', as she
put it. Mrs D., wife of one of the local grandees, seemed to be
in charge, and Miss Crowfoot described the scene when she
arrived at the woman's house after breakfast to collect some
curtains that had to be machined to fit the windows at the village
hall:

Mrs D. on the telephone alternately to London (head evacuation
centre for district) and to everyone for miles around, Mr D.
walking around with lengths of wood to put bunks for children

in one room, B. (daughter, 24, hotel agent) calling for breakfast, and R. (daughter, 23) going to Beccles to settle accounts for a dance they gave. Mrs D. gave me the curtains . . . after continual interruptions took the curtains and P. (son, c.16) down to the hall, as Mrs D. had lost measurements of windows and wanted to get B. (carpenter) to put up the rods.[12]

Later, back at Miss Crowfoot's family home, she sought out blankets for the evacuees and helped transfer some things to the attic rooms where the children's teachers would be accommodated.

H.L. (gardener, married, c. 57) came in after Daddy had gone into Beccles to get the buckets and some other things, and said that the builder was in the village, and did I want him to look at the plaster in the outside lavatory. I told him to get him quick, and when he came back, H.L. said to me, 'Mr H. says that in Beccles they're saying they've begun the war'. I said, 'Rot,' and then asked who had begun war. H.L. said the army had, and I said what did he mean? He said 'They've begun fighting them Poles.' Daddy came in from the car, and I said 'Then we'd better get the blinds up.'

*

At about 12.15 p.m. – even the BBC cannot be more precise – British television screens went blank. The last programme transmitted was a Mickey Mouse cartoon, *Mickey's Gala Premiere*, which contrary to popular myth* was shown in its entirety before being replaced by a 'test card' for a short while until the service was finally shut down.

The day's television programming had already included an

---

* According to legend, the cartoon was abruptly halted before it ended, and after the war when television was resumed (1946) continued exactly where it had left off. This is not true. What actually happened when television resumed was that the well-known pre-war announcer Jasmine Bligh reappeared and addressed the camera with the words 'Remember me?' After this, the cartoon was shown again from start to finish.

outside broadcast from the annual radio exhibition at Earls Court, known as 'Radiolympia'. The audience was robbed by the shut-down of later appearances by Mantovani and his Orchestra, *Cabaret Interlude*, two news programmes (at 3.20 and 10 p.m.), a zoo programme, for the evening a variety show, also broadcast from Radiolympia (featuring the 'Gordon Radiolympia Girls'), a light-classical music show with the BBC Television Orchestra, and, to conclude, a short documentary film about the Scottish Highlands.

The abruptness of the BBC shutdown surprised many, but this procedure had been planned for some time in case of war. An entertainment service for about 20,000 well-off people in the Home Counties could hardly be justified under wartime condi-tions – looking at receiver models available after the 1938 Radiolympia, they included at the topmost level the 'Ekco-Scophony ES 104 Projection', giving a 24″ by 20″ (61 cm x 51 cm) picture by a mechanical scanning process, for a price of 220 guineas. This sum amounted to rather more than a year's wages for the average British worker.[13] In any case, there were anxieties that the Alexandra Palace television transmitter could be used to guide German bombers in on London. Many of the television technicians were put straight to work on radar; govern-ment sources later confessed that one of the reasons for funding public television in the first place had been to progress the cathode-ray-tube technology vital to wartime anti-aircraft tracking equipment.[14]

German television had gone off the air, and the public 'televi-sion rooms' had been closed down, on 24 August, on the orders of the Wehrmacht High Command. Its wavelength was turned over to military use. The regime had always seen sponsoring television as a way of proving superior German know-how rather than as a reliable mass-communications tool. Also, again, in such a militarized society potential anti-aircraft and military commu-nications uses had always played an even more crucial role in the government's furtherance of television technology than in Britain.[15]

On 1 September, the BBC also announced that it was curtailing the number of wavelengths available for public radio transmissions.

The reduced network would from now on be known as the 'Home Service'. This was to make more frequencies available for the military.

In Germany, on 1 September, listening to foreign radio stations had been made illegal under a law named the 'Extraordinary Radio Measures Act'. Should it see fit, the government could now punish transgressors with heavy prison terms.

Even the state's keenest supporters were aware that the popularity of foreign radio stations (such as Radio Beromünster from German-speaking Switzerland – Erich Ebermayer's favourite news source – and the BBC in London, which also broadcast in German) was partly the result of lack of detailed information from domestic sources. Government-controlled stations within the Reich tended to broadcast only official statements about negotiations and provided only the broadest details about the country's preparations for war. Simply to have some real idea, on a continuing basis, of what was going on during a crisis – or to hear opinion or speculation – the listener had to 'go foreign'. As one police report from rural Bavaria admitted shortly before war broke out:

> During the last few days it has moreover become clear that the propaganda efforts of the Reich and the Party have so far not sufficed to fully enlighten the farming population, or are not always popular. The rural population prefers tuning in to foreign stations rather than the 'wireless service'*. This happens, however, not in any way because of its anti-state attitude but mostly in an effort to learn more than the official sources are prepared to say . . . [16]

Once the new law was in place, in Bielefeld the *Gau* leadership's report showed considerable relief, an expression of the depth of official anxiety that the public had been getting too much information from unapproved sources:

---

* The Wireless Service (in German: *Drahtloser Dienst*) was the political news department of the Nazi-controlled radio network, supplying several bulletins every day.

Yesterday's law against listening in to foreign radio stations must be characterized as very important, for enemy propaganda has clearly been having a subversive effect on uncritical spirits here. London has, especially, been working in the German language in a very skilful way.[17]

*

In London, both houses of Parliament had been summoned for an emergency session beginning at 6 p.m. However, as it was a Friday, many MPs had already left the capital for the weekend.

The weather remained good, though more unsettled conditions were forecast. To distract himself from worries about the international situation, Duff Cooper, who had resigned from the government at the time of Munich, played a morning round of golf – very badly, he admitted – near his seaside home at Bognor, in Sussex. Over drinks in the clubhouse afterwards, there was chat about horse racing. Then one of the men turned to Cooper and said: 'Hitler started on Poland this morning.' He then went back to discussing racing. 'That,' Cooper later recalled, 'was how I heard that the Second World War had begun.'[18]

But, despite the news, not everyone was convinced that Britain would go to war for Poland. One young Londoner, A.F. Coles, reported:

Up to today the general opinion was that a way out would be found. Very few believed that Hitler would go to war but would back out at the last minute. When the news came through that Warsaw had been bombed (first in a rumour and then confirmed) people I was in contact with . . . looked upon it as exaggerated rumour and 'couldn't believe we'd have a war'.

In fact, when Parliament did meet, although Chamberlain strongly attacked Germany and reminded Hitler of inevitable consequences, he did not make the expected declaration of war. Response to the Prime Minister's bold-sounding but inconclusive words was muted. A lot of MPs were clearly unhappy. Many would have read the text of the treaty of mutual assistance with

Poland, of which Article 1 promised immediate help for Britain's new ally:

> Should one of the Contracting Parties become engaged in hostil-
> ities with a European Power in consequence of aggression by
> the latter against that Contracting Party, the other Contracting
> Party will **at once** [my emphasis – FT] give the Contracting
> Party engaged in hostilities all the support and assistance in its
> power.

However, Churchill, the arch anti-appeaser, uttered no word of criticism, instead sitting gloomily in his place, in unaccustomed silence. That afternoon, he had accepted Chamberlain's invitation to join the cabinet. As a minister he was no longer permitted to criticize the government in public.[19]

According to Sir Alexander Cadogan, when an official response to the invasion was conveyed to Berlin it was, on Foreign Office advice, 'a warning (not an ultimatum) to the German government, calling on them to withdraw (no time-limit)'. The unofficial answer was rather more raw. Göring's back-channel envoy, Dahlerus, had offered to come to London again and indicated that Hitler would like to discuss the new situation with the British. After consultation with the Prime Minister, Cadogan replied:

> Any idea of [British] mediation while German troops are
> invading Poland is quite out of the question.
>   The only way in which a world war can be stopped is (1)
> that hostilities be suspended and (2) German troops should be
> immediately withdrawn from Polish territory.[20]

By the same token, the Mass Observation diarist A.F. Coles himself wrote in successive unhappy sentences regarding his feel-ings during the early part of that day: 'War very near but a lot of hope for peace. Determination to resist Hitler.'

At Elizabeth Crowfoot's family home in rural Suffolk, 'Miss S.', a family friend, arrived on a weekend visit arranged before the crisis. The family's guest 'never listened to the wireless' and insisted, after being picked up from the station, that there still wouldn't be a war:

> Mummy . . . came back with Miss S., who was still saying it was all right and there wasn't going to be a war, and was quite astonished to be told the Germans and the Poles were fighting . . .[21]

There were clearly still those, especially in the ranks of the British elite, who also did not believe in going to war, even at this late hour. Duff Cooper and his wife, Lady Diana, had dinner in London at the Savoy Grill with Winston Churchill and a small group of friends. As they were leaving, they met the Duke of Westminster, the wealthiest landowner in England, an unbending Conservative and anti-Semite, who had himself just finished dining. He offered them a lift in his Rolls-Royce. No sooner had the journey got under way than the Duke launched into a virulent rant against the Jews – with whom, he said, the Savoy was infested. Cooper held his tongue until the Duke expressed satisfaction that Britain had not yet gone to war with Germany. Hitler must, he said, after all know that 'we are his best friends'. 'I hope,' Cooper retorted, unable to contain himself any longer, 'that by tomorrow he will know that we are his most implacable and remorseless enemies.' The short drive to the Coopers' house in Gower Street, Bloomsbury, concluded in icy silence.

For the man in the street and the man in the Rolls-Royce alike, this would be a weekend of colliding and often mutually contradictory feelings.

*

'The dice have been cast,' wrote Wilm Hosenfeld on 1 September 1939 to his eighteen-year-old son Helmut, who was away on agricultural duty with the Reichsarbeitsdienst. The middle-aged schoolmaster, SA man and reserve officer was with his unit in barracks at Fulda, in Hessen.

Hosenfeld, who had harboured troubling doubts about his Führer's actions during the Sudeten Crisis a year earlier, saw the conflict with Poland as a just war. True, just two days earlier he had still expressed hopes of peace, writing of himself and his comrades that 'we are of the opinion that it will not come to war'. However, the year of propaganda about 'encirclement' had worked its spell, as had the regime's careful elaboration of an alibi in the last stages of the crisis.

> The storm is beginning in the east. The Führer's demands were acceptable, modest, and would have served to preserve peace. It is quite clear to me that England does not want to prevent war, exactly as in 1914, when the German Kaiser made efforts at the final hour on behalf of peace. Germany has become strong too quickly, she has cast off her fetters too quickly, and has begun to become a decisive world power, which England cannot allow. Since 1902 England has followed the ruthless path of encirclement. Even if there had been another government than the National Socialist one in Germany, it would, if it had set its eye on the nation's natural goals, have ended up in conflict with England just like Hitler. There has been a lot of talk and complaining and abuse and criticism – there must now be an end to all that. All differences in world view and political conviction must now retreat into the background, everyone must be a German, standing up for our *Volk*.[22]

War with Poland over Danzig and the Corridor was not viewed with enthusiasm, but it was by no means unpopular. Many Germans neither respected nor liked the Poles, and resented their behaviour since the country had regained its independence. The small war just beginning was, as Hosenfeld believed, and many others were prepared to agree, justified. The Sopade reports for the German Social Democratic Party in exile in Paris repeatedly (and gloomily) pointed out this fact, even before the war actually started. In July, a Sopade agent reporting on the mood of ordinary Germans in Silesia had confessed:

> Until a few weeks ago, there could still be no question of noticeable anti-Polish feeling. Today, one is unfortunately forced

to ascertain that the propaganda against Poland has begun to have an effect, so that even among workers the opinion surfaces to the effect that if Hitler were to strike at the Poles now, he would have a majority of the people behind him.[23]

The propaganda barrage, with its incessant listing of Polish 'atrocities', had obviously achieved its aim. After the beginning of hostilities, the Sopade reports were simpler and even bleaker: 'The action against Poland – in contrast to a war against England and France – is approved of among wide circles of the German people.'[24]

Some of the approval came from surprising sources. One such was Willy Cohn, a fifty-year-old Jewish historian, teacher and writer whose diaries chronicled the Breslau community's suffering under the Nazis. Dr Cohn would write, not long after the war began, even after mentioning that German Jews had been put under curfew as possible saboteurs: 'All the same, I would make myself available if Germany needed me. Despite everything, I consider her cause just.'[25] The Dresden academic and linguist Victor Klemperer, Protestant by religion but Jewish by heritage, had served as a volunteer with a German artillery unit in the First World War. Although thoroughly distrustful of the Nazi regime's motives, and indeed hourly fearing arrest and state violence, Klemperer also could not suppress his feelings during these dramatic days:

> But yet one is so patriotic, when I saw a battery leaving yesterday, I wanted more than anything to go with them![26]

Everywhere, however, the consensus was that, as the Sopade bulletins also noted, there coexisted 'No Enthusiasm for War'. 'The mood of the people is in general not good; no one wants war,' Willy Cohn had observed after walking the streets of his native Breslau on the eve of the conflict.[27]

Confidential Nazi Party reports were, if anything, even less cheerful in tone. A Bavarian Gendarmerie official's report admitted:

Although indications of a fear of war are nowhere to be found, on the contrary, belief in the strong German Wehrmacht is boundless, there can also be no question of enthusiasm for war. The memory of the previous war and its consequences are still much too fresh to allow space for a mood of euphoria. The farming population in particular experiences the loss of human resources and horses and the petrol shortage as particularly drastic, and makes lively complaint against these measures.[28]

'Serious concerns of most family members in the face of new blood sacrifices,' wrote a *Gau* official in Bielefeld, continuing along similar lines to his Bavarian counterpart:

The [previous] World War has returned remarkably vividly in people's memories, its misery, its four-year duration, its two million German fallen. No enthusiasm for war at all. Fear of air attacks.

In those same official circles, there was also a heightened fear that the privileged position of Nazi Party bigwigs would inspire resentment, especially now that so many ordinary people's sons, brothers and fathers were facing danger at the front. Such men were advised, for now, to avoid identifying themselves as members of the elite:

The *Gau* leadership has therefore expressed a verbal wish that any Party comrades who have not been called up should not appear in public wearing Party badges, so that the impression is not created that Party comrades are being protected . . .[29]

Meanwhile, as the first day of the war drew to an end, the troops in Poland were looking to bed down wherever they could. 'The sky is lit with red streaks,' a Wehrmacht signals officer noted as night fell and his unit advanced towards a town not so far from the border. 'Black smoke rises. There are scenes of the devastating fire of war which later we will see even more often.'[30]

The town was Wieluń, and it had been burning since before dawn.

*

Civilians in Britain spent their first night under full blackout conditions.

For some who awoke that Saturday morning, 2 September, in anxious anticipation, the threat of war brought more than concerns for themselves and their immediate circles. Thousands of German refugees, children included, had come to Britain during the past months and years. They realized that if the Polish war did, as it seemed it must, pit Britain and France against Germany, then it might mean the end of Hitler, but on the other hand all sorts of other hopes and possibilities would close down.

Fritz Lustig's aunt Ada had arrived safely in London from Berlin in early August, but as the situation in Danzig and the Corridor deteriorated, he was aware that his parents had still not left Germany. They were nervously awaiting visas to join Fritz's elder sister and her Portuguese husband in Lisbon. Fritz wrote them a postcard and posted it; sadly, it was returned to him a few days later. He saw a seemingly endless convoy of London buses on the road to Cambridge on that Saturday and was told that they were full of evacuees. He helped make blackout curtains, but was almost immediately moved from the German refugee household where he was living to the house of thoroughly English Professor Sutton, who had also played a part in getting him a visa. It was thought that Fritz, still technically a German citizen, would be safer from internment if he stayed with a British family.[31]

Fritz's parents would, in fact, eventually manage to find refuge in neutral Portugal. Others, many others, were not so lucky. Käthe Strenitz's parents and small brother never managed to leave Prague, and would perish in the holocaust. Peter Jordan, who had come on the Kindertransport from Munich in early 1939 as a twelve-year-old, had expected his art-dealer father and his mother – highly secular Jews and ski fanatics who had always taken him up to the mountains every weekend – to come over to England to join him in the summer of that year. However, as he recalled, somehow there always seemed more arrangements to be made, more affairs to be tidied up – and then suddenly it was too late. He too never saw them again.[32]

In Berlin, Ruth Andreas-Friedrich and her circle had, as ever, been forewarned of the coming catastrophe through their contacts in the Nazi elite. Susy Simonis's well-connected cousin, Erich Kordt, had rung her the evening before the attack on Poland. All the overnight warnings imaginable, though, had done no good for Ruth and Leo's Jewish friends. One, Frau Rosenthal, had just received a letter with the news that her visa for Britain was on its way. That hope was now gone. The trap had sprung shut. And Heinrich Mühsam, Andreas-Friedrich's wry Jewish writer friend and almost-lover, was trapped too. '*Mitgefangen – mitgehangen*' – get caught with a criminal, you'll be hanged along with them – as he remarked with his usual grim humour.[33]

Meanwhile, because of the blackout, stars were visible in the dark skies over Berlin for the first time in Ruth Andreas-Friedrich's experience. 'The city returns to nature,' Leo remarked as they made their way home through the moonlit streets on the first night of the war. 'It could almost turn you into a romantic.'[34] In fact, what it turned them into, along with their friends, was a Resistance group (nicknamed 'Uncle Emil') that, among other things, protected and hid Jewish fellow citizens and enabled many to survive the Holocaust.

*

Howard Cowan, an accountant living in the East London suburb of Ilford, was a bachelor in his late thirties and, at least in his own estimation, something of a man about town. He had awoken that Saturday morning after a 'troubled night'. 'Conflict,' he wrote glumly in a report for Mass Observation, 'seems inevitable'. It would not be good for business, or for his hopes of a successful day on the golf course:

> In my happy-go-lucky way I have made no financial provision. Of all the hundreds due to me, I doubt if a *sou* will be paid and I'm absolutely broke. Spent the whole of a glorious afternoon

making screens to black out the windows, when I had been all set to win the Monthly Medal and get my handicap down to single figures. Curse Hitler![35]

Unlike Mr Cowan, who was clearly usually master of his own time, J. Austin, a solicitor employed by the local council and a resident of the West London suburb of Ealing, went into work that morning at the town hall. No one seemed to be doing any work.

> Being sick of having no work to do, I talked my boss into making a job for me, namely, doorkeeper. I had been horrified the previous night by the number of unidentified people wandering in and out of the Town Hall at will. Any ill-disposed IRA man could have blown the place to bits with impunity.[36]

Mr Austin duly spent the whole day dealing with inquiries at the entrance to the building, from people needing gas masks ('a large percentage were foreign refugees') to an octogenarian gentleman who 'tottered in to see if he was wanted' and an equally elderly lady 'with the most charming face and manners imaginable' who appeared already dressed in a nurse's uniform and said she had been through the last war and was ready to face the next: 'I may not be young, but I'm still active.' Another woman, much younger, came in to ask if there were any evacuation arrangements that might help her elderly parents. When Mr Austin said, not yet, she retorted: 'Never mind. I'm sure there's not going to be a war.' 'Good for you,' wrote Mr Austin sarcastically in his report. 'A surprising number of people said the same thing, by the way.'

In Cardiff, Mr C.W. Moir, a civil servant, also went into his office, and like Mr Austin and most other contemporaries, confessed that everyone was talking about the crisis and not getting any work done. The afternoon, after he had returned home, was devoted to putting together blackout precautions.

> Next door neighbour saw me at work and said she had done nothing in that direction yet as she had faith war would not

come. Spent evening listening to wireless hearing same news announcements over and over again but frightened of missing something. Felt very depressed in evening, think we are heading for another Munich and that France is going to let us down . . .[37]

*

In Danzig, as the second day of the war dawned, things were superficially much calmer. Though the Polish garrison was still holding out on the Westerplatte – drawing reluctant admiration from the local Germans – Sybil Falkenberg, née Bannister, had also acquired a little more equilibrium after a night's sleep. She had very little food in the house, and so she ventured out to the grocer's shop on the next street but one to stock up on basics such as butter, cooking fats and coffee. She found her neighbours confident that there would be no wider war:

> Everybody reckoned the Poles would fight to the last man, but that the German army would make short work of them. The war would soon be over. *Nobody* believed the English would move a finger, and they all laughed me to scorn when I said we were in for long and bitter warfare. I never heard anything mentioned anywhere about the French attitude. It was always 'the English'.[38]

As it happened, her husband Kurt had been given a brief compassionate leave from his unit that day and arrived after she got home from her shopping expedition. He also did not think England would declare war; indeed, he 'understood agreement would soon be reached'. Though she wanted to believe her husband, Mrs Falkenberg was doubtful, and still divided in her loyalties. 'On the one hand, I did not want England to leave Poland in the lurch, but I so earnestly longed for a last-minute miracle to stop this awful war . . . between our two countries'.

The feelings of a troubled Englishwoman in Danzig reflected much of the opinion in Britain as the weekend began, and Chamberlain's ultimatum that was not yet an ultimatum remained unanswered. Cadogan's account of that day made it clear that, whatever the British public's mood, the government's response was becoming more, rather than less, confused:

> No answer from Germans. We are simply waiting . . . I found message summoning me to No 10 (3.15). Went over . . . Trouble is the French. We can't simply wait longer for a German reply. But the French don't want to present ultimatum until noon tomorrow, with 48 hrs' notice. Found Ciano [the Italian Foreign Minister] had been ringing up with proposal for 5-power conference. And I think Bonnet [French Foreign Minister] has committed himself to it too far – trying to wriggle out. P.M. committed to making a statement this evening to Parliament. Cabinet in afternoon, who wanted ultimatum to expire at midnight tonight. But we couldn't budge the French. Awful evening, ringing up Bonnet and Daladier [French Prime Minister]. Told Ciano we couldn't look at Conference unless German troops withdrawn. He said useless to press that on Germans. Finally Daladier agreed a statement for P.M. to make at 7.30 – no time limit – merely saying we were consulting French as to procedure. This infuriated the House . . .[39]

Understandably, the Poles were eager for the British and the French to intervene. Air raids in the west would force the Germans to split their own air force in response, thus taking pressure off the eastern front. A thrust by the French army across the frontier might likewise serve to slow the Germans down in the east. Still there was no clear declaration from London or Paris.

German forces had arrived in Wieluń that same morning. The infantry units moving into what was left of the town found it almost entirely empty. Most of the population had taken refuge in the forest. No one had cleared away the bodies. The brutality that would mark the advance of the Wehrmacht during these September days was already in evidence. Several survivors, especially those identified as Jews, were shot. Two women, thought to have learning difficulties, were executed after being accused of signalling to the enemy with lamps during the night. Captain Claus von Stauffenberg, a future leader of the 20 July 1944 conspiracy to kill Hitler, shocked by such behaviour, accused the officer in command. The man was court-martialled – although reportedly later pardoned, having pleaded that the men who took the women out of the building and shot them had misunderstood his instruction to 'get rid of' the suspects.[40]

*

Until August 1939, Stutthof (Sztutowo) was just a fishing village 22 miles east of Danzig, narrowly within the boundaries of the Free City's territory. Shortly before the invasion of Poland, the Nazi-dominated authorities in Danzig decided to build a prison camp there – not formally a 'concentration camp' but an internment camp, though the difference might be considered academic. Although secluded, the site was situated not far off the coastal highway on the way to the Baltic Sea resort of Kahlberg (Polish Krynica Morska). The area was largely surrounded by water: to the north was the Bay of Danzig, to the east the Vistula estuary, and to the west the Vistula river, making escape almost impossible. The land itself was marshy and damp and unhealthy.

Since taking control of Danzig, the local Nazis had been building up a card index of 'undesirables' in the city, mostly Poles. Now they had decided to build somewhere to put those undesirables when the moment came, which they knew could not be far off. A newly formed SS unit was dubbed 'Guard Sturmbann Eimann' (Wachsturmbann Eimann) after its commander, Kurt Eimann, a prominent Danzig SS leader. Given the status of a reserve police unit (these would later become the notorious 'Death's Head' companies), it had begun scouting for a location in July. By mid-August, Stutthof had been selected. Prisoners were transported from Danzig and forced to build a fence and some wooden barracks buildings.

Starting during the night of 31 August/1 September 1939, hundreds of Poles and other individuals deemed suspicious were rounded up by the local police and Nazis in a well-prepared operation. On 2 September, the day after Danzig had been incorporated into Germany, and while its citizens were still scoffing at the idea that 'England' would go to war over their city, the first 150 of these detainees were transported to Stutthof from their impromptu places of incarceration in Danzig. This made it the first functioning concentration camp outside the pre-September 1939 boundaries of the German Reich.[41]

Later in September, hundreds of Jews would be brought to Stutthof, most of whom died soon after. The camp would grow to hold more than 50,000 prisoners, many used as slave labour operating under the most terrible conditions. Although it was not an extermination camp as such, the regime there was among the harshest. Many thousands would die there as a consequence of disease as well as systematic official violence, executions and mistreatment. This was especially true after Stutthof became an overflow facility for Auschwitz.

*

Irene Naylor lay in bed that night in London, having retired early after a long day of organizing evacuees, 'hoping that Chamberlain is not going to back out of his pledges at the last moment'. It was still warm, but the weather had turned unsettled:

> Distant rumblings of thunder can be heard, and the lightning flashes almost continuously. Presently the storm burst right over head with great violence, and deluge of rain. I lie still in bed pretending that it is an air-raid, and practising feeling brave, but am not very successful. Ultimately the storm dies and I go to sleep.[42]

Over in Westminster, the mood matched the weather. The House of Commons had been in session since 3 p.m., but it was 7.45 p.m. before the Prime Minister appeared. He was cheered loudly, and reiterated the government's commitment to the guarantee for Poland, as well as the illegality of the overnight German annexation of Danzig. However, there was, as Cadogan reported, clear disappointment when Chamberlain went on to declare that, even as the second day of conflict came to an end, no immediate military action would be taken. He mentioned the difficulties involved in coordinating a response with the French, making play with Italian mediation efforts and what might be possible if the Germans were to halt their advance and withdraw – indeed, the Hansard report on the speech was headed 'Germany and Poland. Italian Proposals'. It ended up as one of his more limp performances. Cheered to the rafters at the outset, the Prime Minister sat down to near-complete silence.

With Labour leader Clement Attlee in hospital for prostate surgery, Arthur Greenwood, his deputy, rose to reply. A tall, rather stiff Yorkshireman in his late fifties, not known for his eloquence, Greenwood apologized for the fact that he would have to speak *ex tempore* on behalf of Labour. There were shouts of 'What about England!' and 'Speak for the working classes!' – and then, from Leo Amery, a leading Conservative, 'Speak for England, Arthur!' Amery's furious remark rang out loud and clear, and there were loud cheers from all sides. Chamberlain, on the government front bench, turned abruptly and fixed Amery – a member of the Privy Council, an erstwhile friend and cabinet colleague –- with a hard, aquiline gaze. Greenwood, reputedly aided by a tot or two of whisky consumed in the bar beforehand, pressed on and made the short speech for which he has always been remembered, in particular for these words:

> I am gravely disturbed. An act of aggression took place thirty-eight hours ago. The moment that act took place, one of the most important treaties of modern times automatically came into operation . . . I wonder how long we are prepared to vacillate at a time when Britain and all that Britain stands for – and human civilization – are in peril. Every minute's delay now means the loss of life, imperilling our national interests . . .

Robert Boothby, one of Churchill's younger supporters, cried out: 'And our honour.' The Labour man glared back at him. 'Let me finish my sentence,' Greenwood snapped. 'I was about to say – imperilling the very foundations of our national honour.'

At about 8.10 p.m. the short session ended. Margesson, the government's notoriously intimidating chief whip, gauged the mood of the Conservative parliamentary troops and privately informed the Prime Minister that unless war was declared the next day, they would mutiny. MPs leaving the House were confronted by thunder and torrential rain.

*

Not everyone in Britain spent the whole evening as the politicians did, or took early to their bed after an exhausting day, like Irene Naylor. This was, after all, Saturday night. Cecil Moxon, a 25-year-old Mass Observation respondent, sold advertising for the local newspaper, the *Free Press*, in Pontypool, South Wales. Determined to enjoy themselves on what could be the last night of peace, Moxon and a young colleague from work, named only as Horace, decided not to venture into Newport, the largest local town, which was reputedly blacked out and gloomy. Instead, they got the bus to the smaller community of Crumlin.

The pub in Crumlin, the Viaduct (so called after the enormous feat of railway engineering which was the town's main claim to fame), was packed, much busier than usual. This seems, judging from other accounts in the Mass Observation archive, to have been true throughout the country. It appeared as if all of Britain was pre-emptively drowning sorrows still to come.

Moxon and his friend ordered at the bar and chatted with some mineworkers, who 'seemed rather sick about things . . . but they became more cheerful gradually'. They then went into another room where a two-piece band was playing music to dance to. 'There was a rather rough-looking crowd present,' Moxon wrote. 'Three or four soldiers and some worn-looking women.' All the same, the two young men joined in the dancing for a while.

When they arrived back in the bar, the rest of the clientele were well into their cups. A young collier, one of the group they had been talking to earlier, now 'maudlin-drunk', confessed to Moxon that he was a 'yellow rat [a coward]. I'm a bloody yellow rat':

I punched him in the ribs. 'The British army is full of yellow rats,' I said. 'But they don't admit it,' he said. 'I'm not like some people. I do admit I'm yellow.' 'That's the point,' I said. 'Don't admit it and you're all right. I'm yellow too, but I don't say anything about it.' We walked back to the dance together. 'You'll be all right,' I said. The other fellow, who had been sick, didn't say anything, he just looked white in the face; he was in the Terriers*, and had to go off in the morning. I joined Horace. There was a poor baritone singing, we were both getting a bit fed up. We got up, picked up our macs, went over to the boys we had met, shook hands, wished them luck, and left the pub . . .[43]

They caught a late bus back to Pontypool. It was blackout everywhere. The conductor could scarcely make out the stops, or the value of the tickets he was offered for his inspection. A young woman friend of Horace got on and they joined her.

She was talking gaily of her plans, she was going to entertain the troops – 'with my voice' almost an afterthought. The other people scowled at us, it was not right to be cheerful in a time of so much sorrow.

I pitied the bus driver, he could not see a yard along the road. The rain made it worse. At last we were out of the deep narrow glen that joins the Western and Eastern Valleys. It became a little brighter.

*

Young Mr Moxon arrived back in his lodgings at 11.15 that evening after a clearly less than wholly uplifting grand night out.

In London, the cabinet met again at midnight. Like the MPs Margesson had consulted, it demanded immediate action, in the form of a time-limited ultimatum to Berlin.[44]

Shortly afterwards, Cadogan composed a fairly brief and sharp telegram, to be sent in the name of Lord Halifax. The Permanent Secretary then finally left the Foreign Office, arriving home at about 1.30 a.m., 'dead beat'.

---

* The Territorial Army.

The telegram instructed Henderson, the British Ambassador to Germany, to deliver the following ultimatum to the German Foreign Minister at nine o'clock the next morning, Sunday, 3 September:

Sir;

In the communication which I had the honour to make to you on the 1st September, I informed you, on the instructions of his Majesty's Principal Secretary of State for Foreign Affairs, that unless the German Government were prepared to give His Majesty's Government in the United Kingdom satisfactory assurances that the German Government had suspended all aggressive action against Polish territory, His Majesty's Government in the United Kingdom would, without hesitation, fulfil their obligation to Poland.

Although this communication was made more than twenty-four hours ago, no reply has been received but German attacks upon Poland have been continued and intensified. I have accordingly the honour to inform you that, unless not later than 11 a.m., British Summer Time, to-day 3rd September, satisfactory assurances to the above effect have been given by the German Government and have reached His Majesty's Government in London, a state of war will exist between the two countries as from that hour.

*

Early the next morning, Irene Naylor was up early and back on duty at East Acton station.

The A.F.S. [Auxiliary Fire Service] men are now wholly in possession, and do any policing that is necessary. Mothers and babies are being evacuated today. There are still less than expected, but we have two days' programme sandwiched into one and our full allotted time is occupied. The parties are not so well organised or so amenable as the schoolchildren. I abandon the attempt to stay on duty at the telephone, and go up onto the platform, helping to carry children, luggage, etc.,

and to get the parties onto the train. At last all are safely got
away, with no casualties.[45]

The storms had now passed over, and the weather was fine
again. E. Webb, a 26-year-old letterpress machine minder at a
printing works in Bristol, lived in lodgings in the pleasant suburb
of Bishopston along with several other young working men. He
and a couple of friends decided to enjoy the good weather.

> Went to bathe with Bob and Alan. The baths were fairly full
> – mixed bathing. Mostly young people.
> During breakfast – about 9.35 – heard warning of an import-
> ant announcement to be given at 11.15.[46]

*

In Berlin, Sir Nevile Henderson arrived punctually at nine on the
morning of Sunday 3 September at the Foreign Ministry in
Wilhelmstrasse. There he presented the ultimatum that had been
sent to him from London in the small hours. The document gave
the Reich government two hours to abandon its attack on Poland
and promise to withdraw.

Etiquette demanded that the ultimatum be addressed to Foreign
Minister Ribbentrop, but as it happened its actual recipient was
Paul Schmidt, a senior German Foreign Office official who acted
as the Nazi leadership's English interpreter. Schmidt accepted the
document politely, in English, and carried it the short distance
over to the Reich Chancellery, where Hitler and Foreign Minister
Ribbentrop were waiting. Other members of the Nazi elite were
gathered in an anteroom.

Years later, Schmidt would recall the scene:

> Hitler sat immobile, gazing before him. He was not at a loss,
> as was afterwards stated, nor did he rage as others allege. He
> sat completely silent and unmoving.
> After an interval which seemed an age, he turned to
> Ribbentrop, who had remained standing by the window. 'What
> now?' asked Hitler with a savage look, as though implying that

his Foreign Minister had misled him about England's probable reaction. Ribbentrop answered quietly: 'I assume that the French will hand in a similar ultimatum within the hour.'

As my duty was now performed, I withdrew. To those in the anteroom pressing round me I said: 'The English have just handed us an ultimatum. In two hours a state of war will exist between England and Germany.' In the anteroom, too, this news was followed by complete silence.

Göring turned to me and said: 'If we lose this war, then God have mercy on us!' Goebbels stood in a corner, downcast and self-absorbed. Everywhere in the room I saw looks of grave concern, even amongst the lesser Party people.[47]

The French ultimatum would finally be delivered at twelve-thirty and would expire at five that afternoon, but even at this early hour the situation was clear. No one could continue to pretend, for whatever purpose, that this conflict was a police action to adjust the borders between Germany and Poland. Germany now faced a European war, possibly one that would envelop the entire world.

*

The two hours ticked by. People in Britain went on, for the most part, with their Sunday-morning lives. Mr Cowan did the Torquemada crossword in the *Observer* Sunday newspaper. Mr Moxon in Pontypool decided he would 'occupy myself with small tasks. An escapist reaction to things, perhaps, but who is there to criticise? Accordingly, I spent the morning repairing [his land-lady] Mrs Long's bike.' In Surrey, Douglas Mannion got up, had breakfast, did some reading, then decided to drive over to visit a friend. In Armagh, young Mr Harrison and his staunchly Protestant clan went to church, as was de rigueur:

Dad brings us round in the car every Sunday and we all pile in about 1 minute to 11 when church starts. Dad as usual was very impatient and I finished my dressing in the nick of time. None of us listened to any news this morning before church.[48]

Most people seem to have set aside time for the Prime Ministerial broadcast, announcements having been made on the radio at regular intervals through the earlier part of the morning. Kenneth Gee, a young publisher's reader and reviewer staying in London that week, though he usually lived with his parents in Hampshire, described just such a sequence of events:

> When I came down to breakfast there was no fresh news. It was a fine, sunny morning. We had managed to hire a car and a man to drive us down to New Milton [the family house in Hampshire]. We had thought it would be difficult, but I suppose most people who were going away – evacuating – had already gone. The car was due to arrive at 11 a.m. We turned on the news at 10.30 a.m. The announcer said 'the Prime Minister will make a statement to the nation at 11.15'. (Sounded like Hibberd*) Well, we knew what that meant, all right. I felt suddenly rotten in the stomach as I had at the news of the bombing of Poland.[49]

Having got her evacuees off safely, Irene Naylor went up to the temporary office at East Acton Station. Someone had brought a portable radio in with them, and the volunteers sat around on the stairs leading up to the office to listen to the Prime Minister.

E. Webb, with his fellow lodgers in Bristol – including a young man who had just arrived and was identified only as 'the Newcomer' – had also spent the time since breakfast in expectation:

> We are waiting – Bob is reading – cups are clattering downstairs – sounds of hammering in next door's garden.
> It must be 11.05 by now. I think I'll take a photo. I run upstairs for my camera. Our landlady is busy changing the bed-linen. She asks 'A quelle heure mes enfants?' I shout, 11.05.

* Stuart Hibberd (1893–1983) was a well-known announcer and radio personality of the time, famous for breaking the news of the impending death of George V in January 1936 ('The king's life is moving peacefully towards its close').

On my return to the lounge I remark on the activities of next door and we all get up to look through the windows.

They are reinforcing their air-raid shelter – driving in wooden piles. I count 3 working, 3 watching, all various neighbours.

The sun is out again – the sky is overcast in the north. The wireless is blaring again downstairs . . .[50]

The BBC had set up equipment for the interview in the Cabinet Room at Number 10 Downing Street. Speaking for just under five and a half minutes, Chamberlain's tone was firm but betrayed obvious anxiety and regret:

This morning the British Ambassador in Berlin handed the German Government a final Note stating that, unless we heard from them by 11 o'clock that they were prepared at once to withdraw their troops from Poland, a state of war would exist between us.

I have to tell you now that no such undertaking has been received, and that consequently this country is at war with Germany.

You can imagine what a bitter blow it is to me that all my long struggle to win peace has failed. Yet I cannot believe that there is anything more or anything different that I could have done and that would have been more successful.

Up to the very last it would have been quite possible to have arranged a peaceful and honourable settlement between Germany and Poland, but Hitler would not have it. He had evidently made up his mind to attack Poland whatever happened, and although he now says he put forward reasonable proposals which were rejected by the Poles, that is not a true statement. The proposals were never shown to the Poles, nor to us, and, although they were announced in a German broadcast on Thursday night, Hitler did not wait to hear comments on them, but ordered his troops to cross the Polish frontier the next morning. His action shows convincingly that there is no chance of expecting that this man will ever give up his practice of using force to gain his will. He can only be stopped by force.

We and France are today, in fulfilment of our obligations, going
to the aid of Poland, who is so bravely resisting this wicked and
unprovoked attack on her people. We have a clear conscience.
We have done all that any country could do to establish peace.
The situation in which no word given by Germany's ruler could
be trusted and no people or country could feel itself safe has
become intolerable.

   And now that we have resolved to finish it, I know that you
will all play your part with calmness and courage.[51]

Messrs Moxon, Cowan, and co. were not alone in having other
things to do, or being simply ignorant of what was going on. A
woman in London:

Looked out of the window while listening to the speech and
there were a good many people in the street acting as usual, I
said, 'There's a good many not listening in.' I put it down to
the fact that people rose late on Sundays and missed the
announcement of it. There was no excitement at all, just a few
groups talking.[52]

Millions of others were listening intently, however. Shirley
Catlin, daughter of the pacifist and writer Vera Brittain (famous
for her memoir *Testament of Youth*), and later herself a Labour MP
and cabinet minister, was then nine years old. Her mother had
lost a brother, a fiancé, and two other very close friends in the
Great War, so it was not surprising that the atmosphere in their
household on that Sunday morning was very intense. Shirley
Catlin wrote in her memoirs:

I was conscious that my parents, especially my mother, were
distracted. We were sitting in the garden of our cottage in the
New Forest. It was a beautiful summer day, I remember Red
Admirals dancing over the flowers, we had an old radio with
a curved front and somewhat crackly, the old man's voice of
Neville Chamberlain, and the words 'so we are now at war
with Germany' – and that completely underlined the whole

experience because my mother burst into tears. It was like the appearance of the devil in Eden – it was as strong as that in my mind. I sensed complete impending doom.[53]

E. Webb vividly captured the scene in the lodging-house in Bristol and the immediate aftermath of the speech:

11.15. Britain at War!
  Chamberlain –
----- '- a bitter blow - - cannot believe' – etc., etc.
  We listen to the whole of speech in silence.
  Bob is standing near the window. The Newcomer is seated, smoking: a car passes – they are still hammering in the garden. I am writing.
  The announcer continues – –
  I run out to tell the people in the garden that it was war. Then in again to hear more. Instructions continue.
  Everything is quiet.
  Ah! The phone rings. Miss F., who is an ARP warden, flies upstairs to the hall but it is for the Newcomer who was expecting a call. He goes up. The speaker finishes and The King is played. No one stands. Silence.
  Then Bow-Bells – – – – we talk – – – Miss F. comes in and asks me about my 'position'. I declare myself a possible Conshy.*
Bob is at work of National Importance, so is 'Mac'. The Newcomer is now in jeopardy, his job of 'Sales Stimulator' is now cancelled and he is stranded and out of work.
  He enquires about possibilities of work nearby. Miss F. suggests the Filton Aeroworks.† He decides to go. We crack

---

* Conscientious objector.

† The Bristol Aircraft Company (founded in 1910 as the British and Colonial Aeroplane Company) was, by the time war broke out, a major aircraft manufacturer, employing many thousands of workers and producing such famous aircraft as the Beaufighter and the Blenheim bomber on its 25-hectare site on the outskirts of the city. At the time, the Filton plant was the largest single aircraft-production facility in the world.

jokes and Miss F. decides to give us a hot meal. She suggests it may be our last![54]

'Instructions' had followed the P.M.'s broadcast, mandating the closing down of places of entertainment, including cinemas, theatres, sports and football grounds, until further notice, because 'if they were hit by a bomb, large numbers would be killed or injured'. The public were warned, in fact, 'not to crowd together unnecessarily under any circumstances'. Hooters or sirens must henceforth not be sounded by private individuals 'except under instructions of the police'.

Young Douglas Mannion, who had been out in his car trying to visit a friend, at first had no idea that war had been declared. Then 'suddenly, when the engine was running quietly, I thought I heard a siren':

I was not sure, so I stopped the car. There was no doubt that it was an air raid warning. I wondered how the family at home would get on, especially the maids, who are all rather timid, and one rather hysterical. So I decided to get home as quickly as possible. I covered the mile and a half in under three minutes; this included a mile of town and one very steep and windy hill.[55]

So, it was war at last. Mr Mannion arrived home and headed for the shelter that had been constructed in the grounds of the house. He immediately took charge.

I found everyone gathered outside the dugout. The maids looked scared stiff, but mother and Phil [a female cousin who had come to stay on 1 September] seemed all right. In a few minutes the 'all clear' sounded, and we returned to our various jobs.

By the afternoon, the dutiful 'young master' was preparing himself and sorting his things for 'when I am allotted my job'.

An American journalist would claim a year later that 'the democratization of Britain goes on apace . . . Hitler is doing what centuries of English history have not accomplished – he is breaking down the class structure of England.'[56] The scene with the maids and the other women by the dugout was redolent of an old world of ingrained hierarchy and deference that would soon be gone. The domestic employees whom Mannion's class had always taken for granted would soon be called away for war service, including the female staff, whether they were recruited into the women's auxiliary organizations or whether they found (often comparatively lucrative) employment in munitions factories and other branches of industry vital to the war effort. And then there was rationing, requisitioning, a huge new apparatus of government intervention in everyday life, and the heavy new taxes that would affect the British middle and upper middle classes more than any other sector of society.

*

Twelve-year-old Inge Lueg, her sister, and their parents had enjoyed a family vacation on the Baltic during August 1939. They travelled up there from Leverkusen in the family car and then took a detour to visit her uncle and aunt in Rathenow, fifty miles west of Berlin, on the way home. They were there when the European war exploded. All Inge recalled was the look of astonished horror that showed on the adults' faces. Privileged they might be in Hitler's Germany, and grateful to the Führer for much, but what lay ahead now, especially as Leverkusen was bound to be a target for the RAF?[57]

At his country bolthole, Erich Ebermayer and his companion had been up early on a fine morning and taken a bicycle ride through the countryside to Kloster Speinshart, a twelfth-century hilltop monastery. Ebermayer wanted, he said, to be among fellow human beings on what he knew could be a fateful Sunday. The church was full. Ebermayer stood at the back beneath the organ loft. The sermon was 'surprisingly good . . . almost moving in its simplicity and dignity. Not a word of war-euphoria, though admittedly also no clear statement against the war.'[58]

They arrived home, switched on the radio and realized that Germany was at war with Britain:

For 70 minutes now we are irrevocably at war. Now it must
be clear even to Hitler and Ribbentrop that this time England
was *not* bluffing. And now it is clear that this will be no short,
victorious campaign against Poland, no punitive action against
an obstreperous neighbour – it will be a long, a major war.[59]

In Danzig, Sybil Bannister/Falkenberg was forced to face up
to the situation she had feared and hoped to the last could be
avoided: war between the country of her birth and the country
of her husband.

The news that England had declared war on 3 September came
like a bombshell to most people in Germany and Danzig.
Everywhere there were bleak faces and a hushed atmosphere,
as in the presence of death. The realization came to them that
neither the form that it would take, nor the end of the war,
could be foreseen.[60]

The locals' fear was that Britain and France would advance straight
away into Germany from the west, bombing German cities as they
came, and weaken the German advance into Poland. 'Would Danzig
be cut off from Germany and left to starve, or would the Poles
seize the town before German troops could cross the Corridor?'
    Later that same day, ranging further than usual in search of
some extra supplies, a terrified Sybil found herself encountering
unidentified aircraft, screaming in low, apparently to attack
Danzig, though fortunately no bombs or bullets hit the place
where she took cover. Afterwards she found out that these were
German planes attacking the Polish garrison on the Westerplatte.
Danzig had nothing to fear for the moment. Out in the Corridor,
the Poles were already being forced into retreat in many places.
Kurt and Sybil's baby, a boy, was safely delivered – by his father
– on 6 September.
    One place in the Corridor where the Poles were already
preparing a strategic withdrawal was the significant city of
Bydgoszcz (Bromberg to the Germans), on the grand canal that
linked the Neisse and Vistula rivers a little less than a hundred

miles to the south of Danzig. Bromberg had been overwhelmingly German before the First World War, when it was part of the German province of Posen (Poznań). However, after the First World War German numbers had declined drastically, as they had in other parts of the Corridor, in good part because of the new Polish republic's aggressive ethnicity policies.

By September 1939, only around 11,000 of the city's burgeoning 140,000 population were German. Intercommunal relations had deteriorated even further in the previous weeks, and on 3 September, with the war two days old, the Wehrmacht was hourly expected to move towards the city. Bromberg had already been bombed by the Luftwaffe, with twenty-five people killed in a raid on the main station on 2 September. Germans and Poles alike were extremely jumpy.

The real trouble seems to have started when, as the mainly Catholic Polish population left church on this Sunday morning, rumours spread that their troops had come under sniper fire from unknown assailants. The shooting appeared, so it was said, to have come from the tower of the Protestant (and German) church of St Paul. Local Nazi sympathizers and infiltrated German agents – who were, in actual fact, operating behind the lines in parts of the Corridor – were immediately suspected of the attack, perhaps an attempt to seize strongpoints in the city as the Polish army withdrew. The mayor of the town had already organized a citizens' militia, and its members now began an action against the German population.

Estimates differ of the numbers of townspeople, mostly German by ethnicity, who were beaten, tortured and shot by Polish irregulars during the hours that followed, continuing into the next day. Though earlier post-war German authorities claim about a thousand ethnic Germans were murdered in Bromberg alone,[61] the accepted figure is now between three and four hundred within the town boundaries, with perhaps a similar figure for surrounding villages and rural districts, making a total of about seven hundred.[62]

Some Polish sources, though not all, still claim that most of the victims were German agents and that the violence was defensive and therefore justified; the situation is further complicated by a recent document discovered identifying one of the victims as a German intelligence agent based at the Abwehr station in Stettin.[63] However, there is little doubt that this atrocity – and similar actions involving abduction, forced marches, murder, and so on – were inflicted by Poles, mostly irregulars, on ethnic Germans in the days and weeks following the invasion, especially as order broke down.[64]

Whatever the truth, after the town fell to the Wehrmacht, the German propaganda machine leapt eagerly on the Bromberg outrages. The events of 3 September became known, by specific instruction to the German press, as 'Blood Sunday' (*Blutsonntag*). The neutral press was shipped into Bromberg the next weekend. Grisly photographs were published of the dead. Throughout Poland, between two and five thousand ethnic Germans, out of a minority of about 700,000, were killed during the following month or so. These were disturbing enough numbers, but the higher figure was then multiplied by ten in a report early the next year, probably on Hitler's personal orders.[65]

The German press in early September was full of bizarre assertions, including one that British agents had trained and directed the Polish killers. 'Secret Service as Instigators of Murder' as the headline put it.

> No British soldier has fought in Poland. But experts in incite-ment, schooled in the Orient, have been giving the Polish population instructions on how they can organize themselves as ambushers and snipers, and attack the advancing German troops from the rear. Not without reason has London broad-cast the Polish radio's call for the inhabitants of Warsaw to undertake perfidious attacks on regular German forces . . . Hereby, London has lent its agents in Poland support, yet more proof for the unscrupulousness with which Great Britain sacrifices foreign peoples for the naked interests of British policy.[66]

Bromberg – and the other places where ethnic Germans were killed after the invasion – could be manipulated to confirm everything that the German press had said during the tensions of the summer about the treacherous, barbaric and cruel nature of the Polish nation. Accounts by advancing German troops in letters home were the best propaganda of all. Eberhard Gebensleben wrote to his grandmother from Poland the following week of 'the horrible murder of untold thousands of ethnic German *civilians* [his emphasis] here':

> There wasn't a single village that we marched through where 30–40 Germans were not massacred. Some we exhumed, others were still lying in the fields next to the country road. Men, women and children. How human beings can carry out something like this is incomprehensible. They are not human beings, and they have to be treated accordingly. The sorrow of the survivors! Again and again we hear: 'If only you had arrived two days earlier.' Of course, now with the military occupation, everything is quiet. But these were horrible scenes to witness, and they justify *any and all* measures on our part.[67]

The spread of stories about Polish atrocities against ethnic Germans in Bromberg and elsewhere was proving highly effective in justifying the war to the German people at home; so much so that the Goebbels-inspired press quietly buried earlier accusations of alleged Polish border incursions such as the Gleiwitz attack. The German government certainly never produced the 'Polish prisoners' that had supposedly been taken on the night of 31 August–1 September. In February 1940 a second campaign centring on the Bromberg outrages served to ensure that the fast-increasing rate of systematic killing by the occupiers of Slavs and Jews alike inside Poland (thousands were murdered in the vicinity of Bromberg alone in revenge for 'Blood Sunday') could be portrayed as tit for tat. A Goebbels-commissioned book about the Bromberg killings by a prominent Nazi journalist and writer, Edwin Erich Dwinger, entitled *Death in Poland. The Martyrdom of the Ethnic Germans*, was printed in an edition of 150,000. Dwinger of course portrayed the atrocities as proof of natural Polish inferiority.

The instrumentalization of Bromberg served a twofold purpose. It supplied both a retrospective justification of the war for international audiences and an important element in the regime's ultimately successful campaign to win over most ordinary Germans for a conflict they had so evidently not wanted just a year before.

*

Almost anyone who was in London on 3 September 1939 would always recall the fact that the Prime Minister's speech declaring war was followed at once by an air-raid warning. Sirens sounded at 11.30 a.m., just after the announcer had informed his listeners precisely what the warning and all-clear sirens (and the gas-warning rattles, and so on) would sound like. Many people expected that the Germans would attack at once with their much-vaunted bomber force, and of course everyone had heard about Polish towns being bombed. Deep anxiety prevailed. There was a lot of calm masking fear.

Howard Cowan had switched on the radio shortly after the Prime Minister's speech had ended, so knew nothing of developments until the warning siren sounded in his street. His brother, with whom he shared a house, was in the bath at the time and:

> got out quicker than I have ever seen him move in his life. Air raid wardens rush up and down the street – in panic, it seems to me – and I have a queasy feeling in the pit of my stomach. The 'Raiders Passed' signal goes about 30 mins later and I have a feeling in my bones that this has been a try-out . . . My sister and brother-in-law come round later on and decide to bed down with us . . .[68]

Irene Naylor, having got all her evacuees 'safely away', was still at East Acton station when the sirens sounded. She and her colleagues had just finished listening to Chamberlain's speech ('for the first time, I feel in agreement with the greater part of what Chamberlain says') and the subsequent public safety announcements:

We wonder if it is a practice, but decide that it must be the real thing. We scatter about the building in small groups. I go to the basement, where I have previously been working, with about four others. Some of us try on our gas-masks and adjust the straps, etc. somebody puts up the shutters. We sit there keeping perhaps rather self-consciously calm and cheerful. My predominant feeling is one of admiration for Hitler's thoroughness in timing the first raid so accurately. When I afterwards find out that it is a 'wash-out' I feel rather disappointed in him.[69]

The warning was indeed a false alarm, although according to the RAF's records it was not a 'practice' exercise, as many suspected, but had been triggered by the detection of a French aircraft, en route to the United Kingdom, that had not filed a flight plan.[70]

If this was so, the alarm extended a long way out of London. In Gateshead, almost 300 miles north of the capital, a 51-year-old woman also reported an air-raid warning straight after the PM's statement.

Air raid warning. We wonder and look out towards sea – Down comes warden to tell people keep in doors. Hubby at office in Birley on 'overwork'. Asks first shall he bring up car and take us out. I say 'Yes, for Goodness' sake let us get out and about!'[71]

The widespread air-raid warnings brought the reality of war home to the public, perhaps even more immediately than the Prime Minister's declaration. For the Militiamen, who had been called up in July for a relatively cosseted six months' training experience, the awakening was to be even more of a shock.

The official declaration of a state of war had two effects: it filled the army camps with reservists and territorials, and it ended the Militiamen's hitherto uniquely privileged status. They were now ordinary conscript soldiers, just as their fathers had been in the previous war. Ivan Daunt recalls getting ready for church parade that morning at Maidstone Barracks in Kent, his last as a Militiaman:

Then that was all cancelled. I think it was about eleven o'clock that it came out that war was declared with Germany. I think it was about a half hour later that all the sirens went in Maidstone. We took a dive into the fields behind the barracks, taking our positions in the trenches, and just sat there until the sirens went again about half an hour later and we could go back to our rooms.[72]

There was worse to come. Later, at lunchtime 'we went to go to our normal place for our meals but we were turfed out of there down to underneath the sheds and different meals. The reservists were coming and they got our rooms.' As for the sergeants and instructors, they now 'really started to put us through it'. That night, the conscripts camped out in the barracks square. Soon after, with the barracks constantly filled with reservists and regulars in transit, Daunt found himself transferred to join a regular army regiment down in Devon. He was 'a proper soldier' now, and instead of six months he would spend more than six years in uniform.

*

In both Britain and Germany, after all the twists and turns of the past year, acceptance of the situation was near-universal. Enthusiasm or otherwise seemed hardly relevant. War had come and would have to be fought. The ever-evolving technology that had made many millions of human beings' lives so much more comfortable and interesting, and peace more desirable than ever, would now be turned to lethal purposes. The race between international chaos and collaboration was over, and chaos had won. More than 50 million Europeans would pay the ultimate price.

On the afternoon of 3 September, Erich Ebermayer's schedule included a long-arranged appointment for tea with an aristocratic family who lived nearby. They had welcomed him to the area, and seemed good people, so Ebermayer felt unable to cancel despite the world situation. The visit proved a sobering experience for a cosmopolitan, liberal intellectual. An encounter with boundless, uncritical faith:

The experience is shattering. How much stupidity! What delusion among such cultivated and actually clever people! Just unconditional belief in the Führer, delight that 'finally our weapons speak'. The Führer's speech was the most beautiful of his life. Poland's insolent aggression against our borders had to be fittingly resisted . . .

. . . Even more irritating than this political nonsense is the personal aspect, and this is typical for millions of conversations in good German families this afternoon: the young Baron will be volunteering during the next few days, his mother, the Countess, is proud and happy, his friend is already serving with the paratroopers. The son-in-law of the Countess, the husband of her only daughter, has already hurried off to war. Almost grotesque – but even the old Count, who is nearing 80 and scarcely in consideration any more as a partner in conversation because of advanced senility, babbles on about his hope of being called up to the front as a reserve officer.[73]

Ebermayer confessed to saying very little and parting from his hosts as soon as was polite. He did not foresee spending any time with them in future. 'Lonely times are coming,' he wrote, 'at least here in the country. In Berlin it will be different. Surely there will still be like-minded people with whom one can speak openly and rationally.'

Another writer, George Orwell, observing the mood in London on the day war was declared, noted drily:

No panic, on the other hand no enthusiasm, & in fact not much interest. Balloon barrage completely covers London & would evidently make low-flying quite impossible. Black-out at nights fairly complete but they are instituting very stringent penalties for infringement. Evacuation involving 3 m. people (over 1 m. from London alone) going on rapidly. Train service somewhat disorganized in consequence.[74]

Two days later, Orwell was back in his country smallholding at Wallington in Hertfordshire, with all his diary notes exclusively about the condition and stage of growth of his flowers, herbs and vegetables ('Early potatoes rather poor, only about 5–6 potatoes to a plant, but the later ones look as if they would be good. Onions fair. Lettuces have all gone to seed'). The author was, in fact, keen, as a passionate anti-fascist, to make a contribution to the war effort, but had as yet been offered nothing by the powers that be. His health was poor, as it would remain for the rest of his relatively short life. He told a friend: 'They won't have me in the army, at any rate at present, because of my lungs.'[75]

Lower down the social scale, the matter of employment was more urgent. As the 'Newcomer' in E. Webb's report would bear witness, war could bring sudden changes in fortune. A telephone call just minutes after Chamberlain's speech had left him stranded in Bristol without a job. The young man promptly agreed to look for a position at the city's Filton 'Aeroworks.' Military aircraft construction had to be a growth industry.

The 'Aeroworks' all over the country would play a major role in the British war effort. They would build an enormous air force that would learn a lot from the Luftwaffe's attacks on Poland and later on cities in Holland and Britain, including Rotterdam, London and Coventry. On 1 September, President Roosevelt had appealed to the European powers to show restraint in the use of air power. All had agreed (with the usual caveats), but soon it was forgotten by all concerned, first by Germany but later, and especially, by Britain.

The 'Aeroworks' throughout Britain, Canada, and the USA would supply the means of delivery for the massive quantities of explosive and incendiary bombs that enabled the Allies to take aerial warfare to a new level of destructiveness, via Hamburg, Kassel, the Ruhr, Berlin, and finally Dresden. The Nazi regime's ruthlessness, its lack of moral boundaries, was apparent right from the outset. On the Allied side, it took its time, but in the form that it took it also crossed lines that the innocent civilians of 1939 would never have suspected it was permissible to cross.

The German people, in the end, went farther, and for longer, along the dark road that Hitler had ordained than anyone would have thought possible in the autumn of 1938. Then, the notion of a war of conquest had met mostly with sullen reluctance. They had to be persuaded, by one of the most concentrated, relentless, and ruthlessly mendacious propaganda campaigns ever known – and many, if not most, succumbed.

*

Anxiety about what to do with Britain's pets in case of war had been rising during the second half of August. After the Germans attacked Poland, things came to a head. The superficial calm with which the nation appeared to greet the outbreak of hostilities concealed a strange and powerful wave of hysteria, centred on its animal companions. What followed became known as 'the great cat and dog massacre'.

Vets were inundated with requests for euthanization:

> On the first weekend of war people in London did indeed 'do things'. These included sending away children to the apparent safety of the country, making blackout curtains, digging up flower beds to create vegetable patches – and killing the family pet.[76]

In four days, during early September 1939, in London alone, at least 400,000 pets, cats and dogs, were killed by or on behalf of their human companions. This amounted to something like a quarter of all the domestic animals in the capital of the United Kingdom.

There is no record of a similar phenomenon in Germany, where they were not supposed to be so 'fond of animals' as the British.

*

The British author Patrick Hamilton used murder to characterize the final death-throes of what the poet Auden had described as 'a low, dishonest decade'. In the final pages of his novel *Hangover Square*, the events of these final seventy-two hours of peace coincide with the last journey of the story's anti-hero, George Harvey Bone.

The shambling, well-meaning alcoholic, more and more subject to schizophrenic episodes in which he feels drawn to murder, finally snaps. In just such a disassociated state, Bone kills the object of his sexual obsession, Netta Longdon, and her sleazy Fascist boyfriend, then flees London on foot for the quiet Thames-side town of Maidenhead, some 30 miles from London. Here, he imagines in his deranged condition, he will find the peace of mind that has eluded him in London.

Bone picks up snatches of the final crisis during his 20-mile journey, hearing Chamberlain's declaration of war in a seedy eating house close to his destination. Twenty-four hours later, his own personal ultimatum has expired. Out of money, and finding no consolation in his new 'paradise' on the Thames, where the inhabitants seem just as unpleasant as elsewhere, Bone turns on the gas tap in his cheap room and lies down to die. Despite the sensational nature of his death and of the murders that preceded it, Bone's fate attracts little attention in the press. The horror of war trumps all others.

In Germany, the murders were not fictional, though the reasons for delay in their resolution may have been similar. Johann Eichhorn, the 'the Beast of Aubing', had confessed back in the late summer to the appalling murders and rapes that he had committed over so many years, hoping to plead 'diminished responsibility'. It would, however, be the end of November 1939 before he stood trial before a 'special court', accused of being what the regime called an 'element harmful to the *Volk*' (*Volksschädling*). The process was not open to the public, although there was press coverage in the local Munich newspaper. According to these reports, having found out that the state did not accept his attempt at mitigation, Eichhorn at first withdrew his confession, before finally admitting all, perhaps in a last desperate, if unlikely, hope of clemency. He was convicted on 30 November and beheaded by guillotine at Stadelheim Prison in Munich the following day, 1 December 1939. His wife Jozefa had already divorced him and changed her own and their children's names.[77]

The Eichhorn case, although it involved one of the century's most brutal and deranged serial killers, was tried at a time inconvenient to the regime under which he had lived and flourished, but it was not quite so completely hushed up as some have claimed.

His trial had been reported locally, and his execution was mentioned by newspapers throughout the country, in the section regularly dedicated to 'Death Sentences Carried Out'. These short items, taken from the DNB's press release, usually took the form of single-paragraph announcements.

The *Freiburger Zeitung* featured Eichhorn on 2 December 1939 in a sidebar ('in four cases he murdered his victims in a bestial fashion' was the main evidence that this might be an exceptional case). In the *Rheinsberger Zeitung,* published in Brandenburg, 50 miles or so north-west of Berlin, the article that day about the killer's execution was exactly the same but the placing more interesting. Immediately above it stood a longer, more highly coloured piece headlined 'Twice Condemned to Death. Another Polish Murder-Beast Before the Judge'. A Polish army sergeant had been found guilty of shooting a Polish deserter and a German POW (a downed Luftwaffe pilot) in their shared cell at the prison in Grodzisk, west of Warsaw, during the army's hasty evacuation of the town. The Reich had new 'monsters' to vilify, and they were not German.

*

On 2 September, in rural Essex, Ann Magnus, the young English girl who a year previously had stood in their garden with her father during the Sudeten Crisis and watched distant searchlights being tested over a night-enshrouded London was preparing to visit a school friend for a 'sleepover' date. The friend's house was some miles distant, but there was no need for her parents to drive her there. The horse-mad thirteen-year-old would ride her pony.

Ann and her placid steed set off along the quiet, sunlit lanes that in those days saw no traffic worth worrying about. She could rely on the pony to know its way to a familiar destination. As they plodded along, on the eve of the greatest war the world has ever known, Ann took out a book she had been gripped by for some days past, laid it open across the pony's mane, and resumed her reading. The novel was the most spectacular best-seller of the moment, and had just been made into a film. Its title was *Gone with the Wind*.[78]

ACKNOWLEDGEMENTS

My appreciation is due, as ever, to my agent, Jane Turnbull. To Georgina Morley, my editor at Picador, I owe more than I dare admit for her great patience and tireless engagement. Claus Christian Malzahn, as well as giving me the huge benefit of his journalistic knowledge, also guided me to the Otto-Dibelius-Stift in Berlin, where I had some fascinating and often touching conversations with a lively group of eye-witnesses to the events I have tried to describe in the book. Richard Thomas, meanwhile, was kind enough to lend me the use of his flat while I was in Berlin. In Munich, Roswitha Arenz provided introductions and generous hospitality. Dr Helmut Schnatz and Frau Ursula Schnatz were also infinitely generous in their advice and introductions during my stay with them in Koblenz. Finally, to all who agreed to be interviewed for this book, and to the helpful staff at the archives I visited in Germany and Britain – especially the German Diary Archive (DTA) in Emmendingen – my warmest thanks.

NOTES

ONE — SEPTEMBER 1938

1 Author's interview with Ann Forman, née Magnus, Hayle, Cornwall, 3 Feb. 2017.

2 These remarks and the following account of the proceedings in the Wilhelmplatz, from Ruth Andreas-Friedrich's memoir, compiled from notes made at the time and published shortly after the war, *Der Schattenmann*, pp. 10ff. Keys to real identities of Friedrich's circle in Lillian Leigh Westerfield, *'This Anguish, Like a Kind of Intimate Song': Resistance in Women's Literature of World War II*, pp. 81f.

3 Entry of 27 Sept. 1938 in Dilks (ed.), *Cadogan Diaries*, p. 109. Cadogan was Permanent Under-Secretary at the Foreign Office, the F.O.'s most senior civil servant.

4 Ibid., p. 107, entry of 27 Sept.

5 See Olson, *Troublesome Young Men*, pp. 25f.

6 Ibid., pp. 170f.

7 See the recording made by the chauffeur, James Joseph Read, for the Imperial War Museum (IWM) in 1987 (Catalogue no. 9945, Reel 1). The Irish-born Read had also driven Baldwin during his last year as Prime Minister. He was not technically a civil servant but rather an employee of the Trust that ran the house under the terms of the act of parliament through which it had been gifted to the nation by Sir Arthur (later Viscount) Lee, a former officer and Conservative MP, and his wealthy American wife.

8 Entry for 28 Sept. 1938 in Dilks (ed.), *Cadogan Diaries*, p. 109.

9 Andreas-Friedrich, *Der Schattenmann*, pp. 15f. This also recalls the author's feelings after Simonis's revelations.

10 See Meehan, *Unnecessary War*, p. 162.

11 See interview in *Der Spiegel (International)*, 27 Oct. 2010, with Professor Eckart Conze, a historical adviser to the current German Foreign Ministry, 'Historian Calls Wartime Ministry a "Criminal Organization"'.

12 Entries for 6 and 7 Sept. in Dilks (ed.), *Cadogan Diaries*, pp. 94f. 'I shall probably never be able to fill in his name,' Cadogan wrote. 'The man's life is at stake, and I can't jeopardise it by putting his name on paper. I have disclosed it to *no one*, and shall not do so.'

13 According to his testimony at the post-war Nuremberg Trial against Foreign Office officials, including his boss, von Weizsäcker, Kordt further told Halifax: 'I am in a position to assure you that the political and military circles I am speaking for will "take arms against a sea of troubles, and by opposing end them" . . . the army leaders are prepared to act against Hitler's policy. A diplomatic defeat would be followed by a serious political setback in Germany and would practically mean the downfall of the regime.' Quoted in Meehan, *Unnecessary War*, p. 153. Eckart Conze (see note 11) sees some of these post-war statements as unreliable, elements in a concerted attempt to save Weizsäcker from prison (he got seven years but was released after serving only a small part of his sentence) and to sanitize the reputation of the Hitler-era Foreign Office, many of whose officials still hoped to continue their careers in post-war West Germany.

14 Mass Observation Archive (Online) 5090 (Leonard Grugeon), report on 28 Sept. 1938, submitted 4 Oct. 1938.

15 Mass Observation Archive (Online) 5292 (E. Crowfoot), report 20 Sept. 1938.

16 Mass Observation Archive (Online) 1557 (G. Hickling), reports for 26–29 Sept. 1938.

17 Mass Observation Archive (Online) 1078 (C. Miller), report for 28 Sept. 1938. And for the remark about trench digging.

18 Mass Observation Archive (Online) 1557 (G. Hickling), report as above.

19 Hosenfeld, diary entry for 26 Sept. 1938, in Hosenfeld, *'Ich versuche'*, p. 236.

20 Ibid., 27 Sept. 1938.

21 Ibid., 28 Sept. 1938.

22 Deutsches Tagebucharchiv, Emmendingen, Catalogue Sig. 1512,4 O.T. (anonymized), Tagebuch 1938–45, entry for 29 Sept. 1938. At the beginning of the month, the Fascist leadership in Rome, showing its growing alignment with the Nazis, had decreed that no new Jewish

immigration would be permitted, and that all Jews who had settled in Italy since 1919 would be compelled to leave the country.

23 Ebermayer, . . . *und morgen die ganze Welt*, entries for 26 Sept. 1938 (evening), p. 298, and 28 Sept. (midday), pp. 299f. Ebermayer edited and polished these diaries after the war, when he had much to explain regarding his activities under the Nazis, so they should be approached with a certain caution. However, they do provide fascinating insights into the survival methods of a politically 'semi-detached' member of the cultural elite during this period. Bouhler also originated the 'T4' euthanasia programme that pioneered the use of poison gas as a weapon of mass murder, first of the disabled and then, notoriously, of Jews, gypsies and other 'racial undesirables'. He committed suicide in May 1945 while in American custody.

24 Dilks (ed.), *Cadogan Diaries*, p. 110.

25 MacDonogh, *1938: Hitler's Gamble*, p. 238.

26 Richard J. Evans, *Third Reich in Power*.

27 MacDonogh, *1938: Hitler's Gamble*, p. 238.

28 See Faber, *Munich*, p. 409.

29 Ibid., p. 413.

30 For discussion of this case of diplomatic zugzwang see Deist et al., *Das Deutsche Reich und der Zweite Weltkrieg Band I: Ursachen und Voraussetzungen der Deutschen Kriegspolitik* , p. 656.

31 Quoted in Faber, *Munich*, p. 416.

32 See *Manchester Guardian*, 1 Oct. 1938, 'An Anglo-German Pledge'. The first instance had been sixty years earlier, in 1878, when the British Prime Minister Benjamin Disraeli had returned from the Congress of Berlin after signing an agreement that (temporarily) defused the long-running Russian–Turkish conflict in the Balkans (and incidentally gave Britain Cyprus as a colony and military base in the Eastern Mediterranean).

33 Dilks (ed.), *Cadogan Diaries*, pp. 110f. And for the comments on Chamberlain's speech at the aerodrome.

34 Reuth (ed.), *Goebbels, Tagebücher*, entry for 2 Oct. 1938. Goebbels's entries are always dated the day after the events described.

35 Andreas-Friedrich, *Der Schattenmann*, p. 17.

36 See reports for September 1938 for the Social Democratic Party in Exile, reprinted in Sopade 1938, p. 953 (with photographic illustrations of the newspaper pages concerned).

37 Boberach (ed.), *Meldungen*, p. 72 (*Jahreslagebericht 1938*).

38 Report from Party member Mauersberger to Untersturmführer Dr Martin Seyfert, Leiter der SD-Außenstelle Grimmau, 22 Sept. 1938, in StA Leipzig SD-Abschnitt Leipzig No. 6.

TWO – OCTOBER 1938

1 Deutsches Tagebucharchiv, Emmendingen, Catalogue Sig. 975, 2 Hilde Maud H., b. 1922, 'My last Christmas in pre-war London in 1938' (written in January 1997).

2 Dee Moss, Oral History recording 1999 for IWM (Catalogue 19862, Reel 1).

3 Vera Ines Morley Elkan, Oral History recording 1996 for IWM (Catalogue 16900, Reel 5).

4 George Patrick John Rushworth Jellicoe, Oral History recording 1993 for IWM (Catalogue 13039, Reel 1).

5 See Olson, *Troublesome Young Men*, pp. 140–2.

6 Sir Alexander Cadogan, clearly no fan of Cooper, wrote tersely in his diary of the resignation: 'good riddance of bad rubbish'; see Dilks (ed.), *Cadogan Diaries*, p. 111.

7 Cox, *Countdown*, p. 41.

8 See Rüdiger Suchsland, 'Disney in Naziland', in *Jüdische Allgemeine Zeitung*, 20 Aug. 2015, at http://www.juedische-allgemeine.de/article/view/id/23112.

9 *Daily Express*, Friday 30 Sept., p. 1.

10 'A New Dawn', *The Times*, Saturday 1 Oct. 1938, p. 13.

11 John Masefield, 'Neville Chamberlain', *The Times*, 16 Sept. 1938, p. 13.

12 Letter from Neville to Hilda Chamberlain, 15 Oct. 1938, in Self (ed.), *Chamberlain Diary Letters*, vol. IV, p. 362. And for the comments about his popularity in Germany.

13 Letter from Minna von Alten to her granddaughter Irmgard Brester, Braunschweig, 4 Oct. 1938, in Kalshoven (ed.), *Between Two Homelands*, pp. 124f.

14 Deutsches Tagebucharchiv, Emmendingen, Catalogue Sig. 1512, 4 O.T. (anonymized), Tagebuch 1938–45, entry for 2 Oct. 1938.

15 Ciano, *Diary, 1937–1943*, pp. 134f.

16 See Rudolf Jaworski, 'Die Sudetendeutschen als Minderheit in der Tschechoslowakei 1918–1938', in Benz (ed.), *Die Vertreibung*, p. 43.

17 Entry for 27 Aug. 1938 in Groscurth, *Tagebücher*, p. 104.

18 See ibid., 3 Sept. 1938 ('The Führer has ordered that on Sunday the incidents planned by the SDP should be implemented'); 11 Sept. 1938

('New incidents in the CSR [Czechoslovakia]. The Czechs are maintaining almost complete calm – they are not rising to the provocations'); 23 Sept. 1938 ('Free Corps has no money. Demanding 100,000 Reich Marks daily. Admiral [Canaris, Groscurth's chief] manages to arrange the money').

19 Ibid., 24 Sept., p. 124.

20 Rudolf Jaworski, 'Die Sudetendeutsche als Minderheit in der Tschecho-slowakei 1918–1938', in Benz (ed.), *Die Vertreibung*, p. 35.

21 Katerina (Käthe) Fischel (née Strenitz), online Oral History recording 2000 for IWM (Catalogue 20128, Reel 1).

22 See Hermann, *Der Weg in den Krieg*, pp. 222f. and footnotes.

23 See reports for October 1938, *Die Allgemeine Situation in Deutschland*, in Sopade 1938, p. 1040.

24 Fühmann, *The Jew Car*, pp. 45ff., and for the following quote. Fühmann switched from Nazism to communism after the war and, driven like most Sudetenlanders into exile, became a prominent writer in East Germany. He expressed growing disillusion with the communist regime in the latter part of his life.

25 Geoffrey Cox, the correspondent of the *Daily Express* in Prague at the time, reported that on 12 September the SDP leader, Henlein, had cancelled talks with the leader of the British government's mediation mission in Prague, Lord Runciman, claiming that in Eger there had been 'a terrible massacre, with hundreds dead, mostly children'. See Cox, *Countdown*, p. 67. Cox (1910–2008) served as a soldier and diplomat for his native New Zealand during the war and later made a distinguished career in British television news, for which he was knighted.

26 'Herr Hitler at Eger', from Our Special Correspondent, *The Times*, 4 Oct. 1938, p. 14.

27 Käthe Fischel interview for IWM, online Oral History recording 2000 for IWM (Catalogue 20128, Reel 1).

28 Anton Weliminsky, online Oral History recording 1996 for IWM (Catalogue 16580, Reel 1.)

29 Reports for October 1938, *Die Allgemeine Situation in Deutschland*, in Sopade 1938, p. 1041. The large town of Reichenberg, in northern Bohemia near the border with Silesia, was the birthplace of the SDP leader Konrad Henlein. Neuers was a compact industrial town in the south-west of Bohemia with a thriving optical industry.

30 See Groscurth, *Tagebücher*, entry for 3 Oct. 1938, pp. 132f. In his conversation with a relatively moderate SDP *Kreisleiter*, Senator Frank, he was forced to listen to bitter complaints that two hundred or so

members of the so-called Sudeten Free Corps, which Frank had personally founded, had been arrested by the '*Lausbuben der Gestapa*' ('Gestapa'
was an alternative term for the Gestapo) since the invasion on suspicion
of less than total loyalty to the 'Greater German Reich' as opposed to
the Sudeten cause. Trials were held in Dresden, over the border in
Saxony, where accusations against these SDP members also included
homosexual activities. While most of the three hundred finally accused
were simply demoted or expelled from the Party, some, including the
leader of this faction, Walter Brand, ended up in concentration camps
for the duration.

31 *Daily Mirror*, 1 Oct. 1938, p. 9, 'For the Women of England Eileen Ascroft
Writes this Letter'. Eileen Ascroft (1914–1962) was married to the film
director Alexander Mackendrick. She would later marry the press mogul
Hugh Cudlipp and go on to become a very powerful figure in the field
of women's and fashion journalism.

32 Quoted in Beaken, *Cosmo Lang*, p. 184.

33 '19 JEWS DIE IN ARAB RAID', *Daily Mirror*, Tuesday 4 Oct. 1938, p. 5.

34 Winston Churchill's speech available at Hansard Online, HC Deb 5 Oct.
1938, vol. 339, p. 360.

35 See Olson, *Troublesome Young Men*, pp. 151f.

36 'NOVEMBER GENERAL ELECTION IS LIKELY', *Daily Express*, 4 Oct.
1938, p. 1.

37 Cox, *Countdown*, p. 80.

38 MO reports quoted in Wallis, *Britain, Germany . . .* , pp. 183–5.

39 Quoted in Gardiner, *The Thirties*, p. 727.

40 See Watt, *Bitter Glory*, p. 386.

41 Entry for 1 Oct. 1938 in Dilks (ed.), *Cadogan Diaries*, p. 111. Colonel
Josef Beck was Polish Foreign Minister from 1932 to 1939, pursuing a
strict policy of 'Poland First' that made him and his country few friends.

42 Story of the shopkeeper known as 'Hennes' in Christel Pütz, 'Tante-
Emma-Laden – einst und heute', in *Gäster an Hätt, Heimatkundliche
Zeitschrift*, Jahrgang 11 (1988), Heft No. 22.

43 Fühmann, *The Jew Car*, p. 64.

44 Ebermayer, *. . . und morgen die ganze Welt*, entry for 3 Oct. 1938, p. 305f.

45 Andreas-Friedrich, *Der Schattenmann*, p. 18.

THREE – NOVEMBER 1938

1 'David Walker's Talking Shop', *Daily Mirror*, 8 July 1938.

2 For an equally blunt analysis, see David B. Green, 'This Day in Jewish

History/1938: "Nations Discuss Jewish Refugees, Get Nowhere, But Then They Hadn't Planned To'", in *Haaretz*, 6 July 2015.

3 As Golda Meir, Meyerson later became Prime Minister of Israel. Meir, *My Life*, p. 158.

4 See http://fortune.com/2015/11/18/fortune-survey-jewish-refugees for a survey of *Fortune* polls on the Roosevelt administration's policies in July 1938.

5 See 'A Jewish Refuge on Caribbean Shores', in *Haaretz*, 22 July 2013.

6 'After Evian', *Manchester Guardian*, 16 July 1938; 'Finding Homes for Refugees: Committee's Task', ibid., 17 July 1938.

7 Quoted in Hermann, *Der Weg in den Krieg*, p. 328. And for the figures regarding Jews deported in the operation.

8 See 'NAZI GUNS FORCED JEWS INTO POLAND', *New York Times*, 1 Nov. 1938.

9 Some of the Jews were allowed temporarily back into Germany to put their affairs in order, while the Poles also allowed the deportees to find slightly better accommodation, though they were still not allowed into Poland proper. Thousands were still marooned there when Germany invaded a little over ten months later. Most were put in concentration camps and later murdered.

10 SD-Hauptamt II 112, Bericht für Oktober 1938, in Dov Kulka and Jäckel (ed.), *Die Juden . . . 1933–1945*, p. 297.

11 For a brief list of such outrages for English speakers, see Dov Kulka and Jäckel (ed.), *The Jews . . . 1933–1945*, pp. lvff.

12 SD Reports (Außenstelle Hanau) nos 325, 326, 327 (15, 23 and 27 May 1938), in Dov Kulka and Jäckel (ed.), *Die Juden . . . 1933–1945*, pp. 275f.

13 See Longerich, *Goebbels*, p. 383. See also entry for 22 June in Reuth (ed.), *Goebbels, Tagebücher*, p. 1228. Goebbels blamed the botched *Aktion* on ham-fisted tactics by von Heldorf, Police President of Berlin. Helldorf would be executed in 1944 for his involvement in the 20 July plot against Hitler.

14 Regierungspräsident Pfalz, Bericht für Oktober 1938, 'Innenpolitische Lage und öffentliche Sicherheit: Juden', Speyer, 9 Nov. 1938, in Dov Kulka and Jäckel (ed.), *Die Juden . . . 1933–1945*, pp. 301f.

15 SD Hauptamt II 1 Jahresbericht der Zentralabteilung II 1, ibid., p. 300.

16 Quoted in Alan E. Steinweis, 'The Trials of Herschel Grynszpan: Anti-Jewish Policy and German Propaganda, 1938–1942', in *German Studies Review*, vol. 31, no. 3 (Oct. 2008), p. 472.

17 Andreas-Friedrich, diary for 8 and 9 Nov. 1938, in *Der Schattenmann*, pp. 26f.

18 Ibid., diary for 10 Nov. 1938, pp. 28ff. Including the following.

19 Longerich, *Goebbels*, p. 397.

20 Entry for 10 Nov. in Reuth (ed.), *Goebbels, Tagebücher,* p. 1281. See Longerich, *Goebbels*, p. 398.

21 See Reuth (ed.), *Goebbels, Tagebücher*, p. 1282, footnote 131.

22 For the importance of Lutze, see Korb, *Reaktionen*, pp. 1f.

23 *Die Pommersche Zeitung*, 11 Nov. 1938, p. 11, under local news, 'Stettin und Vororte'.

24 Quoted in Longerich, *Goebbels*, p. 398.

25 'Anti-Jüdische Demonstrationen auch in der Kurmark', in *Teltower Kreisblatt*, 11 Nov. 1938, p. 3.

26 Richard J. Evans, *Third Reich in Power*, p. 590.

27 Ebermayer, . . . *und morgen die ganze Welt*, entry for 10 Nov., pp. 320f.

28 Ibid., entry for 11 Nov. (morning) p. 321. This account, and the general mania for looting, is borne out by Heydrich's report to the 12 November meeting at the Air Ministry (for citation see note 39 for this chapter).

29 Smithsonian Institute, Oral History Interview with Ruth Adler Schnee (1923–), November 24–30 2002. Available online at https://www. aaa.si.edu/collections/interviews/oral-history-interview-ruth-adler-schnee-12111. And for the details of the clear-up, the neighbours, and Herr Adler's arrest. Ruth Adler Schnee emigrated with her family to America, where she became a well-known textile and interior designer.

30 Author's interview with Frau Inge Heyl (née Lueg) (1927–), Otto-Dibelius-Stift, Berlin, 15 Sept. 2017.

31 Report of Stapostelle Bielefeld II B2, 'Protestaktion gegen die Juden am 10.11.38', in Dov Kulka and Jäckel (ed.), *Die Juden . . . 1933–1945*, p. 324.

32 'I instruct Wächter in Berlin to have the synagogue in the Fasanenstrasse smashed up. He responds repeatedly: "An honourable assignment."' ['*Ich weise Wächter in Berlin an, die Synagoge in der Fasanenstrasse zerschlagen zu lassen. Er sagt nur dauernd:"Ehrenvoller Auftrag."'*). Not in the published diaries edited by Reuth, but mentioned in Longerich, *Goebbels*, p. 398, and the 10 Nov. 1938 entry reproduced in full with comments by Angela Hermann on the website *100(0)) Schlüsseldokumente zur deutschen Geschichte im 20. Jahrhundert* (http://www.1000dokumente.de/index.html?c=dokument_de&dokument=0118_gob&object=translation&l=de).

33 Report of Landrat Paderborn, 'Aktion gegen die Juden am 10.11.1938',

23 Nov. 1938, in Dov Kulka and Jäckel (ed.), *Die Juden . . . 1933–1945*, p. 320.

34 Report of Landrat Bielefeld, 'Aktion gegen die Juden am 10. November 1938', 18 Nov. 1938, ibid., p. 321.

35 Report of SD-Außenstelle Kochem, 'Bericht für November 1938', 25 Nov. 1938, ibid., p. 326.

36 Report of Bürgermeister Amt Borgentreich, 'Aktion gegen die Juden am 10.11.1983', 17 Nov. 1938, ibid., p. 322.

37 Deutsches Tagebucharchiv, Emmendingen, O.T. (anonymized), Tagebuch 1938–45, entry for 10 Nov. 1938.

38 See Korb, *Reaktionen*, p. 92.

39 During the conference held on 12 November. 1938 at Göring's own Air Ministry in Berlin to decide on further anti-Jewish measures, the Marshal had expressed himself with typical ruthlessness. See 'Stenographische Niederschrift von einem Teil der Besprechung über die Judenfrage unter Vorsitz von Feldmarschall Göring im RLM am 12. November 1938', available online at https://archive.org/stream/TrialOfTheMajorWar CriminalsBeforeTheInternationalMilitaryTribunalNuremberg14Nove /Trial%20of%20the%20major%20war%20criminals%20before%20 the%20International%20Military%20Tribunal%2C%20Nuremberg %2C%2014%20November%201945-1%20October%201946%20 Volume%2028_djvu.txt.

40 'Reichsminister Dr. Goebbels an die Bevölkerung', in DNB, p.m. edn, 10. Nov. 1938, No. 1838, online at the Staatsbibliothek Berlin Website (http://zefys.staatsbibliothek-berlin.de/index.php?id=list).

41 Ebermayer, . . . *und morgen die ganze Welt*, entry for 11 Nov. (lunchtime), pp. 321f.

42 Report and figures of Jewish males arrested quoted in Hermann, *Der Weg in den Krieg*, p. 339.

43 Richard J. Evans, *Third Reich in Power*, p. 584.

44 Ibid., p. 585.

45 Andreas-Friedrich, *Der Schattenmann*, p. 35. And for the following.

46 'Gefahr an der Synagoge beseitigt' ('Danger at Synagogue Eliminated'), in *Pommersche Zeitung* (Sunday edn), 13 Nov. 1938, p. 2.

47 'LOOTING MOBS DEFY GOEBBELS', *Daily Express*, 11 Nov. 1938, p. 1.

48 See Wallis, *Britain, Germany . . .*, p. 185.

49 Cox, *Countdown*, p. 85.

50 'Opinion', *Daily Express*, 21 Nov. 1938, p. 12.

51 'A Strange Conversion. Lord Londonderry Former Friend of Germany Becomes Protector of the Jews', in *Action*, 31 Dec. 1938, p. 4.

52 'Commons Denounce Hitler's Anti-Jew Pogrom', *Daily Mirror*, Tuesday 22 Nov. 1938, p. 2.

53 'Our Live Letter Box', *Daily Mirror*, Wednesday 23 Nov. 1938, p. 12.

54 'Jews Hide in Berlin Woods', *Daily Express*, Monday 14 Nov. 1938, p. 2.

55 'Our Live Letter Box', *Daily Mirror*, Wednesday 16 Nov. 1938, p. 12.

56 Quoted in Wallis, *Britain, Germany . . .* , p. 186.

57 Letter to Hilda, 30 July 1939, in Self (ed.), *Chamberlain Diary Letters*, vol. IV, pp. 433f.

58 For a brief analysis of the desperate state of the Reich's finances at the end of 1938 and the role played by the massive new impositions on Germany's Jews after *Kristallnacht*, see Aly, *Hitlers Volksstaat*, pp. 62f.

59 'Rede Hitlers vor der deutschen Presse' in http://www.ifz-muenchen. de/heftarchiv/1958_2_6_treue.pdf (translation by FT).

60 Hosenfeld, '*Ich versuche*', entry for 12 Nov. 1938, p. 237.

FOUR – WINTER 1938/1939

1   Hilmes, *Berlin 1936*, p. 93.

2   Ibid., p. 97.

3   For Brandt's undercover trip see Merseburger, *Willy Brandt*, pp. 119ff.

4   See Deist et al., *Das Deutsche Reich*, pp. 661ff.

5   See Overy, *The Bombing War*, p. 137.

6   Dee Moss, Oral History recording 1999 for IWM, as above.

7   Marion Bryan née Perkins, Oral History recording 1982 for IWM (Catalogue 6237, Reel 1).

8   Reuben Hyams, Oral History recording 2005 for IWM (Catalogue 27791, Reel 1).

9   Walter Togwell, Oral History recording 1996 for IWM (Catalogue 17494, Reel 1).

10 Mass Observation Online Report Crisis (2) (1040), Miss Dorothy Hughes (23), typist Liverpool, 5 Feb. 1939 (date slightly unclear).

11 'Wait and See', *Daily Mirror*, Wednesday 21 Dec. 1938, p. 11.

12 '207 Boys and Girls are Happy: Julius is Sad', *Daily Express*, Saturday 3 Dec. 1938, p. 5.

13 'Our Live Letter Box', *Daily Mirror*, Friday 16 Dec. 1938, p. 12.

14 Wallis, *Britain, Germany . . .* , p. 189.

15 'Refugees Fund. The Entertainment World. Help of Audiences and Proprietors', *The Times*, 16 Jan. 1939, p. 9.

16 *The Lord Baldwin Fund for Refugees, 1938–39: A Case Study of Third Sector Marketing in Pre-World War II Britain*, Richard A. Hawkins Department of History, University of Wolverhampton, presented at the CHARM (Conference on Historical Analysis & Research in Marketing) Copenhagen 2013. Text available at http://charmassociation.org/CHARM%20 proceedings/CHARM%20article%20archive%20pdf%20format/ Volume%2016%202013/Hawkins%20CHARM%202013%20 Proceedings.pdf.

17 Poll figures in Olson, *Troublesome Young Men*, p. 179.

18 'Those Who Know', *Daily Mirror*, 20 Dec. 1938, p. 11.

19 Deutsches Tagebucharchiv, Emmendingen, Hilde Maud H (b. 1922), 'My last Christmas in pre-war London'.

20 See Jeff Schutts, 'Die Erfrischende Pause: Selling Coca-Cola in Hitler's Germany', in Swett et al. (ed.), *Selling Modernity*, pp. 151f.

21 Author's interview with Dr Maria Müller-Sommer, Berlin 14 Sept. 2017. Maria Sommer studied theatre and gained her PhD in Berlin in 1945, just days before the city fell to the Soviets. After the war, still living in West Berlin, she became a well-known publisher of dramatic texts, and was especially close to the novelist and playwright Günter Grass (1927–2015), whose play *The Proletarians Rehearse the Uprising* she published and promoted internationally, as well as putting in place the connexions that made possible the filming of Grass's most famous novel, *The Tin Drum*.

22 See 'Women in Germany, 1925–1940. Family, Welfare, and Work', in Caplan (ed.), *Nazism . . . Tim Mason*, p. 166, for the child payments and p. 171 for a consideration of the *Mutterkreuz* system.

23 Author's interview with Elly Feliksiak, née Luckow, Derby, 15 Nov. 2017.

24 Entry for 12 Dec. in Ebermayer, *. . . und morgen die ganze Welt*, p. 332.

25 See Horst Daniel, 'In der Pogromnacht zerbrach mehr als Mauern und Glas', in *Nord-West-Zeitung*, 5 Nov. 1988.

26 Deutsches Tagebucharchiv, Emmendingen, Diary of Ruth Thieme, Sig. 1295/I, 2.

27 See Burleigh, *Third Reich*, p. 223.

28 Deutsches Tagebucharchiv, Emmendingen, Diary of Dorothea B., Tagebuch 1938/39 Sig. 1783, 1.

29 See particularly 'Nazi Attacks on British Army. Denials from War Office. "Slanderous"' and 'German Lack of Goodwill', *Manchester Guardian*, 24 Dec. 1938, p. 9. The *Guardian* also mentioned another DNB-sourced piece about the attempts of unemployed marchers to have tea at the Ritz in London – attempts which, predictably, led to a polite but

extremely firm ejection of the applicants. 'There are indeed very few bright spots in the gloomy panorama of Britain spread before German newspaper readers'.

30 'Sonnwendfeier der Freiburger SA', in *Freiburger Zeitung*, early a.m. edn, Friday 23 Dec. 1938, p. 7. 'Ein junges Volk steht Auf' remains a popular song among modern neo-Nazis.

31 Deutsches Tagebucharchiv, Emmendingen, Hilde Maud H. (b. 1922), 'My last Christmas in pre-war London'.

32 'London, Monday night', *Manchester Guardian*, 27 Dec. 1938, p. 8.

33 'Bronchial Empire', *Daily Mirror*, 30 Dec. 1938, p. 9.

34 Articles by David Walker, *Daily Mirror*, 30 Dec. 1938, 31 Dec. 1938 and 3 Jan. 1939.

35 '"No War in 1939" Say French Fortune Tellers', *Daily Express*, 27 Dec. 1938, p. 2.

36 'This is why you can sleep soundly in 1939', by George Malcolm Thomson, *Daily Express*, 2 Jan. 1939, p. 10.

37 'Sir John Anderson ends his holiday as boats sail in A.R.P. trenches', *Daily Express*, 9 Jan. 1939, p. 7.

38 Entry for 4 Jan. 1939 in Dilks (ed.), *Cadogan Diaries*, pp. 133f.

39 'News from Germany. Giant Loan to Ransom Jews', *Daily Express*, 27 Dec. 1938, p. 2.

40 Dalton's speech reported in 'Parliament. Peace Policy After Munich', *The Times*, 20 Dec. 1938, p. 7.

41 Editorial, 'Germany and the Refugees', *The Times*, 22 Dec. 1938, p. 13.

42 'Nazi Finance', *Daily Mirror*, 21 Jan. 1939, p. 11.

43 Included with entry for 24 Jan. 1939 in. Dilks (ed.), *Cadogan Diaries*, pp. 141ff.

44 See 'Mr Chamberlain's Speech. Preparedness of the Nation', *The Times*, 30 Jan. 1939, p. 8.

45 Letter from Neville to Ida Chamberlain, 28 Jan. 1939 in Self (ed.), *Chamberlain Diary Letters*, vol. IV, p. 375.

46 Sequence from entry for 31 Jan. 1939 in Reuth (ed.), *Goebbels, Tagebücher*, p. 1303. And for Goebbels's comparisons of his own personal position with that in 1933.

47 Text of Hitler's speech in English translation, *Manchester Guardian*, 31 Jan. 1939 (continuation), p. 15. As for the following quote.

48 Letter from Neville to Hilda Chamberlain, 5 Feb. 1939, in Self (ed.), *Chamberlain Diary Letters*, vol. IV, p. 377.

49 Landesarchiv Nordrhein-Westfalen (Münster), 'Gauleitung Westfalen-

Nord Hauptleitung' No. 26 Januar 1939 1), *Stimmungsmäßiger Überblick über die gesamtpolitische Lage.*

50 Entry for 1 Feb. 1939 in Reuth (ed.), *Goebbels, Tagebücher,* p. 1304. In fact a Führer order to the military for preparation of a plan to 'dispose of' (*erledigen*) what remained of Czechoslovakia had been in place since 21 October the previous year.

FIVE — SPRING 1939

1 See 'London Bomb Outrages', *The Times,* 4 Feb. 1939, p. 12; also 'The London Tube Station Explosions. Time Bombs secreted in Cloakrooms' and 'Drastic Measures Follow New Bomb Outrages. Luggage Inspection at Stations', *Manchester Guardian,* 4 Feb. 1939, p. 11.

2 See Coogan, *The IRA,* pp. 212ff.

3 Hull, *Irish Secrets,* p. 51.

4 See articles 'Der Nationalsozialismus Ist die Antwort des Deutschen Volkes an das Schicksal', 'Kein Künstlicher Judenstaat, sondern Errichtung eines jüdischen Reservates unter Polizeikontrolle', and 'Eröffnung der Palästina-Konferenz', in *Freiburger Zeitung* (early a.m. edn), 8 Feb. 1939, p. 1.

5 'Sir John Anderson (Pictured As He Talks) Wants 12 A.R.P. Dictators', *Daily Express,* 3 Feb. 1939, p. 1, and 'Twelve A.R.P. Dictators to Run Britain in War', ibid., p. 2.

6 *Daily Express,* 2 Feb. 1939, p. 6.

7 For the Katakombe and the Gestapo report, see Herzog, *Heil Hitler,* pp. 78f. For the 'weapons' joke, ibid., p. 79.

8 For this quote and other references, unless otherwise stated see Jelavich, *Berlin Cabaret,* pp. 248ff.

9 Theodor Wolff, 'The "Berliner Tageblatt". An Epitaph. Liberalism in Germany', *Manchester Guardian,* 1 Feb. 1939, pp. 11 and 12. Wolff was handed over to the Gestapo when Nice was annexed by the Italians in 1943, and after mistreatment in Sachsenhausen died aged seventy-five in Berlin, his birthplace, in September 1943.

10 See 'Efforts to Restructure the Press', in Longerich, *Goebbels,* pp. 340f. The *Frankfurter Zeitung* was finally closed down in 1943 after Hitler was displeased by an article about an early Nazi comrade of his, the writer Dietrich Eckhart.

11 Diary entries for 16 Jan. and 24 Feb. 1939 in Andreas-Friedrich, *Der Schattenmann,* pp. 50f.

12 Smithson, Oral History Interview with Ruth Adler Schnee, as in ch. 3 n. 29 above.

13 Diary entry for 6 Mar. 1939 in Andreas-Friedrich, *Der Schattenmann*, p. 52.

14 See Heinrich Bodensieck, 'Das Dritte Reich und die Lage der Juden in der Tschecho-Slowakei nach München', in *Vierteljahrshefte für Zeitgeschichte* Jahrgang 9 (1961), Heft 3, pp. 249ff., and for the following unless otherwise indicated.

15 See Hermann, *Der Weg in den Krieg*, pp. 414f.

16 Ripka, *Munich, Before and After*, p. 251. Dr Ripka (1895–1958) was diplomatic editor of the influential Czech newspaper *Lidové noviny* and an adviser to Edvard Beneš during the 1930s. He followed him into exile.

17 See Lohmann, 'Das "deutsche Prag"'.

18 Anton Weliminsky, online Oral History recording for IWM, as in ch. 2 n 28 above.

19 See 'Erbitterte Slowakische Proteste gegen Prag', deadline Preßburg (Bratislava), 10 Mar. 1939, in DNB (a.m. edn), 11 Mar. 1939.

20 Karmasin quoted in 'Slovakia Breaks With Prague', *Daily Express*, 11 Mar. 1939, p. 2.

21 'Five I.R.A. men get 20 Years Each', *Daily Express*, 11 Mar. 1939, p. 1.

22 'Hoare Suggests 5-Year Peace', *Daily Express*, 11 Mar. 1939 p. 1, with full report on his speech at p. 13.

23 'A Golden Age?', *Manchester Guardian*, 13 Mar. 1939, p. 8.

24 All these taken from the front page of the *Freiburger Zeitung* (evening edn), 13 Mar. 1939.

25 'Will They Call It Bohemia?', *Daily Express*, 14 Mar. 1939, p. 10. And on the same page 'Opinion' for the editorial.

26 See Hermann, *Der Weg in den Krieg*, p. 443.

27 Ebermayer, . . . *und morgen die ganze Welt*, entry for 23 Mar. 1939, p. 363.

28 See Richard J. Evans, *Third Reich in Power*, p. 683.

29 'Proklamation des Führers', reprinted in *Freiburger Zeitung* (evening edn), 15 Mar. 1939, p. 1.

30 Lohmann, 'Das "deutsche Prag"', p. 79.

31 Käthe Fischel interview for IWM as above.

32 Groscurth, *Tagebücher*, pp. 170f. And for his report on the trip into the Czech lands with Hauptmann Dingler.

33 Ibid., p. 171.

34 Deutsches Tagebucharchiv, Emmendingen, Catalogue Sig. 1708, 10 Wilhelm Sölter, 'Der Weg', entry for 16 Mar. 1939.

35 'Mr Chamberlain's Plain Words to Hitler', report and text of the speech, *Manchester Guardian*, 18 Mar. 1939, pp. 18f.

36 Reuth (ed.), *Goebbels, Tagebücher*, p. 1308, entry for 19 Mar. 1939.

37 See report for March 1939, 'Die Allgemeine Situation in Deutschland', in Sopade 1939, p. 280.

38 Ebermayer, . . . *und morgen die ganze Welt*, entry for 18 Mar. 1939, p. 359.

39 See report for March 1939, 'Die Allgemeine Situation in Deutschland', in Sopade 1939, p. 278.

40 Ibid., pp. 283f.

41 Ibid., p. 284.

42 Letter from Minna von Alten to her granddaughter Irmgard Brester, Braunschweig, 22 Mar. 1939, in Kalshoven (ed.), *Between Two Homelands*, p. 137.

43 Ebermayer, . . . *und morgen die ganze Welt*, entry for 24 Mar. 1939, p. 363.

44 Report for March 1939, 'Die Allgemeine Situation in Deutschland', in Sopade 1939, p. 268.

45 Mass Observation Archive Online, MJ Hill, Huddersfield (2478), 20 Mar. 1939.

46 'The Way the Wind Blows', *Daily Mirror*, 18 Mar. 1939, p. 2. For the paper's views on conscription and beefing up the cabinet, see the following Monday's edition, p. 15.

47 'Miss Mitford Attacked – by 1,093 of our readers', *Daily Mirror*, 22 Mar. 1939, p. 14.

48 Mass Observation Archive Online, Miss D. Hughes (1040), 'Crisis', 21 Mar. 1939.

49 Mass Observation Archive Online, no name (4153), 'Crisis', Mar./Apr. 1939.

50 Mass Observation Archive Online, A. Elliott (1032), 'Crisis', 20 Mar. 1939.

51 Mass Observation Archive Online, G. Bowles (1041), 'Crisis Directive', 20 Mar. 1939.

52 First published in *The Left Forum*, September 1939, but clearly written at the time the first Militia trainees were being called up. Available online at https://www.marxists.org/archive/orwell/1939/democracy-army.htm.

53 'Opinion', *Daily Express*, 17 Mar. 1939, p. 10.

54 'Opinion', *Daily Express*, 18 Mar. 1939, p. 12.

55 Mass Observation Archive Online, D.M. Hill (1407), 'March Crisis', 18 Mar. 1939.

SIX — APRIL/MAY 1939

1 *Neue Zürcher Zeitung*, 20 Apr. 1939.

2 Andreas-Friedrich, *Der Schattenmann*, diary entry for 20 Apr. 1939, p. 55.

3 Phayer, *The Catholic Church and the Holocaust*, p. 45.

4 Terveen, 'Filmbericht über Hitlers 50. Geburtstag', p. 82. And for Hitler's instructions to Ribbentrop regarding choice of guests.

5 Entry for 21 Apr. 1939 in Reuth (ed.), *Goebbels, Tagebücher*, pp. 1319f.

6 Ibid., p. 1319, n. 40, and Terveen, 'Der Filmbericht', pp. 75–84. The entire 19.19-minute-long *Wochenschau* of the birthday events is (as of April 2018) available online at www.youtube.com.

7 *Neue Zürcher Zeitung*, 20 Apr.1939.

8 See the round-up of the Nazi press in Report for April 1939, 'Die Allgemeine Situation in Deutschland', in Sopade 1939, p. 438.

9 Reproduced with other poems and essays in reports for April 1939, ibid., p. 445. The German text reads:

> *Führer*
>
> *Wir haben dir einmal geschworen.*
> *Nun sind wir auf immer dein.*
> *Wie Bäche im Strome verloren,*
> *Münden wir in dich ein.*
>
> *Auch wenn wir dich einmal nicht fassen,*
> *Werden wir mit dir gehn.*
> *Einst wirst du uns schauen lassen,*
> *Was du vor uns gesehn.*
>
> *Herzen wie erzene Schilde*
> *Haben wir um dich gestellt.*
> *Und es ist uns, als hielte*
> *Gott durch dich seine Welt.*

10 Otto Dietrich, quoted in *Neue Zürcher Zeitung*, 20 Apr. 1939.

11 Ebermayer, . . . *und morgen die ganze Welt*, p. 372.

12 'Birthday March in Berlin. New A.A. Guns. Führer Takes Salute', *The Times*, 21 Apr. 1939, p. 16.

13 'Crowd Keep Hitler from "Merry Widow"', by Selkirk Panton, and 'London Nazis Toast Hitler', *Daily Express*, 21 Apr. 1939, p. 15.

14 See reports for April 1939 in Sopade 1939, p. 442.

15 Ibid., p. 452.

16 Ibid., p. 435.

17 'Truth Prevails. Czechs' Protest in Prague', *The Times*, 21 Apr. 1939, p. 16.

18 Boberach (ed.), *Meldungen*, p. 316.

19 Gauleitung Westfalen-Nord Hauptleitung Februar–März 1939 1) 'Stimmungsmässiger Überblick über die gesamtpolitische Lage', at Landesarchiv NRW Münster.

20 Ibid., April–Mai 1939 23/23a) 'Schwierigkeiten in der Versorgung', at Landesarchiv NRW Münster.

21 Ibid., Februar–März 1939, 23) 'Schwierigkeiten in der Versorgung', at Landesarchiv NRW Münster.

22 Ibid., Januar 1939, 1) 'Stimmungsmässiger Überblick über die gesamtpolitische Lage', at Landesarchiv NRW Münster.

23 See n. 18 in Reuth (ed.), *Goebbels, Tagebücher*, p. 1306.

24 Tooze, *Wages of Destruction*, pp. 135f.

25 Aufzeichnungen aus der Autobiographie von Josepha von Koskull (1898–1996) aus Berlin (DHM-Bestand; Inv.-Nr.: D02 98/501) online at https://www.dhm.de/lemo/zeitzeugen/josepha-von-koskull-kriegsbeginn-1939.html.

26 Gauleitung Westfalen-Nord Hauptleitung 6) 'Stimmungs- und Lagebericht für August–September 1938', at Landesarchiv NRW Münster.

27 Sopade 1939, 'Der Arbeitseinsatz', p. 723.

28 Ibid., p. 735.

29 See Overy, 'Blitzkriegswirtschaft? . . .', pp. 383f.

30 See 'Ungewöhnliche Gäste im "Ritz"', in DNB a.m. edn No. 2094, 23 Dec. 1938. For comparison, see 'Scene in West End Restaurant. Workless Demonstrate. Asked for Tea at the Ritz', *Manchester Guardian*, 23 Dec. 1938, p. 10.

31 See http://www.allcountries.org/uscensus/1027_motor_vehicle_registrations.html.

32 For British driver figures see the page at the Coventry Transport Museum website, http://www.transport-museum.com/visiting/the_growth_of_the_motor_industry_1918_to_1939.aspx. German figure and details about relative costs and savings scheme from Tooze, *Wages of Destruction*, pp. 150–6.

33 Author's interview with Frau Inge Heyl (née Lueg), Otto-Dibelius-Stift, Berlin 15 Sept. 2017.

34 Klemperer, *Diaries*, entry for 6 Mar. 1936, p. 148.

35 See König, 'Adolf Hitler vs Henry Ford', p. 252.

36 Part of a lengthy report on the KdF-Wagen in Sopade 1939, p. 489.

37 Ibid., p. 488.

38 'Wie kommt man schnell zum KdF-Wagen?', in *Pommersche Zeitung*, 12 Nov. 1938, p. 6.

39 Ibid., pp. 489f.

40 Boberach (ed.), *Meldungen*, p. 177 (*Jahreslagebericht 1938*).

41 Tooze, *Wages of Destruction*, p. 156.

42 See König, 'Adolf Hitler vs Henry Ford', p. 260.

43 Günter Hätte in http://www.dhm.de/lemo/zeitzeugen/guenter-haette-kindheit-im-1000-jaehrigen-reich.html.

44 Schanetzky, *Kanonen statt Butter*, p. 108.

45 See the account of this first television transmission from German public broadcaster WDR at https://www1.wdr.de/archiv/rundfunk-geschichte/rundfunkgeschichte130.html.

46 See Peter Hoff, 'Das Bild des Führers in Alle Deutsche Herzen', in Uricchio (ed.), *Anfänge des Deutschen Fernsehens*, pp. 210f.

47 Article by Kurt Wagenführ, quoted in Monika Eisner, Thomas Müller, Peter M. Spangenberg, 'Der Lange Weg eines schnellen Mediums: Zur Frühgeschichte des deutschen Fernsehens', in Uricchio (ed.), *Anfänge des Deutschen Fernsehens*, p. 196.

48 See Peter Hoff, 'Das Bild des Führers in Alle Deutsche Herzen', ibid., p. 223.

49 See Currie, *British Television, 1930–2000*, p. 17.

50 John Macadam, 'Boon Fight Put a New Industry on the Map', *Daily Express*, 26 Feb. 1939, p. 17.

51 James Agate, 'Agate Takes Notes', *Daily Express*, 18 Mar. 1939, p. 12.

52 'Opinion', in *Daily Express*, 13 Feb. 1939, p. 10.

53 Letter from S. Johnson, quoted in 'Letters', *Daily Express*, 4 Jan. 1939, p. 8.

54 For this and other problematic considerations see Peter Hoff, 'Das Bild des Führers in Alle Deutsche Herzen', in Uricchio (ed.), *Anfänge des Deutschen Fernsehens*, especially p. 233.

55 Monika Eisner, Thomas Müller, Peter M. Spangenberg, 'Der Lange Weg eines schnellen Mediums: Zur Frühgeschichte des deutschen Fernsehens', ibid., p. 199.

56 See Tooze, *Wages of Destruction*, pp. 157ff.

57 Kompisch and Otto, *Bestien des Boulevards*, p. 159. See also Arz, *Todsicheres München*, pp. 97–103.

58 Flanner quoted in Olson, *Troublesome Young Men*, p. 190.

59 See 'Military Training Bill. Labour's Opposition Not to be Taken to Point of Obstruction', *Manchester Guardian*, 8 May 1939, p. 11.

60 Quoted in 'Conscription Plan the Way to Peace', *Daily Mirror*, 27 Apr. 1939, p. 8.

61 'More Men for Our Army', *Daily Mirror*, 28 Apr. 1939, p. 32.

62 Ebermayer, . . . *und morgen die ganze Welt*, p. 373.

63 Albert 'Tony' Cameron, Oral History recording 1992 for IWM (Catalogue 12918, Reel 2).

64 Albert Davies, Oral History recording 1990 for IWM (Catalogue 12709, Reel 1).

65 James Edward Plant, Oral History recording 1997 for IWM (Catalogue 17616, Reel 1).

66 Ivan Daunt, Oral History recording 2000 for IWM (Catalogue 20461, Reel 2).

67 Text reprinted in British Blue Book, available online at http://avalon. law.yale.edu/wwii/blbk20.asp.

68 Longerich, *Goebbels*, p. 411.

69 See Hermann, *Der Weg in den Krieg*, p. 478.

70 See Deist et al., *Das Deutsche Reich*, p. 671.

71 Hermann, *Der Weg in den Krieg*, p. 473.

72 For descriptions of the reception see 'Our London Correspondence', *Manchester Guardian*, 4 Apr. 1939, p. 10, and 'All Wore Top Hats to Meet Col. Beck but – Col. Beck Was Top-Hatless', *Daily Express*, 4 Apr. 1939, p. 3.

73 'The Daily Worker Says . . .', *Daily Worker*, 4 Apr. 1939 (1st edn), p. 1; 'Poland Mortgaged to Jewry' in *Action*, 8 Apr. 1939, p. 3; 'Our London Correspondence', *Manchester Guardian*, 4 Apr. 1939, p. 10.

74 See 'Loan to Arm the Poles', *Daily Mirror*, 3 Apr. 1939, p. 1.

75 Ebermayer, . . . *und morgen die ganze Welt*, entry for 11 Jan. 1939, p. 341.

76 See Hargreaves, *Blitzkrieg Unleashed*, p. 55.

77 'Deutsche Flüchtlingsstrom infolge polnischen Terrors', in DNB 2nd night edn No. 715, 5 May 1939.

78 See photographic reproductions in Sopade 1939 , pp. 547–50.

79 See Bonacker, *Goebbels' Mann beim Radio*, p. 56.

80 Entry of 9 May 1939 in Dilks (ed.), *Cadogan Diaries*, p. 179.

81 Quoted in Olson, *Troublesome Young Men*, p. 192.

82 Quoted ibid., p. 193.

83 Sopade 1939, p. 408.

84 Ibid., p. 545.

85 Ibid., p. 554.

SEVEN — JUNE/JULY 1939

1 Schanetzky, *Kanonen statt Butter*, p. 101.

2 Quoted ibid., p. 104.

3 Rudolf Urbahn in https://www.dhm.de/lemo/zeitzeugen/rudolf-urbahn-das-ns-regime.html.

4 Baranowski, *Strength through Joy*, p. 166.

5 Ibid., p. 122.

6 Ibid., p. 153.

7 Ibid., p. 137.

8 Ibid., p. 171.

9 See Shelly Baranowski, 'Selling the "Racial Community": Kraft durch Freude and Consumption in the Third Reich', in Swett et al. (ed.), *Selling Modernity*, pp. 144f.

10 Baranowski, *Strength through Joy*, p. 170.

11 Ibid., p. 168.

12 See ibid., pp. 155–61.

13 'Stimmen aus dem Landvolk', in *Freiburger Zeitung*, 4–5 Mar. 1939, p. 16.

14 Karl Christian Führer, 'Pleasure, Practicality and Propaganda: Popular Magazines in Nazi Germany, 1933–1939', in Swett et al. (ed.), *Pleasure and Power*, p. 145.

15 Thamer, *Verführung und Gewalt*, p. 516.

16 For accounts of this visit and the political and social/ideological background, see 'When Hitler's Perfect Woman Came to Call', *BBC History Magazine*, Mar. 2014, and Julie V. Gottlieb and Matthew Stibbe, 'Peace at Any Price: The Visit of Nazi Women's Leader Gertrud Scholtz-Klink to London in March 1939 and the Response of British Women Activists', available online from Sheffield Hallam University Research Archive (SHURA) at http://shura.schu.ac.uk/12142/.

17 See *Daily Mirror*, 8 Mar. 1939, p. 21.

18 See 'Frau Schotz-Klink bei der Anglo-German Fellowship', in *Freiburger Zeitung*, 9 Mar. 1939 (early a.m. edn), p. 2.

19 'When Hitler's Perfect Woman Came to Call', in *BBC History Magazine*, Mar. 2014.

20 Quoted in Gottlieb and Stibbe, 'Peace at Any Price', as cited in note 16 above, p. 17.

21 Doris Kirkpatrick, 'Role of Women in Germany: She Works Because She Must and She Fears That Another War Will Take Her Sons', *New York Times*, 26 Sept. 1937, p. 89.

22 Claudia Koonz describing an encounter with Scholtz-Klink in 1981 in *Mothers in the Fatherland*, p. xxi. The former *Frauenführerin* (women's leader) died in 1999, aged 97.

23 Ibid., p. 145.

24 Grunberger, *Social History of the Third Reich*, p. 324. And for the proportion of working women.

25 Ibid., p. 325.

26 Thamer, *Verführung und Gewalt*, p. 516.

27 Figure for UK/USA working women in Schanetzky, *Kanonen statt Butter*, p. 118.

28 See Stephenson, *Women in Nazi Germany*, p. 32.

29 Grunberger, *Social History of the Third Reich*, p. 329. And for the following. Quotes from Scholtz-Klink.

30 Glenn Collins, 'Women in Nazi Germany: Paradoxes' (interview with Dr Claudia Koonz), *New York Times*, 2 Mar. 1987.

31 Letter from Neville to Hilda Chamberlain, 29 Apr. 1939, in Self (ed.), *Chamberlain Diary Letters*, vol. IV, p. 412.

32 Ibid., letter to Hilda Chamberlain, 28 May 1939.

33 Ibid., letter to Hilda Chamberlain, 17 June 1939.

34 Ibid., letter to Ida Chamberlain, 25 June 1939.

35 See White, *Britain and the Bolshevik Revolution*, note on p. 296.

36 Monthly Weather Reports for 1939 available online at https://www.metoffice.gov.uk/learning/library/archive-hidden-treasures/monthly-weather-report-1930s.

37 See the website of the George Formby Society http://www.george-formby.co.uk/gf_story/report.html.

38 Account of holiday in Blackpool quoted in Cross, *Worktowners at Blackpool*, p. 136. 'Worktown' was the cotton-textiles-producing centre of Bolton, north of Manchester.

39 For a detailed account of the disaster see A.S. Evans, *Beneath the Waves*, pp. 184f., and Booth and Deighton, *Thetis Down*, an unsensational account that debunks the worst of the conspiracy theories.

40 Jesse Lionel Shepherd, Oral History recording 1990 for IWM (Catalogue 11626, Reel 1).

41 Edward Findley Gueritz, Oral History recording 1997 for IWM (Catalogue 17394, Reel 1).

42 'Our Live Letter Box – Thetis! Widespread Criticism', *Daily Mirror*, 7 June 1939, p. 10.

43 'Opinion. Grim Drama', *Daily Express*, 3 June 1939, p. 10.

44 See Booth and Deighton, *Thetis Down*, p. 201.

45 'King, Queen at Hot Dog Picnic', *Daily Mirror*, 12 June 1939, p. 3.

46 William Hickey, 'These Names Make News. Envoy Suburban', *Daily Express*, 9 June 1939, p. 6.

47 'Freche Polnische Drohung an Danzig' and 'Neuer Mord an Volksdeutschen. Polnische Verbrecher gehen straflos aus', in *Freiburger Zeitung*, 12 June 1939 (a.m. edn), p. 2.

48 See the tribute to Gottschalk on what would have been his 100th birthday by Klaus J. Hennig, '. . . oder geht man zugrunde', in *Die Zeit*, 1 Apr. 2004.

49 See Irit Neidhardt, 'Einführung zum Film *Aufruhr in Damaskus*', at the website of the German Historical Museum, Berlin (Deutsches Historisches Museum) https://www.dhm.de/fileadmin/medien/relaunch/zeughauskino/Neidhardt_Aufruhr_in_Damaskus.pdf.

50 *Aufruhr in Damaskus* can be downloaded from the internet and freely viewed on YouTube.

51 'Sir O. Mosley Restates His Policy. Free Hand in East for Germany', *Manchester Guardian*, 17 July 1939, p. 12. And for the details of the speech that follow.

52 Full text of his speech available, surprisingly, as a recent paperback, or at https://www.oswaldmosley.com/britain-first-rally-1939/.

53 'Blackshirt Caesar! Cassandra reports on last night's great rally in London', *Daily Mirror*, 17 July 1939, p. 12.

54 Deutsches Tagebucharchiv, Emmendingen, Diary of Ruth Thieme Sig. 1295/I, 2.

55 'Opinion', *Daily Express*, 19 June 1939, p. 12.

56 'La politesse', in 'Our Live Letter Box', *Daily Mirror*, 7 June 1939, p. 10.

57 A mix from author's interview with Fritz Lustig, London, 24 June 2017, and his privately published autobiography, *My Lucky Life*. Quotation here from p. 106. Details of move to Cambridge pp. 107f. Mr Lustig, who died in December 2017, was the father of the well-known British journalist and broadcaster Robin Lustig.

58 Katerina (Käthe) Fischel (née Strenitz), online Oral History recording 2000 for IWM (Catalogue 20128, Reel 2).

59 See especially Finch, *A View From the Hill: A History of Sibford School*. This

Quaker boarding school in Oxfordshire provided a safe haven for dozens of Jewish refugee children. With thanks to the late David Laity.

60 'New Army – All Present and Correct – By 3 pm', *Sunday Express*, 16 July 1939, p. 13.

61 'I Join the Army With a £10 Bonus from the Firm', *Daily Express*, 15 July 1939, p. 5.

62 'Please Send Me My Ukelele – Says Militiaman', *Daily Express*, 20 July 1939, p. 3.

63 'Militiamen Granted Leave on Their First Day', *Manchester Guardian*, 17 July 1939, p. 5.

64 'The Rally of Youth. 34,000 Militiamen Report for Training', *Observer*, 16 July 1939, p. 15.

65 'Democracy and the Militia', *Daily Worker*, 18 July 1939, p. 3.

66 Andrew Gwynn Curry Jones online Oral History recording 1995 for IWM (Catalogue 14925, Reel 1).

67 Hamilton, *Hangover Square*, p. 101.

EIGHT – 1–22 AUGUST 1939

1 See the 'Einstein Letter' online at the website of the Roosevelt Library http://www.fdrlibrary.marist.edu/archives/pdfs/docsworldwar.pdf.

2 See Lev Besymenski, 'Die sowjetisch-deutschen Verträge von 1939', published on the website of the Katholische Universität Eichstätt-Ingolstadt http://www.ku.de/forschungseinr/zimos/publikationen/forum/zeitgeschichte/besymenski-sowjetisch-deutsche-vertraege/.

3 Ericson, *Feeding the Eagle*, p. 54.

4 Ibid., p. 55.

5 'Not Counting Niggers', in George Orwell, *Collected Essays, Journalism and Letters*, vol. 1, p. 396.

6 Details in 'Nazis Howl at Paper "War"', *Daily Mirror*, 7 July 1939, p. 4.

7 'Plumpe englische Bauernfängerbriefe' (Crude English Swindler Letters), published in *Völkischer Beobachter*, 14 July 1939, and in DNB, 14 July 1939, spread over three issues: 1st early a.m. edn (1042), 2nd early a.m. edn (1043), and a.m. edn (1044), with additional material to follow.

8 Quoted in 'Latest Nazi Howler', *Daily Mirror*, 18 July 1939, p. 28.

9 See the article 'Privater Krieg mit Goebbels', in *Der Freitag. Das Meinungsmediium* at https://www.freitag.de/autoren/friedhelm-greis/privater-krieg-mit-goebbels.

10 See 'Propaganda by Post', *Daily Express*, 28 July 1939, p. 8.

11 King-Hall, *Total Victory*, p. 285. See also the website devoted to the life

and career of King-Hall, which carries detailed information about the origins and reckoned effects of the letters sent to Germany. https://sites.google.com/site/kinghallconnections/7900-the-next-ten-years-1929-1939.

12 Report on impact of the King-Hall leaflets part of report 'Die Allgemeine Situation in Deutschland', July 1939 in Sopade 1939, p. 830.

13 Longerich, *Hitler*, p. 659.

14 See Dennis Clark, 'Boomerang! . . . or . . . It hurts them more than it hurts us', *Daily Express*, 28 July 1939, p. 8.

15 'Hitler: New Bid for Gag', *Daily Mirror*, 21 July 1939, p. 2.

16 'Propaganda by Post', *Daily Express*, 28 July 1939, p. 8.

17 'Communication from the German Government to the British Government, Handed by Joachim von Ribbentrop, Minister for Foreign Affairs, to the British Ambassador (Sir Nevile Henderson) at 11:20 a.m. on 3 September, 1939', online at http://www.ibiblio.org/pha/policy/1939/1939-09-01e.html.

18 See Longerich, *Hitler*, p. 660.

19 Ciano, *Diary, 1937–1943*, entries for 11 and 12 Aug. 1939, pp. 118f.

20 Longerich, *Hitler*, p. 663, n. 97.

21 'Krieg gegen das Deutschtum. 204 Überfälle klagen gegen Polen', in *Freiburger Zeitung*, 12 Aug. 1939 (early a.m. edn), p. 2.

22 Dilks (ed.), *Cadogan Diary*, entry of 12 Aug. 1939, p. 195.

23 Meehan, *Unnecessary War*, pp. 230f.

24 'Englands Kochtopf', 'Englands Armee in Streik getreten' and 'Schlappen in Londons Nervenkrieg', in *Freiburger Zeitung*, 14 Aug. 1939 (evening edn), pp. 1 and 2.

25 'Die größte Baustelle der Welt', in *Freiburger Zeitung*, 15 Aug. 1939 (evening edn), p. 2.

26 Selkirk Panton, 'Nazis Talk of Five-Day Victory Over Poles – Without General War', *Daily Express*, 22 Aug. 1939, p. 2.

27 Kurt Elfering, 'Die Schlesienfahrt 1939', at https://www.dhm.de/lemo/zeitzeugen/kurt-elfering-die-schlesienfahrt-1939.html. And for the following.

28 See Wehler, *Deutsche Gesellschaftsgeschichte* Bd.4 p. 705. See also https://www.dhm.de/lemo/kapitel/ns-regime/alltagsleben.html.

29 'Opinion. Harvest Time', *Daily Express*, 8 Aug. 1939, p. 8.

30 See https://warwick.ac.uk/fac/soc/economics/staff/sbroadberry/wp/totwar3.pdf.

31 See *Daily Express* Agricultural Reporter, 'If No Food Ship Reached Us for

a Year – Britain Could Not Starve', *Daily Express*, 25 Aug. 1939, p. 9.

32 Elfering, 'Die Schlesienfahrt 1939', as cited in note 27 above.

33 Ebermayer, . . . *und morgen die ganze Welt*, entry for 9 Aug. 1939, p. 405.

34 'Sir Barry Domvile, the Link chief, says he was told in Germany: "Hitler Offered to Defend the British Empire". But Plan Was Turned Down', *Daily Express*, 9 Aug. 1939, p. 9. Domvile was arrested and interned in the summer of 1940 under Defence Regulation 18B, as were Sir Oswald Mosley and up to a thousand other potential 'fifth columnists'.

35 'Home or Foreign' Report for Mass Observation April 1939 SxMOA1/1/4/3/1 (A16) p. 8 for the figures on support for foreign policy and p. 6 for opinions on relative importance of foreign and domestic politics.

36 See Todman, *Britain's War*, pp. 149–51, for an analysis of the by-elections and the calculations of Conservative strategists.

37 For a year-by-year summary of Hitler's consistency in this regard, even from the first weeks after his seizure of power in 1933, see Maser, *Das Regime*, pp. 204ff.

NINE – 23–31 AUGUST 1939

1 'Das hatte die Welt keineswegs erwartet. Großdeutschlands Diplomatie bereitete dem Ausland eine Sensation. Ereignis von weltpolitischer Bedeutung', in *Freiburger Zeitung* (evening edn), 22 Aug. 1939, p. 1.

2 See Landesarchiv Nordrhein-Westfalen (Münster), Gauleitung Westfalen-Nord Hauptleitung No. 29, 31 Aug. 1939, *Berichterstattung über die Stimmung in der Bevölkerung*.

3 'Russia Signs Trade Pact with Nazis', *Daily Express*, 21 Aug. 1939, p. 1.

4 Dilks (ed.), *Cadogan Diaries*, p. 201.

5 Footnote by David Dilks to entry for 22 Aug. 1939, ibid., p. 199.

6 Meehan, *Unnecessary War*, p. 233.

7 See *Daily Express*, 23 Aug. 1939, front page and p. 2.

8 Meehan, *Unnecessary War*, p. 235.

9 Dilks (ed.), *Cadogan Diaries*, p. 200.

10 Ibid., entries for 23 and 24 Aug. 1939, pp. 201.

11 DNB, 18 Aug. 1939, p.m. and evening edn, No. 1174.

12 Taken from DNB, 25 Aug. 1939, evening edn,, No. 1212.

13 'Scheinheilige Phrasen wie 1918', in DNB, 25 Aug. 1939 (night edn), No. 1213.

14 See 'Die Stunde der Befreiung kommt', in *Freiburger Zeitung* (early a.m. edn), 26 Aug. 1939, p. 1, and 'Verwahrloste polnische Jugend', ibid., p. 4.

15 Entry for 22 Aug. 1939 in Burdick and Jacobsen (ed.), *Halder War Diary 1939–1942*, p. 31. For analysis of the various accounts of the meeting and their plausibility, plus extensive quotations from these documents, see Winfried Baumgart, 'Zur Ansprache Hitlers vor den Führern der Wehrmacht am 22. August 1939. Eine quellenkritische Untersuchung', in *Vierteljahrhefte für Zeitgeschichte*, Jahrgang 16 (1968), Heft 2, pp. 120–49.

16 Baumgart, 'Zur Ansprache Hitlers', as cited in note 15 above, pp. 133f.

17 See editor's note to entry for 27 Aug. 1939, in Dilks (ed.), *Cadogan Diaries*, p. 202.

18 Andreas-Friedrich, *Der Schattenmann*, entry for 22 Aug. 1939, pp. 61 and 62f., for their experiences in Berlin too.

19 Landesarchiv Nordrhein-Westfalen (Münster), Gauleitung Westfalen-Nord Hauptleitung No. 29, 31 Aug. 1939, *Berichterstattung über die Stimmung in der Bevölkerung*. And for the following conclusions.

20 Author's interview with Frau Anna Marie Gramling, Stuttgart, 22 Sept. 2017.

21 Landesarchiv Nordrhein-Westfalen (Münster), Gauleitung Westfalen-Nord Hauptleitung No. 29, 31 Aug. 1939, *Berichterstattung über die Stimmung in der Bevölkerung*.

22 Ebermayer, *. . . und morgen die ganze Welt*, entry for 28 Aug. 1939, p. 419.

23 Deutsches Tagebucharchiv, Emmendingen, Catalogue Sig. 146 1 (Albert Joos 1919–), Kriegstagebuch 28 Aug. 1939.

24 See Fairfield, *Trial of Peter Barnes and Others*, pp. 21f. Also useful, Adams, *Sabotage Plan*, pp. 63ff. Internet sources include 'Coventry IRA bombing: The "forgotten" attack on a British city', at http://www.bbc.co.uk/news/uk-england-coventry-warwickshire-28191501; also http://www.historiccoventry.co.uk/articles/s-shaw.php, And see also Taylor, *Coventry, Thursday, 14 November 1940*, pp. 17ff.

25 For these details see Fairfield, *Trial of Peter Barnes and Others*.

26 See the comprehensive list of IRA actions, including the Coventry incidents mentioned, ibid., Appendix 5, pp. 260ff.

27 'Bomb Found at a Flat: Charges Against Five Men', *The Times*, Saturday 9 Sept. 1939, p. 3.

28 '5 Killed By I.R.A. Bicycle Bomb', *Daily Mirror*, 26 Aug. 1939, p. 3.

29 See also www.historiccoventry.co.uk, as above.

30 'Anti-Irish Demonstration in Coventry', *Manchester Guardian*, 29 Aug. 1939, p. 10.

31 'Into the Sun', *Sunday Express*, 13 Aug. 1939, p. 10.

32 'Parents Day for Militia', *Daily Mirror*, 21 Aug. 1939, p. 19.

33 'Is There a Pet in Your House?', *Daily Mirror*, 28 Aug. 1939, p. 12.

34 See Kean, *Great Cat and Dog Massacre*, pp. 53f.

35 'Guard Your Pets', *Daily Mirror*, 30 Aug. 1939, p. 4.

36 'Dogs and the Crisis', *Daily Mirror*, 31 Aug. 1939, p. 10.

37 'Ivor Lambe's Tales', *Daily Mirror*, 29 Aug. 1939, p. 11. The 20th Baron Willoughby de Broke would in fact serve with the RAF in the war, commanding the control room for Fighter Defences in South-East England during the Battle of Britain, and reached the rank of Air Commodore.

38 'Record Crowd Fly Back to Croydon', *Daily Express*, 26 Aug. 1939, p. 6.

39 'Americans, Britons Rush Home', ibid.

40 William Hickey, '8 Lives Left?', ibid.

41 Mass Observation Archive Online, Naylor I.M.A. (5382), 'War Diary, 1939'.

42 Mass Observation Archive Online, Harrison, S.J.C. (5102), 'Mass Observation Diary'.

43 'IT WAS A GRAND DAY OUT FOR THE CHILDREN', *Daily Mirror*, Monday 29 Aug. 1939, across pp. 14–15.

44 Hilde Marchant, 'MOTHERS WEEP AS CHILDREN MOBILISE IN SCHOOLROOMS', *Daily Express*, Monday 29 Aug. 1939, p. 4 ('Home Crisis News').

45 See Dargleff Jahnke, 'Erster Weltkrieg: Bomben trafen Freiburg', in *Badischer Zeitung*, 26 July 2014, available at http://www.badische-zeitung. de/freiburg/erster-weltkrieg-luftangriffe-trafen-freiburg–87935635. html#kommentare.

46 Major Mohneck, 'Das Luftverteidigungsgebiet', in *Freiburger Zeitung*, 22 Aug. 1939 (early a.m. edn), p. 4.

47 'Freiburg—nur im Mondschein', in *Freiburger Zeitung*, 31 Aug. 1939 (early a.m. edn), p. 5.

48 Armin Peez, 'Bessere Atmosphäre?', in *Freiburger Zeitung*, 30 Aug. 1939 (evening edn), p. 1.

49 See editor's note to entry for 28 Aug. 1939 in Dilks (ed.), *Cadogan Diaries*, p. 203. And for the account of Henderson's subsequent meeting with Hitler.

50 See editor's note to entry for 30 Aug. 1939, ibid., p. 205.

51 Kotze (ed.), *Heeresadjutant bei Hitler*, pp. 60f.

52 Entry for 29 Aug. 1939 in Burdick and Jacobsen (ed.), *Halder War Diary*, p. 41.

53 See editor's note for 30 Aug. 1939 in Dilks (ed.), *Cadogan Diaries*, p. 205.

54 Quoted in Deist et al., *Das Deutsche Reich*, p. 698.

55 Ebermayer, . . . *und morgen die ganze Welt*, entries for 29 and 30 Aug. 1939, pp. 421f.

56 See 'Ein Schwerverbrecher gefasst. Einer der größten Sittlichkeitsverbrecher aller Zeiten', in *Freiburger Zeitung*, 27 Aug. 1939, p. 18.

57 Quoted in Arz, *Todsicheres München*, p. 103.

58 Kompisch and Otto, *Bestien des Boulevards*, p. 159.

59 Ibid., p. 158.

60 Müller, *Canaris*, p. 129.

61 Ibid., p. 155.

62 See 'Jablunka Pass. Vorhut im Wartesaal', in *Der Spiegel*, 14 Mar. 1966 12/1966, pp. 78f. It should be added that when war did actually break out, the tunnel was blown sky-high within minutes.

63 'Unvorstellbare Leiden der Bevölkerung in Ostoberschlesien', in DNB, 28 Aug. 1939 (early a.m. edn), No. 1219. For a front-page reprint in the German provincial press, see, e.g., 'Jablunka-Tunnel gesprengt', in *Rheinsberger Zeitung*, 28 Aug. 1939, p. 1.

64 See text of Naujocks's post-war statement to American forces for this and the following unless otherwise stated. Available online at https://www.ns-archiv.de/krieg/1939/sender-gleiwitz/naujocks.php.

65 See Spieß and Lichtenstein, *Unternehmen Tannenberg*. Also available in shorter form as the series 'Unternehmen Tannenberg. August 1939: Wie die SD den Überfall auf Polen vorbereitete', in (Teil I) *Der Spiegel*, 6 Aug. 1979 32/1979, pp. 62–74, (Teil II) *Der Spiegel*, 13 Aug. 1979 33/1979, pp. 67–74, (Teil III) *Der Spiegel*, 20 Aug. 1979 34/1979, pp. 68–78.

TEN — 1–3 SEPTEMBER 1939

1 Bannister, *I Lived Under Hitler*, p. 66. And p. 67 for the following quotation.

2 Quoted in Joachim Trenkner, 'Ziel vernichtet', in *Die Zeit* 07/2003, 6 Feb. 2003, online at https://www.zeit.de/2003/07/A-Wielun. And for other quotes unless otherwise indicated.

3 See Professor Davies's article 'We must not forget the real causes of the war', in *The Independent*, 29 Aug. 2009, online at https://www.independent.co.uk/voices/commentators/we-must-not-forget-the-real-causes-of-the-war-1778973.html.

4 Snyder, *Bloodlands*, p. 119.

5 Quoted in Trenkner, 'Ziel vernichtet', as in note 2 above.

6 'Der Führer an die Wehrmacht', in DNB, 1 Sept. 1939, No. 1241 (a.m. edn).

7 Hitler's appearance in Reichstag and his speech in full in 'Historische Reichstagssitzung', in DNB, 1 Sept. 1939, No. 1245 (1st p.m. edn), and continuation, ibid., No. 1246 (2nd p.m. edn).

8 Groscurth, *Tagebücher*, entry for 31 Aug. 1939, p. 195. Morale comment, 1 Sept. 1939, p. 196.

9 Mass Observation Archive Online, Naylor I.M.A. (5382), 'War Diary, 1939'.

10 Mass Observation Archive Online, Harrison, S.J.C. (5102), 'Mass Observation Diary', entry for 1 Sept. 1939.

11 Mass Observation Archive Online, Mannion, D.E. (5142), 'Crisis Diary'.

12 Mass Observation Archive Online, Crowfoot, E. (5292), report for 1 Sept. 1939. And for the following until otherwise mentioned.

13 See http://www.thevalvepage.com/tvyears/1938/rlymprep.htm.

14 See the official BBC website: https://www.bbc.co.uk/historyofthebbc/research/general/tvstory9.

15 Unlike in Britain, however, television made a comeback from October 1939 under military control as a way of providing entertainment for the troops, and especially for entertaining wounded soldiers in military hospitals. The German television service even maintained a studio in occupied Paris, operating out of the French broadcasting system's transmitter in the Eiffel Tower. See http://www.fernsehmuseum.info/1939-der-2-weltkrieg-naht.html. Military uses included television transmissions of V-1 and V-2 rocket tests at Peenemünde, enabling technical staff to observe blast-off from a safe distance.

16 Monthly report of Gendarmerie in Ebermannstadt, near Bamberg, 29 Aug. 1939, quoted in Maser, *Das Regime*, p. 216.

17 Landesarchiv Nordrhein-Westfalen (Münster), 'Gauleitung Westfalen-Nord Hauptleitung', Report No. 29, 2 Sept. 1939.

18 Olson, *Troublesome Young Men*, as above, pp. 202f. And for Ronald Cartland's experience.

19 Ibid., p. 204.

20 Entry for 1 Aug. 1939 (written on 3 Sept.) in Dilks (ed.), *Cadogan Diaries*, p. 211.

21 Mass Observation Archive Online, Crowfoot, E. (5292), report for 1 Sept. 1939.

22 Hosenfeld, letter to his son Helmut, 1 Sept. 1939, Hosenfeld, '*Ich versuche*', p. 245.

23 Report for July 1939, 'Die Allgemeine Situation in Deutschland: b) Oberschlesien', in Sopade 1939, p. 818.

24 Report for August–October 1939, 'Der Krieg. 1. Zum überfall auf Polen', in Sopade 1939, p. 965.

25 Cohn, *Kein Reicht, Nirgends*, Band 2, diary entry for 11 Sept. 1939, p. 690. Cohn, his wife and two of his children were 'deported' in November 1941 to Lithuania, where they were murdered.

26 Klemperer, *Diaries*, p. 295.

27 Cohn, *Kein Reicht, Nirgends*, Band 2, entry for 31 Aug. 1939, p. 681.

28 Monthly report of Gendarmerie Ebermannstadt, quoted in Maser, *Das Regime*, pp. 215f.

29 Landesarchiv Nordrhein-Westfalen (Münster), 'Gauleitung Westfalen-Nord Hauptleitung', Report No. 29, 2 Sept. 1939.

30 Quoted in Hargreaves, *Blitzkrieg Unleashed*, p. 122.

31 See Lustig, *My Lucky Life*, pp. 10ff. He was briefly interned in the summer of 1940, but then joined up and spent the rest of the war serving with the British Army, latterly in the Intelligence Corps.

32 Author's interview with Peter Jordan, Didsbury, Manchester, 3 Nov. 2017. His parents were arrested and transported to Lithuania, where they were killed in one of the many mass shootings of Jews in November 1941. Curiously, family photographs of Peter Jordan and his parents from the 1920s and 1930s are included, without identification, in W.G. Sebald's novel *The Emigrants*. Sebald had been a friend of the Jordan family since renting a room from them as a student in the 1970s.

33 Andreas-Friedrich, *Der Schattenmann*, p. 66. Mühsam was arrested and murdered in 1941.

34 Ibid., pp. 65f.

35 Mass Observation Archive (Online), Cowan, H.D. (128), Report for 2 Sept. 1939.

36 Mass Observation Archive Online, Austin, J. (5014), 'Crisis Diary' for 2 Sept. 1939.

37 Mass Observation Archive Online, Moir, C.W. (5156), Report for 2 Sept. 1939.

38 Bannister, *I Lived Under Hitler*, p. 69. And p. 70 for her husband's remarks and her response.

39 Entry for 2 September 1939 in Dilks (ed.), *Cadogan Diaries*, p. 212.

40 See Joachim Trenkner, 'Ziel vernichtet', as in note 2 above, and Jens

Mattern and Hans-Michael Kloth, 'Stukas über Wielun', in *Der Spiegel* 26 Aug. 2009, online at http://www.spiegel.de/einestages/kriegsbeginn-1939-a-948468.html.

41 See the website of the Stutthof Museum, http://stutthof.org/english/node/8, also https://www.jewishvirtuallibrary.org/stutthof-sztutowo-poland,

42 Mass Observation Archive Online, Naylor I.M.A. (5382), 'War Diary, 1939', entry for 2 Sept. 1939.

43 Mass Observation Archive Online, Moxon, L. (5161), diary 2 Sept. 1939.

44 For the scene in the House and afterwards see Olson, *Troublesome Young Men*, pp. 208–11. For full texts of Chamberlain's and Greenwood's speeches see the transcript of the debate in https://hansard.parliament.uk/commons/1939-09-02/debates/621e8d90-8e86-4856-b0b8-a2b5bd2ea776/GermanyAndPolandItalianProposals.

45 Mass Observation Archive Online, Naylor I.M.A. (5382), 'War Diary, 1939', entry for 3 Sept. 1939.

46 Mass Observation Archive Online, Webb, E., (5224), 'Crisis Directive. Personal Diary', entry for 3 Sept. 1939.

47 Schmidt, *Hitler's Interpreter*, pp. 157f.

48 Mass Observation Archive Online, Harrison, S.J.C. (5102), 'Mass Observation Diary', entry for 3 Sept. 1939.

49 Mass Observation Archive Online, Gee, K. (5080), Diary for 3 Sept. 1939.

50 Mass Observation Archive Online, Webb, E. (5224), 'Crisis Directive. Personal Diary', entry for 3 Sept. 1939.

51 Transcript of Chamberlain's speech on 3 Sept. 1939 available on the BBC website at http://www.bbc.co.uk/archive/ww2outbreak/7957.shtml?page=txt. Available to listen in its entirety including the subsequent public announcements at https://www.youtube.com/watch?v=xcSnKArKz8E.

52 Quoted in Mann, *Out of Harm's Way*, p. 8.

53 Also quoted ibid.

54 Mass Observation Archive Online, Webb, E. (5224), 'Crisis Directive. Personal Diary', entry for 3 Sept. 1939.

55 Mass Observation Archive Online, Mannion, D.E. (5142), 'Crisis Diary', entry for 3 Sept. 1939. And for the following.

56 Cable from a correspondent for the *New York Herald-Tribune* quoted in 'London Carries On. "Business at the Old Stand". An American Witness', *Observer*, Sunday 22 Sept. 1940, p. 9.

57 Author's Interview with Frau Inge Heyl (née Lueg) (1927–), Otto-Dibelius-Stift, Berlin, 15 Sept. 2017.

58 Ebermayer, . . . und morgen die ganze Welt, entry for 3 Sept. 1939, p. 432.

59 Ibid.

60 Bannister, I Lived Under Hitler, pp. 70f., including the following.

61 See Horst Rohde's description in Klaus A. Maier, Horst Rohde, Bernd Stegemann, Hans Umbreit, Das Deutsche Reich, Band 2: Die Errichtung der Hegemonie auf dem Europaischen Kontinent, p.144.

62 For a balanced discussion of the controversy about numbers and differing opinions of German and Polish historians regarding the Bromberg massacre, see Markus Krzoska, 'Der "Bromberger Blutsonntag" 1939. Kontroversen und Forschungsergebnisse', in Vierteljahrshefte für Zeitgeschichte Jg 60 (2012), H.2, pp. 237–48. Comments in the text are based on Krzoska's summaries unless otherwise stated.

63 See Böhler, Auftakt zum Vernichtungskrieg, p. 136.

64 Curiously, one of the chief 'witnesses' quoted by modern German far-right websites (which usually give vastly inflated numbers of dead) is Sybil Bannister/Falkenhagen, who moved to German-occupied Bromberg in November because of her husband's transfer to a hospital there. In her memoirs, Mrs Bannister cited accounts she had heard later from German survivors, which make terrible reading, but she also – speaking in 1993 to the British Imperial War Museum – took a balanced view, describing the outrages, in the context of earlier relations between Poles and Germans in the city, as 'rather like the situation in Bosnia, in a way . . . although they had been friendly before'. See Sybil Bannister, Oral History recording 1993 for IWM (Catalogue 13648, Reel 5).

65 See Richard J. Evans, Third Reich at War, pp. 7f.

66 'Secret Service als Mordstifter. Bromberger Bluttat Vorbereitet – Polenbanditen Bewaffnet', in Freiburger Zeitung, 12 Sept. 1939, p. 1.

67 Letter from Eberhard Gebensleben to his grandmother Minna von Alten, Poland, 13 Sept. 1939, in Kalshoven (ed.), Between Two Homelands, p. 133.

68 Mass Observation Archive (Online), Cowan H.D. (128), Report for 3 Sept. 1939.

69 Mass Observation Archive Online, Naylor I.M.A. (5382) ,'War Diary, 1939', entry for 3 Sept. 1939.

70 See the RAF's explanation at https://www.rafmuseum.org.uk/research/history-of-aviation-timeline/interactive-aviation-timeline/british-military-aviation/1939.aspx.

71 Mass Observation Archive (Online), Mason, Mrs (1016), 'Crisis Directive Diary', entry for 3 Sept. 1939.

72 Ivan Daunt, Oral History recording 2000 for IWM (Catalogue 20461,
Reel 4). And for the following.

73 Ebermayer, . . . und morgen die ganze Welt, pp. 434f. And for the following
quote.

74 Orwell, Diary of Events Leading up to War, entry for 3 Sept. (Greenwich)
in Davison (ed.), The Orwell Diaries, p. 208.

75 Davison (ed.), Orwell. A Life in Letters, letter to Geoffrey Gorer, 10 Jan.
1940, p. 174.

76 See Kean, Great Cat and Dog Massacre, pp. 46ff.

77 Kompisch and Otto, Bestien des Boulevards, pp. 160–2.

78 See 'Todesurteil vollstreckt' in Freiburger Zeitung, 2 Dec. 1939, p.3, and
'Zweimal zum Tode verurteilt' plus 'Vollstreckung eines Todesurteils' in
Rheinsberger Zeitung, 2 Dec. 1939, p.3.

79 Author's interview with Ann Forman, née Magnus, Hayle, Cornwall, 3
Feb. 2017.

SOURCES

Adams, Ian, *The Sabotage Plan: The IRA Bombing Campaign in England 1939–1940*, Raleigh, N.C. (pb), Lulu.com, 2011

Aly, Götz, Hitlers Volksstaat: Raub, Rassenkrieg und nationaler Sozializmus, Frankfurt-on-Main, S. Fischer, 2005

Andreas-Friedrich, Ruth, *Der Schattenmann*, Berlin, Suhrkamp Verlag, 1947

Arz, Martin, *Todsicheres München. Die spektakulärsten Kriminalfälle*, Munich, Hirschkäfer Verlag, 2009

Ball, Stuart (ed.), *Parliament and Politics in the Age of Churchill and Attlee: The Headlam Diaries 1935–1951*, Cambridge, Cambridge University Press, 1999

Bannister, Sybil, *I Lived Under Hitler*, London, Penguin Books, 1995

Baranowski, Shelley, *Strength through Joy. Consumerism and Mass Tourism in the Third Reich*, Cambridge, Cambridge University Press, 2004

Baumgart, Winfried, 'Zur Ansprache Hitlers vor den Führern der Wehrmacht am 22. August 1939 Eine quellenkritische Untersuchung', in *Vierteljahrhefte für Zeitgeschichte*, Jahrgang 16 (1968), Heft 2

Beaken, Robert, *Cosmo Lang: Archbishop in War and Crisis*, London, I.B. Tauris, 1988

Benz, Wolfgang (ed.), *Die Vertreibung der Deutschen aus dem Osten. Ursachen. Ereignisse, Folgen*, Frankfurt-on-Main, Fischer, 1985

Boberach, Heinz (ed.), *Meldungen aus dem Reich: Die geheimen Lageberichte des Sicherheitsdienstes der SS, 1938–1945*, Band 2, Herrsching, Pawlak Verlag, 1984

Bodensieck, Heinrich, 'Das Dritte Reich und die Lage der Juden in der Tschecho-Slowakei nach München', in *Vierteljahrshefte für Zeitgeschichte*, Jahrgang 9 (1961), Heft 3

Böhler, Jochen, *Auftakt zum Vernichtungskrieg: Die Wehrmacht in Polen 1939*, Frankfurt-on-Main, Fischer, 2006

Bonacker, Max, *Goebbels' Mann beim Radio. Der NS Propagandist Hans Fritzsche (1900–1953)*, Munich, R. Oldenbourg Verlag, 2007

Booth, Tony, and Deighton, Len, *Thetis Down: The Slow Death of a Submarine*, Barnsley, Pen & Sword, 2008

Burdick, Charles and Jacobsen, Hans-Adolf (ed.), *The Halder War Diary 1939–1942*, Novato, Presidio Press, 1988

Burleigh, Michael, *The Third Reich. A New History*, London, Pan Books (pb), 2001

Caplan, Jane (ed.), *Nazism, Fascism and the Working Class. Essays by Tim Mason*, Cambridge, Cambridge University Press, 1995

Ciano, Count Galeazzo, *Ciano's Diary, 1937–1943* (ed. Hugh Gibson), New York, Doubleday, 1946

Cohn, Willy, *Kein Reicht, Nirgends. Tagebuch vom Untergang des Breslauer Judentums 1933–1941*, Band 2 (ed. Norbert Conrads), Köln Weimar Wien, Böhlau Verlag, 2007

Coogan, Tim Pat, *The IRA*, London, HarperCollins, 1996

Cox, Geoffrey, *Countdown to War: A Personal Memoir of Europe, 1938–1940*, London, William Kimber, 1988

Cross, Gary, *Worktowners at Blackpool. Mass Observation and Popular Leisure in the 1930s*, Cirencester, Lacy Books, 1990

Currie, Tony, *A Concise History of British Television, 1930–2000*, Bridgewater, Kelly Publications, 2003

Davison, Peter (ed.), *George Orwell. A Life in Letters*, London, Penguin Books, 2011

Deist, Wilhelm, Messerschmidt, Manfred, Volkmann, Hans-Erich, and Wette, Wolfram, *Das Deutsche Reich und der Zweite Weltkrieg*, Band I: *Ursachen und Voraussetzungen der Deutschen Kriegspolitik*, Stuttgart, Deutsche Verlags-Anstalt, 1979

Dilks, David (ed.), *The Diaries of Sir Alexander Cadogan, 1938–1945*, London, Cassell, 1971

Dov Kulka, Otto, and Jäckel, Eberhard (ed.), *Die Juden in den geheimen NS-Stimmungsberichten 1933–1945*, Düsseldorf, Droste Verlag, 2004

Dov Kulka, Otto, and Jäckel, Eberhard (ed.), *The Jews in the Secret Nazi Reports on Popular Opinion in Germany, 1933–1945* (revised English language version translated by William Templer), New Haven and London, Yale University Press, 2010

Ebermayer, Erich, *. . . und morgen die ganze Welt: Erinnerungen an Deutschlands dunkle Zeit*, Bayreuth, Hestia-Verlag, 1966

Ericson, Edward E., *Feeding the German Eagle: Soviet Economic Aid to Nazi*

Germany, 1933–1941, Westport, Praeger Publishers, 1999

Evans, A.S., *Beneath the Waves: A History of HM Submarine Losses 1904–1971*, London, William Kimber, 1986

Evans, Richard J., *The Third Reich at War: How the Nazis Led Germany from Conquest to Disaster*, London, Allen Lane, 2008

Evans, Richard J., *The Third Reich in Power, 1933–1939: How the Nazis Won Over the Hearts and Minds of a Nation*, London, Allen Lane, 2005

Faber, David, *Munich: The 1938 Appeasement Crisis*, London, Simon and Schuster (pb), 2009

Fairfield, Letitia CBE, MD (ed.), *The Trial of Peter Barnes and Others (The I.R.A. Coventry Explosion of 1939)*, London & Edinburgh, William Hodge & Co., 1953

Finch, Michael, *A View From the Hill: A History of Sibford School 1842–2010*, York, Sessions Books, 2010

Fühmann, Franz, *The Jew Car* (translated by Isabel Fargo Cole), Chicago, Seagull Books/University of Chicago Press, 2013

Gardiner, Juliet, *The Thirties: An Intimate History*, London, HarperPress (pb), 2011

Groscurth, Helmut, *Tagebücher eines Abwehroffiziers 1938–1940 Mit weiteren Dokumenten zur Militäropposition gegen Hitler* (ed. Helmut von Krausnick and Harold C. Deutsch in collaboration with Hildegard von Kotze), Stuttgart, Deutsche Verlags-Anstalt, 1970

Grunberger, Richard, *A Social History of the Third Reich*, London, Phoenix (pb), 2005

Hamilton, Patrick, *Hangover Square: A Story of Darkest Earl's Court*, London, Penguin Books, 2001

Hargreaves, Richard, *Blitzkrieg Unleashed: The German Invasion of Poland, 1939*, Barnsley, Pen & Sword, 2008

Hermann, Angela, *Der Weg in den Krieg 1938/39: Quellenkritische Studien zu den Tagebüchern von Joseph Goebbels*, Munich, Oldenbourg, 2011

Herzog, Rudolph, *Heil Hitler, das Schwein ist tot! Lachen unter Hitler – Komik und Humor im Dritten Reich*, Frankfurt-on-Main, Eichhorn, 2006

Hilmes, Oliver, *Berlin 1936: Sixteen Days in August* (translated by Jefferson Chase), London, Bodley Head, 2018

Hosenfeld, Wilm, '*Ich versuche jeden zu retten*'. *Das Leben eines deutschen Offiziers in Briefen und Tagebüchern*, in *Auftrag des Militärgeschichtlichen Forschungsamtes*, ed. Thomas Vogel, Munich, Deutsche Verlags-Anstalt, 2004

Hull, Mark M., *Irish Secrets: German Espionage in Ireland, 1939–1945*, Dublin, Irish Academic Press, 2003

Jelavich, Peter, *Berlin Cabaret*, Cambridge, Mass. and London, Harvard University Press, 1993

Kalshoven, Hedda (ed.), *Between Two Homelands: Letters across the Borders of Nazi Germany* (translated from the Dutch by Hester Velmans and from the German by Peter Fritzsche), Urbana, Chicago & Springfield, University of Chicago Press, 2014

Kean, Hilda, *The Great Cat and Dog Massacre. The Real Story of World War II's Unknown Tragedy*, Chicago and London, University of Chicago Press, 2017

King-Hall, Sir Stephen, *Total Victory*, London, Faber & Faber, 1941

Klemperer, Victor, *The Diaries of Victor Klemperer 1933–1945. I Shall Bear Witness to the Bitter End* (abridged and translated from the German edition by Martin Chalmers), London, Phoenix Press (pb), 2000

Kompisch, Kathrin, and Otto, Frank, *Bestien des Boulevards. Die Deutschen und ihre Serienmörder*, Leipzig, Militzke, 2005

König, Wolfgang, 'Adolf Hitler vs Henry Ford: The Volkswagen, the Role of America as a Model, and the Failure of a Nazi Consumer Society', in *German Studies Review* 27/2 (2004)

Koonz, Claudia, *Mothers in the Fatherland: Women, the Family and Nazi Politics*, London, Methuen (pb), 1988

Korb, Alexander, *Reaktionen der deutschen Bevölkerung auf die Novemberpogrome im Spiegel amtlicher Berichte*, Saarbrücken, VDM, 2008 (consulted online at https://www.academia.edu/2373997/Reaktionen_der_deutschen_Bev%C3%B6lkerung_auf_die_Novemberpogrome_im_Spiegel_amtlicher_Berichte_2nd_Edition_)

Kotze, Hildegard von (ed.), *Heeresadjutant bei Hitler. Aufzeichnungen des Majors Engel*, Stuttgart, Deutsche Verlags-Anstalt, 1974

Krzoska, Markus, 'Der "Bromberger Blutsonntag" 1939 . Kontroversen und Forschungsergebnisse', in *Vierteljahrshefte für Zeitgeschichte*, Jg 60 (2012)

Lohmann, Nina, 'Das "deutsche Prag" 1939–1945. Ein Beitrag zur Erforschung der besetzten Hauptstädte Europas', Charles University, Prague, PhD Dissertation 2014, available online at www.https://is.cuni.cz/webapps/zzp/download/140035716

London, Louise, *Whitehall and the Jews, 1933–1948. British Immigration Policy, Jewish Refugees and the Holocaust*, Cambridge, Cambridge University Press, 2000

Longerich, Peter, *Goebbels: A Biography*, London, Vintage, 2016

Longerich, Peter, *Hitler: Biographie*, Munich, Siedler Verlag, 2015

Lustig, Fritz, *My Lucky Life. The Memoirs of Fritz Lustig*, London, Self-published, 2017

MacDonogh, Giles, *1938: Hitler's Gamble*, London, Constable (pb), 2010

Maier Klaus A., Rohde, Horst, Stegemann, Bernd, Umbreit, Hans, *Das Deutsche Reich und der Zweite Weltkrieg*, Band 2: *Die Errichtung der Hegemonie auf dem europäischen Kontinent*, Stuttgart, Deutsche Verlags-Anstalt, 1979

Mann, Jessica, *Out of Harm's Way. The Wartime Evacuation of Children from Britain*, London, Headline, 2005

Maser, Werner, *Das Regime. Alltag in Deutschland 1933–1945*, Munich, Bertelsmann, 1983

Mattern, Jens, and Kloth, Hans-Michael, 'Stukas über Wielun', in *Der Spiegel*, 26 Aug. 2009

Meehan, Patricia, *The Unnecessary War: Whitehall and the German Resistance to Hitler*, London, Sinclair-Stevenson, 1992

Meir, Golda, *My Life*, London, Weidenfeld & Nicolson, 1975

Merseburger, Peter, *Willy Brandt, 1913–1992*, Munich, Deutsche Verlags-Anstalt, 2002

Müller, Michael, *Canaris. The Life and Death of Hitler's Spymaster* (translated by Geoffrey Brooks), Annapolis, US Naval Institute Press, 2007

Olson, Lynn, *Troublesome Young Men: The Rebels who Brought Churchill to Power in 1940 and Helped Save Britain*, London, Bloomsbury, 2007

Orwell, George, *Collected Essays, Journalism and Letters,* vol. 1: *An Age Like This: 1920–1940*, London, Secker & Warburg, 1968

Orwell, George, 'Diary of Events Leading up to War' in *The Orwell Diaries* (ed. Peter Davison), London, Penguin Classics (pb), 2010

Overy, Richard J., 'Blitzkriegswirtschaft? Finanzpolitik, Lebensstandard und Arbeitseinsatz in Deutschland 1939–1942', in *Vierteljahrshefte für Zeitgeschichte*, 36. Jahrgang, 3. H (July 1988)

Overy, Richard, *The Bombing War*, London, Penguin (pb), 2014

Phayer, Michael, *The Catholic Church and the Holocaust*, Bloomington, Indiana University Press, 2001

Reuth, Ralf Georg (ed.), *Josef Goebbels, Tagebücher,* Bd. 3: *1935–1939*, Munich, Piper, 2000

Rieger, Bernhard, *The People's Car: A Global History of the Volkswagen Beetle*, Cambridge, Mass. and London, Harvard University Press, 2013

Ripka, Hubert , *Munich, Before and After: A Fully Documented Account of the Crises of September 1938 and March 1939*, London, Victor Gollancz, 1939

Schanetzky, Tim, *Kanonen statt Butter. Wirtschaft und Konsum im Dritten Reich*, Munich, C.H. Beck, 2015

Schmidt, Paul, *Hitler's Interpreter*, London, William Heinemann, 1951

Self, Robert (ed.), *The Neville Chamberlain Diary Letters,* vol. ɪv: *The Downing Street Years, 1934–1940*, Aldershot, Ashgate, 2005

Snyder, Timothy, *Bloodlands. Europe between Hitler and Stalin*, London, Bodley Head, 2010

Sopade 1938 (Deutschland-Berichte der Sozialdemokratischen Partei Deutschlands (Sopade) 1934–1940) *Fünfter Jahrgang 1938*, Salzhausen and Frankfurt-on-Main, Verlag Petra Nettelbeck/Zweitausendeins, 1980

Sopade 1939 (Deutschland-Berichte der Sozialdemokratischen Partei Deutschlands (Sopade) 1934–1940) *Sechster Jahrgang 1939*, Salzhausen and Frankfurt-on-Main, Verlag Petra Nettelbeck/Zweitausendeins 1980

Spieß, Alfred, and Lichtenstein, Heiner, *Das Unternehmen Tannenberg*, Wiesbaden and Munich, Limes-Verlag, 1979

Steinweis, Alan E., 'The Trials of Herschel Grynszpan: Anti-Jewish Policy and German Propaganda, 1938–1942', in *German Studies Review*, Vol. 31, No. 3 (Oct. 2008)

Stephenson, Jill, *Women in Nazi Germany*, Abingdon and New York, Routledge, 2013

Swett, E., Wiesen, S. Jonathan, and Zatlin, Jonathan R. (ed.), *Selling Modernity: Advertising in Twentieth-Century Germany*, Durham, N.C., and London, Duke University Press, 2007

Swett, Pamela E., Ross, Cory, and d'Almeida, Fabrice (ed.), *Pleasure and Power in Nazi Germany*, Basingstoke and New York, Palgrave Macmillan, 2011

Taylor, Frederick, *Coventry, Thursday, 14 November 1940*, London, Bloomsbury, 2015

Terveen, Fritz, 'Der Filmbericht über Hitlers 50. Geburtstag', in *Vierteljahrshefte für Zeitgeschichte*, Jahrgang 7 (1959), Heft 1

Thamer, Hans-Ulrich, *Verführung und Gewalt. Deutschland 1933–1945*, Berlin, Siedler, 1986

Todman, Daniel, *Britain's War. Into Battle 1937–1941*, London, Penguin Books (pb), 2017

Tooze, Adam, *The Wages of Destruction: The Making and Breaking of the Nazi War Economy*, London, Alan Lane, 2006

Trenkner, Joachim, 'Ziel vernichtet', in *Die Zeit* 07/2003, 6 Feb 2003

Uricchio, William (ed.), *Die Anfänge des Deutschen Fernsehens: Kritische Annäherungen an die Entwicklung bis 1945*, Tübingen, Max Niemeyer Verlag, 1991

Wallis, Russell, *Britain, Germany and the Road to the Holocaust*, London, I.B. Tauris, 2014

Watt, Richard M., *Bitter Glory. Poland and its Fate 1918–1939*, New York, Barnes & Noble, 1998

Wehler, Hans-Ulrich, *Deutsche Gesellschaftsgeschichte*, Bd. 4: *Vom Beginn der Ersten Weltkrieges bis zur Gründung der beiden deutschen Staaten, 1914–1949*, Munich, Beck, 2003

Westerfield, Lillian Leigh, *'This Anguish, Like a Kind of Intimate Song': Resistance in Women's Literature of World War II*, Amsterdam/New York, Editions Rodolpi, 2004.

White, Stephen, *Britain and the Bolshevik Revolution*, Basingstoke, Palgrave Macmillan, 1980

Contemporary Newspapers 1938/1939 (consulted at online archives)

BRITISH

Action (British Union of Fascists newspaper)
Daily Express and *Sunday Express*
Daily Mirror
Manchester Guardian
The Times
Yorkshire Post

GERMAN

DNB (*Deutsches Nachrichtenbüro*, German News Bureau, official press releases)
Freiburger Zeitung
Pommersche Zeitung (Stettin) (for November 1938)
Rheinsberger Zeitung
Teltower Kreisblatt

AMERICAN

New York Times

Archive Research (details as noted in text)

Landesarchiv Nordrhein-Westfalen Detmold
M1 I P
Nr 637

Regierung in Minden
Aus der Tätigkeit der Staatspolizei
SD Bielefeld

Landesarchiv Nordrhein-Westfalen Duisburg

RW 134
Nr 32
Chef des Hauptamtes, Vorsorgungs- und Fürsorgeamt-SS

Landesarchiv Nordrhein-Westfalen Münster

4.1.1. Nichtstaatliches Schriftgut/Nationalsozialismus

NSDAP Gauleitung Westfalen-Nord/Hauptleitung Nr 14
Stimmungs und Lagebericht für den Monat Juli 1938

NSDAP Gauleitung Westfalen-Nord/Hauptleitung Nr 6
Stimmungs und Lagebericht für August und September 1938

NSDAP Gauleitung Westfalen-Nord/Hauptleitung Nr 26
Januar 1939 Stimmungsmässiger Überblick über die gesamtpolitische
    Lage

NSDAP Gauleitung Westfalen-Nord/Hauptleitung Nr 27
Februar/März 1939 Stimmungsmässiger Überblick über die gesamtpoli-
    tische Lage

NSDAP Gauleitung Westfalen-Nord/Hauptleitung Nr 21
April/May 1939 Stimmungsmässiger Überblick über die gesamtpolitische
    Lage

NSDAP Gauleitung Westfalen-Nord/Hauptleitung Nr 29
Berichterstattung über die Stimmung in der Bevölkerung 31 Aug. 1939
02 Sept. 1939 (Rundfunk/Allgemeine Stimmung)

Sächsische Archivverwaltung/Staatsarchiv Leipzig

StA Leipzig SD-Abschnitt Leipzig Nr. 6
(Correspondence between Pg Mauersberger and SD-Untersturmführer
    Dr Martin Seyfert 1938–1939)

Deutsches Tagebucharchiv Emmendingen

Catalogue Sig. 975, 2 Hilde Maud H., b. 1922 'My last Christmas in
    pre-war London in 1938'

Catalogue Sig. 1512, 4 O.T. (anonymized)
Catalogue Sig. 1295/I, 2, Tagebuch Ruth Thieme
Catalogue Sig. 1783, 1, Dorothea B., Tagebuch 1938/39
Catalogue Sig. 1708, 10 Wilhelm Sölter 'Der Weg'
Catalogue Sig. 146 1 (Albert Joos 1919-) Kriegstagebuch

Mass Observation Archive Online (via British Library)

(References as individually noted)

Imperial War Museum, London
Online Recorded Interviews referred to in text

Bryan, Marion (née Perkins)
Cameron, Albert 'Tony'
Curry Jones, Andrew Gwynn
Daunt, Ivan
Davies, Albert
Elkan, Vera Ines Morley
Fischel, Katerina (Käthe) (née Strenitz)
Gueritz, Edward Findley
Hyams, Reuben
Jellicoe, George Patrick John Rushworth
Moss, Dee
Plant, James Edward
Read, James Joseph
Shepherd, Jesse Lionel
Togwell, Walter
Weliminsky, Anton

Interviews conducted by the author
(asterisked where directly quoted or referred to in text)

Britain

Enid Watson, Derby, 23 January 2017
Marjorie-Ann Lowenstein, London, 25 January 2017
Ann Forman, née Magnus, Hayle, Cornwall, 3 February 2017*
Anne Queensberry, London, 23 June 2017
David Laity, St Austell, Cornwall, 4 May 2017*
Ken Brockley, Derby, 3 July 2017
Peter Jordan, Didsbury, Manchester, 17 November 2017*

Fritz Lustig, London, 24 June 2017*
Allsop Smith and Ken Brindley, Derby, 3 July 2017
Mary Wilson, Derby, 3 July 2017
Elly Feliksiak, née Luckow, Derby 18 November 2017*

Germany

Dr Maria Sommer, Berlin 14 September 2017*
Joachim Trenkner, Berlin 15 September 2017
Dr Günter Schulz, Berlin 15 September 2017
Heinz Oldenburg, Berlin 15 September 2017
Inge Heyl, Berlin 15 September 2017*
Hannelore Pfeffer, Berlin 15 September 2017
Helmut Wald, Berlin 16 September 2017
Irmgard Klingst, Berlin 16 September 2017
Renate Rehor, Berlin 16 September 2017
Dr Johanna Schmid, Munich 18 September 2017
Luisa Haar, Stuttgart, 22 September 2017*
Anna Marie Gramling, Stuttgart 22 September 2017*
Helmut Schnatz, Koblenz 23 September 2017

INDEX